P9-CAB-584

D A

Lake Superior

Eastport, ME

Burlington, VT

Duluth, MN

Lake Michigan

Lake Huron

Lake Ontario

Sioux Falls, SD

Holland, MI

Lake Erie

Erie, PA

Allentown, PA

Vermilion, OH

Pittsburgh, PA

Gaithersburg, MD

Missouri R.

Columbus, OH

Washington, DC

Charleston, WV

Ohio R.

Louisville, KY

Wichita, KS

Greer, SC

APPALACHIAN MOUNTAINS

Greenville, SC

Columbus, MS

Mississippi R.

West Point, MS

Birmingham, AL

ATLANTIC
OCEAN

Starkville, MS

Caddo Lake, TX

Demopolis, AL

St. Marys, GA

GULF OF MEXICO

Towns visited in:

2013          2014

2015          2016

# OUR TOWNS

# OUR TOWNS

*A 100,000-Mile Journey into the Heart of America*

James Fallows and Deborah Fallows

*Pantheon Books, New York*

All rights reserved. Published in the United States by Pantheon Books, a division of Penguin Random House LLC, New York, and distributed in Canada by Random House of Canada, a division of Penguin Random House Canada Limited, Toronto.

Pantheon Books and colophon are registered trademarks of Penguin Random House LLC.

Portions of this work are based in part on previously published articles that originally appeared, in different form, in TheAtlantic.com between 2013 and 2016.

Names: Fallows, James M., author. Fallows, Deborah.
Title: Our towns : a 100,000-mile journey into the heart of America / James Fallows and Deborah Fallows.
Description: First edition. New York : Pantheon, 2018.
Identifiers: LCCN 2017052007. ISBN 9781101871843 (hardback).
ISBN 9781101871850 (ebook)
Subjects: LCSH: Public opinion—United States. Social surveys—United States. United States—Social conditions—Public opinion. United States—Politics and government— Public opinion. Fallows, James M.—Travel—United States. Fallows, Deborah—Travel— United States. BISAC: TRAVEL / United States / General. HISTORY / United States / 21st Century. SOCIAL SCIENCE / Sociology / Rural.
Classification: LCC HN90.P8 F35 2018 | DDC 306.0973—dc23 LC record available at lccn.loc.gov/2017052007

www.pantheonbooks.com

Jacket photography by Jessica Remmey
Jacket design by Janet Hansen
Front-endpaper map by Beehive Mapping
Rear-endpaper photograph courtesy of the authors

Printed in the United States of America
First Edition
4 6 8 9 7 5 3

For our next generation: Jack, Tide, Eleanor, Navy.

This is your country.

# Contents

# *Authors' Note*

This book is the story of journeys that took place over more than four years, from preliminary and planning trips late in 2012 through our final cross-country travel at the start of 2017. Our goal has been to portray the people we spoke with and places we visited at specific moments in time.

Time has not stood still in any of these cities, and inevitably circumstances have changed from what we originally saw. Some people we interviewed have changed jobs, retired, gained or lost political office, moved to different parts of the country. At least one of them has died. Many of the businesses we describe have grown and prospered. At least two of them have failed. Cities and their populations have gone through political and cultural changes—some for the better, but not all. In a few important cases we have noted these changes, but for the most part we have left our account faithful to what we saw and heard when we were on-scene. This account draws on extensive notes we made each night while on the road, a practice based on the belief that we'd remember and capture impressions more vividly during the same day than ever afterward. It also draws on reports we posted along the way on *The Atlantic's* website, and on later follow-up interviews. Reflecting this mix of reporting over an extended period, some of the narrative is left in present tense, describing what we saw at the time: "the downtown is recovering." Other parts are in past tense: "the mayor told us. . . ."

For most of the cities we describe here, we made two or even three reporting visits, initially to get our bearings and then to follow leads or observe specific events. Usually those trips were only a few weeks apart; a few were separated by months. For clarity we've combined the results of the separate trips in our accounts of each town. In one case we discussed findings of a later journey—to Louisville, in 2016—in a sequence of earlier reports, because of the thematic connections. For completeness, the map on the front endpaper of the book includes cities that were important to us in our travels, among them a few that are not extensive parts of the final narrative. In some cases, the year-by-year grouping of cities within the text differs from the color-coded travel dates shown on the map; that is so we could better connect related themes in the book. For instance, the long flight from the East Coast to the West that began our West Coast travels occurred at the end of 2014, but for narrative coherence it is presented as the introduction to 2015.

Alternating sections of the book are written by James and Deborah Fallows. A small symbol at the beginning of each section indicates its author: an airplane for Jim, a quill pen for Deb.

—Redlands, California, 2018

# OUR TOWNS

# Introduction

## 2017: A Last Trip West

*Montgomery County traffic, Cirrus Four-three-five Sierra*
*Romeo taking Runway one-four, VFR departure to the west.*
*Montgomery.*

 DEB FALLOWS

And with that, we were off, flying away from frigid Washington, D.C., and its political postelection turmoil, on a southerly route to California.

We had flown nearly one hundred thousand miles in nearly four years in our small plane, with Jim as pilot and me in the right seat. We began in my home territory of the Upper Midwest, then headed over to Maine and flew south through New England and the Mid-Atlantic states to Georgia and Florida. We swept farther through the Deep South, to Texas and the Southwest, up the Central Valley of California to Oregon and Washington, and closed the loop after leaving Montana. All the while we snaked in and out of the so-called flyover country, through Wyoming, Kansas, Missouri, Oklahoma, West Virginia, and much more.

We have landed in dozens of towns and cities along the way, anticipating in each of them local stories that would organize themselves into some kind of composed narrative about the backbone and character of the region and maybe beyond that, to help explain the character of the country. We began by looking for towns with positive energy, with signs of rebound from some kind of shock or shift, like a mine or factory that had closed or waves of people who'd departed or newcomers who'd arrived. We ended up adding towns with down-and-out reputations where we truly feared for what we might find. Life upon landing was never quite what we'd planned.

We have stayed in towns for weeks at a time. We have often revisited them, following threads from one person, or one group or town institution or movement, to the next, settling into the local rhythm. We have gone to town plays and musicals, sat in on civic meetings, hung out at coffee shops and brewpubs, spent days at schools, libraries, and ball games, taken tours of downtowns, visited factories, start-ups, and community college classes, taken boat rides and bike rides, swum in local public pools and run on high school tracks, borrowed cars, and stayed in motels, private homes, and one-off eco-hotels. We remained long enough to begin to imagine how much we didn't know, but also to appreciate the unusual opportunity we've had, in seeing a broader sampling of modern America's realities than most of its citizens will ever have a chance to do.

This time we were heading to Jim's hometown of Redlands, in the orange-growing country of Southern California, to write this book. Our final flight west would mark both a leave-taking from frenetic Washington, D.C., and a homecoming. After so many miles, we knew that flight in a small plane is rarely routine. There are dramas when you're airborne: weather, birds, parachute jumpers, mechanical blips, crop dusters, and drones. And perspectives unfold among the clouds or over the sights below: rangy forests, tamed farmlands, strings of quarries, hours of desert, well-defined prisons, pop-up small towns.

Our departure was not auspicious. Cold, wind, snow, and icy conditions in Washington gave us a few more days to organize at home and winnow the next six months' belongings into the 140 extra pounds the plane could carry besides us and a lot of fuel. Clothes, flight gear, electronics, emergency supplies, water, books, a little food.

By now, I knew *Travels with Charley* the way some people know the Bible, and I was more than a little envious that Steinbeck could stock his trusty outfitted truck Rocinante without limit, including what he described as "far too many clothes" and a week's worth of food, plus liquor! Steinbeck could pack quadruple what he needed until Rocinante's springs overloaded, but if we did so we would never get off the runway.

Tuesday was still a blustery twenty-nine degrees outside, but the clouds were high enough that we could fly below them without worry about ice forming from their moisture collecting on our wings. We bundled into clothing layers so thick that I had to loosen my seat belt, a complex system of straps not unlike those in toddlers' car seats. I stretched my headset to fit over a heavy knit cap. Jim unplugged the plane's engine from its overnight warming station. After all that, the sound of the motor turning over quickly—and, I would add, proudly—was our signal.

The air traffic controllers (ATCs), my heroes of the sky, guided us through the busy Dulles airspace on a shortcut south. We were ready for headwinds, but not the strong 40 to 50 knots straight at us that slowed our ground speed from our accustomed 170 knots (about 200 mph) down to as low as a measly 109. I was grateful for my natural sea legs, dating back to a childhood of pounding over waves in small sailboats, which translated well to the bumps from gusty winds aloft.

In autumn, if we flew north, we would watch the green leaves near the Mason-Dixon Line fade to yellow, then pivot to a bright orange and red, until the foliage all but disappeared over northern New England. On this trip, the snowpack over Virginia melted thinner into the Carolinas, then gave way to dry land just south of Greenville. Clipped diction from the ATCs along the busy Eastern Seaboard slowed to a more languid drawl, and outside the temperature began inching up. We flew over Georgia's catfish farms and the erratic geometry of forest-clearing, chasing the late-afternoon sunset in Demopolis, Alabama, our destination. Jim had spent a good part of the summer of 1968 around Selma, Montgomery, and Demopolis as a teenage cub reporter for a civil rights newspaper called *The Southern Courier*. We wanted to give the town at least a quick look.

Morning in Demopolis was downright balmy. In the Best Western breakfast room, Miss Nettie was making grits and biscuits for us and the out-of-town crews who had come in to monitor the planned outage at the cement factory.

Two small things stood between us and our progress west. One was a problem with our onboard weather system; the software wasn't communicating to bring in the weather updates. Before this technology existed, we had flown without radar depictions of the weather. But once you've had new tools, it's hard to go back, especially with some iffy weather forecast for the next few days along our route. The closest place to arrange for that repair was Dallas, but conditions by the time we could get there forecast crosswinds gusting above 30 and even 40 knots, far beyond safe landing guidelines for us.

We settled in for an extra unexpected day in Demopolis, as we had in other places, like Red Oak, Iowa, and Cheyenne, Wyoming, and Hickory, North Carolina. Luckily—and we have found there's usually good luck to match the bad—we had ended up the night before at a cozy Demopolis bistro and found ourselves in conversation with owner Mike Grayson, who turned out to have been the mayor of Demopolis for the previous eight years. He was full of suggestions for what to see and do there.

Our first stop was the Demopolis Public Library. My favorite institution. Inside public libraries, we had learned from visiting them in nearly every town on our journey, you see the people, programs, problems, and answers that offer a genuine look into the heart and soul of a town. This public library, housed in a former furniture company store and warehouse, is as elegant and graceful as any Carnegie library I've seen. A wraparound balcony on the second-story mezzanine overlooks the main reading room, with its wooden Mission-style worktables and lamps. Oversized photos of some of the town's historic moments lined the walls. One showed Woodrow Wilson, who'd visited nearly a century ago for the then-legal cockfighting, at a fund-raising auction to build a bridge over the Tombigbee River.

More recently, Bill and Melinda Gates visited in 1998 to check out one of the first computer donations made by their Gates Library Foundation. Connie Lawson, who worked at the library then and still does now, recalled the visit as if it were yesterday. They had spent days cleaning the building "down to the baseboards," nervous about making a good impression. Lawson said that the Gateses were as nice as could be. She didn't wear a touch of makeup; he held his tie in place against the wind with a piece of tape. "The world's richest man had no tie clip," Lawson marveled nearly twenty years later.

After a second morning's grits and biscuits from Miss Nettie, we headed for Dallas, passing over Meridian and Jackson, south of the startlingly booming new heavy-manufacturing center of Mississippi's Golden Triangle. This was territory familiar to us from at least three earlier reporting trips, where we'd seen a helicopter factory, a drone plant, a sophisticated state-of-the-art steel mill, the ground breaking for a Yokohama Tire plant, and East Mississippi Community College, which was training former textile workers for the new skilled jobs arriving in the area.

I always looked forward to crossing the Mississippi River. We've done that from just about every state through which the mighty river flows, especially in the Upper Midwest: Minnesota, Wisconsin, Iowa, Illinois. There it would be today as we left the state of Mississippi, below us just around Vicksburg. I was worried about even getting a glimpse because of the low clouds. We watched the navigation maps on the cockpit monitors, and just as we approached the river, the clouds parted. Jim banked the plane to dip the wing for a good view from my right-side seat. I stole enough of a look to recognize the powerful Mississippi.

The following day, a cool drizzle moved in over Dallas as we were preparing to depart, reminding us why we'd avoided winter during most of our flying in the last three years. We filed an instrument plan, and for the next three hours, we were either in the thick cloud layer or just above it, barely seeing the vast stretches of West Texas below us or the sun above.

I think Jim enjoys the challenge of this kind of flying. He is always on the instruments, pushing buttons, checking gauges, switching screens, and testing the redundant systems. The total focus of piloting spirits him away from every single earthly concern. For me, the opaque flying is unpleasant; I find it a little spooky and am unnerved by the absence of orientation to the ground.

I'm not a pilot, which is often an uncomfortable admission. I don't share the zealous passion for flying that I have seen in most pilots, and my eyesight has always been, well, wanting. If Jim says, "Do you see the runway?," I'll mumble something in return. But after a thousand hours of being in the right seat, I know a lot about flying the plane. I know its repertoire of gurgles and agitations as well as I knew those of our infant children. I am very familiar with the gauges, navigation, radio work with ATC, steering the plane, and I know how to pull the parachute, which deploys from the fuselage and settles the plane in a true emergency. The parachute of the Cirrus, now the best-selling small aircraft in the world, eliminates night-before-flight worries for me.

For distraction on days of long flights, there is always the radio. The air traffic controllers were busy over West Texas, with its vast stretches of military airspace. There were many calls between the ATCs and "Fighter 25" and "Fighter 26," who were no doubt on training missions. I tallied at least five medevac flights in the air that day, which seemed like a lot until I considered the long, desolate stretches of road between sick or injured people and medical attention. Pilots this day requested vectoring to get to places with names that sounded exotic and evocative: Amarillo, San Angelo, Dalhart, Alpine, El Paso. When the ATC chatter faded out, we switched to SiriusXM radio and toggled around.

Road Dog Trucking warned about winter road conditions and impending ice storms over Omaha and St. Louis. In one of my favorite segments on Road Dog Trucking, called *Worst Load Ever,* drivers would call in with stories and try to outdo one another. One trucker was driving north to Saskatchewan through burning country, with flames along both sides of the highway. "We were on fire," he said, with twenty-eight hundred gallons of aircraft fuel aboard. Helicopters were dropping water bombs alongside him. "It was kind of hot," he continued undramatically, "a bad-load trip through kind of a shitty time. Ain't too many people who could say: I hauled a load of jet fuel through a forest fire. What've you done?" Background music by The Band faded in: "I pulled into Nazareth, was feeling 'bout half past dead."

Rural Radio offered up local crop prices and advice on pest control. Entire stations were dedicated to Willie Nelson, or Bruce Springsteen, or coffeehouse music or jazz, or the irreverent guys on the Catholic Channel.

We ascended to 10,000 feet to cross the southernmost remnants of the Rockies, the Guadalupe Mountains, on our way to Las Cruces. This reminded me of the tail end of a stretch of the Great Wall of China in Gansu Province; we'd climbed a section near where the crumbling remains had become little more than an obstacle for farmers to work around in their fields. Finally, the cloud cover was dissipating.

Our little cabin, about the size of a sedan, isn't pressurized. Legally, you can fly without oxygen up to 14,000 feet. We carry small bottles of oxygen on board for emergency. (A technical note: after thirty minutes at 12,500 feet, the pilot is required to use oxygen.) Even at 10,000 feet, I felt myself involuntarily taking longer, deeper breaths. And I also started checking the color of my fingernail beds for any tinge of blue, which signals oxygen deprivation. We were fine, of course.

We stopped in Las Cruces in search of cheap fuel and a late-afternoon lunch. We never knew what kind of food we would find. Many times, vending-machine peanut butter crackers were the best we could do. I worried about this a lot in our early days. Our go-to provisions were a cool sack with dried fruit, nuts, granola bars, carrots, hummus, grapes, cheese, Vitaminwater—you get the picture. Over time, the list became leaner and leaner. By now, more than three years later, we'd actually become aficionados of jerky: beef, buffalo, reindeer, elk, spicy, lime-ginger, teriyaki. One Uber driver who drove us on an unscheduled stop in Wyoming went on for twenty minutes with stories about his home-made jerky from a personal drying machine. When lunch in Las Cruces didn't work out, jerky it was.

We pressed on for another hour or so to Tucson. The mountains deflated into undulating brown hills. We flew over flatlands with occasional volcanic outcroppings and long stretches of almost surreal desert landscapes that looked like pointillist paintings.

In Tucson were some threads we had left unraveled over Arizona. I wanted to trace a few more steps taken by Isabella Greenway, one of the extraordinary women I had stumbled onto. She was a lifelong friend of Eleanor Roosevelt's, twice a widow to two of Teddy Roosevelt's Rough Riders, a builder and shaper who brought the beautiful copper-mining town of Ajo, Arizona, to its heyday. She was Arizona's first female representative in Congress, as part of FDR's New Deal Democratic majority. And she also built and opened Tucson's Arizona Inn, which was, I had heard, still thriving today under the family eye.

So, a visit to the Arizona Inn was very special (and a splurge for us), and it turned out to be exactly what I had imagined. Isabella Greenway herself described it as "a simple, home-like, cottage hotel," but it is much more than that, with high-ceilinged, oversized rooms, furniture from its own shop, quiet green spaces, a big pool (almost twenty meters by my stroke count), wonderful food, and a hospitality still imbued with the family's sensibility.

On a whim, I e-mailed the current proprietor, Patty Doar, the granddaughter of Isabella Greenway. To my surprise, she e-mailed right back. The next morning, we met with her and her son and co-proprietor, the writer Will Conroy, to swap photos and stories about the different pieces of Isabella's life that we each knew.

We left Tucson reluctantly but with strong tailwinds, the first of this cross-continental trip. We hadn't really been expecting tailwinds, since we were flying into the prevailing westerly winds, so this was indeed special and appreciated. Just north of Gila Bend, Jim and I were chatting about our first trip here a few years back on our way to Ajo, a tiny oasis of a town in the Sonoran Desert.

The ATC interrupted our reminiscing to say he could no longer see us on his radar. This wasn't so surprising; it often happened with a relatively low-altitude flight, or in remote areas far from controllers, or with natural impediments like mountains that block radar beams. Jim recycled the transponder, a click of one button that often cleared up the connections. This time, nothing.

Then the dials and gauges on the cockpit monitors—showing ground speed, wind direction, location, just about everything—began to go haywire. They spun around randomly, showing a 150-knot headwind, then a tailwind, then no wind. I thought of *The Exorcist*. The moving map, with our location, waypoints, obstacles like mountains, restricted airspace, and other airplanes, suddenly blanked out as if it had no idea where our plane actually was. Red warning signs popped up on the dual GPS guidance systems (almost everything in the plane's critical instrumentation has a backup), indicating lost signals. Then the urgent robo-voice was yelling, "TERRAIN! TERRAIN!" We looked around instinctively, confirming a flat desert floor but no high terrain of any sort.

All this was getting Jim's attention. He switched to his pre-GPS, old-school backup navigation systems. It was dark comfort to hear a call from United 404, reporting to the ATC that they had also lost their GPS. At least it wasn't just our plane. I studied the dials, thinking, overdramatically, that this was how the world as we know it might look during some kind of nefarious global technological takeover.

The ATC said calmly—controllers are always calm—that there must be a military test exercise of GPS jamming happening today. Later, on the ground, Jim learned that the air force was indeed running a month-long trial in that area, testing the effects of intentional GPS outages. *Thanks for letting us know,* I thought.

As we flew over Palm Springs, the aerial road signs were becoming familiar: the mountains north and south, the desert settlements below, the wind farms, the Banning Pass through to the Los Angeles basin. We had been here several times before. We flew over Redlands, our destination, to San Bernardino and the long, wide runways that had once accommodated B-52s when this site was Norton Air Force Base. Jim guided our Cirrus in, hovering near touchdown in the wind gusts for the final few hundred feet.

*Landed.* What were we supposed to feel now, some twenty-five hundred miles and four days later? Or one hundred thousand miles and four years later? Maybe like Mark Twain, I thought, one of the writers whose account of an epic journey I had read. At the end of twenty days by stagecoach, the *Washoe Zephyr,* from Missouri to the territory of Nevada, Twain wrote, "It had been a fine pleasure trip; we had fed fat on wonders every day; we were now well accustomed to stage life, and very fond of it; so the idea of coming to a stand-still in a village was not agreeable, but on the contrary depressing."

We, too, had indeed "fed fat on wonders every day." Our ending didn't feel as sad as Twain described his, but he was young then and didn't understand yet that you can craft many adventures in a lifetime. I knew we would head on to many more adventures, and that this ending was, again, another beginning.

JIM FALLOWS

We began this project with one purpose in mind: we wanted to take a fresh look at the country, its disappointments and its possibilities. We ended up wondering about questions and trends that were different from what we'd expected, and with a story to tell that we could barely have imagined when we were starting out.

By the end of the journey, we felt sure of something we had suspected at the beginning: an important part of the face of modern America has slipped from people's view, in a way that makes a big and destructive difference in the country's public and economic life. Despite the economic crises of the preceding decade and the social tensions of which every American is aware, most parts of the United States that we visited have been doing better, in most ways, than most Americans realize. Because many people don't know that, they're inclined to view any local problems as symptoms of wider disasters, and to dismiss local successes as fortunate anomalies. They feel even angrier about the country's challenges than they should, and more fatalistic about the prospects of dealing with them.

We wanted to look at parts of the country generally missed by the media spotlight. That would mean reporting in the places often considered as "flyover country." Such cities, medium-sized or below, and rural areas usually made their way to national attention only after a tornado or a mass shooting; during presidential-campaign season; or as backdrops for "concept" pieces like "The Private Prison Revolution" or "After Coal: What?" We were interested in places that had faced adversity of some sort, from crop failure to job loss to political crisis, and had looked for ways to respond.

Since the late 1990s, we had flown at low altitude in little single-engine, four-seat propeller planes, seeing the sorts of landscapes, communities, and cultures that can be hard to reach. Once we had stopped unexpectedly in Red Oak, Iowa, a tiny farming center usually neglected even during the saturation coverage, every four years, of the Iowa caucus. There we learned about an enclave of Central American immigrants who had set up successful operations in what would be considered a classically insular, non-diverse part of America.

When we touched down at the small airport on the evening of our arrival, taking our place in the landing sequence among the crop dusters that were buzzing in and out to fertilize or apply insecticide to the surrounding corn and soybean fields, we saw a group of junior-high-school-aged boys, plus one girl, gathered in the small airport building. They were clustered around a grizzled-looking flight instructor, who was teaching them about aerial navigation as part of the weekly meeting of local cadets in the Civil Air Patrol. We stayed for a while and talked with students and instructors, learned about some other efforts under way to add life and attract residents to what had been a declining small town, and left the next day with an impression we frequently found ourselves with: that of an intensity of local civic life that generally escaped any outside notice. It was the kind of activity that readers take for granted in Tocqueville-era accounts of the American genius for "association," or in Frank Capra–era depictions of the most appealing sides of mid-twentieth-century American life, but also the type assumed to have vanished in this era of social-media silos.

Wherever we stopped, we saw things of this sort. On a trip through the Mountain West, bad weather forced us to make an overnight stay in the rough mining town of Rock Springs, Wyoming. It had been famous in the nineteenth century for a race riot, in which white mine workers beat and shot and burned the houses of Chinese immigrants who had come to the western United States to build the transcontinental railroads but then stayed to work in the mines. Mainly white miners killed at least twenty-eight Chinese workers during that riot in 1885. When we visited, more than 125 years later, Rock Springs was booming again as the world's main source of a mineral called trona, which, when converted to soda ash, is a necessary component for countless industrial processes around the world. (Glass, detergents, baking soda, kitty litter, and many other products all depend on trona mined in Rock Springs.) We saw Rock Springs' modern Chinese community, its African-American miners, and others improbably attracted to a city we had come upon by happenstance. We had a similar sense—*Wait, there is more here than we imagined*—after stops in Scotts Bluff and Grand Island, Nebraska; and Richmond, Indiana; and Eau Claire, Wisconsin; and Astoria, Oregon; and Yakima, Washington.

In late 2012, we began planning a journey. We knew we were looking for medium-sized or smaller towns. The definition was flexible; we ended up visiting places as sizable as Columbus, Ohio, the fifteenth-largest city in the country, though most were much smaller, like Eastport, Maine, population less than 1,500. Early in 2013, I put an item on *The Atlantic*'s website, asking for suggestions from readers on why it would be worth learning the story of their town. More than one thousand entries arrived, at least seven hundred of them extended essays, and we began compiling a list.

In June we began our travels. Early on was a week-long stop in the little lakeside town of Holland, Michigan, a longtime manufacturing center that had managed to avoid the general fate of Rust Belt decline, and a city that had also coped with what we have come to see as a much broader pattern of ethnic change.

Before our time in Holland and on a return trip afterward, we went to Sioux Falls and Rapid City, in South Dakota, which had their own economic, cultural, and political surprises. We spent several months working our way up and down the West Coast, from the tiny town of Ajo, Arizona, built next to what was once one of North America's largest copper mines, to the troubled and now-famous California city of San Bernardino—and northward to Fresno, in California's Central Valley, Bend and its neighboring cities in central Oregon, and the twin cities of Lewiston, Idaho, and Clarkston, Washington. On the East Coast, we've been as far north as Eastport, the very last city on Maine's Down East coast before the Bay of Fundy and Canada, and as far south as St. Marys, Georgia, which is east of the Okefenokee Swamp and just north of the Florida border.

By the end, we'd made extended visits, usually totaling two weeks in each of twenty-five cities across the country, with shorter visits to another two dozen.

There are dozens more we would like already to have visited, and that we plan to spend time in and learn about in the next wave of our travels. These are places like Rochester and Buffalo, New York; Chattanooga and Knoxville, Tennessee; Dayton and Youngstown, Ohio; South Bend and Gary, Indiana; the Batavia area and Moline, Illinois; Stockton and Fremont, California; Brownsville, Texas; Lakeland and St. Petersburg, Florida; Danville, Kentucky; Eau Claire, Wisconsin; greater St. Louis, Missouri; Roanoke and Hampton Roads, Virginia; Frederick, Maryland; Lewiston, Maine; Huntsville and Mobile, Alabama; Reno, Nevada; Coeur d'Alene, Idaho; and many more. With each new city we've spent time in and learned about, the list of places we'd like to go next continues to grow.

This is an ongoing project: we ask readers to send a tweet about their cities to @JamesFallows or @FallowsDeb, with the tag #ThisIsMyTown, or a longer message about where you live and why to TheStoryOfMy Town@gmail.com.

\* \* \*

There is a high-toned tradition of road trips as a means of "discovering" America, from Lewis and Clark and Tocqueville through John Dos Passos, John Steinbeck, and William Least Heat-Moon. Apart from other obvious points of contrast, our project is different in that rather than going by car (or wagon or pirogue), we've gone from city to city in our family's small single-engine propeller airplane, a Cirrus SR22. This was a decision made for convenience, for beauty, and for edification.

The convenience comes from the simple fact that almost any settlement in America is within close range of a place where a small airplane can land. Some five thousand public landing facilities, many of them built for military purposes during and after World War II, are scattered about the United States, making many remote hamlets more easily reachable by air than by other means.

The beauty comes from the unending fascination of watching the American landscape unfurl below as you travel at low altitude. At the dawn of powered flight, a century ago, it was assumed that writers and painters would want to become aviators, and vice versa—Charles Lindbergh, Amelia Earhart, and Ernest K. Gann were fliers who wrote; Beryl Markham, Antoine de Saint-Exupéry, and Anne Morrow Lindbergh were writers who flew—because of the unique perspective on civilization and nature offered by the aerial view. The late novelist James Salter, who was a Korean War fighter pilot and retained his passion for flight, was a midcentury example; William Langewiesche, a longtime book and magazine writer, and the son of Wolfgang Langewiesche, whose *Stick and Rudder* is the flying world's equivalent of *The Elements of Style,* is a recent one. Mark Vanhoenacker, a 747 pilot who writes about flight with extraordinary elegance in his book *Skyfaring,* is another.

From ground level, America is mainly road—after all, that's where cars can take you. From the sky, America is mainly forest in the eastern third, farmland in the middle, then mountain and desert in the West, before the strip of intense development along the California coast. It's also full of features obvious from the sky that are much harder to notice from the ground and are difficult to pick out from six miles up in an airliner. Some of the most striking are quarries at the edge of most towns, to provide gravel for roads and construction sites; prisons, instantly identifiable by their fencing (though some mega–high schools can look similar), usually miles from the nearest town or tucked into locations where normal traffic won't pass by; and the vast sea of parking-lot spaces surrounding shopping malls, on the edges of towns. We never tire of the view from this height, as different from the normal, grim airliner perspective as scuba diving is from traveling on a container ship.

The edification comes from lessons in history, geography, urban planning, and environmental protection and despoliation that are inescapably obvious from above. Why is St. Louis where it is? Ah, of course!

It's where the Missouri and Mississippi Rivers come together. Why were mill towns built along the fall line of the Appalachians? Because of the long north-to-south series of waterfalls. As you cross South Dakota from east to west, from the big city of Sioux Falls, at the Iowa and Minnesota borders, toward Rapid City and the Black Hills and beyond, you can see the terrain change sharply. In the East River portion of the state, between Sioux Falls and the Missouri, you see flat, well-watered farmlands and small farming towns. Then past Pierre you reach West River, with rough, dry badlands, some grazing cattle, and very few structures. Everyone who has looked at a map "knows" about the effect of topography and rainfall, but it means something different as it unfolds below you, like a real-world Google Earth.

You can also see the history of transportation in the way towns are settled. Even in South Dakota's fertile East River area, you can easily trace, from low altitude, what the railroads ushered in 150 years ago, and how their impact has ebbed. As we flew along one of the east-west lines that brought settlers into these territories and carried crops out to markets, we would see little settlements every few minutes. In the 1800s, they were set up at roughly ten-mile intervals, an efficient distance when farmers were delivering their harvests by wagon. Now it seems that four out of five of those towns are withering, as farms are run with giant combines and crops are hauled by truck.

With each city we visited and stop we made, the list of future places we hoped to learn about only grew. But as the months and years went on, we developed a picture of on-the-ground realities different from what we had assumed when the journey began.

# 2013

*Sioux Falls, South Dakota*

*Rapid City, South Dakota*

*Holland, Michigan*

*Burlington, Vermont*

*Eastport, Maine*

# Sioux Falls, South Dakota

We arrived in Sioux Falls on our wedding anniversary. That evening, we headed from our motel to the nearby Granite City brewery: it was an introduction to the reality that we would be able to find brewpubs almost every place we went. (Granite City started in St. Cloud, Minnesota, and was at that time spreading across the Plains States.)

Our anniversary, on the summer solstice in June, is the longest day of the year. In the long, late night of the northern plains on June 21, we watched the sun spread a slanting light over the city's bike path and talked with a group of young women who were out on the town on some sort of celebration. It turned out they were all nursing students, and all from smaller cities around the plains. Did they like Sioux Falls? we asked. Oh yes, they began telling us in detail. It was growing. It was friendly. (Proving their point, they bought us beers when they learned that it was our anniversary.) It was big enough to have everything—especially with a growing medical community—and small enough to be approachable and easy. "It's a big small town," one of them said—the first but not the last time we heard that.

The excitement of the young nurses about the opportunities in the city, and their emphasis on the just-rightness of Sioux Falls, turned out to be no accident. The profound impact of the *local* circumstances—the farm economy, its position as capital of this part of the prairie, its central location within the continent—were ingredients in the economic strategy that made Sioux Falls work.

Every city that is trendy or successful in some way attracts people from someplace else. The biggest, hottest international magnet cities—Los Angeles and San Francisco, New York and Washington, D.C., Boston and Chicago and Miami and Seattle and whatever you'd add to the list—draw people from around the country and the world. If someone from South Dakota shows up at a research lab in Boston or a tech team in the Bay Area or a TV show in Los Angeles, the standard coastal narrative would be that the person had "made it" out of the heartland and into the big time.

The dominant tone we heard in Sioux Falls was of people who feel that they have "made it" precisely by getting to the state's biggest city from the farms or tiny hamlets where they grew up. The big-box malls all around Sioux Falls are a disappointingly familiar part of its look, versus the more homegrown look of its restored and revived downtown. But those malls also symbolize the city's role in the region, which, in turn, gives so many people there a sense of being in the right place at the right time—of having come *to* a place, rather than just having left wherever they were from. Many people we met, like the nurses that first night, talked about Sioux Falls as occupying a sweet spot: big enough to offer most of what is attractive about very large cities (shopping, medical care, entertainment, and an increasingly rich food-and-drink life) but small enough to be manageable, inexpensive, and—something we often heard—"safe."

* * *

Our first impression of Sioux Falls was dominated by three great features. One was the falls themselves, on the Big Sioux River. They are in the center of town, and a dozen years ago they had been crime-ridden and graffiti-covered. As part of a civic cleanup program, they had been surrounded by a polished-seeming Falls Park—an attraction for tourists, a destination for local families. The park's improvement came in parallel with a similar large civic effort: the twenty-mile bike and walking course that circles the entire town. We didn't realize it at the time, but the falls and the trail were markers for something we'd encounter almost every place we went: restoration or revival of civic attractions, like the falls, and creation of bike and walking paths. Deb eventually formulated a law: the mark of a successful city is having a river walk, whether or not there is a river.

The second prominent feature, dominating a hill overlooking the falls and the adjoining part of the bike path, is the state penitentiary. We learned that it was the subject of a hoary local joke. Back in the 1880s, when the Dakota Territory was preparing to become two states, the prospective South Dakota state government offered what was then (and still is now) its largest city, Sioux Falls, a choice: Would it prefer to be the home of the state university? Or of the state penitentiary? The joke was that the penitentiary offered steadier work for locals, so that is what they took. The University of South Dakota wound up in the much smaller town of Vermillion, but Sioux Falls now has an assortment of public and private universities.

The third major feature, the most evocative of all, is the giant downtown abattoir generally known as John Morrell's, where thousands of pigs go to their deaths each day. In many parts of the United States, you might complain that it's hard to "see" the economy anymore. There are too many indistinguishable office blocks, too few old-economy structures where "real" work is done. In downtown Sioux Falls, where the slaughterhouse is an unavoidable visual and aromatic reminder of the realities of the modern food chain—and where it has a distinct social significance, as well—you would never say that. In the century-plus since John Morrell opened the slaughterhouse, in 1909, it has been an arena for wave after wave of ethnic and economic change in this part of America. Eastern Europeans and Germans worked for Morrell during the pre–World War I era of mass immigration. As a high-wage unionized employer for half a century after that war, despite the physical and psychological hardships of the jobs, Morrell was part of the road to the middle class for people in the area. People we met at the newspaper, the universities, the city governments, the banks had family stories that began with versions of "We came to town when my dad got a job with Morrell's." By the 1980s, it was a center of bitter labor strife, which led to a strike and the breaking of the union.

Now it symbolizes two aspects of the global connection of even the most removed-seeming parts of the American topography. One is its workforce, which has become part of the area's refugee fabric. From Somalia, from Sudan, from the Congo, from Burma and Nepal, the latest round of immigrants are working in this plant. The other is its ownership. In the 1990s, the Morrell company sold to Smithfield, which, in turn, was sold in 2013 to the Chinese firm Shuanghui. As we'd known from our previous years in China, Shuanghui and other higher-end food companies were in a desperate race to demonstrate to customers that they offered safer, less adulterated products, ones that met international standards.

Thus from the slaughterhouse in the center of town, in this corner of Plains States America, you had a little parable for globalized connections, regardless of changing political sentiments. Every morning, pigs that have spent all but the final days of their lives in Iowa, which has more permissive legislation on large-scale pig-rearing, cross the Big Sioux River into South Dakota and proceed toward their fate. In the slaughterhouse, workers—mainly refugees who have come from every corner of the world—put the pigs to death and convert them into meat, and then a Chinese company, relying on the United States' reputation for higher food-safety standards, ships much of the meat to customers who are rapidly moving up the protein chain in China.

There was one other significant aspect of Sioux Falls' appearance, which took us a while to notice but whose significance eventually became plain. That is the city's sprawl—taken for granted as part of the automobile-era American landscape, but with additional meaning for Sioux Falls and places like it.

Some cities look smaller than they actually are. When living in Shanghai, we tried to make sense of statistics showing that our immediate walking-and-shopping neighborhood had a population of more than one million, or maybe two. Sioux Falls is the reverse. The official population is above or below two hundred thousand, depending on how much of the surrounding area you take in, but the sprawl and physical extent is that of a much larger place. If the footprint of Sioux Falls were laid down anywhere in China, you'd expect a population at least twenty times as great. We later learned what reasons, apart from standard-issue sprawl, accounted for the city's footprint.


An improbable part of the region's economic base is its role as a financial center. The next time you receive a credit-card statement, check the address. Odds are that your payment is headed to Sioux Falls. That is the result of an effort by state leaders in the late 1970s, when they used the state's heart-of-the-country location as part of a winning argument that Citibank and other major credit-card companies should move their processing centers there from high-cost locations in New York. At the time, Nevada, Delaware, Missouri, and several other states, including South Dakota, were in a race to the bottom to relax their usury laws, so that financial companies headquartered there could charge whatever interest rates they wanted. But in itself that wasn't enough to make Sioux Falls plausible as a next home for operations historically based on the East Coast. "And that's where Benjamin Franklin and Wernher von Braun come in," as Robert E. Wright, an economics professor at Augustana University in Sioux Falls, wrote in "Wall Street on the Prairie," an online history of Citibank's decision.

The Benjamin Franklin part of the decision involved the U.S. Postal Service, of which Franklin was the first postmaster general. For reasons involving the great efficiency of Sioux Falls' transportation system and the congestion of its counterparts in the East, South Dakota officials argued that a payment mailed in from one of the five New York boroughs would reach Citibank more quickly if it had an address *in South Dakota* than if that same check was sent right to its headquarters in New York. "That sounds incredible and is almost certainly apocryphal marketing hype," Wright wrote, "but what mattered is that Citibank officials believed that payments and other correspondence sent from most places in the country would reach Sioux Falls before they would hit New York's financial district."

The Wernher von Braun part of the equation was shorthand for the Cold War–era space systems, military and civilian, that the United

States deployed with help from scientists who had once worked for the Nazis, like von Braun. These included strategic bomber bases and ICBM sites in the Dakotas—which, in turn, meant an advanced telephone and, eventually, Internet communication system that happened to link Sioux Falls with the outside world in a reliable and very high-speed way. In those days when "long-distance" calls were still expensive—either for the customers or for the company offering a 1-800 system to absorb the cost—it was cheaper, on average, for callers from around the country to phone into relatively central Sioux Falls than to call New York. Beyond that, the accent of Sioux Falls residents sounded "normal," rather than regional, to callers from most other states. "People could understand us!" Wright said, when I met him at Augustana. "And on the phone, we were nice. There's a culture of education and work here."

The city willed itself into a role as a back-office financial center. By 1982, one-third of all the mail going through its very efficient post office was for Citibank. By the time we visited, a generation later, 10 percent of the local workforce held finance-related jobs, roughly twice the national average.

Sioux Falls also created an advantage in the realm of high tech, with two facilities that, in their fields, are now world-famous.

One of them, Raven Industries, ended up here through a combination of effort and happenstance. During the all-out militarization of the U.S. economy during World War II, a time in which Henry Ford's car-making company became one of the world's largest producers of airplanes, General Mills, of Minnesota, the same company best known now for breakfast cereals, also served as a military contractor. After the war, General Mills set up the Aeronautical Research Division, which specialized in high-altitude balloons. In those pre-satellite days, balloons were uniquely valuable for carrying sensors and surveillance cameras. By the mid-1950s, four General Mills engineers were ready to leave and start a balloon company of their own. For reasons ranging from airport congestion (airports in the Twin Cities were very crowded; Joe Foss Field, in Sioux Falls, was more welcoming) to prevailing-wind patterns, they decided to start their new company in Sioux Falls.

The company has become dominant in a number of tech-intensive fields, all of them involving advanced balloons. First is Raven's Aerostat line: great big surveillance balloons used by the Customs Service, the U.S. military overseas, and similar customers. We went to a hangar at a Raven location, in the middle of a cornfield ten miles north of the city, to see some of these huge devices.

Another part of the balloon-tech division makes the cartoon-character balloons familiar from Macy's Thanksgiving Day parades in New York. In the summer of 2013, five months before that year's parade, Deb and I enjoyed the frisson of seeing the then-secret designs on the hangar floor. And the third high-tech balloon effort was providing the launch vehicles for Google's Project Loon—an ambitious plan of that era to provide very low-cost "Internet for everyone" to underserved parts of the world, via a network of high-altitude balloons. Raven was making the balloons—sixty feet tall, designed to fly at 66,000 feet—there in Sioux Falls and preparing them for launch.

Raven has also been developing the agricultural version of self-driving cars. These involve GPS guidance systems for farming vehicles so tall, wide, and complex that the word "tractor" seems disrespectful. By whatever name—combine, behemoth—these have been part of a digitized revolution in farming. GPS guidance allows farmers to plow furrows longer and straighter than had ever before been possible; to apply fertilizer to the exact points where seeds have been sown; and in countless other ways to speed the age of "precision agriculture."

Not long after Raven's arrival, Sioux Falls also became the home site of an even more broadly significant aerial-technology company. In the late 1960s, the Pentagon, NASA, and the CIA were looking for a safe central location for the rapidly increasing flow of satellite imagery of the earth. South Dakota's senator Karl Mundt worked with Sioux Falls officials to demonstrate that their area was ideally situated to receive data from satellites as they passed over the United States. In the early 1970s, they opened the Earth Resources Observation and Science Center, or EROS, in a cornfield just north of Sioux Falls. Now it is a repository of more digital images of the earth—military, civilian, environmental, cartographic—than any other. Much of what you have seen on Google Earth originates from a master file at EROS, as did most of the graphics used in international climate talks. Because of EROS, hundreds of scientists have come from around the world to work in Sioux Falls.

We spent most of a day touring EROS, seeing its huge antennas, onto which satellites download their data, and the sequence of historic photos that show the loss of tree cover in the Amazon ("Since the Brazilian government began using our photos, they've slowed the rate of deforestation!" Tom Holm, chief of the policy and communication office at EROS, told us); urban growth in China ("You can see how Beijing emptied out during the Cultural Revolution—and the development since then"); and the changing size of lakes and robustness of wheat fields in the Great Plains States during wet years and dry.

"I have the best possible combination," Holm told us. He had grown up near Sioux Falls, done his undergraduate work at South Dakota State nearby and spent a summer as an intern at EROS, and then headed off for graduate school before returning. "I work in one of the most exciting places on earth, and I am home."

There's more in the town: a significant health-care establishment, part of it funded by a local credit-card entrepreneur made good named Denny Sanford. Diverse community colleges and universities. A start-up tech sector and, for most of the years since 2013, the lowest unemployment rate in the country.

The Sioux Falls area has its severe problems as well. We saw signs of the opioid crisis there. The state's numerous tribal reservations are mainly far to the west, but the chronic economic and health problems of many of their residents affect life statewide. Floods, drought, climate shift, and volatile world markets affect the farming industry; and on down the list. But while the outside world might easily have assumed these and a score of other challenges, how *much* was going on in this part of inland America would, we thought, come as a surprise.

We weren't surprised to find that Sioux Falls had become the move-to town for aspiring residents of many of South Dakota's rural towns. What we hadn't expected was the great number of people in another group, those who were instantly distinguishable from South Dakotans of German and Scandinavian heritage. These are the foreigners, of so many different colors and ethnic groups.

Beginning in the 1970s Sioux Falls welcomed wave after wave of refugees. The city is well known in the refugee and migrant community for having a strong supportive system. The population is large and diverse. Take the schools as a proxy. Nearly 10 percent of the students in Sioux Falls public schools are designated as ELL (English-language learner) students. They are native speakers of some sixty different languages. Sixty. Can you even name sixty languages?

When the Sioux Falls public schools opened their doors in 2013, the biggest single group of these students, about one-third of the total (according to school district figures), were the 700 Spanish speakers, many of whom arrived in migrant worker families. As for the other two-thirds, when we visited, there were 259 Nepali speakers, 135 who spoke Arabic, 129 Swahili, 101 Somali, 93 Amharic, 84 Tigrinya (a Semitic language from the Horn of Africa), and 77 French. A very long tail of other languages included many I've never heard of, and I have been studying languages and linguistics all my life. Mai Mai had 27 speakers in the city, Nuer had 7, and then there were Grebo, Lingala—the list goes on.

The Jane Addams elementary school is an immersion school for the newly arrived non-English-speaking children. The students can stay in the program for up to two years before integrating into mainstream schools. It is part of a strong, textured Sioux Falls infrastructure of support, from health services to jobs to churches to housing to sports.

The school programs start in the classroom and extend to tutoring, summer school, free lunches, and bus passes. They also look to whole-family success. Home-to-school liaisons do things like help schedule parent-teacher conferences and round up translators. Sometimes, translation involves the children's game of telephone, where speakers pass on a message from one language to the next and the next, and then back again. Such details are fundamental to keeping the entire system working.

The refugees and those who work with them told me about some of the cultural differences:

*Gender:* Many of the immigrants come from countries and cultures where education for girls is an afterthought. Arriving in the States, girls lag far behind in their school experience or may even be starting school for the first time, no matter what their age. The academic and social cost to the girls is obvious. Boys often have another advantage. In a word: soccer. Being a good athlete translates into many advantages, starting with positive attention from teammates, classmates, coaches, and fans.

*Birthdays:* Many refugee kids share a January 1 birthday. Coincidence? A mother of ten from one refugee family told me that if she, instead of her husband, had been the one to answer questions during the blur of the final entry paperwork, she would have provided the proper birth dates. The default was January 1.

*Lunch:* Many students told me that because of their sketchy schooling in refugee camps and their native countries or just being on the move for years, they aren't competitive enough academically to get into the classes with the "American kids," as they call them. That leaves lunch as a potential hangout time to mix and mingle. They also said that while friendships at least have a chance to start at lunch, they usually also end at lunch. After-school jobs, transportation issues, and the preferences of some families to keep their children close can complicate the after-school social scenes for newly arrived kids. I heard from coaches who would personally drive some of their immigrant athletes to and from practices, so they could be part of the team.

*Being Muslim:* Administrators noticed that it seemed particularly cruel for fasting students to sit idly in the cafeteria during Ramadan while everyone else was eating. To address that, the school provided a place for those students to spend that time.

*The basics:* Where do you start acculturation with the ocean-deep discrepancies among the children? In refugee-rich Burlington, Vermont, one school's population includes the daughter of the principal and a little boy whose life experience is so raw that he pees in the corner of the classroom because he can't imagine a toilet in a restroom.

*Reaching for dreams:* A refugee from Darfur, a high school soph-omore, told me with pride that she had joined Junior ROTC at her school. She said she liked the history lessons and the activities the program provided. A big disappointment, however, was not being allowed to wear her hijab along with her ROTC uniform to school on Dress Day. She would have to choose.

It was beyond me, from my adult perspective, that this girl's preoccu-pying problem at sixteen years old was her apparel conflict. She had been through more tragedy and miracle by the time she was six years old than most of us will experience in a lifetime. When Muslims fled Darfur on foot across Sudan to escape death, she was separated from her family and lost in the chaos of war. At six years old. Later, in a miracle of odds that expunged her bad fortune, she was reunited with her family in a camp.

I heard some months later that ROTC officials at her school had appealed her case all the way to the top, and she was allowed to dress as she wished on formal dress day.

During our first week in town, I mentioned to a local college professor that the place seemed "over-retailed." Its shopping malls, chain stores, and specialty shops were part of the overall sense that it had a larger physical layout than its population would normally indicate. The his-toric downtown was in the middle of a comeback, with new restaurants and shops and breweries, as well as metal and stone statuary. But the edges of town, especially where interstate highways entered from east and west, north and south, were occupied by huge shopping malls, plus motels and chain restaurants. Sioux Falls is roughly the same size as Bur-lington, Vermont, which we would visit a few weeks later. But it has an incomparably larger number of McDonald's and Subway franchises, plus Sonics, Olive Gardens, and Taco Bells, and every other standardized eat-ing, shopping, lodging, payday-loan-giving establishment you would find anywhere. Walmart and Sam's Club, Michaels and Lowes, big-box stores of any kind—they are all around, including in what has become the state's largest tourist draw (yes, exceeding Mount Rushmore), the Empire Mall.

How, I wondered, did they possibly stay in business? Sioux Falls is not *that* big a town. "You'll notice," the professor said, "that we're also 'over-lawyered.' And over-banked, and over-doctored and over-hospitalized, and over-serviced in any way you want to name."

The reason, he explained, was the city's emergence over the past generation as the economic capital of the region as a whole. If you lived within a couple-hundred-mile radius and needed to do back-to-school or special shopping, get a medical checkup, or spend money on entertainment, you were less likely to look in your own tiny Dakota town and more likely to go into Sioux Falls. The city's economic-development leaders refer to this as its "fringe city" advantage, as the nearest biggish city for the surrounding rural areas in both Dakotas, Iowa, southern Minnesota, and northern Nebraska. The next level of bigger cities are "the Cities," Minneapolis and St. Paul to the east, Denver to the west, and Omaha to the south, all more than casual-driving distance away.

This pattern is obviously bad for the much-smaller cities in the area—we heard about those who had lost their clinic or their school or their grocery store, as services concentrated in metropolises like Sioux Falls—but changed the character of Sioux Falls in a way we hadn't expected, and that was a reminder of some classic chronicles of boom-era towns in the American West. What were some of the signs? Once we were alerted to watch for them, we saw more and more.

For all our days in Sioux Falls, we stayed in a bargain "extended-stay suites" motel right near the famed Empire Mall. The place was jammed on each of our visits: during the week, mainly with business visitors, but starting Thursday nights and through the weekend, mainly with families from farms and tiny towns who had come to shop and see the city. People also came for medical treatment at the area's two big competing (both nonprofit) health-care systems, Sanford and Avera.

When we talked with college students at Augustana, the private Lutheran college, or the public universities, the most typical story was: I am from Spearfish (or Mitchell, Watertown, Brookings, Huron, Pierre, a farm twenty miles from the nearest town) and I've made it out of there for college. From them and other college-age people in the area we heard: Back in my town, the public school is shrinking or being consolidated (so we go to a regional school); the local grocery store is closing (because the owner got too old), so we take big shopping trips; the post office is closing; it's only my parents (or my uncle, my grandparents, our old neighbors) who are back there, because it doesn't take much manpower to run the farm.

We talked over pizza with a dozen students who had just graduated from a Sioux Falls public high school and were all headed off to college—most in the immediate area, one to the University of Nebraska, another to a small private school farther away. They were as bright-eyed and, yes, bushy-tailed as you'd expect from young kids from the Midwest, and we all gathered at the home of one of them. We asked how many of them had lived on a farm, and one or two hands went up. How many had immediate relatives still on farms or in small farming towns? All but one person.

"Our overall growth rate has been about one-third births, one-third people from smaller places in state, and one-third from out of state," Reynold Nesiba, an economist from Augustana University (and later one of South Dakota's few Democratic state senators), told me. (When I checked with him a few years later, he said that the international arrival rate had gone down, and the local birth rate had gone up.) "There are lots of people for whom this *is* the big city. And lots of people who grow up here may head off to Omaha or Minneapolis, but when they have their own families, they recognize that it's a very nice place to live."

One question on my mind as we set off to see the country and landed in South Dakota was "How will it sound?" Would the regionalisms of language be strong and obvious, or would the edges of American English have been flattened into submission by our shared national media, our easy communications, and the popularity of travel?

It didn't take long before the first examples of regional language popped out, reassurance to me that they are alive and well.

On that Sunday in Sioux Falls, when Jim and I borrowed bikes from friends to ride the twenty-mile circuit circling town, we stopped to watch a fisherman casting into the stream that runs alongside a long section of the path. Just then, a serious fellow biker screeched to a stop and backtracked toward us.

I instinctively braced myself for the rebuke "GET A HELMET!," which I hear when I sometimes ride helmet-free on the Capital Crescent Trail along the Potomac in Washington, D.C. To my surprise, the Sioux Falls rider started in with a friendly litany of "Are ya lost? Can I help? Ya need some direction?" I was caught off guard, then surprised at my own surprise by his friendly gesture here in the heart of the Midwest.

I also heard plenty of classic Dakota phrases. There were "You betchas," sometimes in response to "Thank you." And "Are you coming with?," where the preposition hangs out there gratuitously, when "Are you coming?" would have been quite enough. A number of people suggested that the dangling "with" was a holdover from the German *mitkommen,* which would be comfortable for the 40 percent of South Dakotans of German heritage. *Kommen Sie mit?* Or literally "Come you with?"

I listened closely to people's language during the interviews and conversations we had in Sioux Falls, with politicians and educators, city administrators, schoolkids, academics, newspaper editors, businesspeople and regular people. These happened in offices, at factories, or at pizza dinners with high school kids, during tours at public schools, home visits, casual encounters in restaurants, standing in lines, at museums, at local shops, at swimming pools, and, of course, over beers.

A number of Sioux Falls words and phrases popped out frequently, starting on our first night in town with the young women in the restaurant. All together, they formed a surprisingly coherent story of the culture of Sioux Falls. Opposite is the word cloud I put together, and what it taught me about Sioux Falls. The bigger the font, the more often I heard the word or phrase.

*Who we are:* So many words and phrases described how people felt about each other. *Modest, nice, humble, nonconfrontational,*

*inclusive.* One person's *nice* or *humble* in Sioux Falls is another person's *passive-aggressive* and *too much like-minded.*

*How we live:* Here is the stuff of everyday life. *Safe, safety, a real safe place* came from the homegrown teenagers and their parents, who felt the kids could have the run of the town. It also came from recently arrived refugees who were either assigned to Sioux Falls or had found their way there as a second resettlement town, after hearing on the refugee grapevine that Sioux Falls was a safe place.

*Easy life* meant logistically easy, as in short commutes and drive times for errands or school. But here is how relative that description can be: one high school girl, a refugee who had walked across lawless South Sudan to her freedom, said that in Sioux Falls, she could walk merely a mile from her house to the grocery store, where she both worked and shopped. A mile, with groceries, in the South Dakota winter, I remember thinking at the time, and this was her definition of an *easy life.*

*Our town:* Sioux Falls is *a big small town,* said so many people. They clarified that they meant the town was small enough to protect and nurture, yet big enough that high school kids say they would like to stay or return one day, and the older generation extols its arts, higher education, recreation, and job possibilities.

If I heard this once, I heard it a thousand times: the references to *East River* and *West River.* I am sure everyone in South Dakota knows this, but for the rest of you, the demarcation refers to the Missouri River, which splits the state in half, not only geographically but also culturally, historically, politically, agriculturally, and economically. Locals could barely refer to it enough.

Two Sioux Falls words, *honesty* and *collaboration,* turned out to portend what I would hear later everywhere around the United States. At first, I thought they were special to Sioux Falls, but I soon learned that they are part of the new national vocabulary. *Honesty*, as in "I'll have to be honest with you," "honestly," or "let's be honest." References to honesty caught my attention as I wondered why people in the Midwest would need to lean on such a qualifier. Weren't they always honest? But once I noticed "honesty" in Sioux Falls, I started noticing it everywhere. Uttered by national pundits or chatty media, it arrives at my ears as a framing phrase that is less about honesty and more like "You may not like what I'm about to say, and I may not be comfortable with it either, so be prepared for what's coming." By the end of our journey, I'd heard these phrases used so frequently that they seemed whitewashed and barely registered anymore. As for the word *collaboration*, that's another story. Remember it for later.

*The grand finale: I love Sioux Falls!* There is something about this phrase that is very disarming and genuine. I came to think that in its unabashed simplicity, it pretty well sums up how the residents of Sioux Falls talk about their town.

# Rapid City, South Dakota

We ended up flying in circles around the Midwest that first warm summer; three times to Sioux Falls, with Holland, Michigan, and Rapid City in between. Luckily, those distances by small plane weren't far. We also managed to squeeze in a trip to Colorado and the western part of Wyoming, with a quick visit back to D.C. as well.

We knew even before the approach to KRAP—the unfortunate call sign for the airport at Rapid, as we soon learned to call the town—that it was a good decision to take a rest stop for a few days. This was Mount Rushmore territory. Seeing Mount Rushmore from ground level almost defies belief. Seeing it from overhead, we agreed, was so great that we shouldn't really tell anyone about it. For me, it goes into the category of "why we fly." Jim said the presidential busts from the sky reminded him of Japanese netsuke figures, in the surprising subtlety of their carving that you can see from above.

We were meeting one of Jim's pilot friends there, David Schwietert. Pilots share a special camaraderie, and they are as friendly and welcoming to each other as are those in two other groups I've met around the world: Esperanto speakers and members of the Baha'i faith. If you're part of these groups and show up somewhere, anywhere, fellow members of the group will take care of you.

David and his wife, Rhonda, drove us west and north toward Lead and Deadwood, deep into the beauty of the Black Hills. David pointed out the damage already done by the rampage of the pine bark beetle, which survives the now-warmer winters and is killing the glorious ponderosa pines. It is turning the forests to a shade of rust that reminds me of autumn in the Alleghenies, and it is paving the way for epic fires that local firefighters predict in terms of "when," not "if."

Our destination was the Pathways Spiritual Sanctuary, a labor of love by Dave Snyder, who, after a career as a pig farmer in Nebraska, decided to create a refuge for reflection. He bought two hundred acres of forest and meadowland in the low hills and tamed paths and resting spots, where he placed statues and rock collections, and then he opened the sanctuary to the public from dawn to dusk daily. Japanese-inspired torii gates mark meditation spots within the forests. There is a copy of a majestic bronze sculpture called *The Invocation,* by western artist Buck McCain, that Snyder had recast and brought in from Santa Fe for reassembly by local artisans. People walk, meditate, and record their thoughts or impressions in journals that he provides in weatherproof Tupperware containers along the way. We read accounts by grateful visitors from Japan, Germany, all parts of the United States. Snyder's pet llamas graze near his elegant, rustic house.

We didn't realize it at the time, but this peaceful commune with art and nature was the first of several we would appreciate around America over the next four years.

Rapid won its way into our hearts in another surprising way: hotels. During his travels with Charley, Steinbeck slept mostly in his converted camper truck, Rocinante. Mark Twain slept in stagecoaches, trains, and at frontier travelers' lodgings. William Least Heat-Moon slept along blue highways in his van named Ghost Dancing. Up until Rapid, we slept mostly in hotels and motels, especially those with "suites" in their name, for more space, a kitchenette, and laundry facilities, which were invaluable when we were traveling for a long time. By the end of our journey, we would have visited about forty of those. We stayed with friends, with friends of friends, in eco-hotels, restored vintage hotels of varying quality, a motel with a bear theme, at a truck stop, and we were destined to stay once in quarters above a prison call center. We never slept in the plane or under its wing, although die-hard fliers would say we missed something by not doing that. That's okay by me.

We stumbled, quite by accident, into a jewel of a hotel in Rapid, called the Adoba. The Adoba, which has since changed its name to the Rushmore Hotel and Suites, was built more than thirty years ago and had a bumpy history of bankruptcies before it was bought in 1995 by its current owners, the Merali family, whose forebears were from India, and who came from the Congo via Belgium, England, Canada, and several spots in the United States before landing in Rapid City.

Sacha Merali, the family's handsome third-generation twenty-something, has been leading the drive to make the Adoba into a LEED-certified "green" hotel. That word, "green," had fixed itself in America's vernacular during the years we were away in China, from 2006 to 2009. I asked Sacha for some show-and-tell to help me understand what "green" means for a hotel.

We toured the construction of a guest room. The original door had been retained and wrapped in a new cover, for looks. The entry floor was floating laminate planks, made from crushed paper and grooved to eliminate gluing. The carpet had been jigsawed together from individual tiles made from recycled natural grass, stone, and fibers from other carpets. Its backing had been made from sugar, salt, sand, and rubber. I began to think that in case of emergency, I could eat this room.

Sacha Merali was passionate about functionality and user experience in his hotel. The desk in our room was a sleek ten-foot stretch with plenty of outlets, no marketing clutter, and an amenities tray made from a recycled metal road sign. Above the full length of the desk was a custom mural of iconic Rushmore and wildlife sites drawn with soy ink on washable, wipeable canvas.

Most of the room's furniture had been custom-made by companies within a five-mile radius of Rapid City—a conscious decision, said Sacha, to support local businesses, reduce transportation costs, and be creative and collaborative with design. A second full-wall mural was a photograph of a local forest scene, shot by the hotel's multitasking chef-photographer. According to Sacha, the nanotechnology of the photo-wallpaper absorbs odors.

My favorite discovery was desk chairs with a back designed to serve as a hook on which to hang a purse. No more purses taking up a chair or parked on the floor.

Other parts of the green list: sheets made from organic cotton and eucalyptus (cool); window shades adjustable for sheer or blackout (heat and light); pillows made from recycled water-bottle fibers (comfy); a 100 percent wool mattress (natural, breathable); chemical-free room paint; toilets that use only 1.5 gallons per flush; LED lighting for the entire room that consumes only as much electricity as a single 75 watt bulb (bright enough).

I would have loved to stay longer in this gem, but we were pressing on at that point, getting back to our original plan with a destination of Holland, Michigan.

# Holland, Michigan

At first glance, Holland's downtown may strike a visitor as kitschy, with its posters of tulips and reproductions of works by Van Gogh and other Dutch artists. The local airport where we landed was called Tulip City Airport. It has since switched to the less distinctive name, West Michigan Regional Airport. Holland's city museum has a display on the history and technology of windmills, and a windmill shipped over from Holland stands by Lake Macatawa, which feeds into Lake Michigan. A long-popular restaurant, Russ', has as its emblem a wooden-shoe-wearing Dutch boy carrying a hamburger to waiting customers. But downtown Holland has many other faces as well, and they don't take long to discover. Parks with walking and biking paths, a lakeside venue for outdoor public concerts in the summer, graceful white churches, the campus buildings of Hope College.

When you walk downtown Holland's streets, volunteer "greeters" will gently step in if you pause, offering brochures and explanations of the bronze statues scattered around town, mentioning the public events that are happening, suggesting the pointers for local shops and restaurants, the university and museum.

We quickly noticed traits that we eventually learned to associate with towns on the rise. Residential buildings and new hotels. Multiple restaurants, and a brewery. Viable stores that are not part of a national chain.

Corporate headquarters that have moved downtown. A nearby college student base, from Hope College, which is located downtown, but also from several other schools in the vicinity.

We also felt the downtown's micro on-the-street sense: almost all of the shop fronts were occupied. Strikingly, almost none of them were lawyers' or doctors' offices, financial consulting firms, or other "dead" professional space that does almost nothing to attract casual foot traffic. Most of the second- and third-floor spaces above the shop fronts create permanent vitality with apartments or offices, and there were also two large "senior-living" facilities right in the downtown. One of the local experts I asked about downtown, Greg Holcombe of a civic group called Riverview, said that the overall occupancy rate in the downtown area was around 95 percent. And, in a way I hadn't seen in exactly this form elsewhere, the private, religious-based Hope College runs seamlessly into the edge of the downtown district, without any suggestion that the environs are a standard college town. The downtown is small, but—compared with most towns I know of this scale—it all seemed to be working, especially on the warm summer nights we were in Holland. The street fair was jammed, and we had trouble finding room at restaurants.

One very surprising and very purposeful step, unique to Holland, has made a big difference in extending this summer success into the winter—for a town that is, after all, in the Upper Midwest.

The surprising story involves Edgar Prince, one of the many very successful industrialists in town. Prince (who is ethnically Dutch; his original surname was Prins) proposed that the city install on its downtown sidewalks and streets something he had tried in some of his factory loading docks: a snowmelt system. It would be a way to increase the allure of downtown in the face of a challenge from the big-box malls.

Prince proposed and partly underwrote taking hot water from the cooling system of the giant downtown coal-powered electric plant and running it through a set of orange plastic pipes placed under the city's streets and sidewalks, to keep them free of snow. (He personally put in $250,000, and the city matched that figure. Prince guaranteed that if the annual operating costs came to more than $30,000, he would cover any amount over that. The costs have stayed below that level.) "It was only a five–three vote in the council, and it was intensely debated," Jim Timmermann, then the opinion editor of *The Holland Sentinel,* told us. "It was really rough, because you had six months of the downtown being entirely chewed up, and some of the smaller businesses didn't make it." (Timmermann died two years after our visit, of a bone-marrow disorder, in his midfifties.)

But the heating system worked, and twenty-five years later, it not only persists but has been expanded. It originally covered some 200,000 square feet; by the time of our visit, the area had more than doubled, and by 2017 it had expanded farther to 600,000 square feet, and nearly five linear miles. When we visited, the coal-fired plant was about to be phased out and replaced by one using natural gas. The city has an ambitious "district heating" plan to use its waste-heat cooling water to expand the snowmelt system, heat the college, and so on.

Everything about Holland, we quickly learned, was connected to the culture of *creating.* San Francisco has a culture of people who start new Web companies; D.C., people who start new blogs or interest groups or think tanks. In this part of western Michigan, it's a culture of people who start companies that make things. "When you don't know what to do, you think of the next product you could make," Dann Engels, a local entrepreneur and manufacturer we'd known for years, told us soon after we arrived.

"This has remained a place *that makes things,*" said Randy Thelen, from an area-development group called Lakeshore Advantage. "It still has the engineering base, the industrial design base, and all the rest that comes with that. Around the world, there are going to be pockets of manufacturing—and ours will be one of them."

The economy of Holland and its western Michigan neighbors, of which the best known is Grand Rapids, is about 40 percent manufacturing based, or roughly twice the average for the country as a whole. The "Big Three" of the world's office-furniture industry—Steelcase, Herman Miller, and Haworth—are here or in the immediate environs. Although the city has no single huge factory, on the model of the auto plants of Detroit or the old steelworks of Pennsylvania and Ohio, it has countless smaller, higher-value, supply-chain facilities. This factory makes glass; this one makes windshield wipers; the next one makes seats. Some of the auto-industry suppliers still have viable plants, and others have shifted to different product lines. Korea's LG company had its biggest battery factory outside of Asia in the area. A shop that had once made sailboats now makes enormous wind turbine blades. This is not even to mention the world's largest pickle-processing plant. The city's museum tells the story of the original boat-builders and other craftsmen who had come there in the late 1800s, mainly from (of course) Holland. Their influence is felt still.

There is considerable family blood in the veins of Holland's manufacturing. Of course, everybody knows that family-owned and personally owned businesses can behave differently from publicly traded firms. For the big corporations, it is a compliment rather than a criticism to say that ultimately they care most about dividend growth and "maximizing shareholder value." Toward that end, layoffs, outsourcing, cost-cutting, cheese-paring, union-busting—you name it, if it can arguably lead to greater long-run corporate profitability, then by definition it is what management should do.

A family-run or privately held business can do things differently, for better and worse. Worse: management jobs for relatives, whether competent or not. Better: sometimes deciding to take a temporary loss or settle for less-than-maximized profit in exchange for some other goal. Through its decades of collapse, the newspaper industry has illustrated these trade-offs. Family ownership has led to its excesses: Hearst, McCormick, Murdoch. But also to some great ambitious traditions: Binghams (until they sold), Chandlers (until they sold), Grahams (until they sold), Sulzbergers, et cetera.

Many of the area's strongest manufacturers make auto-industry and aerospace components for customers in North America and beyond. Haworth, Herman Miller, and nearby Steelcase sell into the world office-furniture market. The Padnos family's scrap and recycling company has big markets in China. The Amway corporation, founded and run not far away, is, of course, a global titan. But an unusually large amount of Holland's economic activity comes from companies that have their headquarters right in the vicinity or are still owned and run by people who live in the immediate area. And every single person we spoke with emphasized the difference that this awareness of local circumstances, this involvement in local long-term prospects, and this latitude of policy for family-owned companies made in the region's life.

Jeff and Peggy Padnos, longtime residents, happen to offer one of Holland's finest examples of what family-owned business can do for a town. Deb and I had known them since college in the 1960s, when Jeff was—like us—a small-towner who had come to the East. He was from the most prominent family in Holland's very small Jewish population; Peggy's family hailed from Jamaica, and she had grown up in New York. As their relationship became serious, she learned that anyone who was going to marry Jeff was going to move back to Holland and convert to Judaism. They were in love; they moved back; she converted; and they are civic and business pillars of their town.

The Padnoses are the third generation of their family to run what started out in 1905 as the Louis Padnos Scrap Iron Company. Louis Padnos, Jeff's grandfather, came to the United States as part of the great wave of turn-of-the-twentieth-century immigration and made his way to this small manufacturing town. "I've sometimes introduced myself by saying that my grandfather was a 'junk dealer,' my father and uncle were 'scrap processors,' and that my brother, cousins and I are 'recyclers,'" Jeff Padnos notes on the company's website. "More recently, I've started to add that, with the next generation, we are moving into 'sensible sustainability.'"

In practice, what this means is a sprawling facility on the east side of town where almost anything that is discarded in modern American life—from the cardboard that goes into recycling bins to the bumpers and interiors from scrapped automobiles—is separated, cleaned, pulverized, or in some other way prepared for reuse and shipped to facilities (largely in China) to be put back to use again. The company employs some six hundred people, among them a significant number of people who had served time for offenses and who the Padnoses thought deserved a new chance. Around town are pieces of public art the Padnos family has sponsored or created.

On our first weekend in Holland, Jim and I went in search of bikes to rent. From the air, biking looked like a good way to cover a lot of the town at ground level, from the downtown through the residential areas, around the river to the public beaches along Lake Michigan.

I called several shops only to discover that bikes were available on Saturday but not on Sunday. When I asked one shopkeeper if she knew of another shop that might be open on Sunday, she responded with an undertone of "Did I need to ask?" "No," she said, "Sunday is Family Day." Family Day! And sure enough, every bike shop in this churchgoing, family-centric town was closed, even during the height of the summer tourist season. I began noticing signs in shop windows: "Closed for Family Day." Sunday closures are not new, but Family Day closures were new to me. I didn't recall them from my youth in the Midwest, and I've certainly never seen them in our hometown of Washington, D.C.

Two other families' philanthropic marks are everywhere. We saw the vast DeVos Fieldhouse sporting complex at Hope College and met people who worked at the nearby Van Andel Institute, a medical research center. They have also been involved in political tangles, at the local and national levels. The DeVos family originally made its money from the Amway company. The best-known current member of the family is Betsy, who at the time of our visit was a leading figure in Michigan Republican politics, and who later became secretary of education under Donald Trump. She grew up as Betsy Prince, daughter of Edgar Prince of snowmelt fame and his wife, Elsa. Her brother is Erik Prince, a onetime navy SEAL who became head of the private security firm Blackwater.

While the influence of leading families may not always be positive or comfortable, we came across evidence of local industrial families pitching in for the city's development time and again. For instance:

- "Mr. Prince [of the snowmelt plan] and others thought it was very much in their interest to create a dynamic downtown," said Randy Thelen, of Lakeshore Advantage. "Prince was a huge factor in improving the downtown," noted Jim Timmermann of *The Holland Sentinel.* "He bought up properties and held on to them until he was confident that the right purchaser or tenant had come along." Prince's wife, Elsa, who remarried after his death, is still involved in downtown-development work.

-  At the arts council, the symphony, the museum, the colleges, and almost any other civic site you can mention are plaques acknowledging gifts from the same list of local family-business names.

- In the public school system, and at the private-religious Hope College, we heard repeatedly about the networks and programs locally based businesses have created to place graduates in jobs.

- Local business families have also been leading a lake-cleanup effort and a community energy-efficiency program.

- A striking dog-that-didn't-bark counterexample is the enormous downtown Heinz pickleworks, the oldest major factory in town and the biggest pickleworks in the world. The pickleworks doesn't pull its weight in Holland, we often heard, in terms of its civic-leader profile. The extensive and remarkable efforts the Heinz family has undertaken in Pittsburgh, its hometown, haven't reached the same way to Holland, where there is no family presence.

"What makes the city what it is?" Jim Timmermann of the *Sentinel* asked when we talked with him. Timmermann grew up in Southern California but came to Holland with his wife, a Hope College professor, in the early 1990s. He answered his own question: "It's because of the local entrepreneurs who started their companies here, kept them here, and remained active in the community."

Jack Groot, founder and owner of the very popular JP's Coffee, downtown, across the street from New Holland Brewing, summed up what Holland's long, deep investment has meant to encouraging his generation, and others to follow, toward success. He came to the city about twenty years earlier, as the downtown recovery was beginning.

Groot's start-up story is what people in any industry would recognize as a classic sequence. He thought coffeehouses could be popular, although "ninety-five percent of the people I talked with thought I was crazy"; he saved money and borrowed from his parents, and it all worked. "It didn't hurt that I have a Dutch name!" he added. But he also made a particular point, at the beginning and end of our talk: "I would not be here, at this level, without what is all around me"—by which he meant a revived downtown, snow-free streets, long-term "patient capital" investment to redo the other shops, a systematic effort to lure chefs from big-city restaurants to start businesses in Holland. The emphasis on rising and falling together was something I heard a lot—in this politically very conservative area. "I have the best location in all of western Michigan!" said Groot.

(Groot's shop was successful enough that in 2014, a year after our visit, a larger local coffee and nut firm offered to buy it, and he accepted. The shop was remodeled and rebranded, under a different name. Groot worked for the company for a while, left under a non-compete agreement that kept him from opening a new coffee shop, and went into another business in the area.)


Through the entirety of our travel, we were interested in the local and regional story, so we started (and usually ended) on that theme. National politics rarely came up, well into 2016.

Although a number of contentious national politics debates were under way, we guessed that if one were volunteered for discussion in Holland, it would probably be Obamacare (given the region's abundance of small-business owners affected by its regulations—and rich families affected by its high-end taxes) or gay marriage (given its dominant conservative-Christian tone). In fact, the theme that came up most frequently was immigration, and in a way we had not foreseen.

We heard about it most dramatically from Brian Davis, a Michigan native who had become Holland's superintendent of schools. Throughout the previous generation, the main challenge for the school system had been a local variant of a familiar national pattern. White parents kept moving with their children across town borders to the suburban districts or shifting their children to the numerous religious and charter schools in town. Mainly non-white immigrants and migrant workers kept arriving with their families. Thus by 2005, Holland was in the familiar situation of having a mainly non-white public school population in a mainly white small town.

This shift mattered because of the nature of Michigan's school funding, which works differently from that of most other states. In most of the country, each district mainly funds its own schools. Rich districts do better—including when rich, childless families are still paying for the local schools. Poor districts do worse. Michigan's school system is more centrally funded than most. Districts send their money into the state. The state sends money back to the schools, based on how many students they enroll. Thus a migration of kids to private or religious schools, which reduces the public school headcount, undercuts public school funding more directly than it does in most other places.

The Holland public school system, which had been in trouble for a while, took its biggest step toward addressing this problem by getting a big local bond measure passed, with a comfortable margin, even though this was during the nationwide financial crisis, and even though a majority of residents in this politically conservative city had no children in the public schools. (We would later see a similar development in the otherwise very different town of Dodge City, Kansas.) Brian Davis told us that the bond was only one part of a much broader strategy for improving the schools, but that it was a very consequential step.

"Had that bond measure not passed, I really believe it would have contributed to the slow death of the institution of public education as we know it today," he told us during our visit. "We could have evolved into a district that served largely at-risk kids. There is nothing wrong with that, but it further segregates out resources and opportunities."

"We have children who come from homes with a million-plus annual income, and ones who come from homes with incomes under twenty thousand dollars," he said. "Just under ten percent of them are considered homeless. When you factor all those variables in, it's the future of what public education looks like."

# Burlington, Vermont

Burlington: you have to start with Bernie, as the country has come to know him. The dominant political figure in Burlington's modern history is Bernie Sanders—an independent senator from Vermont since 2007, the state's only House member before that, and, through the Reagan years, from 1981 to 1989, the embattled and effective mayor of Burlington. Running for mayor as an independent, Sanders beat a long-time Democratic incumbent by ten votes. Through the next year, the Democratic-dominated city council tried to thwart every appointment, proposal, and piece of legislation Sanders put forward. "They thought my election was a fluke—they called it a fluke!" Sanders told me in 2015 in Washington. "Their strategy was to prevent me from doing anything, so the people would realize their mistake and get rid of me next time. At the first city council meeting, they fired my only appointee." He drew the obvious comparison to the GOP's strategy of hamstringing and waiting out Barack Obama.

The difference, as Sanders has not been shy in pointing out, is that he directly fought back, and overcame rather than compromised with his main opponents. His city attorney and the state attorney general sued the Central Vermont Railway for control of waterfront property then used for petroleum storage and a rail siding. They won, and now the land is the site of an aquarium and science center, bike paths, and other public facilities. "We put together a grassroots coalition and made the city as open as we could," Sanders told me. "Unions, workers, low-income people, women, environmentalists—that's the kind of politics I believe in."

Sanders pushed to create a "land trust," a kind of permanent endowment for low-cost housing in the city. His economic-development agency concentrated not on recruiting big outside employers but on "helping the small businesses we had grow." Sanders started after-school programs that are now popular at all the city's schools.

"He just turned that city around," noted Chris Graff, a longtime Associated Press correspondent in Vermont and the author of a book on the state's politics, *Dateline Vermont*. "People will tell you, 'What Burlington is, is because of Bernie,' and they are right." Melinda Moulton, who moved to Vermont in the early 1970s and has led waterfront reconstruction through the Main Street Landing company, which she co-founded with Lisa Steele, told us, "He really is a socialist, and thinks that what is good about the city should be available to everyone."

Sanders told me that his "major political achievement" came when he ran for reelection in 1983, after two years in office. Voter turnout doubled, and he won an easy victory: "People saw something happening in the city, and they wanted to be involved." He eventually served four terms, in his last election defeating a candidate who was running with both Republican and Democratic support.

Deb and I realized after several visits to Burlington that people elsewhere almost assumed we should apologize for including it in our travels. It could seem almost too special, too nice.

Burlington has built-in advantages and hard-won achievements. It has a natural scenic location, right on the shores of Lake Champlain. It has lake walks, bike trails, parks, a science center, and an arts center directly overlooking the water. Its downtown is thriving. On warm evenings— and even cool ones—the restaurants on the pedestrian street are usually overflowing.

The beloved state university, the University of Vermont (generally known as UVM) has a sizable student population to buoy local business (plus visiting families to stay in hotels and go to restaurants) and academic staff from around the world to enrich its cultural and creative base and generate spin-off businesses. Students from other parts of the country get a look at the area through UVM or Burlington's two smaller colleges, Champlain and St. Michael's, and some decide to stay.

It's the largest city in the self-consciously separate and special realm of Vermont—which means it has an ability to choose its own path more easily than other places might. Burlington's main political division is not between Democrats and Republicans, as in Washington, D.C., or between Tea Party and mainstream Republicans, as in many "red" states, but between the Democratic Party and the socialists (the Vermont Progressive Party), of which Senator Bernie Sanders was a prominent member during his rise as a crusading mayor of Burlington.

The scale of the entire state of Vermont—with just over 600,000 people in the entire state, ranked 49 on the list of states, ahead of only Wyoming—and of Burlington in particular makes concerted action feasible there, on projects that would be much harder at greater scale. (The square mile where we lived in Shanghai had a much higher population than the nearly ten thousand square miles of Vermont.) For the record, Vermont is also the very whitest state in the country; as of the 2010 census, its population was about 95 percent white. (The next four whitest are, in order, Maine, West Virginia, New Hampshire, and Iowa, a reminder that the crucial two first contests in a presidential primary are the fourth and fifth whitest states in the union.)

Like all cities, Burlington has its problems. The drug culture is apparent, starting with the multitude of signage downtown that warns people against loitering for no good reason. Even before the modern opioid and heroin epidemic had proven devastating in the Midwest and Appalachia, its effects were evident in Vermont. On the cultural side, there are tensions between old-family Vermont residents and new arrivals. Every tension of have and have-not America also affects this thriving college-and-tech town in a largely poor state. Still, the town's success is notable, and it didn't happen by itself.


While in Burlington, we often heard a comparison to a smaller city across Lake Champlain, Plattsburgh, New York. Both cities enjoyed a big boost in their economies through shares of the military-industrial complex. In the 1950s and 1960s, the Strategic Air Command based its East Coast B-52 squadrons in Plattsburgh, a start that ended in a consequent blow when Plattsburgh Air Force Base was shuttered in the 1990s, after the Cold War ended. For its part, Burlington has had an Air National Guard contingent based at its airport, which all of its politicians, including Bernie Sanders, have fought to preserve. But Burlington's big post–World War II turning point came with the arrival in the late 1950s of what eventually turned out to be one of IBM's major semiconductor works, in the suburb of Essex Junction, just east of Burlington. At its peak, the IBM factory employed some eight thousand engineers and technical workers. Its staff fell to about three thousand (and IBM has sold the works to another company, a Silicon Valley spin-off called GlobalFoundries). But its influence on Burlington remains profound.

"When IBM came, a whole different type of person was moving to town, and new businesses came from that, too," Chris Graff said. We kept running into people whose parents had relocated to the area to work for IBM, and we kept hearing that this was one of the "everything was different after that . . ." watershed events for the local economy, even beyond the direct payroll effect. After that: the schools got better, the universities got better, there was a different talent pool, and a different sense of plausible businesses to start up and run in Burlington. More times than not, when we asked the founder of a start-up or his or her employees why they were doing business in Vermont, the answer began with either "We were up here for school" or "My parents came here with IBM" or "My parents were looking to get away from the big cities." This was Burlington's version of the comments we heard about college and the Morrell slaughterhouse in Sioux Falls and how it became the go-to town.

Mayor Miro Weinberger, who had been elected the year before our visit, said that he thought of IBM as the beginning of the tech economy, with everything flowing from that. "Tech companies want to locate in places that are great places to live," he noted. Jude Blanchette, a China scholar whose parents moved to Burlington in the 1960s, said, "People *like* living here, and they define success as finding a way to stay."

The start-up culture and the encouragement of local companies in Burlington has made for a variety of different businesses: Seventh Generation is a major supplier of natural and "green" cleaning and personal-care products; NRG sells wind-turbine instruments around the world; Burton is a leading snowboard and recreation company; the Dealer.com company provides websites and tech infrastructure to auto dealers. When we visited in the fall of 2013, Dealer.com was a little bit of Silicon Valley in the northern woods: live video screens in its Burlington headquarters linked its roughly eight hundred employees there with the branch office in Manhattan Beach, California. (Soon thereafter, Dealer.com was acquired for $1 billion by another auto-related company, which, in turn, was acquired for $4 billion by the parent company of Kelley Blue Book and other auto-related businesses.) And, of course, there is Ben & Jerry's.

What's at least as remarkable as anything else about the town is that Burlington has an enjoyable commercial airport. It was one of the first in the country to offer yoga rooms, private booths for nursing mothers, wooden rocking chairs in nooks with views of the runway, free Wi-Fi and abundant plugs before other airports started providing them, outlets for Vermont's famous microbreweries, and a location for the Skinny Pancake. "We're trying to create the sense of a lot of separate spaces where people can go," Eugene Richards, the airport's director, told us as he showed us around. "Anything to make the experience seem more relaxed."

Like Sioux Falls, Burlington has been a resettlement city for refugees for decades. It, too, has refugees from all over the world, and it, too, has embraced the sense of becoming a richer, better city for having them.

During our first days in Burlington, I sat in on a workshop at the Vermont Refugee Resettlement Program (VRRP) in Burlington, where nearly twenty very newly arrived Bhutanese were learning the cultural ropes for their new jobs. Get to work on time. Check bus schedules on holidays. Call your boss if you are sick. Be friendly to your colleagues.

Smile. Sit with workmates at lunch, even if language is a barrier. Wear deodorant and clean clothes every day. The language sounded very blunt. But softening the delivery with the sorts of qualifiers that native English speakers are used to—the shoulds, mights, coulds we use for politeness—would also have risked diluting the message.

Among the adult refugees, there are those who left behind menial jobs or no jobs at all. There are also those who abandoned professional jobs as lawyers, administrators, doctors, and teachers. They all arrived in the United States as equals, and they are all now scrambling to patch together lives.

Hai Blu, and his wife, True Tender, are among them. Hai Blu (pronounced like *hey blue*) is Burmese, and his name means "Brings Luck." His life began with such unimaginable bad luck that his name might seem like a cruel joke. But later, it turned toward fortune so good that he met his "Brings Luck" destiny.

Hai Blu is from the Karen ethnic minority group of southern Burma, which had been involved in conflicts with Burmese rulers for many decades. In the 1980s, his parents fled to a refugee camp in Thailand, where he was born, raised, married True Tender, and lived for a total of twenty-three years. That is the bad luck start.

Then Hai Blu's luck changed. In a world where there are too many refugees for all of them to be considered equally, he had many attributes that would be attractive to resettlement administrators. He was young, strong, and stable. He and his wife looked like good candidates to be anchors for a new community of Burmese. That was enough. Hai Blu received his official refugee status, making him eligible for resettlement outside the camp. Hai Blu, his pregnant wife, True Tender, and their young son became the first Burmese to resettle in Burlington, Vermont, in April 2008.

Hai Blu quickly landed a temporary job at the Autumn Harp lipstick factory, where he worked in packaging and labeling. Factory work, a VRRP counselor told me, is attractive to refugees for its good pay, reliable hours, and sense at the end of the day of a tangible product, like boxes and boxes of lipstick. And employers quickly come to appreciate the reliability, determination, and work ethic of refugees. We later heard a further comment about refugee employees in Erie, Pennsylvania, where employers reported appreciatively that refugees shunned the drug culture.

Then Hai Blu got another lucky break. He was hired as a dishwasher by Benjy Adler, the co-owner of Burlington's fast-growing, hip crêperie, Skinny Pancake. Reliable dishwashers are hard to find, but as Adler told us, they are a critical foundation in the restaurant hierarchy. If the dishwasher doesn't show up, then it's up to the manager or the owner to step in. Hai Blu quickly moved up into the role of food processor, which means he works in the bulk preparation of Skinny Pancake ingredients. Three or four people in Burlington had mentioned Hai Blu to us by this point; he had become something of a local rock star.

Hai Blu and his wife bought a car, which they both drive, and they are studying for their citizenship tests. When Hai Blu's wife passes her test, I would guess she could become the first American citizen with the name True Tender.

I talked to Hai Blu again, three years after I first met him and True Tender. He is still working at the Skinny Pancake; they are still on track for citizenship. And True Tender is studying to become a nurse. They have the patience of refugees who spent their first twenty-three years in a camp in Thailand.

Miro Weinberger, mayor at the time we visited, is himself an example of Burlington's draw for its particular kind of human capital. Weinberger's parents, from Long Island, moved north during the Vietnam War "to opt out and find a different value system," Weinberger told us. He is one of many forty-something children of that migration who stayed in Vermont. "You'll hear a lot about public-private partnerships," he told us on our first visit. "This is a place where it's really true." In Vermont, these efforts—to teach nutrition and sustainability courses in the schools, to find work for some of the Burmese and Bhutanese refugees being resettled in the area, to foster tech start-ups—are often called "social responsibility" efforts, a part of the brand we came to think of as being classically Burlington. "Civic engagement is the absolute heart of what keeps the city palpitating," said Melinda Moulton, of the Main Street Landing company. "People go to events; they are part of groups. It's like Tocqueville."

Burlington's Sustainability Academy is a public magnet school in the Old North End of town. Like charter schools, magnet schools usually orient their academics around a theme or focus. Here, that focus is on what the name says: sustainability.

That seemed to me a perfect match to the town of Burlington, the home of Bernie Sanders, the base for Seventh Generation and its environmentally friendly plant-based products, and the site of the 360-acre fertile Intervale, which hosts a community agriculture system—from growing to marketing to consuming. We visited the Intervale Center and chatted with local farmers who were part of Burlington's robust refugee population. They were growing a small vegetable called garden eggs, which we recognized as a favorite in West Africa from our months there decades earlier. Burlington is also home to conservationist Shelburne Farms, socially conscious Ben & Jerry's ice cream, and the wind-power company NRG. Burlington's sustainability list is endless.

"Sustainability Academy" is a lot of syllables for the name of an elementary school. But in Burlington, no tongue stumbles over it. "Sustainable" may be Burlington's most popular word. I heard it invoked all over town—by those involved in the "locavore" food movements, in the leading-edge pedestrian-only commercial zone for restaurants and shops, the smart and user-friendly recreation developments, the entrepreneurial ventures, city hall, companies' mission statements, and on and on. The Sustainability Academy partners with most of the above to serve their children and with more in-kind help from the bike shop, ski shop, and sailing center, the YMCA, and others.

Five years earlier, the Sustainability Academy was known as the Lawrence Barnes Elementary School, a failing school in the needy, sketchy part of Burlington, home to a mix of the down-and-out and the frontier pushers, and also the first stop for many of Burlington's constant influx of refugees and immigrants. About 95 percent of the kids were on free or reduced lunch (the nation's usual proxy for poverty). Test scores were very low, and enrollment was declining.

The town and school district decided that rather than redistrict, bus kids, or shut the school down, they would try a different and radical approach. Barnes became one of Vermont's first magnet schools and adopted the theme of sustainability, a nationwide first in elementary magnet schools.

I found then-principal Brian Williams in the lunchroom of the Sustainability Academy. He was easy to spot: the biggest guy in the room, sitting on a very small chair, talking with an eight-year-old tousle-haired boy who was having trouble with his writing. It was noontime, and Principal Williams asked me if I would like some of today's lunch: "Beef stew. I made it myself."

I was about to blurt out, "Sure, sure," when I stopped and thought that maybe he *had* actually made the stew himself. It seemed like a place where the principal might also be the cook.

A few minutes later, when Principal Williams was called out, I found myself eating beef stew, sitting on a tiny chair, talking with that little boy. His problem, he told me, was that he didn't know what to write about. I empathized and told him that when I was in that spot, I found that one way to start was to just write down what people say, and that might be a good way for him to start, too. He took a blank page from my reporter's notebook and started in.

Moments like these, impromptu conversations with a teacher or a young student, were what I was always looking for in learning about a school. They were more genuine than test scores and mission statements, and they opened windows into the soul of a school.

The school identifies its mission as sustainability in economic, environmental, and social-justice terms. But how, practically and academically, do these lofty goals fit into the day-to-day life of the students?

The environmental part seemed easiest. The older kids can learn about energy and electricity by examining ways to heat and cool their own school, which was retrofitted to use solar and geothermal sources. The younger kids can study cycles of nature firsthand via the garden's compost and recycling systems.

What seemed harder to address were the other pillars of the definition: the quality of economic and social life. How do you start when you've got a population of kids whose parents' experiences range from being lifelong professionals to being lifelong refugees? How do you introduce the idea of a parent-teacher organization to parents who have never been to school themselves? How do you begin to shape a culture in a neighborhood where there are drug busts on one side of the school and chic urban delis and Himalayan food markets on the other?

The Sustainability Academy's answer is that you do *everything,* and you do it as well as you can. You draw on the special community that is Burlington, going beyond the businesses and civic groups to include the parents and local talent who will help construct anything you want to build or paint, and you rely on the police to forewarn you when a drug raid is about to happen in the neighborhood. And instead of fencing the school to keep an elderly neighbor from picking a few vegetables from your gardens, you offer her a recipe on how to use them. You try to help the kids understand why the rock garden they all worked to build was vandalized the first (and only!) time, and you encourage them to rebuild.

You have big dreams for the future—a new playground, tree houses. And you make immediate goals for the present: everyone will learn to ride a bike and how to swim. That's where the bike shop and YMCA and access to the local beach can help. You make a compost heap, build raised gardens, create an open-air classroom, and paint the school with murals. You procure a few items for the school that are very useful for hands-on kids, like a washing machine.

You go to the local universities and ask them to send you "only the best" of their talent to help you out. And you become so good that you eventually get a critical mass of teachers, parents, and invested community neighbors, friends, and advocates, who step in when they see a need. You might even make the beef stew yourself. In essence, you create a world where children can see and process all these examples, which are all true.

In Burlington, we found *Seven Days,* a print newspaper that is influential in local and statewide politics and has been a business success. Defying the trend of most publications across the country, its print circulation was three times higher, when we visited, than it had been at the paper's inception as an alt-weekly in the mid-1990s; it employed more people than it ever had before; and it was on pace to have much higher total revenue than its previous high, before the crash of 2008.

One successful paper is not an answer to the dire pressure on local journalism across the country. But *Seven Days* had used the scale of Vermont, and its potential to be a statewide news source, to fill some of the gap in "serious" reporting to go along with its role as a food-music-culture source. For instance, the issue that came out during our first visit had a detailed cover story about the specific ways in which the Obamacare/health-exchange era would affect people of different ages, incomes, and health situations. Each time we returned to Burlington, the paper looked thicker, and we saw it at more places around town. We met young staffers who had moved to Vermont from New York, from Philadelphia, from the West Coast, some with hopes of staying in Vermont and some because of *Seven Days'* reputation as a training ground for ambitious talent.

What made their paper different, I asked Paula Routly, its publisher, co-founder, and co-editor. "People look at our paper, and it makes them happy and interested to *be here,*" she said. It was a vehicle of local consciousness and involvement. "That motivates them to do something, and participate—which makes it more a community, and gives us something to cover. It's a cycle that works."

# Eastport, Maine

After a brief spell at home in Washington, we were flying up the coast toward Maine, before it got really cold. During the flight we were reminded of one of the truths about air travel that had motivated us in the first place.

Flying across the landscape on a clear day at low altitude predictably reveals things you had not known, or noticed. From 1,500 feet up, about the height of the Empire State Building, you are far enough from the ground to discern patterns not visible at street level but close enough to pick out details that to airline passengers would be just blurs. From 2,500 feet above the ground, nearly the height of the world's tallest building, you can see far enough in all directions to notice how cities interleave with suburbs, or how the course of a river, a ridge, or a tree line shapes the farmland and settlements around it.

Often the speed and perspective of the aerial view make economic and social gradients amazingly vivid. This was certainly the case on this leg of the journey as we flew, at 2,500 feet, along the full extent of the Maine coast, from the New Hampshire border north. An hour in, when we passed over Bar Harbor and Acadia National Park on Mount Desert Island, it became clear that we were simultaneously crossing not just a geographic but a gentrification line.

Behind us, to the south and west—in Kennebunkport, in the thriving city of Portland, in Rockland and Camden and other well-known resort towns—houses with big porches had faced out toward the sea, the waters had been crowded with sailboats and other pleasure craft, and we could see families with children walking or taking bicycle rides. As the miles past Bar Harbor wore on, the houses got smaller and less summery, the sailboats gave way to commercial fishing rigs, and the major sign of human activity was the occasional pickup truck bouncing down a road. This was too far for most vacationers or second-home shoppers to come. The population of Maine is poorer (and whiter) than America as a whole, and much older. The communities generally get poorer and older as you move north and east, a shift whose effects were quite visible even from above.

We were headed that day to the easternmost point in the state—and, for that matter, the entire country. This was the tiny town of Eastport, population 1,400, which sits across a mile-wide strait from Campobello Island, which is on the Bay of Fundy in the Canadian province of New Brunswick.

The flight up the Atlantic coast was notable mainly for the increasing beauty of the scenery as we moved along the Maine coast. We passed the big city of Portland, the sailboat-studded waters of the coastal resorts along the way, the big airports at Brunswick and Bangor. While we were still about thirty miles from Eastport, the air traffic controller at Bangor said we were moving beyond her radio and radar range. She bid us adieu, and we switched to the local frequency to alert any other planes that might be in the area. There weren't any—and, in fact, the air strip in Eastport was so uncrowded on our first arrival that, just as we were lining up for our final approach course, someone drove right onto the runway, in front of us, with a rideable lawn mower. It was time to trim the grass at the runway edges: What were the odds, he must have figured, that someone would be landing just then? (He had a headset on and didn't hear us—until I put in full engine power to "go around" and circled back for another approach.)

Fortunately, someone else in town had been listening for our arrival and rolled over in his truck just as we were getting out of the plane and beginning to tie it down. This was Captain Bob Peacock, one of many outsized personalities in the town. We'd gotten his name from mutual friends; we told him that we'd like to learn about Eastport's challenges and plans, and through the several days of that visit and our subsequent trips, he took us on his boat, to his house, and to the locations he had known all his life.

Physically, Eastport resembles the more celebrated resort areas along the Maine coast. Rocky fingers reach out into the sea; pine trees line the low hills; and the downtown waterside structures are mainly two- and three-story brick storefronts, most of them built soon after a fire in 1886 destroyed all the wooden buildings of the old downtown. Eastport's residential areas are mainly classic New England clapboard, at dramatically cheaper prices than in other seaside sites. You could buy a three-bedroom house in town or a nearly three-acre buildable lot for well under $100,000. Eastport is so compact that as we circled over Campobello, famous as the summer home of Franklin Roosevelt's family, to land at Eastport's small airport, we could easily keep all its houses, office buildings, and retail shops and cafés in view. That same view took in the twenty large, round enclosures in the bay in which five hundred thousand farmed salmon were swimming in circles nonstop.

A century ago, Eastport was a center of the Atlantic Seaboard's sardine-canning industry, and its population was more than 5,000. The population has decreased in every census since then, and Maine's state economist recently projected that if current trends prevail, by 2025 it will fall below 1,000. The people who remain in town are old even by Maine's standards, with a median age of fifty-five. (The national median is thirty-seven.) By national standards they are also quite poor: across the country, the median household income was about $50,000 in 2012; in Eastport, it was less than $27,000. The income is even lower in the adjoining Passamaquoddy tribal reservation.

We had come to Eastport because we had heard that this little hard-pressed town was the scene of an audacious and creative recovery attempt.

Maine's fjord-like coast gives Eastport the deepest natural harbor in the lower forty-eight states. (Valdez, in Alaska, is slightly deeper.) As the easternmost point in America, it is set apart from the rest of the country and the state. It's well over four hours by car from Portland, at least two from Bangor, with mainly woodland in between. "We like to think we're ideally positioned," remarked Chris Gardner, a lifelong Maine resident and former policeman who, as the Eastport Port Authority director over the past five years, has overseen a major increase in shipments through Eastport. Gardner spoke very quickly and kept up a jaunty wisecracking patter, noting, for example, "We're a day closer in sea time to Europe than New York is." (He says this with a wink, aware that the other transport and commercial connections coming into Eastport are, to put it mildly, not comparable to New York's.) As the melting Canadian Arctic permits more northwest passages to Asia—such passages were not possible without icebreakers ten years ago, but they are expected (or feared) to be routine ten years from now—Eastport becomes by far the closest U.S. Atlantic Seaboard port to China, Korea, and Japan, Gardner told me. "We automatically wake up with an advantage."

Depth and location do not in themselves ensure a port's commercial success. Eastport's lack of a rail connection to the rest of North America is a major handicap to the port. The money that shippers save in seafreight costs because of Eastport's favorable location is often less than the extra money they have to spend to bring cargo in on trucks. The city has been lobbying hard for state and federal help in restoring the rail link that connected Eastport with the Maine Central Railroad until it was abandoned in 1978. But even without a rail connection, Eastport steadily increased its shipments by sea. One of its specialties is container ships full of (live) pregnant cows, bound for Turkey.

Pregnant cows? European beef and dairy herds, reduced by mad cow disease and other factors, are being replenished, largely with American stock. When cows make the sea voyage while pregnant, their calves can be born on European soil and have the advantages of native-born treatment. To put it in American terms, the mother cows would not be eligible to run for president of Turkey, but the calves would. A company called Sexing Technologies, based in Navasota, Texas, devised a sperm-sorting system to ensure that nearly all of those calves will be female, a plus for dairy herds. Chris Gardner convinced Sexing Technologies that

Eastport would be an ideal transit point, and since 2010 some forty thousand cattle have been loaded aboard ships there. "When they asked if we could handle it, I immediately said yes," Gardner told me. "My answer to everything is yes. Then we work out the details of what it would take."

Nearly every person we met in Eastport had a tale about cows that escaped their shipping containers and galloped through town, pursued by the Texas cowboys who accompany them on the entire trip. The cowboys ride with the cows on their truck journey from farms across America. When they get to Eastport, the cows are loaded fourteen at a time into modified shipping containers, with ventilation ports, fans and cooling systems, and openings where the cows can look out. The cowboys continue to chaperone them on the ship and shovel wood chips into the containers each day to absorb the cows' excreta. On arrival in Turkey, I was told, they pass through something like a cow car wash to get cleaned up.

Captain Bob Peacock took us on a tour of the port, one of the many spots in Eastport he knew intimately and where he was greeted like a family member. Captain Bob is a native of nearby Lubec who worked around the world as a tanker captain starting in his twenties and, in his sixties, serves from Eastport as the chief operating officer for a global fish business whose main facilities are in Norway and Vietnam. He is also one of two local pilots who guide enormous cargo ships through the tricky straits off Eastport to their docking point in Eastport. He seems to be everywhere.

The port is breathtaking in its magnitude and larger-than-life operations. On our first visit, we watched a steady stream of eighteen-wheeler trucks, each laden with tons of white, high-quality paper pulp made from the Maine woods, roll toward waiting freighters at the dock. As each truck neared, local stevedores attached lift chains around the edges of the truck bed, and after an all-clear signal, a crane lifted the entire load into the ship's hold. Then the truck rumbled out, and another rolled in to take its place. The pulp was bound for China and Korea, where it would be used for glossy magazines and books.

The decline of the newspaper-publishing industry is reducing demand for some kinds of wood products from Maine. The onslaught of global

warming has increased demand for low-carbon fuels. Torrefaction—
the technique's name was taken not from a person but from the Latin
word *torrefacere,* meaning to heat and dry (as in "torrid")—is a process
designed to convert pulp and wood by-products, including stumps, into
briquette-like pellets. European utility companies substitute these for
coal in electric-power plants, which allowed them to meet European
standards for reduced coal consumption. With state and federal aid, the
Eastport Port Authority invested $9 million in an enormous conveyor-
belt system that will make Eastport the fastest, cheapest site for sending
pellets and wood chips to Europe.

"A group of consultants looked us over long ago and said we would
be lucky to do 50,000 tons of cargo a year," Chris Gardner said. "It's a
good thing we didn't listen to them, because now we have done about
450,000 tons of wood pulp alone in a year." The port's sixty-plus stevedores are unionized, but they work on an on-demand basis for an average
of a week or two a month. The other days, they run lobster or sea urchin
boats, work as lumberjacks or handymen, or care for their families. The
port jobs are some of the most sought-after in town because, even for
part-timers, the union deal includes health insurance.

The Bay of Fundy is famous for some of the world's most powerful tidal forces. The volume of water that flows in and out each day is
equivalent to that of all the world's rivers combined. In the early 2000s,
a group of engineers and investors decided that Eastport should be one
of two places (the other is Cook Inlet, off the coast of Alaska) to test,
design, and develop tidal-power electricity-generating systems made
by their Ocean Renewable Power Company. "Generating electricity in
seawater poses some obvious challenges," noted Bob Lewis, an Eastport
native who has been with the company since its start in Eastport. "But
it has great advantages. Water is so much denser than air—832 times as
dense!—for turning turbines. And it is predictable. You can't look out
a year from now and know which way the wind will be blowing or how
hard. But you know exactly what the tide will be doing."

The company was funded by private investors and research grants
from the Department of Energy in roughly equal amounts. Since 2012,
it has run multi-month trials of a large turbine in Cobscook Bay, off Eastport. The carbon-fiber foils were arranged to keep turning in the same

direction, even as the tide ebbed and flowed. The initial trial confirmed the concept: the system fed power into Maine's electric grid and survived the harsh undersea environment. The company has refined its technology with subsequent trials and projects in Alaska, Ireland, Canada, and elsewhere.

"We like to think we are the Kitty Hawk of hydrokinetic power," Lewis told me. "I don't know that the Wright brothers could have envisioned today's Boeing and Airbus. We are trying to stimulate people to tinker and experiment and improve on what we've done."

The town is developing another kind of renewable energy as well, through its arts. Eastport native Hugh French with his wife, Kristin McKinlay, returned to town in 2002. Hugh and his brother Ed, the editor of the weekly *Quoddy Tides* with his wife, Lora Whelan, grew up in the town; their father was one of two doctors, and their mother had started the newspaper. The population of the town has been declining since 1900 and was nearly three times bigger when the French kids were growing up than it is now.

Hugh and Kristin purchased the old Eastport Savings Bank and painstakingly transformed it into a town museum, which they called the Tides Institute & Museum of Art. "Tides" was chosen to signal the broad reach of both the United States and nearby Canada, and "Institute" to announce that their vision was for something bigger than a museum. The building is just across the street from the Peavey Memorial Library, where I stopped in to see a copy of the just-published *Passamaquoddy-Maliseet Dictionary*, of the language of the local tribe. The dictionary, with its side-by-side English explanations, was thirty years in the making, and with eighteen thousand entries filling twelve hundred pages, is more intimidating than my unabridged *Oxford English Dictionary*.

French and McKinlay started populating the museum with their family's collection. They encouraged others from the area—many of whom knew and trusted the family name—to contribute their treasures as well. Today, the holdings include architectural drawings, maps, furniture, musical instruments, and a forty-five-hundred-volume library. Also Native American basketry, ceramics, boat models, portraits of ships, and photographs from the old sardine canneries.

In 2011, French and McKinlay purchased Water Street's twin buildings, the former clothing factory and retail store, to create an artists' studio, with working space, common areas, and lots of both elaborate and basic equipment. During our last visit, we strolled down Water Street and went in through the studio's wide-open door to meet Richelle Gribble, the young California artist-in-residence at the time, and hear about what she was up to. In the back room, Richelle showed us the fruits of her scavenging around the water's edge and hikes overland. (The Tides Institute also owns shoreland in Eastport.) She had laid out netting, shells, bits of driftwood, plastic, and glass, with the care and categorization of an archaeologist.

Part of the idea behind the studio is that the artists who work there will engage with the town to help the residents and visitors feel close and connected to the art being made there. The studio's open door did exactly that for folks like us, who were strolling nearby and walked right in.

The institute has expanded into a half-dozen nineteenth-century buildings around the town, including churches, a Civil War veterans hall, and a private residence, where the visiting artists live. Some were purchased, and some were donated.

Hugh French handed us the keys to the institute's Free Will North Church one morning and suggested we walk over to take a look at the new installation there. We fiddled with the side door's key for a while, then finally let ourselves in to prowl around the empty church, dusty with the trappings of installing the amazingly giant sculpture. It was called *Undertow;* its creator, Anna Hepler, describes it as "the hull of an empty ship in . . . the nave of an empty church." We peered at it from all angles—underneath from the pews, up above from the balcony, along the sides by the stained-glass windows.

The Tides Institute anchors one end of Water Street. You can't walk to the other end of Eastport (it'll take you about five minutes) without spotting Don Dunbar's photo gallery across the street, and then passing several art galleries and gift shops that display and sell all kinds of cre-

ations from local artists. More than thirty buildings in the Eastport Historic District have been transformed. We stopped by wine-and-cheese
openings at galleries on several nights, and attended a performance of
*The Glass Menagerie* by the local theater group at the Eastport Arts Center. The ticket taker that night was none other than newspaper editor Ed
French. And the stage manager, Jenie Smith, was by day the barista at the
coffee shop, the nephrologist at the town clinic, and the new owner of a
dog kennel. Everyone in Eastport seems to be a multitasker and an artist.

The fish-farming industry had a rough start in the Eastport area some
thirty years ago. Diseases swept through the overcrowded pens, and the
large corporations that then dominated the business pulled out of the
local operations. A family-owned Canadian firm, Cooke Aquaculture,
set up salmon farms around Eastport and has been more successful.

"We have come so far since then," Dave Morang told me. Another
local native, he became director of Cooke's salmon-farming operations
around Eastport. These days, he said, fish are segregated by age group,
so that diseases will not spread from one generation to another. The fish
are fed at dawn and dusk through a computer-controlled system that
resembles a lawn sprinkler, shooting out pellets as it rotates. Each of the
pellet shooters is in the center of a circular net enclosure one hundred
feet across; within each of these enclosures, some twenty-five thousand
salmon grow to roughly ten pounds apiece. From a nearby floating control room on a barge, a Cooke employee monitors underwater cameras
showing the fish as they eat, so that he can turn off the sprinkler before
the fish have had their fill and start letting the pellets drift down.

On our flights into and out of Eastport, our approach and departure
routes would usually take us over the fish pens in the water. From above
they looked like a cupcake-tray array, five rows of four pens each. You
could tell when it was feeding time in one of the pens by the frothed
surface of the water there, as fish snatched for their food.

As needed, fish are sucked into a tanker boat and exposed to water
treated with hydrogen peroxide. This kills some of the "sea lice"—a kind

of parasitic crustacean that occurs in the wild but can be a problem in concentrated populations of farmed salmon—and makes most of them fall off the fish. (The peroxide dissipates and does no known environmental harm.) When the fish are about eighteen months old, they are pulled out, killed, and processed. Then that pen is left fallow for two months to a year before the next crop of fish arrives—and, yes, people in aquaculture do use these farming terms.

How, I asked Morang, should consumers feel about farmed fish? "Myself, I'm a beef eater," he said. "But the reality is that Americans import ninety percent of our fish, and we're the third-largest consumer of seafood in the world. The wild catch is not there, so we need to grow the fish." One of Morang's sons works at the salmon farm, and Morang said his goal was to make the business sustainable enough—economically and environmentally—that some or all of his six grandchildren would have that choice.

Lobsters are another important part of the marine economy. It's a seasonal business, so the lobstermen of Eastport are also the stevedores, and the clammers, and the boatyard workers. Depending on the season, they supply the Asian markets not just with lobster but with sea urchins and sea cucumbers.

Whenever I asked any lobstermen—they were all men—how business was going, each complained about the plummeting price per pound. When I asked other people, they said, "There's never been so much money coming in over the docks." I didn't know which observation was more true—worst of times, best of times—but two other relevant factors are the steady warming of the seawater, which is drawing lobsters north, and the devastating overfishing of Atlantic cod. Cod, I was told, had been the main predator of juvenile lobsters; now more lobsters survive to feed the current predator, man.

Was the current boom in abundant, cheap lobster the prelude to another overfishing disaster? I asked Captain Bob Peacock. He and others contend that, for the moment, and in the absence of the cod, the increased lobster catch was sustainable.

Another local fishery focuses on scallops. The typical North Atlantic scallop boat might spend two weeks at sea and return to port with a catch that has been on ice for many days. The waters in Cobscook Bay are the last good scallop grounds in Maine, and the local fishermen (some of them are also the stevedores, et cetera) can bring in their catch each day. But until now, they had no way to distinguish their fresh day-boat scallops from the commercial norm on the market. Will Hopkins—who grew up on a Maine island, went off to and dropped out of Harvard, ran a variety of businesses in Boston, and came to Eastport twenty-one years ago—headed a community organization called the Cobscook Bay Resource Center. When we visited, he was getting ready to open the group's latest facility: a dockside processing house and distribution center, which would get Eastport's scallops marketed as a premium brand. It was also designed as a community center, for the hoped-for future in which more visitors would bring more business, which, in turn, would draw more residents and more activities.

This is not even to mention the locavore farmers; the new boat-making company; the quiet defense contractor I kept hearing about (but was never able to visit) that makes hazmat suits for the Pentagon and police departments all around the country; or the century-old Raye's Mustard Mill, which ships jars of specialty mustards all around the country. All of this in a city with fewer inhabitants than one wing of an apartment building we lived in while we were in Beijing.

After a few return trips to Eastport, we felt like we knew most of the residents. They certainly knew us. One day, we hiked out to Raye's shop to purchase a heavy case of mustard to take home and asked if they could deliver it on a trip into town. The next morning, we found it at break-fast at the WaCo (pronounced *wack-o*) Diner, right next door to where we were staying. The waitress said Raye's had dropped it off; they didn't want to wake us with the delivery, and they guessed we would be coming by later.

Right in front of the fishermen's pier on Eastport's Water Street stands a larger-than-life twelve-foot statue of a bearded sailor that strongly resembles the captain on the box of Gorton's frozen fish sticks. The statue was erected for a Fox reality-TV show, *Murder in Small Town X,* whose crew had arrived in the winter of 2001 to do some filming. The crew literally lit up the quiet town that winter, especially at night. Everyone enjoyed it. When the crew members packed up, they left the giant fisherman behind. The Eastport residents decided to preserve the kitschy statue in place as a reminder to themselves of what's possible and to believe in your dreams.

Enter, then, the Women of the Commons. Six women—Linda Godfrey, Nancy Asante, Meg McGarvey, Sue Crawford, Alice Otis, and Ruth Brown, longtime friends and residents of Eastport—got together one morning in Eastport and decided that they wanted to "make something real happen to benefit the community of Eastport."

They set their sights on an abandoned building between the WaCo Diner and the pier, just next to the fisherman's statue. Because of the building's unbeatable water view, the women saw it as a fine place for a gallery that could showcase local artists' work and a space that would offer small public programs and lectures. There would also be enough room on the second story for two small apartments for tourists or visitors to rent, and a storefront with community edibles for sale. So the six women pooled their resources and bought the building. They resolved to name it the Commons, in the democratic spirit of their vision.

The Women of the Commons intended a profitable venture for themselves and an inspirational one for the town. While others might look at a town with the size and economic state of Eastport and think "scarcity," these women instead thought about what they had learned from Stephen Covey *(The 7 Habits of Effective People)* and focused on "abundance," in deference to the town's people, attitudes, networks, and potential.

Three additional partners were invited to complement the thinking and reach of the Commons: Alice Gough, from across the bay on Campobello Island, in Canada, would be their "international partner"; Vera Francis, a poet and a leader in the Passamaquoddy tribe, down the road, would be their "wisdom partner"; and Anna Baskerville, a southern black woman who had moved to town, would be their "spiritual partner."

A crew of men came on board to renovate the building, seasoned craftsmen as well as apprentices from the Passamaquoddy tribe. The women set the ground rules for how the show would go: No smoking, drinking, drugs. No inappropriate language and no comments about women. Show up on time, work a full day. Period. Paragraph.

The workers might have wondered what hit them, but the operational rules had strong upsides: this wouldn't be the standard piecemeal or seasonal work; it would continue year-round inside the building, which would be shrink-wrapped and warmed during the winter months. All this, the women intended, would translate into the workers' feeling of "ownership" of the project and the town's sense of the seriousness of the women.

It worked. The building was completed, and local artists, about 90 percent of them women, poured in with their work. There were traditional woven baskets, burl bowls, jewelry, photographs, note cards, paintings, hand-knit sweaters, creative collage art. The apartments became popular as rentals, including as sabbaticals for writers and artists. A small number of programs were held in the gallery.

Next up is the renovation of the currently derelict Seacoast Canning Company building, which, during Eastport's era as a capital of the sardine industry, housed a tin-can-producing factory. The women plan to develop the old factory into a multiuse downtown center for retail, entertainment, office space, meetings, and hotel and apartment use that could make Eastport attractive for many people and purposes.

I asked the Women of the Commons what I should understand, if anything, about their being a women-only endeavor. Their answer was quick. Each of the baby-boomer-generation founding women came from households of strong women—mothers, aunts, grandmothers, sisters. Some went to all-women's colleges and found strong mentors there. Many were political activists themselves, working for the Equal Rights Amendment. The role of prominent Maine women, including their senators and congresswomen, was impressed upon them. And they lived in the lee of the ghost of Eleanor Roosevelt, whom you could channel visibly across the sound at the Roosevelt summer home on Campobello. Further, they explained, a historical factor was the seaporting heritage of Eastport. This is a town of fishermen, who are on the water for long periods of time, and thus have always left the women onshore, charged with keeping everything together, under harsh circumstances, with no promise of their men's return. This deal-with-it sensibility doesn't leave a lot of room for softness or moseying around in Maine, in Eastport, or among the Women of the Commons.

Language has always been important to the Women of the Commons, partly in a branding sense, but also in a sense of self-reflection and self-consciousness. They were open to changing their lexicon to pay new attention to things they considered worth spotlighting. For example, they swapped the dreary word "fog" with "seasmoke," especially in winter. They enhanced the name of the "Old Sow" tidal whirlpool by calling it an "aqua vortex." And they expanded the familiar description of Eastport as "land of first sunrise" to include "first moonlight" and "first stars."

The people of Eastport, Maine, have turned local language into a power tool of their development. Usually, a language change in the spoken vernacular happens in response to something in society. Maybe people mimic a new hero or superstar. Maybe a new concept goes begging for a word, like "locavore." Maybe the meaning of a word waxes fat or thin, like "quality," which has in my lifetime absorbed the entire semantics of "good quality."

In his American travels in the early nineteenth century, Tocqueville, not the easiest travel writer to read, reported with shades of astonishment how frequently Americans shaped and reshaped their language, unlike their British forebears (and certainly unlike the French).

Tocqueville ascribed the shifting of American English to American democracy, writing that "the continual restlessness of democracy leads to endless change of language." He meant that new ideas pop up, old ones are chopped up, and the language reacts. Because of democracy? Well, maybe. But the interesting point to me was that Tocqueville noticed this trait of American English back then, just as he might have noticed a twist on it two hundred years later.

In Eastport, the language change was a little different and less organic. With a number of examples, the townspeople set out with a self-conscious and deliberate effort to engineer local language usage to create a positive energy for their town.

Linda Godfrey told me how she and some other women noticed several years back, when Eastport was beginning to show its colors, that the media seemed stuck in how they were referring to Eastport.

She pointed to what they called the *de-* words: "The most-used *de-* words were words like: 'depressed,' 'dependent,' 'decline,' 'despair,' and were usually used in comments about economics, services, schools, population." Godfrey continued: "It just seemed the *de-* words were ever-present, even if a story about Eastport was a positive one."

So, the group set forth to crowd out the *de-* words with *re-* words, words like 'rebound,' 'rediscover,' 'redesign,' 'reverse,' 'renew,' 'reenergize,' 'reemerge.' They encouraged reporters and politicians to substitute the more positive words.

Gradually, Godfrey reported, their campaign seems to have worked. She recently harvested a few dozen Eastport stories written in the last several years, and not a single one ended in a downer with one of the *de-* words.

Eastport residents told me versions of another deliberate vocabulary shift, this one involving their nearby neighbor Canada, an important partner to this region for trade, culture, tourism, and recreation. Putting a positive spin on how they refer to the dividing line between the two countries, they said, "We don't call it a *border*, we call it an opportunity."

At the end of each conversation we had in town—at least fifty in all, a statistically significant sample in a town this small!—I asked whether Eastport seemed to still be declining, to have leveled off, or to have begun an ascent. "We're beginning the ascent," people told me, or "We're poised."

"We've always thought of this as a twenty-year effort," Hugh French said. "We're ten years in."

Can Eastport make it? If it does, one of its keys will be civic booster-ism, a central part of American culture since long before Sinclair Lewis wrote a whole book about it, *Babbitt*. But if willed optimism sometimes deludes people, it can also empower them. "I think it was Henry Ford who said, 'Whether you think you can do something, or think you can't, you're right either way,'" Chris Gardner told me. In practical terms, a belief that you can shape your fate is more useful than a belief that you cannot.

Captain Bob summed up Eastport for us one day. So, I asked him as I looked around at his minuscule hometown, why are you living here?

"This is where I'm from," he said. "Where the hell else would I want to be?"


It's no fun to fly on the East Coast in the winter. You're out on the run-way; the wind is cold; the days are short; you're more likely to have to worry about ice when you're in the air and about starting a chilled engine after it has sat overnight on the ground. So we returned to Washington after the exposure to Vermont and Maine.

We thought about what we had learned, which began with momen-tum and extended to the power of the local.

We realized, of course, the limits. "Positive attitude," civic responsibil-ity, and what I have come to think of as local patriotism matter only so much when matched against the largest forces of geography, of demo-graphics, of economic change.

In Eastport, the location on the Bay of Fundy was a fundamental plus, because of its unique tidal flows. But the town's distance from centers of wealth was a perhaps insuperable challenge. Could younger, better-educated people really be lured that far away from the benefits increas-ingly concentrated in larger cities?

These limits are real: no amount of positive thinking can change a city's location or, at least in the short run, offset its demographic or transportation obstacles.

But—and here we come to the positives—the farther we went on this journey, the more impressed we became with the importance of the stories people tell themselves about their city's or region's success.

They have to think of themselves as a city—a distinct region and culture, not as part of an urban sprawl. The places we've been most definitely have a sense of themselves as distinct entities, with their own traits and strengths.

# 2014

Greenville, South Carolina

St. Marys, Georgia

Columbus, Mississippi

Caddo Lake, Louisiana-Texas

In the Air

Columbus, Ohio

Louisville, Kentucky

Allentown, Pennsylvania

In the Air

Duluth, Minnesota

Pittsburgh, Pennsylvania

Charleston, West Virginia

# Greenville, South Carolina

This year, first we went south, with extended periods in South Carolina and Mississippi and a shorter pass through Georgia and Louisiana; and then we headed to the industrial north, to Allentown, Pittsburgh, Columbus (Ohio), and other venues. As things turned out, all but one of the states we visited during this initial period, north and south, ended up going for Donald Trump in 2016. But when we visited, none of them displayed anything like the seething fury described by the media during that campaign.

We'll start with South Carolina. One of the most popular city names across the United States—along with Franklin, Washington, and Springfield—is Greenville. When we hear that name, we now think automatically of Greenville, South Carolina.

You know you're somewhere when people say, "Katy, bar the door!" in the middle of a conversation. And you know it's a place where people don't cautiously measure out their language, wary of sound bites.

I heard the phrase from a revered father figure of Greenville, a man whose southern storytelling prowess made me think I was somehow back in Spoon River. He was recounting part of the history of Greenville's downtown rehabilitation. One piece of the plan called for demolishing the heavily trafficked bridge over the Reedy River, a bridge that hid the view of falls beneath it, and for prettying up the space around the falls with a park complex. Fifteen years of controversy roiled over an idea that was embraced by some and met with strong resistance by others. "Why take down a perfectly good bridge?" asked the people who were happy to let things be and who didn't see river revitalization as a welcome proposition. They pointed out that the river was not at all attractive, being flanked by kudzu and poison ivy. These folks, our narrator recounted, were all about "Katy, bar the door!"

Well, the bridge did get demolished, and the new Falls Park area with the elegant pedestrian Liberty Bridge was dedicated in 2004.

As for the fruits of the huge redevelopment effort: "Dadgum if we didn't do it!" he said.

Every city has a cliché anecdote or slogan. By the sixth or seventh time you've heard it, you have a clearer idea not so much of the community's reality but of what people believe that reality to be. For New York: "If you can make it there . . ." For Washington: "The most important city in the world." For Austin, Burlington, Boulder, Seattle, Santa Monica: variations on "We're lucky to live here." For Sioux Falls, South Dakota: "I grew up in a little farming town."

After a few days in Greenville, South Carolina, we thought of its characteristic phrase as "Greenville? Are you kidding?" We heard it from many people, but here is the version told by Knox White, a Boomer-era lawyer who grew up in Greenville as part of an old local family and who, since 1995, has been its mayor. "I heard from the CEO of a company in Houston," he told us. "It was transferring a division here, and one of their key talents said, 'Greenville? Are you kidding?' They wouldn't come here—until they came here, kicking and screaming, and the next thing you know, they'd bought a house."

We heard that story from a restaurant entrepreneur (plus several of his staffers), the founders of a start-up software firm, engineers originally from Germany and France, newspaper reporters, and on through a long list. Behind it is a conception of the town—*people think we're hicks, but we know we've developed something great*—evident in a series of specific achievements.

The best known of those is the economic transformation of the part of inland South Carolina that abuts Georgia and North Carolina and is locally known as "the Upstate." For much of the twentieth century it was one of the world's major textile-producing hubs. Greenville and its neighboring cities lie along the East Coast's famous Fall Line, where the plateau stretching from the Appalachian Mountains meets the Atlantic coastal plain. This is also where rivers spill down from the mountains as rapids and waterfalls, and thus (as with their counterparts in New England) where the region's first water-powered mills were set up. "Low Country" Carolinians grew cotton and rice on their plantations, and "Up Country" merchants built water wheels to power their mills and made their area one of the South's manufacturing centers.

For a century after the Civil War, Up Country Carolina grew steadily as a textile center, built in part by mills that moved south from New England in search of cheaper labor. "As late as the early 1990s, textiles seemed to be a viable business employing tens of thousands of people," we heard from Steven Brandt, a Philadelphia-area native who took a job in Greenville in the late 1970s, liked it, and became the publisher of the Gannett-owned daily *The Greenville News*. NAFTA took effect in 1994, and the World Trade Organization was created one year later. Both accelerated the inevitable move of textile mills to lower-cost sites in the Americas and Asia. Greenville County alone lost six thousand textile-related jobs, and the state at least fifty thousand.

South Carolina is still poor, usually ranking in the bottom ten states in per capita income. But the Greenville region has had lower unemployment and faster growth, largely because of what it did to offset the loss of its dominant industry. Foreseeing the decline of the textile business before it became a certainty, civic leaders worked with a business-promoting state government to convince big American and international companies that this was the next place to expand. General Electric opened a plant in Greenville in the 1960s and produces gas turbines and other advanced products there. Michelin made its first Upstate investment in the 1970s and now has its North American headquarters near Greenville. Other auto-parts makers followed Michelin, and in the early 1990s BMW announced that it would build a major auto-assembly plant midway between Greenville and neighboring Spartanburg.

When I asked for the story behind these decisions, most people treated the question as if I were asking why the stock market was in New York—where else would it be? The details include low wages and anti-union "right to work" laws in South Carolina; the belief of the governor at the time of the BMW decision, a Greenville native named Carroll A. Campbell Jr., that personal sales calls to recruit businesses from around the world were the most important use of his time; and the fact that Europeans had long done business in Greenville. During the textile mills' heyday, much of the high-end equipment came from Europe, and international textile and fashion conventions in Greenville brought European business representatives there. They added up to the larger idea that the area had done everything it could to make itself an economically, environmentally, and culturally attractive venue for newcomers.

Business recruitment was a statewide effort. The more interesting, city-specific, and mayor-driven transformation was the one Greenville wrought on its then-decrepit downtown starting in the 1970s. Study groups come from cities around the world to analyze how Greenville has brought an assortment of restaurants, national and local retail outlets, high-end hotels, bars, theaters, in-town residences, public art, and riverfront pathways to what had been a boarded-up crime- and drug-ridden area. Presumably to spare themselves from telling the story over and over, in 2013 the mayor, Knox White, and a local writer, John Boyanoski, published a book whose title conveys the city's view of its achievement; it is called *Reimagining Greenville: Building the Best Downtown in*

*America*. The steps the book delineates include the decision in the 1970s to narrow the city's main shopping street from four traffic lanes to two, so as to simultaneously discourage driving and encourage strolling on broadened sidewalks lined with rows of now-stately shade trees.

In the urban-planning world, noting that Greenville has a walkable and gracious downtown is like mentioning that Seattle has good coffee. When we asked during our time in town and in follow-up phone calls afterward, we heard more or less the following set of reasons for the city's success:

The downtown recovery effort was heavily guided by city officials— a series of mayors and a cadre of professionals in the city's planning and economic-development agencies. The first of the influential modern mayors was Max Heller, who had fled Vienna after the Nazi takeover, found work in a shirt factory when he arrived in Greenville, and eventually owned a shirt-making company himself. As mayor starting in 1971, he led the effort to make the downtown more European—that is, walkable. He faced opposition from threadbare downtown merchants, who feared that making driving less convenient would push their remaining customers out toward the suburban malls. Now there is a heroic statue of him amid the bustle of Main Street.

Heller's latest successor, Knox White, overcame resistance in locating a baseball stadium for a minor league team downtown, at the site of an eyesore, an abandoned lumberyard a few blocks from city hall ("Even my wife thought that was crazy—where would people park?" White says); in requiring the stadium developers to build adjoining condos as part of the project ("I told them, 'This is how we do things'—and the condos sold like hotcakes!"); in working with the county to develop the Swamp Rabbit walking-and-biking trail, which now extends for seventeen miles; and, most of all, in removing the concrete highway bridge that since the 1960s had blocked off the Reedy River waterfalls from the city that had grown up around them. Now Falls Park is the featured attraction of downtown, with the falls area ringed by clubs and restaurants and surmounted by an elegant 345-foot-long suspension bridge for pedestrians, the Liberty Bridge, conceived of by the same firm that designed Boston's Leonard P. Zakim Bunker Hill Memorial Bridge.

There is a parade of bronze statues along Main Street, which affected us the way it was probably intended to—giving us an excuse to slow down and even linger a bit, taking in the story of the town as we walked from one block to the next.

There's Max Heller, the 1970s town visionary who rose from janitor to entrepreneur to civic leader, and imagined how downtown would look today.

There's Joel Poinsett, a diplomat, legislator, and botanist who brought the eponymous plant from Mexico to root it forever in the U.S. holiday season.

There's Shoeless Joe Jackson, who spent three decades disputing his part in the "Black Sox Scandal" of 1919. He removed his cleats from his blistered feet during a game in Greenville. You'll pass him on the way to Fluor Field, which Knox White had told us about, and which is now the new home of the Class A Boston Red Sox affiliate, the Greenville Drive.

Roy Fluhrer, a leading figure in Greenville arts, helped me begin to understand what art can mean not only to a community's own sense of itself, but to all those who happen to come by there. Art, he said, "lets the world know there is a community in South Carolina that values the human soul."

That's true of many other towns where we had been or would visit: bronze statues of presidents in Rapid City, the gateway to Mount Rushmore; statues of gunslingers, desperadoes, and Wild West characters in silhouettes and statues in Dodge City; a "peace walk" with larger-than-life-sized statues of larger-than-life heroes like Gandhi and Martin Luther King Jr. in Riverside, California; statues representing the remarkable and everyday people and moments of the town's history in Holland, Michigan.

We continued on to the Swamp Rabbit Trail along the Reedy River. You see everything on that trail: fit bikers, wedding photo shoots, strollers pushed by moms and by nannies from France and Germany, old folks strolling hand in hand, especially along the easy-for-walkers rubbery stretch of the trail. If you look high up the wooded hill across from Liberty Falls, you'll spot a collection of striking buildings in a campus-like idyllic green setting, yet nearly in the middle of town. "Oh, that's the governor's school," people told us, with pride.

The Governor's School for the Arts and Humanities is a public boarding school specializing in the arts: dance, drama, visual arts, music, and creative writing. To repeat: a public boarding school. It was founded as a summer program in 1980, by musician, teacher, and apparent force of nature Virginia Uldrick, who had a vision of creating a nontraditional arts conservatory. Greenville donated more than eight beautiful acres, the former site of the Furman University men's campus. The $27 million Uldrick campus opened in the fall of 1999 to its first class of juniors.

There is a loose network of a few dozen governor's schools around the country. They are all a bit different. Some are summer programs only. Others, like Greenville's, are for juniors and seniors. Some focus on the arts and humanities, others on science and math. South Carolina has one of each. They are all supported by a combination of state funds and private donations. Students in Greenville pay modest fees, as they are able.

The students are admitted from all over South Carolina. Some are from larger towns like Greenville and Columbia, others from towns that kids described as remote, being mapped in their parts as near the "third bend in the river." Some students arrive with impressive portfolios or experience at the governor's school summer programs. Others are "discovered" in the old-fashioned way by admissions officers who scour the state.

According to school officials, about a third of the students qualify for free or reduced lunch. I was told that the school naturally attracts mostly lower- and middle-class students, because it is a harder sell to kids from wealthier families, who don't want to give up their own rooms, cars, and TVs.

The school complex is, in a word, stunning. There are multiple dance studios, a performance hall, art spaces for silversmithing and ceramics, a brass foundry, more studios for drawing, music rooms for practicing, a computer lab for graphic design, a gorgeous library, and ad-lib rehearsal areas in broad glassed-in halls.

One of the days I visited, a student violinist was playing on the stage in the theater, performing for her peers and a guest artist. The visitor, who would be featured that evening as part of a public series that is a draw for many Greenville residents, was critiquing the young violinist's performance. We tiptoed into an art room, where a seventy-something male model, clad only in running shorts and with musculature that made you wonder how he could be for real, stood statue-still while students sketched him.

We watched a practice session preparing drama students for upcoming auditions in Chicago. One young woman was performing Desdemona for the drama teacher and her fellow students. The teacher was tough on her, describing the changes he was looking for and instructing her to "try it again" at least three times before we slipped out. She was tough right back. "They break you down and build you back up," another student told me.

This is a school for those with passion. Several students talked about their transition from feeling disengaged and out of sync in their hometown high schools, to being wholly consumed, involved, and at home in this place the likes of which they had never imagined. They call themselves Govvies.

The students are driven—or more accurately, they drive themselves. "One-half dream, one-half plan" is how one student described his life at the school. Dreaming big at the governor's school means Broadway, Hollywood, Carnegie Hall, Pulitzer, Pritzker. Planning big means half of every day in practice, rehearsal, studio, workshop, training, rewrite, instruction, all alongside the usual high school academics.

The dance teacher described the commitment, even obsession, of her students: "You're a dancer from the minute you get up in the morning," she said. And the dancers, some as young as fifteen years old, told me how they orient and ground themselves day by day: "This is how I think of myself. Dance is the place I go to work through my issues. I am comfortable here."

By the metrics, the governor's school has proven itself: National Merit finalists, Presidential Scholars in the Arts, 100 percent acceptance to colleges or professional schools, including RISD, Juilliard, Eastman, Peabody Conservatory, and awards and scholarships of all sorts. Many alumni are already on their way to successful careers on the stage, on the screen, and in television.

Upstate South Carolina is politically conservative, to put it mildly. Greenville County was the very last one in South Carolina (which was the very last state) to observe Martin Luther King's birthday as a holiday. Mitt Romney beat Barack Obama by ten points in South Carolina, and by twenty-eight points in Greenville County (whose rural areas are even more conservative than the city). Donald Trump carried the state by fifteen points over Hillary Clinton and the county by twenty-five. Bob Jones University is based in Greenville; the area's congressional representatives have included Jim DeMint and Trey Gowdy.

But the political divisions and passions remained remarkably separate from the area's effort to attract new businesses and improve the community. "Whatever happens here, it has to be about business," Nancy Whitworth, the city's director of economic development since the 1990s, told us. "This has always been a business-first town." So how does such a town account for the record of its success? We heard the answer many times each day: the power of "public-private partnerships." It was public-private partnerships that brought the big manufacturers to South Carolina, that made the downtown come alive, that are now supporting high-tech incubators in the city and science and engineering programs in the public schools.

The bigger surprise, other than the major factories, involves all the aspects of civic life that have evolved here. These range from public art, to environmental and public-spaces initiatives, to a revitalized downtown that urban-planning teams from around the world visit to study, to an in-town minor league baseball stadium, to educational innovations we have not seen in other places and had not anticipated here.

There is a larger lesson here. To wit: if we can find ways to name strategies so that they sound acceptable and soothe rather than raise hackles, we can get a surprising amount done. Had a politician labeled Greenville's strategy "picking winners" or "industrial policy," it would have been stillborn. As a series of "public-private partnerships," it is a source of civic pride.

It was hard to get people in Greenville to actually name a school we should visit; they would demur with a kind of "we love all our children equally" tone. There were just so many good ones, they would go on, the magnet schools, STEM schools, arts schools, charter schools, IB schools, et cetera.

But one sounded irresistible, the A. J. Whittenberg Elementary School of Engineering—that's right, *engineering*. Whittenberg is a public school that sits at the edge of the city's central area, which was described to me as highly distressed, meaning high poverty, unemployment, and crime, and lots of single-parent households.

The school is located next door to the expansive Salvation Army Ray & Joan Kroc Corps Community Center (Kroc as in McDonald's), where the students can walk for lessons in swimming, golf, rock climbing, tennis, and soccer. The school is also a ten-minute walk along the Swamp Rabbit Trail to the Peace Center of the performing arts, which coordinates with Whittenberg on special projects with the children.

When Whittenberg was preparing to open, in 2010, few people had gotten wind of it. High schoolers were hired to canvass the school's neighborhood, introducing the school to parents and encouraging them to enroll their youngsters. By the second year, word was out, and out-of-district parents camped in front of the school for a week before registration, hoping to secure a first-come, first-served spot. The demand was so high that the local Lowe's home store offered discounts on camping supplies. Registration day spun out of control. Videos showed parents stampeding the doors when they opened. The next year, the school switched to a lottery system. Now, a Whittenberg administrator told me, Green-ville real estate agents advertise the location as a plus for houses listed in the Whittenberg district.

Whittenberg is a beneficiary of the business, manufacturing, and higher-education mecca that is Greenville. This is where the city's cor-porations, private donors, government agencies, NGOs, and universities demonstrate their deep commitment to public education and the future workforce of Greenville. Whittenberg alone lists more than three dozen partners, including General Electric, Michelin, BMW, Duke Energy, Lockheed Martin, Fluor, the Greenville Drive, Hubbell Lighting, Jacobs Engineering, Furman, Whole Foods, and Walmart.

During January's "engineering week," young professionals from GE were on campus, wearing purple T-shirts and teaching lessons. That week, they were teaching about hydro, wind, and solar power sources. One volunteer, who looked about the age that the kids' dads would be, was boiling water in a glass beaker; this produced steam, which drove a pinwheel to spin. Another was demonstrating the evolution of light bulbs, measuring the amount of heat the bulbs produced, and engaging fourth graders in a discussion of what it meant to a bulb that much of its energy was spent on producing heat instead of light. It was an example of how engineering is folded into every available step of Whittenberg's traditional academic curriculum.

The school halls can be disorienting. The walls of the fourth-and-fifth-grade corridor are bare, except for digital screens. In fact, almost every-thing in the fourth and fifth grade is digital. All the schoolwork is done on tablets, students enter their work into folders, teachers use a stylus to comment on work, and parents are encouraged to open the folders and monitor the entirety of their children's work.

The kids are introduced to their digital world from the get-go. Kin-dergartners begin practicing on unplugged keyboards. By second grade, they each have a personal iPad. Soon they learn PowerPoint, which is a favored application of every engineer I've ever watched give a presenta-tion. The students learn block-letter printing, but not cursive. When I talked with the administrators about the absence of cursive, which even they had originally questioned, they told me that they'd realized that the only necessary example for cursive in the students' future lives would be a signature, which they could print in block letters. Writing letters in cursive? Nope, they'll type them. Research notes? Nope, laptops. I tried to think of one to stump them.

The first graders showcased the synergy between engineering and the Greenville arts scene. The nearby Peace Center (named for its original donors, the local Peace family), with its broad outdoor plaza and welcoming glass atrium, features a Broadway series each year. That year, one play was to be *The Wizard of Oz*. First graders at Whittenberg were studying the production from every angle. They studied the physics of getting the Wicked Witch up into the air. They broke into teams to design their own rope-and-pulley systems to hoist a flying witch. They marched the Swamp Rabbit Trail to the Peace Center to learn how the stage lighting works, how the orchestra pit operates, how the scenery is set up. They all learned the songs from the musical; they read the book; they made their own pop-up books of the story. The winning design team earned tickets to a performance at the theater.

In 2013, the Lego Robotics Team won the right to compete in Germany—the only elementary school in the United States to do so. This meant the first airplane flights and first passports for lots of kids. They returned with so much excitement that, not surprisingly, now everyone wants to be on the Lego Robotics Team. The mascot of the school is a robot, and the team members are the "engineers."

Environmental service is a schoolwide effort. First graders compost. Second graders collect recycling waste from classrooms every Thursday. They sort it, count it, and rate the classrooms' recycling bins, awarding points for volume of recycled material and logging demerits for candy wrappers. Third graders measure air quality and post signs outside promoting a no-idling campaign for cars. Fourth graders study water quality and give instructive PowerPoint presentations to the other classes. (A curious fact: at least four people in Greenville told me that the city boasts the "best-tasting water in North America." No one could tell me where the accolade comes from, but the water was good enough that everyone we saw ordered tap water over bottled water, even at high-end restaurants.) Fifth graders learn how to conduct home energy audits.

The kids and adults built an organic garden out behind the school, including a greenhouse constructed of recycled plastic bottles. They learn to categorize foods as green, yellow, and red—Go, Slow, and Whoa—to help them understand proteins, veggies, low-sugar fruit, carbs, high-sugar fruit, cookies, and cakes and to plan their own menus. They bake their own bread and make their own homemade soup. That year, they planned to launch a project to grow and harvest cotton, tying that process into the history of textile mills of yore here in the Upstate of South Carolina.

Rounding out the curriculum is art. Many lower-grade corridor walls explode with 3-D extravaganzas. The children have created all manner of decor. There are paper trees growing out of walls, fluffy snowmen popping out, suspended robots, and mystery things that protrude and hang and dangle.

Each classroom of the lower grades that I entered was a creative heaven—sculptures hanging from ceilings, bursts of color everywhere, students busy at various work stations, clusters of buzzing activity, books, furniture, photos, and a lone and empty "thinking chair."

When the kids age out of Whittenberg, some go on to the brand-new Phinnize J. Fisher Middle School, which recently opened with a STEAM curriculum, adding an *A* for "arts" to the more familiar science, technology, engineering, and math, or STEM, curriculum.

STEM versus STEAM is a hot topic in the education world. Proponents of STEAM argue that infusing more liberal arts into a highly technical curriculum will build more well-rounded, richer lives for the students. Part of the push to STEAM for Fisher came from Greenville's business community, which wanted to nurture a future workforce steeped in the world of technology, but also one that would be comfortable and practiced in the softer skills of communicating, teamwork, organizing, and public speaking.

Fisher is on the east side of town, adjacent to the campus of Clemson University's International Center for Automotive Research.

"Is that a school?" is a question that Fisher's principal, Jane Garraux, says she often hears people ask as they drive by the award-winning, modernistic glass buildings, which don't look like a conventional school. The buildings were designed around the curriculum, she explains, rather than the other way around.

If you took several walks around Fisher's complex, you'd be likely to see something different each time, even over the course of the day. Classrooms have big glass-paneled garage doors, which lower for a cozier feel or rise to create an open space with adjoining common areas. Tables and chairs can be pushed around and fit together like puzzle pieces. Indoor-outdoor classroom spaces and an innovation lab are so big that you can drive a car right inside them.

The school is bright and airy. Its lighting responds automatically to the degree of sunlight pouring in. The infrastructure of the buildings is exposed. Brightly painted ceiling pipes, color-coded for their functionality, and see-through walls into electrical closets let the kids absorb lessons in engineering just by walking around their school.

Students work in red, blue, or green so-called learning communities, where classrooms can spill into those big shared spaces. There are studios, design labs, arts-and-media centers, and music and seminar rooms. There is no need for student lockers because the laptops, which hold e-books and digital papers and homework, can easily fit into a backpack. Those were strewn about, kid-style, or lined up against the walls.

Fisher's STEAM curriculum is taught through a method called project-based learning (PBL). Students address a real-world challenge or problem and then work to explore and respond to it. They are encouraged to collaborate, think critically, be creative, and solve problems.

Anne Kelsey-Zibert, a veteran teacher of twelve years and a newly trained PBL teacher, took me step-by-step through an example of project-based learning in her class. The students were studying World War I, and Kelsey-Zibert wanted her students to connect real, everyday life in those times to the actual events they were studying. The students would construct a tool or artifact of the era, using today's materials, and then present the object to the class. This exercise would fold in research, design, construction, writing an essay about their creation and its relation to the historical event, and then making a public presentation to the class. With a kind of *Shark Tank* twist, each student received $1,000 (fake, of course) to invest in their favorite project, the one they found most promising. One was a bazooka like gun, one was a tinfoil-covered submarine, and another was an extensive medical kit for field use.

Like Whittenberg, Fisher benefits from strong Greenville community involvement. Employees from Michelin were at Fisher the day I visited, demonstrating catapults to the middle schoolers. Zike, a Greenville company that makes a human-powered hybrid scooter-bike, donated twenty bikes to the school. Another local company donated a 3-D printer. Staff and faculty at the next-door campus of Clemson offer tours and mentorship programs to Fisher, and some Clemson professors hold regular office hours on their campus for Fisher faculty members.

That same day was the morning after huge winds had blasted through Greenville in a fierce overnight rainstorm. Outside, clusters of sixth graders were picking up and patching together the remnants of shelters they had designed and built from found goods like cardboard, plastic bags, wooden pallets, and old newspapers. They discovered that the location of some of their shelters, a protected-looking corner near the outdoor amphitheater, actually turned out to be a wind tunnel. The storm had wreaked havoc on the shelters, injecting a big dose of reality, as the students must have considered how lucky they were not to have actually been sleeping out overnight.

These issues—construction, shelters, wind tunnels, weather, homelessness—were on the students' mind, as they were concurrently reading a popular novel called *Maniac Magee,* about an orphan looking for a home, and woven through with themes of homelessness and racism.

At Fisher, the library is called the media center. The space is drenched with light from the two-story windows and is the first thing you notice driving up to the school. Inside, kids can curl into comfy sofas or sprawl on colorful rugs. There are relatively few actual books. The director of the center told me that Fisher students were comfortable with the style and operations of the media center, which means doing their research, browsing for books, reading, and producing their papers mostly digitally.

In Burlington and Sioux Falls, we began wondering why high-value companies end up where they do, and how and where new companies get their start. In Greenville, we spent a very interesting afternoon at the locally well-known firm the Iron Yard, which was housed in a new tech-incubator building that said NEXT out front.

The NEXT program was run by the Greenville Chamber of Commerce, with "public-private" guidance from local officials, businesses, developers, and so on. But it is located separately from the main chamber of commerce building and is designed to look and feel like a start-up center in Boston, San Francisco, Brooklyn or southern China, rather than some standard corporate building. When we visited, John Moore, a chamber executive who runs NEXT, told us that it tried to run in a lean start-up style, too. "We had the advantage of starting with a blank sheet of paper," he said.

"Because there were no existing entities to protect their turf, we were able to leapfrog," Moore said—much as some developing countries jump entirely past the wired-telephone stage to create nationwide wireless networks. "We went from the idea for the center, to finishing the building and opening it, to having it full, all within three years. If we'd had to start with a university or an existing city facility and tried to change its model, it would have been a lot harder and slower."

The purpose of NEXT is to make it easier for new companies to get a foothold in the Greenville area. Moore pointed out that while this Upstate region of South Carolina had become famously effective in recruiting big, established firms like GE, BMW, and Michelin, "we may not have done enough to develop our own." NEXT and related enterprises connect start-ups with angel investors, provide physical space for them to get off the ground, offer advice from mentors and start-up veterans, and generally supply the sort of surrounding entrepreneurial information and advantage that can come automatically from being in start-up centers from Boston to San Francisco.

Had it made any difference? Can it make any difference, I asked Moore, given the scale and distance handicaps of a smallish place like Greenville?

"If you'd asked me five years ago, during the toughest times economically, I would have said, 'I hope so,'" Moore told us. "We had eight software companies in our program in 2006. They hadn't known each other. Now we have one hundred and thirty-four companies, all new, in all kinds of industries, from manufacturing to genomics to game software." He said that he expected two hundred local start-ups to be involved with NEXT soon. The main building has space for only twenty to twenty-four; the rest are part of a network for advice, financing, and other services. Moore said the companies NEXT is looking for are ones "that can compete on a global scale but are based here."

"They're now coming without recruiting," he noted. "It's become a kind of flywheel. The momentum, the acceleration—it all shows the potential. But, of course, I'm from the chamber of commerce, so you'd expect me to say that!"

Indeed, but then he put it in more tangible terms, gesturing to an office across the hall: "A few years ago, people like Eric Dodds would never have stayed here."

Eric Dodds, whom we met at the NEXT building, is a co-founder and the chief marketing officer of the Iron Yard, a multipurpose software start-up based in Greenville that also had operations in Spartanburg, nearby Asheville, North Carolina, and other southeastern locations.

Dodds grew up in Greenville and always dreamed of getting away. "Boulder, Portland—that's where My People would be." Then, after going to Clemson and working for national branding companies, he came back and noticed that the place where he'd started out had changed. The Iron Yard's co-founder and CEO, Peter Barth, grew up in Florida and had worked in New York and the Midwest and was planning to work in Charlotte. He stopped in Greenville for lunch, walked through its famously renovated downtown, and decided that this was where he wanted to stay.

The Iron Yard's business model was a combination of "code academy," business incubators, kids' classes, and other features. The code academy charged $10,000 for a three-month session and offered a full refund if graduates could not get an appropriate job. "We can guarantee an entry-level job, but entry level in this field might be $65,000 or $75,000," Barth told us.

In the years after we met Dodds and Barth, the Iron Yard expanded very rapidly across the South and into the Midwest. Then, in the summer of 2017, as part of a general contraction of "code academies," it said it would suspend operations by the end of the year. Some start-ups succeed; most fail. The significance of the Iron Yard's story was what it showed about this area's ability to attract and retain people like Barth and Dodds—whom you might normally expect to find in Boulder, Portland, or Boston.

"Greenville is great once you get here, but it can be hard to get people to come and take a look," Peter Barth said. ("Greenville—are you kidding?") Eric Dodds added, "It's been really interesting rubbing shoulders with people in our classes who say, 'I've gotten here, I'm going into your program, and this is my ticket Out.' Then, after a while, they say, 'I've seen this culture; I think I'm going to stay around here.'"

After several visits to Greenville, we began thinking of the places it reminded us of and differed from. The resemblance started, unexpectedly, with the place we had visited only a few weeks before, Burlington.

In principle, you would compare Greenville and the Upstate with Burlington and northern Vermont only to highlight the unbridgeable chasms in American politics: one of the most right-leaning regions versus one of the most left-leaning.

But if you looked at Burlington and Greenville as cities, for their amenities and feel and civic sense, and for the history of public-private interactions behind today's cityscapes, you would find more similarities than you might expect. The waterfront is very important to the character of each town—the Reedy River and its waterfalls in Greenville's case, Lake Champlain in Burlington's. Thirty years ago, the cities were similar in that their waterfronts were off-putting rather than attractive: Greenville's because of the highway that made it hard for people to get to the river; Burlington's because of a railroad right-of-way that ran along the lake. The shopping, cultural, and recreational life of each city (and its surrounding region) now centers on its lively downtown. Greenville's is called Main Street, Burlington's is Church Street, but, with allowances for the difference in climate, you would have a hard time telling them apart. As with the waterfronts, these were deliberate public-private creations. Led by strong mayors, each city changed the physical look of the street, redid parking arrangements, commissioned public art, ran concerts and fairs, and took the lead in bringing new life to a battered downtown. Each city has a very popular minor league baseball team. Greenville has a software and design start-up community with a critical mass of entrepreneurs who have chosen a smaller-town life. Burlington has a critical mass of entrepreneurs who have chosen the outdoor life and political tone of Vermont. Both cities have commercial airports that are bigger and nicer than you might expect, given the cities' size—yet small enough to be quick and convenient to travel through. And despite their deep dissimilarities on most issues of national politics, the leaders and voters of each city have relied steadily on public-private partnerships, in which state and city governments have taken active steering roles for corporate and philanthropic efforts.

And what about the contrasts? For all of Greenville's likenesses to Burlington, we saw differences with the other major city of the Upstate—Spartanburg, some thirty miles to the east. They have roughly the relationship of Dallas and Fort Worth or Minneapolis and St. Paul, with the larger, richer city of each pair—Greenville, in this case—unavoidably looking down on its neighbor, which, in turn, looks right back with pride in its scrappy authenticity. Midway between Greenville and Spartanburg is the tiny former textile town of Greer, which is the home of the BMW factory, the major commercial airport for the region, and the brand-new Inland Port, which offers shippers a streamlined, speedy rail connection to the ocean port two hundred miles away in Charleston. Greer is also the closest attempt in the region to replicate the Greenville formula.

If you have seen the Greenville model, the parallels in Greer are evident. First the problem: the collapse of the textile business that had been the local mainstay. Then the response, via a public-private effort called the Partnership for Tomorrow: rebuild the downtown, which is tiny but has most of its original brick structures. "We're very fortunate to still have good bones intact," said Rick Danner, who ran a landscape-design firm in Greer and then worked for a local bank and had been Greer's mayor since 2000. He was referring to Greer's classic-American turn-of-the-century downtown architecture. "That's been the foundation for our downtown-revitalization plans." Create new parks and public spaces. Invest in infrastructure for the long run.

Apart from the Inland Port—a joint project between a railroad company and the South Carolina Ports Authority—the local airport, Greenville-Spartanburg International, is the most dramatic instance of a long-term public-private bet. When I first saw it from above, en route to the small airport in downtown Greenville, I assumed it must have once been a Strategic Air Command base, so enormous were its runway and surrounding buffer of open land. In fact, it was a purely local undertaking, led by the Spartanburg textile magnate Roger Milliken, who decided in the late 1950s that the Upstate needed an airport that would never limit its potential growth. "They said, 'Let's not only build an airport, let's build one that will be here for generations,'" Rick Danner said of the public-private airport commission, led by Milliken, that developed the airport. (Milliken was still active locally until 2010, when he died at age ninety-five.) "They own thirty-five hundred acres of land all around it for expansion," Danner noted, "their land reaches right to the Inland Port, and they have a literal fifty-year plan, updated continuously, for how they intend to grow."

"The good news is that it was possible to do all this," Steven Brandt, of *The Greenville News,* told us about the recovery process in Greenville and, by extension, in Greer and other small towns like Travelers Rest and Duncan. "The bad news, for anyone trying to do it overnight, is that it required a purposeful and organic process for more than thirty years, with so many shoulders to the wheel."

## St. Marys, Georgia

We were warmed up to the extravagance of southern talk by the time we flew south to Georgia and spent a day in the Okefenokee Swamp. Our guide, a veteran of swamp tours, worked his language for all it was worth. He knew everything about the swamp. There was plenty to talk about: mama gators, baby gators, liddel ol' bitty baby gators, each with a liddel ol' tooth on the end of its nose.

He was "swampwise," or *swampwahse,* as he pronounced it, his diphthongs sliding off into long, slow single monophthong vowels. The *i* sound, which northerners like me pronounce as the diphthong *ai,* in words like *nine, right, stripe, mile, I,* and *five,* became *ah,* to produce *lahk, nahn, raht, strahp, mahl, ah,* and *fahve.* Those words popped up in his swamp lessons about cypress knees and the value of pine straw or when he pointed out moonshine islands where old-timers made white lightning.

There was also an issue with how our guide would address us. He alternated between *y'all* and *guys,* with a few *you guys* thrown in for good measure. In just three minutes by my watch, I counted seven uses of *y'all* and seven of *guys.*

From the treasure trove of the very popular 2003 Harvard Dialect Survey, I learned that the favored term around the country as the way of addressing a group of two or more people is *you guys.* Some 43 percent of people say that nationwide, compared with a mere 11 percent in Georgia. By contrast, 71 percent of Georgians choose *y'all,* as compared with 14 percent nationwide. (The study didn't offer *guys* as an option, just *you guys.* That was 2003, and popular language can change quickly.) As we moved through the South, I heard plenty of all of these terms, including lots of variations; my favorite is the possessive form *you guys's.*

Around the world, when people think of coastal Georgia, they are likely to think of the resorts at Hilton Head, or the wildlife preserves of Sapelo and Cumberland Islands, or the stylishness of Savannah.

Deb and I think of those places as well, especially Savannah, where long ago we spent several months as young volunteers on a Ralph Nader project combating pollution in the broad (and now much cleaner) Savannah River. But we also think of the little town of St. Marys, the scene of literal life-and-death dramas in that same period.

The small town of St. Marys, Georgia, differs from the other places we have visited in the basic structure of its economy. When we first went there in the 1970s, it was still what it had been for many decades: a company town, in the good and (mostly) bad senses of that term. Now it has become a surprising variant of the same thing: a small-town economy whose well-being revolves around one huge employer. That is a circumstance the city and county officials were trying to change when we visited. Yet something else we discovered was the real surprise of the city for us.

Back in the early 1970s, when a young Jimmy Carter was making his run for governor of Georgia, St. Marys was a caricature of the isolated Southern Gothic company town. The company in charge was the Gilman Paper Company, which was a formidable political and economic force throughout the state and essentially its own law in the southeastern corner that included St. Marys. "Gilman Paper Company is the only major Georgia industry south of Brunswick and east of Waycross," its manager said in a speech that was reported in local papers around that time. "It can safely be stated that not less than seventy-five percent of the economy of Camden County is directly dependent on Gilman Paper Company."

In those days, St. Marys was the most bleakly Dickensian of the places we visited. The mill paid good wages, in exchange for all-encompassing political and social control. Its corporate attorney was also the state representative, and he was the county attorney, too; the result in tax policy and environmental regulation was predictable. The mill's manager was the local Big Man. The company's owners the Gilman brothers of Manhattan—lived an art-patron life far removed from the harshness of their family's company town. In the past few years, whenever I have gone to brutal, polluted, boss-run factory towns in remote China, I have thought back to St. Marys. It wasn't that long ago that China's current reality was tolerated in the United States.

The good of the old company-town arrangement was that the giant mill of the Gilman Paper Company provided paychecks for the over-whelming majority of families in the area. Indeed, the air and water pollution was so heavy, and the location was so remote, that a job with Gilman was the most obvious reason anyone would choose to live there. The bad included not simply the expected distortions of a town entirely dependent on one company but also a range of extralegal offenses. One of those was hiring a hit man to eliminate a local critic—that critic being a man who became our friend, Wyman Westberry.

The sequence of what happened is appropriately full of Gothic con-volutions, but in brief: the young millwright named Wyman Westberry, who had become disgusted by what we'd now consider China-scale despoliation of the local river and marshlands, drew press attention to what was happening in this little enclave. He called me in Savannah late one night, we went down to learn about his town, and we wrote about him in our report. Eventually, *60 Minutes* and national and statewide media got interested in St. Marys. In the midst of the furor, the local Big Men put out a contract to have Westberry killed (the going rate was $50,000, only the would-be hit man decided to keep the money but not carry out the hit). The administration of new governor Jimmy Carter began paying attention; and, at the end of a tale worthy of Elmore Leonard or Carl Hiaasen, Wyman Westberry ended up surviving, and then prospering as a major real estate investor and entrepreneur, and much of the local establishment either ended up in prison or died before coming to trial.

In some ways, the city is unrecognizably different now. When we first visited, the pollution from the paper mill was so thick and caustic that, as in a scene from modern China, even the Spanish moss had been poisoned from the trees. Now the trees are once more heavily draped with moss. Back then, there was a perpetual layer of ash on cars and houses downwind of the mill. Now the historic downtown of St. Marys, the part not subject to strip-mall sprawl a few miles away from I-95, has the little restaurants and shops of other aspiring revived downtowns we have seen, plus the Oak Grove Cemetery, just steps from the waterfront, which was founded when George Washington was president and whose headstones, beneath oaks dripping with Spanish moss, record the different waves of residents, black and white, and the epidemics, wars, and other misfortunes that did them in. One part of its lore, which we heard from Kay Westberry, Wyman Westberry's ex-wife, on an extensive and partly spooky tour, is that during an epic flood in St. Marys, the coffins from the black deceased, who had been interred in the low-lying part of the cemetery, floated up and out.

The Gilman Paper Company is no more—not as a business entity, not as part of the physical landscape in St. Marys. The family managers squabbled; the paper business itself was troubled; what had been the largest privately owned paper mill in America was sold to a Mexican firm, and soon thereafter that firm, too, declared bankruptcy. In 2002, the mill shut down, eliminating some nine hundred jobs. In 2007, the remains of the mill were blown up, despite some local efforts to retain and reuse them as start-up sites, light-industrial buildings, or even monuments. Piles of concrete are what remain.

\* \* \*

The good news for St. Marys and surrounding Camden County was that another mammoth employer had arrived even before Gilman went down. That was the U.S. Navy. During the administration of the former submarine officer and loyal Georgia native Jimmy Carter, and with the support of Georgia's Senators Sam Nunn and Herman Talmadge, then big powers on Capitol Hill, the U.S. Navy decided that Kings Bay, immediately north of St. Marys, would be the East Coast home of America's nuclear-submarine fleet. (The West Coast home is near Seattle.)

Everything about the city was changed by the navy's arrival. While in Gilman's heyday the manager claimed that 75 percent of the people in the county owed their living directly to the mill, these days local officials told us that perhaps 70 percent of the regional economy was now related to the base—a figure that includes rental housing, retail, construction, and the other spillover effects of growth itself.

This is the part of small-town life that didn't change: the outsized importance of a single big-gorilla economic engine. Gilman Paper Company, the previous gorilla, had been "local" but not in a good way. The local managers behaved as mini-tyrants, and the owners lived in New York City and seemed to view the mill mostly as a hinterland source of wealth. The U.S. Navy, the current gorilla, is by all accounts faultlessly well-behaved and good-citizen-like in its local relations. The submarine officers and seamen are an elite within the military—older, better educated, and more carefully selected than the norm, and not any source of trouble in town. But by definition a military presence is transient—and while some navy officials come back to the area after retirement, the navy represents an economic power that is in but not of the town. Much of the growth it has induced has been "just" growth—malls, restaurants, fast food establishments, and the like on the fringes of town.

The officials we met from St. Marys and Camden County are perfectly well aware of the imbalanced nature of the local economy. One school official described it, during the Gilman era, as the "Uncle Bubba" phenomenon: "If a kid was slacking off in school, you couldn't tell him to try harder, because he'd just say, 'My uncle Bubba will get me a job at the mill.'" Uncle Bubba can't get people into the navy, but another person noted, "Most places talked about economic development, but we really didn't need to worry about that. Around the time Kings Bay leveled off, the housing industry started to grow. We kind of thought, Well, we don't need traditional economic development. We kind of got our eyes off the ball." But now, he said, "We have looked in the mirror and, for the first time in my life, found the political will to pull together."

People in the city said they are trying to think about using things they do have, to foster the growth of what they now lack. Their ideas include several facets.

Chief among them is the pretty downtown, which resembles better-known and more popular resort cities but with dramatically lower real estate costs. Tourists now troop into St. Marys for holiday celebrations like its classic Fourth of July parade through the downtown (or they sail in, along the Intracoastal Waterway) and to take the ferry over to the Cumberland Island National Seashore, historically a resort for the Carnegie family. Plans are under way to add more attractions, hotels, and other local venues that would entice people to stay for a day or two rather than just pass through.

Of the entire Atlantic Seaboard, this stretch of coastal Georgia is one of the best preserved and most beautiful parts, in addition to having great ecological significance for its wetlands. Beautiful places, especially by the coast, are increasingly where people with a choice of where to live want to live. You can rebuild infrastructure, but you can't manufacture an ocean view.

The commercial space-launch business is growing. According to local officials, this part of Georgia was in the running when Cape Canaveral was chosen as NASA's main site in the mid-twentieth century. And so they are making a twenty-first-century push to build a new "spaceport" in a former industrial area (and onetime Thiokol rocket test site) just north of town, where companies like SpaceX would be able to launch their vehicles.

But none of these seemed to be embraced with the do-or-die spirit we had seen in some other small cities. What was revolutionary, and served as our introduction to an important area of education, was the local high school.

———

The Camden County High School, or CCHS, is famous throughout Georgia for the success of its football team. But it's also home to a revived form of education, one that took us by surprise.

CCHS is the only high school in the county, drawing a total of some twenty-eight hundred students from the cities of Kingsland (where it is located), St. Marys, and Woodbine, plus unincorporated areas. Each year's graduating class is around six hundred students. The school's size has helped make it a perennial athletic powerhouse. In the ten years before our visit, it had won the state football championship three times. It also has another advantage that I recognized from my own time as a student in a diverse community with only a single high school: in a region with relatively few private or religious schools, it provides an enforced region-wide communal experience, across class and race, rather than the separation-by-suburb paradigm of many public schools.

Demographically, the CCHS student body reflects the surrounding area: about one-quarter black, most of the rest white, and small numbers of other ethnic groups (including from navy-related families). According to school officials, about 40 percent of the students qualify for reduced-price lunches, and about 60 percent go to post–high school training of some sort. Each year, a small number go away to out of state schools, including selective ones. In 2001, only half of the school's students graduated from high school. Now that is up to 85 percent, a change that Rachel Baldwin, the CCHS career academy instructional specialist who showed us around, attributed mainly to the school's application of programs from the Southern Regional Education Board. CCHS has the best AP (Advanced Placement) record of high schools in its part of the state.

What struck us about the school was the very practical-minded and well-supported embrace of what used to be called "vocational education" and now is called the "career technical" approach.

In effect, what this meant was dividing a large, sprawling campus and student body into six "academies," each with different emphases. One of them is the Freshman Academy, to get the new students acclimated. ("I don't know if you've seen ninth graders recently," one person there told us. "But some of them look big and old enough to be parents of some others. It's a big range, and it helps to have a special place for them.")

The other five academies each have a "career technical" emphasis. After freshman year, all students enroll in one of the five. While they still take the normal academic-core range of subjects, they also get extensive and seemingly very well-equipped training in the realities of jobs they might hold.

A few examples:

- In the "law and justice" curriculum, which is part of the Government and Public Service Academy, a former navy–Kings Bay NCIS official named Rich Gamble trained students in conducting mock crime investigations and in preparation for testimony in court.

  On the day we were there, he had staged a mock robbery in which the perp grabbed a cashbox from an office, ran through the hallways, and dumped the box as he was escaping. (The students acting out the scenario wore their white CSI lab coats, so other teachers would know what they were up to.) Then Gamble divided his students into three teams to investigate the crime— making plaster casts of footprints, taking evidence, filing reports, preparing a case. "We emphasize a lot of writing," he said. "I give them issues where they have to defend themselves, in very few words, because courts don't like you to waste words. Some of these papers are as good as any written by NCIS."
- In the Engineering, Architectural, and Industrial Academy, students design and build doghouses and other structures, which they sell in the community; do welding (and compete in state and national welding competitions); run an auto-repair shop that handles county vehicles; do extensive electrical work, and complete other activities.

  This same academy also includes computer-aided design and robotics programs, under the direction of Fred Mercier. We saw architectural models of houses that students had designed and built with 3-D printers, and robots they had entered in a national robotics competition.
- In the Health and Environmental Sciences Academy, students

were preparing for certification tests by administering care to dummies representing nursing-home patients.

The other two academies are Business Administration and Fine Arts. CCHS has an industrial-scale kitchen and catering facility, overseen by a former navy chef. It has a very large auditorium, where students not only perform plays, dances, and concerts but also learn to build scenery and make costumes. There are more illustrations, but the point is already clear.

Here is why we found this interesting and surprising. Among the non-expert U.S. public, the conventional wisdom about today's education system is more or less this: At the highest levels, it's very good, though always endangered by budget cuts and other problems. At the lower ends, it's in chronic crisis, for budgetary and other reasons. And overall it's not doing as much as it should to prepare students for practical job skills, especially for the significant group who are not going to get four-year college degrees. Sure, the Germans are great at this, with their apprenticeship programs and all. But Americans never take "voc ed" seriously.

One high school doesn't prove a national trend. But what struck us at Camden County High was its resonance with developments we were seeing elsewhere: serious training for higher-value "technical" jobs. "Non-college" often serves as a catchall term, covering everything from minimum-wage-or-worse food-service jobs to highly skilled hands-on technical and engineering jobs that may be the next era's counterpart to the lost paradise of assembly-line jobs that paid a family-living wage in the 1950s and 1960s.

# *Columbus, Mississippi*

After writing about the Greenville governor's school in our ongoing blog of our travels, I opened my in-box one morning to find an e-mail from Thomas Easterling, an English teacher at the Mississippi School for Mathematics and Science. In a gentlemanly southern way, Easterling was throwing down the gauntlet, basically saying: You think the governor's school in Greenville is so great? Come see ours in Mississippi.

That was enough. We put Columbus, Mississippi, on our map.

We headed for Mississippi on Easter Sunday, feeling a little sorry for ourselves. Our families were gathered thither and yon; somehow we couldn't make our timing work to get to any of the corners of the country where they were living. By chance, changes in the winds and weather pushed us toward a small runway in the middle of lush Georgia hills; this was KTOC, the Toccoa–Stephens County Airport. We landed, and Jim taxied over to the fuel pump while I headed for the FBO (the universally used abbreviation for Fixed Base Operator, the management of a small airport), praying for at least a vending machine. The quaint brick building with a broad porch featuring a row of deep plantation rocking chairs suggested that people liked to gather there to watch the planes take off and land. I opened the door and then: a miracle.

The aroma of roast ham and baking yams, macaroni and cheese and biscuits. And pies! At the end of the hall, in one of the pilots' rooms, was a fully laid-out potluck Easter banquet, part of a multigenerational, multifamily celebration. We gratefully accepted the hosts' southern hospitality to join them for a meal, including all of the above plus greens, broccoli, creamed corn, deviled eggs, salads, and trimmings of all sorts.

Some of the pilots strode out to look at our Cirrus. While this model of plane is not new to the market anymore, seeing one in person is often an attraction. Pilots are interested in the avionics and the parachute packed into the fuselage; passengers admire the comfortable seats and big windows. As we were preparing to leave, Jim told the airport manager, "We feel very lucky to have ended up here just now." And he responded, "Or you could say you were blessed. You'll remember us, either way!"

Fat and happy, we flew toward the Lowndes County airport in Columbus, Mississippi. By now, my patience for long, slow southern conversations was limitless. In fact, a few weeks later in Columbus, I spent some considerable time in an elevator with the housekeeper of the hotel floor where we were staying. She had asked how I was doing; I replied and inquired back after her. A good twenty minutes later, after lots of pressing on the Door Open button so the conversation could continue, I had heard about her plans to attend an afternoon wedding, the dress she would be wearing, the flavor of cake that was under debate and finally ordered, and the likely number of guests and accoutrements like flowers and music.

We approached Columbus slowly for landing; I could see the many, many church spires and the old downtown, which promised elegant antebellum houses with big, wide-columned porches. I could also spot the derelict abandoned factories; we were so low on the approach that I could make out the tufts of weeds growing through the asphalt parking lots around them. We later learned that one was a factory where blue jeans had been stitched (before that work moved to the Caribbean) and that in another, toilet seats had been made (until most of that work moved to Mexico).

It was nearly Sunday evening by now, a slow day with no signs of life at the FBO. Finally, a guy came along in a pickup truck and offered us a ride into town, which we gratefully accepted. No taxis and no Ubers here.

In Mississippi, we knew that whatever economic challenges the whole country faced would appear in more acute form here, in what is chronically dead last in any economic ranking of the fifty states. At the time of our visit, the median household income for the United States as a whole was a little over $50,000. It was about $37,000 for the state of Mississippi, and closer to $30,000 for the region we were about to visit.

The region was part of the so-called Black Prairie of Mississippi and Alabama, so named because of its rich soil type. The geological Black Prairie also coincides with the historical and sociological Black Belt of these two states; that designation refers to the area's high concentration of slave-labor plantations before the Civil War and of African-American population ever since then. One Mississippi portion of this Black Prairie has renamed itself the "Golden Triangle." It is the area in east-central Mississippi, along the border with Alabama, that includes the medium-sized cities of Columbus, Starkville, and West Point. It has become, improbably, a new industrial zone of the South.

The three cities have different stories and situations. Starkville is the home of the leading research university in the area, Mississippi State, and has the greater stability and higher-end amenities that come with being a university town. West Point is the smallest of the three and, in recent years, has been the hardest hit by economic change. In 2007, Sara Lee closed a nearly century-old meat-processing plant that had employed more than one thousand workers, fully a tenth of the town's population. Since then, West Point's unemployment rate has been near 20 percent. Columbus was historically the richest of the cities, and it still has many mansions from the plantation era. But through the past generation it had been hit by the one-after-another collapse of low-wage manufacturing jobs that had come there through the mid-twentieth century. It has relied very heavily on the nearby Columbus Air Force Base, which Mississippi's powerful congressional delegation has defended through wave after wave of base-closing measures.

The whole area is poor.

Like the Greenville Governor's School for the Arts and Humanities, the Mississippi School for Mathematics and Science—or MSMS, as it is fondly called—is a public two-year boarding school. It draws students from big towns like Hattiesburg and small ones in the impoverished delta.

MSMS was founded in 1987, shortly after the administration of educationally progressive governor William Winter, who five years earlier had introduced sweeping reforms for the state, including mandating kindergarten for all students and compulsory school attendance until age sixteen. MSMS was the fourth such specialized secondary school for math and science to be established in the United States. Despite its veteran status, today MSMS remains modestly financed, primarily by state funds, with some additional foundation and private support.

The school occupies a number of plain buildings on the grounds of the elegant Mississippi University for Women, traditionally called "the W." (The men who have enrolled at the W since it became coed say they always have a time explaining themselves to those not in the know.) Students come to MSMS to spend their last two years of high school in accelerated science, math, and computer courses, as well as in a deeply rich selection of arts and humanities classes.

Few kids arrive with a portfolio of science genius, but they learn fast. While we were there, I saw a fascinating array of projects in progress.

In one corner of the glassed-in entry to a main classroom building was a grandfather clock, probably about eight feet tall, constructed by one of the students out of brightly colored plastic pieces. On the hour, a golf ball would roll down a chute, tripping levers to ring a small chime.

Upstairs in one of the science rooms was a 3-D printer, a rough-and-ready contraption that reminded me of a homemade boat. Within a few more weeks, it should actually be printing, said Donely Gunn, who'd made the 3-D printer himself.

A dozen or so students in the robotics class were testing the robots they had built for an upcoming national competition. There were three robot missions: search and rescue; a mock sumo-wrestling match; and a bell lift, where the robot scooped up a bell and delivered it to a destination.

The humanities classes at MSMS were described as the school's "secret weapon" by Wade Leonard, an alumnus who works at the school. Just spend a little time in Thomas Easterling's English class, where, when I visited, they were reading a Bharati Mukherjee short story, and you get that. The students, busy being teenagers, were in high spirits. "Curb your enthusiasm!" Easterling called out at one point. Most of the students were taking notes on laptops; one was multitasking his laptop work with a task on his phone. An Indian girl in the class was quietly correcting the pronunciation of the Indian names in the story. The pupils seemed fascinated by Mukherjee's life story, and—adolescents that they are—were comfortable and attentive in a discussion about self-discovery. Easterling drew them into talking about whether a person's immigrant status accelerated their self-discovery. "Abso-stinking-lutely!" was one hearty response that pretty much revealed the energy and engagement of the class.

In Chuck Yarborough's U.S. history class, students research the lives of individuals buried in the town's Friendship Cemetery. Columbus was a small town of about six thousand people during the Civil War. Being near a rail line, Columbus received many mainly Confederate casualties of war, which led to its becoming well known as a hospital town.

By the war's end, some twenty-five hundred Confederate soldiers were thought to have been buried in the Friendship Cemetery—along with, according to the National Archives, thirty-two Union soldiers as well.

Yarborough's students from the year-long "Tales from the Crypt" research and performance class choose an individual who died before 1930, locate his or her gravestone, then plumb the town's archives of Union and Confederate Civil War records, county court records, family files, and more at the local library, the county courthouse, and university collections. They learn how to conduct the very hands-on work with original documents. Archivist Mona Vance-Ali at the Lowndes County Library, young, attractive, and modern like so many women I have met who work at public libraries across the country these past few years, took me into the archives vault. We drew out a file, and she walked me through the exercise the kids learn, donning gloves and carefully turning pages, trying to interpret what they find in the county register of slaves, court case transcripts, and secrets of the community—making real the racial history of their state.

Yarborough's African-American history class also stages a cemetery production, called "The Eighth of May Emancipation Celebration." The students perform in-costume reenactments that they write themselves, with music, based on characters from among those buried in the town's African-American Sandfield Cemetery. As Yarborough describes it, students in both these projects must wrestle with the tangles of Mississippi's history "to research and tell stories that reflect the racial, ethnic, gender, and spiritual diversity of our area."

The performances are exercises in reconciliation for the students as well as for the residents of Columbus who attend. Yarborough e-mailed me with an update a few years after we saw a production for ourselves; a huge crowd, over two hundred people, showed up at the cemetery. He wrote that the students were "particularly engaged this year [it was a time of heightened racial troubles in the United States.] considering past periods of increased racial/ethnic cooperation in our story and how our communities might foster a return to those realities."

Selling the school to Mississippi parents is hard—even a school that regularly sends state champion teams to national science fairs and scoops up half the writing awards in the state, that turns out winners of Gates Millennium scholarships and in 2015 had one of its alumnae chosen as the first African-American woman Rhodes scholar from Mississippi. Several students told me that their moms were scared, or nervous, or didn't want them to leave home. And the students themselves mentioned the compromises they had to make, particularly abandoning extracurriculars that weren't available at MSMS. But those comments were invariably a warm-up to their feelings now: "I am so happy to be here. I have so many opportunities. I am so fortunate."

At MSMS, it's not surprising to meet a student who grew up in a shack or a double-wide. And to find them being friends now with others who came from private schools and affluent families. The kids were all in it together at MSMS, and many talked about how it had opened their

Mississippi eyes. An African-American girl from a nearby town even smaller than Columbus said that her hometown high school was 100 percent black and she appreciated being in a diverse environment now. A white girl from a larger town in the south of the state said that her private school had been all white, and she echoed her friend's comment exactly, adding, "My roommate is from India. I had never met someone from India before." A black boy from Columbus said his high school had been somewhat mixed, but it was really all about football. He said he appreciated being in a place where football didn't dominate everything.

Many MSMS alumni have already reached their dreams of becoming doctors, aerospace engineers, veterinarians, academics. Gunn, the student who built his own 3-D printer, was on his way to Harvey Mudd College. He said he would like to get cheap 3-D printers to resource-deprived third-world countries, because such printers could help their dreamers make what they need to build the products they might imagine. And after that, he continued, he wants to return to Mississippi to build his own engineering company, which would also do its part to address the education problems in Mississippi. "I am very blessed. I'll never forget where I am from. I see the struggle," he said, also adding that it is about more than football.

The most modern-looking aspects of this part of Mississippi are centered around the Golden Triangle Regional Airport, built at an approximate center point of the triangle's three towns and offering commercial airline connections to Atlanta. Just beyond it is a sprawling, modern steel mill owned at the time of our visit by the Russian Severstal company (it was later sold to an American firm). Nearby are large factories making truck engines, helicopters, drones, and other advanced devices, paying wages equal to several multiples of the local household income. Not far away, Yokohama Tire, of Japan, was building a major new plant, which opened about a year after our visit.

In all, the Golden Triangle region has brought in some $6 billion in capital investment in the decade before our visit, creating about six thousand new jobs, in an area of concentrated poverty where this influx has made an enormous difference.

Why so much? Why here? And to what effect?

The answers go in every direction. The search for non-union labor that has drawn companies from the Northeast and Midwest to the South is a central factor. Incentives from the state and local governments are another. Plain old political logrolling has been crucial to Mississippi and some other southern states: its representatives are tough on federal spending, and even tougher about keeping earmarked projects coming here. And on down the long list.

But there are countless places that offer incentives, and discourage unions, and would love to have the factories. Each of the big employers that has recently chosen the Golden Triangle considered scores or hundreds of other possibilities, many in the South and some in Mexico or the Caribbean, before coming here. Why here?

Allowing for all the other explanations, it still seemed clear that a handful of forceful people made the difference in shaping the region's economy as a whole. In a way, this is consistent with the pattern we were beginning to see around the country. A stalwart group is determined to give Eastport, Maine, a chance; a series of civic leaders shifted the Greenville area of South Carolina to a new civic and economic footing; successful businesspeople who retained a strong local identity made a huge difference in the character of Holland, Michigan, and Sioux Falls, South Dakota.

In this part of Mississippi, it is harder to identify purely civic leaders who have played a comparable role. But it is harder still to ignore the difference that the area's economic-development team has made, including Joe Max Higgins and Brenda Lathan and their colleagues at a regional organization called the Golden Triangle Development Link and Raj Shaunak of East Mississippi Community College.

This was brought home in our first visit to the area. One day I was taking a tour of the major industries around the Golden Triangle Regional Airport with a group of investors from the Midwest who had put money into the region and were considering investing more. On the bus back to the airport—where several of their own jets were ready to fly them back home—one of the investors told me, "There are entire states that can't come close to what this team has done here," meaning Higgins and Lathan. Lathan is an imposing black woman who grew up in the area; Higgins is an imposing white man who is a relative newcomer. Together they have led a transformation of a left-behind area of a famously left-behind state.

During that visit, Deb and I sat with Higgins in his office and asked him to describe the sequence of development in the area. Higgins grew up in Arkansas as the son of a sheriff and cultivates a southern-sheriff bearing. We asked him what the turning point in the region's recovery was.

He had a long list, but he focused on Eurocopter—the facility, part of Airbus, that makes helicopters for both civilian and U.S. military use.

"Eurocopter was really, really, a big deal," he said. "It was important because they make *helicopters*! In a county and a state where most people think the women are all barefoot and pregnant, all the men got snuff up in their lip, we're all members of the Klan—now we're making *shit that flies*! That genuinely changed our psyche. It was monumental. When Eurocopter came in, people started walking upright a little bit."

It's a story he had told before, and he reveled in the "barefoot and pregnant" effect and apologized pointedly to Deb a few times when he thought his language might offend her. But he was talking about something real.

On his pickup truck, Joe Max Higgins had a vanity license plate that read, "2EQLAST." He explained it to us, using a joke he had clearly told before: In the economic-development business, coming in second equals coming in last. You get the deal, or you don't—and there's no reward for a near miss or giving it a good try. It's a subtler version of the standard signature line in his e-mail messages: "Live every second as if your ASS is on fire."

You expect talk like this from any number of football coaches, and Higgins's talk about his region's prospects is very much that of a coach.

One example was his description of how he ended up in this part of Mississippi. It started with a recruitment call in the early 2000s, a dozen years before we met.

"When the headhunter called," he told us, "and said, I want you to look at a position in Mississippi, I said, You gotta be kidding me! I hear 'Mississippi,' and I hear poverty, despair, no future, and no hope for a future!

"Then we drove through here—the azaleas were in bloom; it was pretty. My wife said we should at least look the place over. We looked at what God gave 'em, and what they were doing with it. And I said, There's no reason in the world these folks aren't winning! But they're not."

Within "they're not" was the whole range of local economic woes, from a starting point of low income and high unemployment to a recent wave of factory closures among the low-tech, low-wage small firms that have moved to the South from the Depression era onward.

Higgins went back to the headhunter. "I said, Here's what I want: audited financial statements, budgets, all this kind of stuff. I spent weeks just looking at it. I came to the conclusion, these guys should be hitting home runs, but they're not even getting to the plate. That's an opportunity." So he signed on and has gone at full speed ever since.

On what had happened since then, Higgins showed us a very detailed chart of all the industries that had included the Golden Triangle in their site selection during his time there, the number that went ahead, what that meant in terms of capital investment and tax revenues, and what it meant in jobs. "If you take it strictly on investment, deals we won versus deals we lost, we're batting .442! And some of those deals we lost are ones we said, Go away, we're not interested. But now, in jobs, we're batting .241. So how good are we, really? Two-forty-one is maybe better than most, but it won't get you into the hall of fame, not unless you can play second base like a champ. But .442 will get you into the hall!" And then Higgins continued on to an argument about why the average had to go up.

Everything about Joe Max Higgins's talk, walk, body language, and comportment is go, go, go; do, do, do. A profile of him by William Browning in the Columbus-based *Catfish Alley* magazine pointed out that Higgins, who is burly by anyone's standards, used to go through two six-packs of Diet Coke per day. By the time we met, he had backed down to just eating packs of an "energy powder" called Spark.

* * *

The Golden Triangle's first big win was its certification as a TVA "Megasite" in the mid-2000s. The Megasite system was a way for the TVA to speed investment within its region by pre-clearing certain sites as being project-ready. They had the infrastructure, they had the permits, they had enough contiguous land, they had everything else. As a Federal Reserve report described them: "The Tennessee Valley Authority coined the term in 2004 for sites in the TVA region that could be deemed worthy of large-scale development—1,000 acres in size, environmentally clean, and accessible to transportation and utilities, among other criteria." A Federal Reserve Bank of St. Louis assessment a few years later was positive: "Megasites Spur Big Turnaround for Mississippi Region."

Higgins and his colleagues at the Golden Triangle Development Link wholeheartedly threw themselves into the competition to be awarded Megasite status. "The TVA was tired of every bean field, cotton field, cornfield in Anytown USA saying, 'We're going to have the next Toyota-Nissan-Mercedes plant!'" he told us. So they hired a prominent national consultant to design the criteria for certification.

"Everybody showed up. The could-bes, the wannabes, the never-weres and thought-they-weres, they all showed up." All the candidate regions were asked to provide simulations of how they would handle major new investments, and to supply specs on every economic, infrastructure, labor-market, and environmental consequence of economic growth.

"They had a two-foot-high book of specs," Higgins said. "We worked twelve hours a day, six days a week. Optioning the sites, doing the soil borings, everything." To cut to the conclusion: in August 2004, the TVA certified its first two Megasites. One was Hopkinsville, Kentucky, and the other was near the Golden Triangle airport in Columbus.

"The worm turned then," Higgins told me. "That TVA decision was the inciting incident that changed this community forever. I'm serious. Before that, I'm working little projects. I'm working a sweet potato plant here and a small, small automotive plant there. That was it. To be honest, when I took this job I thought, I'll hit a couple of singles, maybe a double, and then I'll get a bigger, better job somewhere else."

Soon after that, Higgins and his team got their first big commitment, with the $600 million steel plant from SeverCorr, later called Severstal. Then they began applications for a second Megasite, which also succeeded. (The TVA has certified only eight altogether, including the two in Columbus.) Then they proceeded on, through the list of other successful industrial recruitments, which in all have brought in billions of new investment, and something like 5,600 new jobs, to an area where the unemployment rate, even with this new work, is still around 15 percent.

The latest big investment news for the region was from Yokohama Tire, which when we visited was building a $300 million new plant near West Point, the most depressed part of the Golden Triangle area. It was to employ five hundred people when it opened the following year, toward a planned total of two thousand.

As part of the courtship process, Higgins's group arranged a site visit by the Yokohama corporate high command: helicopter tours of the area; green tea and hot, moist towels to refresh the visitors at each stop; galoshes to protect their shoes from the Black Prairie mud after a rainstorm.

During the aerial tour, Higgins took Yokohama's chairman over the ruins of what had been, for nearly a century, the economic foundation of West Point. This was the meatpacking plant, locally owned for decades by the Bryan family and then taken over by the firm that eventually closed it, Sara Lee.

"I told the chairman [of Yokohama] that this was an area that placed a lot of stress on long-term relationships," Higgins told me. "People worked for Bryan for generations. When that plant left, it tore the heart out of the whole community. I said, You can be the phoenix rising up, for the next generations."

Hokey, yes. But Higgins said that the helicopter then did several circles around the plant, while the chairman stared down at the devastation. "He looked over at me, and nodded," Higgins said. "I told the pilot, We can go now."

What has it cost, and what has it brought? During our visits to town, we talked with newspaper reporters, black and white civic and labor leaders, people who had been laid off and people who had found new jobs. Most of what we heard was positive: the area had been heading down, and now it was looking up.

But for any aspect of the modern American economy, the next question, the real question, is this: *Who* was being helped and hurt? Who was getting new opportunities? Who was being left behind?

Everything about Mississippi is, of course, shaped by the history of race. That is true for the United States in general, and perhaps most of all in this state. But by all measures we could observe, the industrial boom was offering more to poor people of all races than they had expected a decade earlier.

The biggest industrial employers, Severstal and Paccar, told us that the racial balance of their employees is "representative of the region." On the visits I made—three to the steel mill, two to the engine factory—the workforce appeared slightly more white than black, like the population of the region as a whole (which is about 50 percent white and 40 percent black, with Asians, Latinos, and others making up the rest). Certainly it was closer to being racially diverse in the fashion of a military unit than being overwhelmingly white in the fashion of many corporations or, especially, high-tech firms. The average earning for hourly employees at Severstal at the time, according to Joe Max Higgins, was around $80,000 before benefits—or more than twice the median household income in the area. At Paccar, it was less but still well above the median household income in the area. Some of the line employees I spoke with, black and white, had come back to the area after holding jobs elsewhere. One I met had previously worked at Sara Lee and then come to the steel mill. Several others had always lived in the vicinity.

"I'm not even interested in factories that aren't going to pay a lot more than people are already making here," Joe Max Higgins told me. "Why would I be? If you are going to create jobs at that level, you are forever dooming your area."

He mentioned a conversation he'd had with the mayor of a small town in Tennessee. "I'll never forget when he told me. 'I can't wait for the blue jeans plant to close in town!' You never hear a politician say that. He said, 'We got to get those ladies to community college and get their skills up. I can't run my town on minimum wage.' I thought that was the deepest thing I ever heard."

One day in Columbus, we toured the distressed facilities of a factory that had made toilet seats and the abandoned pants factory. Before winding up at the bricked up marble headstone factory, one of our hosts mentioned that we would pass near the orphanage.

"Orphanage! That is so sad," I blurted out, envisioning something Dickensian or out of the dark side of Harper Lee.

"Actually, the children live very well," rebutted our host gently.

I set out the next day to visit the orphanage, which everyone I met in Columbus called the Palmer Home.

The Palmer Home for Children, first known as the Palmer Orphanage, was started in 1895 by the First Presbyterian Church of Columbus with help from all the other churches in town. It still retains its strong Christian heritage. Like any institution that has endured for more than a century, the Palmer Home has felt the effects of wars and economic ups and downs, as well as, in its particular purview, a shift away from the public embrace of classic orphanages, the wane and wax of government engagement with child welfare issues, and major shifts in the demographics of the American family. There was also a fire.

One big change that affected the everyday and overall lives of the children came in the 1960s, when the Palmer Home began moving its children out of big traditional dormlike buildings, which today are mostly used for administration and communal cooking and dining, to on-campus individual homes. This idea, which was new to the times and especially new in the South, was a move toward more family-style living. The cottages, as the houses are quaintly called, were designed for six to eight children to live with a set of house parents, the overall effect resembling a much more "normal" family life.

Our guide around the Palmer Home told me a particularly poignant story, about the background of one of the early cottages. In 1967, there was a catastrophic midair collision between a Piedmont Airlines Boeing 727 and a twin-engine Cessna over Hendersonville, North Carolina. Everyone aboard the two planes was killed, eighty-two people in all, including three from Columbus: J. Dudley Hutchinson, the owner of a wholesale food company; his son of the same name; and a new employee, C. L. Hutcherson. They did not leave orphans, but they did, in effect, leave a gift to the orphanage, which came in the form of a memorial fund from the people of Columbus. Today that is Hutchinson House, one of the first of the seven cottages there now.


The cottages, long one-story ranch-style buildings, are set around the main lawns with a playground, basketball court, and lots of running space. Horses and stables are off to one side, a baseball diamond and a swimming pool off to another. There is also a gym. When I visited, some boys were playing basketball, and one girl was skipping across the lawn and another was trotting by on a horse. The campus sprawls over 110 acres, amounting to a small farm with vegetable gardens, orchards, and twelve big greenhouses, which were abloom with all sorts of flowers, including my favorite, gerber daisies.

The farming is a source of revenue for the Palmer Home, from produce they sell at the local farmers' market to their new venture, a community-supported agriculture (CSA) program where people buy a season subscription for fresh produce. It is also a way for the children to learn farming skills and to earn pocket money by working on the farm.

Most of the children fan out to public and private schools around town, whichever seems to be the best match. A few are homeschooled at the Palmer Home. There is an abundance of outside opportunities and support—camping and fishing trips, trips to Disney parks, service trips, tutors, therapists.

The cottages reminded me of the houses of some childhood friends who came from big Catholic families of seven or ten or even a dozen kids. Everything in those homes seemed industrial-sized to me, organized to ladle out life and love in well-managed, huge portions. The living space in the Palmer Home cottages was similarly expansive, and stretched out along a long hallway with double bedrooms, decorated as individually as new college freshmen dorm rooms, and bathrooms connecting pairs of bedrooms. The laundry room had double sets of washers and dryers; in this house, the kids who were old enough to manage each had a day to wash her own clothes.

I saw some of the seven girls living in the house I visited, along with their small but very strong-looking house mom, who had a new baby of her own. House parents in each cottage live three weeks on and one week off; often R&R is taken in a separate small cottage on campus. Sibling orphans often live together in the same cottage.

Which brings us to the terminology: orphan, double orphan, social orphan, children waiting, foster child, foster care, orphanage, group home, house parents, caregivers, residential care, out-of-home care. Which words to choose? The nuances of meaning have shifted with the social contexts of the times. Yesterday's orphan is not today's orphan.

An orphan, technically, has no living biological parents. A double orphan is another way of saying this. Social orphans may have a biological parent, but that parent is not able to care for them. Foster children are in the legal care of someone besides a biological parent. A child waiting is legally able to be adopted. And on and on.

Drake Bassett, who came recently from a completely different corporate world to be the president and CEO of the Palmer Home, described his puzzlement, early on, at how he should refer to the children at Palmer Home. "Are they orphans or not?" he asked a colleague. They talked over the many possible terms and finally decided, "They are children. Let's call them children." This felt right and freed them to attach whatever descriptive phrases they needed to suit the situation.

So who believes in this Mississippi orphanage? Plenty of people, as it turns out. The home is privately funded, beginning with the smallest checks and proceeds from its farm and thrift shops, and growing to more substantial support from many churches, private donations, foundations, estates, and from industry giants including Monsanto, Chick-fil-A, and the nearby Severstal steel plant, which donated a computer lab for the home, as well as the founder of Gary's Pawn and Gun shop, who dedicated funds to the Palmer Home in honor of his daughter Ginger, who passed away.

The orphanage was another surprising example to me, like MSMS, of where Mississippi excels.

The factories brought work to this part of Mississippi. But solving one problem opened up several more.

When you create thousands of high-wage, high-skill jobs in an area with a very low median income, poorly ranked schools, and a history of farming and low-end factories rather than advanced manufacturing, you raise another question: Where are companies going to find the right people to do these jobs? Sure, lots of people need work. But the ones who have been laid off from packinghouses or "cut and sew" minimum-wage garment plants, or who have not held a steady job at all, may not be ready to help run a billion-dollar modern steel mill or an Airbus helicopter factory.

This is where East Mississippi Community College, or EMCC, comes in. What we had seen in Camden County—a revolution in "career technical" training with significant social and economic effects—was under way here.

Back at the dawn of time, when I was in high school, "vocational ed" had a patronizing, loser tone. The modern "career technical" programs that we were beginning to see across the country, in contrast, aspire to help people avoid the minimum-wage service-or-retail trap with better-paid jobs as skilled repair technicians, in health care, in construction and design, in advanced modern factories, in law enforcement, and in other "living wage" categories.

Many of these schools naturally operate on a dispersed public-good principle. They have no way of knowing where the students they're training will end up working ten or twenty years from now. So they proceed on the belief that the area will always need more welders and more nurses, and it will be better for the region to have a larger pool of better-skilled workers. (Also, it increased the prospects that some large corporation might open a branch there, and new start-up businesses might arise.) And it is obviously a plus for the students to have more skills and options, whether they stay nearby or leave.

EMCC's current ambitions are more targeted. The good jobs are coming to its Golden Triangle region, thanks to the efforts of its promoters. The big new factories have already brought in thousands of higher-skill, higher-wage jobs. An enormous plant from Yokohama Tire will bring more. The challenge is to prepare local people to qualify for them.

This is the challenge Raj Shaunak has undertaken.

\* \* \*

Raj's family is Indian; he was born in Kenya; and as a teenager he moved with his family to England, where he went to college. I will refer to him as Raj because that is how everyone seems to know him locally. When he picks up the phone, he says slowly and in a deep voice, "*Rajjjj . . .*" or "This is Raj. . . ." His accent is an arresting combination of U.K. Indian and Mississippi southern.

In 1972, Raj paid a visit to Mississippi to see his brother, who was then at Mississippi State University in Starkville. He ended up staying and building a very successful manufacturing business with other family members.

In 1989, the family sold the business, and Raj was freed from workaday economic concerns. On October 31 of that year, he dramatically threw his wristwatch into the Tennessee-Tombigbee Waterway outside Columbus, and began the next stage of his life. (Me: "Raj, could I call you at eleven a.m. tomorrow?" Raj: "Jim, I have no watch—call me when you would like.") Two years later, he was teaching adult-education courses and math. By 1994, he had begun what is now his major commitment: "workforce development," or preparing people in the community for the jobs that the economic-development commission is trying to attract.

The results can be seen in various ways around this part of the state. EMCC has brochures, billboards, ads, and other publicity all over town, letting people know about its programs. Students who enroll go through what Raj calls "skills-based pathways," which essentially assess the skills and disciplines they do and don't have, and train them accordingly. In the EMCC training facilities, students work on real versions, or sometimes scaled-down models, of the machinery and products being made in the local factories. I saw them dealing with real engines from the nearby Paccar factory, and real computer-controlled machine tools.

"What happens to the ones who don't get hired?" Raj asked me, anticipating the question, after he had shown me through a mock assembly line where the workers were trained. "They will have much higher skills, and they will be more marketable—either when Yokohama opens its next phase"—another five hundred jobs—"or anywhere else."

He explained further: "We cannot guarantee a job for anyone. We are in the business of training people to be part of a qualified pool of applicants. We're trying to move people from dependence to enterprise and independence."

There may be an underside to EMCC and the programs it is carrying out; I didn't pretend to be launching a detailed investigation. But at face value, the people I asked—students at the school (without Raj or other officials present), alumni in the factories (some one-third of whom had been through EMCC), people around town—all described it as a plus. Just before our visit, the state's lieutenant governor had come to town to praise Raj and others at EMCC for what they had achieved.

Mississippi has the highest proportion of African-Americans of all states, at around 38 percent. All the classrooms, cafeterias, libraries, and factory sites I saw were racially mixed—if not exactly in the 50/40 white/black ratio for the Golden Triangle region, then with a much larger black presence than mere tokenism. Raj, by the way, seemed to enjoy and make the most of his "other" status on the black-white racial grid. He works very closely with Joe Max Higgins. I heard him on a call with Higgins, who was in a rush (as always) and had to hang up. "Joe, Joe, you never have time for the brown man," Raj said, obviously using a familiar joke line between the two.

On our third visit to town, Raj took me to a catfish buffet at Lion Hills, a former private (and formerly segregated) country club that has now become a EMCC dining center and golf course, as well as a training facility for its restaurant-management, chef-training, and turf-management programs. He worked his way through the racially mixed group of diners and students there, seeming to slightly code-switch his accent from group to group. In most big U.S. cities where I have lived, "How are you?" is a pro forma question to which no one expects a real answer. In this part of Mississippi, people treated it as an actual query, deserving an extended reply. Thus Raj moved around the room shaking hands, patting people on the back, taking time to exchange words with everyone dining—and working—there.

* * *

Does any of this matter, the industrial-recruitment efforts and the training of a workforce? People in the state think it does. "The industrial boom in the Golden Triangle happened because leaders in the Golden Triangle made it possible," Tate Reeves, the lieutenant governor, said at a local event. "When you are competing for businesses, you have to have the infrastructure, you have to have the quality of life, you have to have the land," Raj told me over the phone. "But most places that are competing have those things. We now have a critical mass of trained and trainable workers. Companies have told us that this makes the difference."

The southern cities we'd visited in the first half of 2014 had all undergone some sort of deep economic shock. For Greenville and the surrounding communities of the Upstate, it had been the rapid loss of the textile companies that even in the early 1990s had been major employers. For

St. Marys and its environs in the coastal Georgia pinelands, it was the sudden disappearance of the region's dominant industry—followed, fortunately and thanks mainly to Georgia's political pull, by the arrival of the U.S. Navy. For northeastern Mississippi, the departure of low-wage workshops like the toilet-seat factory and blue jeans plant compounded economic and social problems that were decades—even centuries—in the making. But each of these areas, like others we'd visited, were experimenting to find ways ahead.

Starting that summer, we headed north, toward areas that in their prime had been the symbolic and, at times, the real hearts of American manufacturing greatness. These were places that contemporary Americans think of as the Rust Belt (and that boosters would like to rebrand as the Chrome Belt). They include cities like such onetime world leaders in steelmaking as Pittsburgh, at the western end of Pennsylvania, and Allentown and Bethlehem, in the east. We went, as well, to Charleston and its surroundings in West Virginia, where during FDR's era most families in the state drew their incomes directly or indirectly from coal mining.

We went to Duluth, Minnesota, which grew rich in the late nineteenth century as the westernmost Great Lakes terminus for the grain, the timber, the iron ore, and the other bounty coming from the American plains and prairie to customers on the East Coast and beyond. (Some of the Gilded Age novels by Theodore Dreiser, like *The Financier* and *The Titan,* use "Duluth" as a shorthand for the opportunity and social upheaval that new technologies and global markets had brought in the late 1800s, much as "Detroit" symbolized in the early 1900s and "California" at midcentury.) We went to Columbus, Ohio, whose immediate economy had long been based on state government, as Ohio's capital city, and by all the activity generated by the Ohio State University. But Columbus has been tied, as well, to the ups and downs of Ohio's manufacturing economy and its still surprisingly important farming sector. Head a few miles in any direction outside the city and you're in farmland; overall, agriculture makes up more than a tenth of the entire Ohio economy.

What we found in most of these places was a certain kind of public and civic life that was consistent with what we'd seen across the country over the preceding year, and at odds with what "politics" had come to mean in national coverage. Public decisions in these towns didn't always turn out right, they weren't always fair in their effects and benefits, they weren't always free of special-interest distortions. But compared with the big showdowns in national politics of the past few presidencies, or even most policy making at the state level, what these cities had done to prepare for long-term challenges, to take advantage of new opportunities, and to minimize posturing and polarization was impressive. The stories of their mayors and other civic leaders obviously oversimplify the reasons for their success. But they struck us as useful shorthands for why these cities had done the things they had.

# Caddo Lake, Louisiana-Texas

We usually began our city visits talking about dollars-and-cents topics—how the economy was doing, whether businesses were moving into downtown or away from it, how the schools were funded and how well they were preparing students for opportunities in the area or beyond.

But time and again we found that the same forces of local patriotism that motivated young people to start their families or businesses in a smaller town, or that convinced mature people to stay there and assume civic responsibilities, also showed up strongly in non-commercial realms. These ranged from promoting the arts to supporting local sports and recreation to protecting the environment. Our stop in the remote area of Caddo Lake, which straddles the border between Texas and Louisiana, illustrated the latter point. It was an unusual conjunction of a prominent personality with local loyalties, and a long-term effort to make a difference in the environment.

Caddo is the largest natural lake in the South, and one of the very few natural lakes of any size in the state of Texas. There most bodies of water, like Lake Travis near Austin or Lake Conroe near Houston, are the result of dam-building projects from the late 1800s onward. Caddo now has a weir at the far eastern end of the lake, but it was formed by two natural if unusual-sounding phenomena. One was the effect of the "Great Raft," starting about one thousand years ago. This term refers to an enormous, wholly natural pileup of tree trunks, branches, and other debris in the shallow twists and oxbows of the local Red and Atchafayala Rivers. At its greatest extent the logjam stretched for more than one hundred miles, and it blocked the rivers' flow sufficiently to create an impounded lake behind it.

The other was a series of major earthquakes in the early 1800s, originating from the New Madrid fault line in the Mississippi River Valley north of Memphis and near the "boot heel" of Missouri. Those quakes, including four that were each as strong as nearly any that have struck California or Alaska, occurred from the fall of 1811 through the spring of 1812. They are thought to have lowered the ground level in the Caddo area enough to create the current natural lake basin. U.S. government observers from the James Madison administration were not in the region to record the effects in Caddo, but the earthquakes play a major role in histories of the Caddo Nation, a confederation of tribes who lived throughout the Southeast. They were taken as an omen of troubled days ahead for the Caddo, which of course arrived in the form of Andrew Jackson and the era of anti-Indian warfare and extirpation. By the 1830s, the Caddo had "sold" their lake-area land to the U.S. government under President Jackson for a token sum and were moved west. They are still recognized as a nation, with official headquarters in Oklahoma.

The two centuries after the earthquake were times of trouble for the lake itself. In the early 1800s, white explorers speculated about removing the Great Raft, to allow waterborne commerce from the ports of the Gulf Coast into the Mississippi Valley. Through the 1830s, an engineering-minded riverboat captain named Henry Miller Shreve supervised a program of blasting, hauling away, and otherwise removing the logs that made up the Great Raft. The work was completed after the Civil War, lowering the lake level by some ten feet, taking commerce away from several inland ports that had grown up along the Caddo, including a town called Jefferson that had become the second-largest city in Texas at the time, and transferring it to a major downriver settlement now known as Shreveport, in Shreve's honor.

In the early 1900s, the oil-discovery boom in Texas and Louisiana spread to the Caddo area. What is thought to be the first-ever offshore rig was built in Caddo Lake in 1911, by the predecessor to Gulf Oil. Modest-level oil production has continued ever since; one of the settlements on the Louisiana side of the lake is called Oil City. During World War II the military established its Longhorn Army Ammunition plant at Caddo, manufacturing bombs and rocket fuel and heavily polluting the lake itself. After the munitions plant finally closed in the 1990s, local developers attempted to transfer its water-use rights to new heavy industries they wanted to attract to the area.

In short, this twenty-five-mile-long body of water in the swampy South has been through the sort of battering usually associated with Lake Erie in its most troubled, pre–Clean Water Act era. Its human and industrial history means that Caddo Lake is anything but pristine. But by the time of our visit, after a flight west from the Golden Triangle of Mississippi over Caddo Lake to the nearest airport, in Marshall, Texas, the lake *looked* pristine. More: it looked and felt serene, set apart, timeless, undisturbed. We later learned that the appearance was misleading in one important way: a site that had endured the dirtiest of modern industrial activities—drilling, blasting, poisoning—had become the object of ecotourism from around the world, and one of only two dozen marsh or wetland areas in the United States to win international designation under the Ramsar Convention as a "Wetland of International Importance."

How had this happened? Why here?

The answer, improbably, involves the rock musician Don Henley—who grew up in the nearby East Texas town of Linden, who spent summers of his childhood in the 1950s fishing on the lake with his father, and who now says it is "the most beautiful place I know on earth."

By the mid-1970s, Henley had left Texas for Los Angeles, and had become famous as drummer, singer, and songwriter for the Eagles. But amid the other distractions and activities of his career, Henley decided relatively early to direct some of his name-brand influence and rock-star wealth toward environmental causes. In the late 1980s, he was part of a bitter battle against the Boston-based real estate developer Mortimer Zuckerman—by coincidence, then also the owner of the *Atlantic* magazine—over Zuckerman's plan to turn a parcel of land near Walden Pond into a commercial complex. This was *the* Walden Pond of Henry Thoreau fame, which Thoreau had described in early issues of the *Atlantic* among other venues. Henley and an alliance of conservationists went against Zuckerman, celebrity against celebrity, and eventually the conservationists won. Henley organized and helped fund The Walden Woods Project, which bought the contested property and put it into permanent-protected status. The project's institute operates by the pond, and Henley still visits frequently and raises funds for it.

Because of Walden's location, just outside Boston, and its international renown, that conservation project drew much more media attention than the parallel effort Henley was launching at about the same time to restore Caddo Lake from the damage done by decades of oil drilling and munitions work, and to protect it from future threats of pollution and overdevelopment.

In the early 1990s, along with a Colorado-based attorney and environmental activist named Dwight Shellman, Henley founded and largely funded the Caddo Lake Institute. It bought and preserved land, sponsored research projects, and blocked proposed construction of a commercial-barge channel through the lake, as part of the effort that won Caddo its protected status under the Ramsar Convention. It worked with other nonprofits and with government agencies, from the Corps of Engineers and the U.S. Fish and Wildlife Service to nearby city councils, toward its goal of "protecting the ecological, cultural, and economic integrity of Caddo Lake." Henley hit back at accusations that he was an outside-agitator celebrity by pointing out that he'd grown up just miles away and still took his children to stay in a double-wide trailer he owns by the lake (in addition to a house). A quarter-century after the Caddo Lake Institute's founding, Henley is still chair of its board and does fund-raisers and promotional interviews and videos for it.

We had learned about Caddo and Henley's involvement through a further string of improbabilities. While living in China, I wrote an

*Atlantic* article about the country's tragic dilemma involving coal. China couldn't stop using coal if it hoped to sustain its all-out pace of industrialization. But it couldn't keep using coal if it hoped to protect its people against currently toxic air (or reduce its carbon emissions). The way out of the dilemma, I argued, was for Chinese and U.S. technologists to work together on clean energy and cleaner-coal innovations.

Henley read the article and sent me an unexpected e-mail suggesting that we meet during the Eagles' upcoming concert tour in China. On a bitterly cold night in early 2011, Deb and I went from our apartment on the east side of Beijing to what had been the 2008 Olympic volleyball stadium, on the west side, to join an ecstatic and sold-out crowd of Chinese fans of all generations, on their feet, singing along with "Desperado" and "Hotel California." The Eagles had been among the first Western rock groups to win popular favor in China, and this was their first appearance on Chinese soil in years. The next day, we went with Henley to a coal company's environmental research center an hour outside Beijing.

We stayed in touch with Henley on environmental matters, and heard from him about Caddo. We flew to Marshall on our trip west, rented a car and drove to the settlement of Uncertain, Texas, on the west shore of Caddo Lake. Henley was preparing to embark on a European tour just then, so his longtime friend and environmentalist ally, Rick Michaels, showed us around. (Why is the little town named Uncertain? No one seemed to know for sure. It apparently started as a bureaucratic mistake, and has lasted as a novelty.)

From three feet above water level, our perspective on the pontoon boat in which Rick Michaels toured us around the lake, at first glance Caddo looked like a slightly less Spanish-moss-laden version of the Okefenokee Swamp of Georgia. But the farther we ventured into its bayous and across its silent stretches, the more it seemed distinct from any place we'd ever seen before.

Stumps and living trunks of bald cypress rose from the dark water. The name "bald cypress" makes the trees sound inelegant. But as they taper up from their broad bases, their trunks have the straight, austere beauty of western redwoods, and something like their scale and age.

Nearly all the bald cypresses in North America grow along the southern Atlantic and Gulf coasts. The tallest rise more than 120 feet above water level; the oldest known specimen, in North Carolina, is at least 1,600 years old. According to Michaels some of the trees around us in Caddo were more than 400 years old. The more ancient the tree, the more it was surrounded by several-foot-tall thin stumps called cypress knees.

Turtles slid off rocks or tree trunks into the water as we drew near. Egrets flapped overhead. Herons prowled through the marshes and stabbed for frogs or fish. Caddo Lake is on a major migratory-bird flyway, and tens of millions of flying creatures—ducks, geese, smaller birds—pass through each year. "The songbirds may be the most remarkable," Rick Michaels said. "This is the only place I know of where you look around and see a red bird, and a blue bird, and an orange bird, or an orange-and-blue bird, all at the same time. We have eagles and alligators." We were motoring in the midday sunlight so we didn't see the other wildlife that Michaels said abounds in the region and comes out at night or in the half-lit crepuscular hours: wildcats, possums, snakes. The waters support more than seventy species of fish—including, recently, a prehistoric-looking creature called the paddlefish, with a long saw-toothed snout. The paddlefish is the oldest surviving fish species in North America. It once abounded in these waters and, in a partnership between the Caddo Lake Institute and the Fish and Wildlife Service, has been reintroduced.

"Caddo is almost as significant for what it is not," the Texas author Joe Nick Patoski wrote in *The Texas Observer* in 2005. "No condos, no high-rises, no chain motels or restaurants, no resorts, no gated, planned communities, no margarita bars, no chains, no pretension, none of the trappings of modern Texas Lake Culture.... Caddo Lake may be in northeast Texas and relatively close to urban centers in all directions, but for those who get Caddo, it is a natural jewel just as worthy of protection."

"There is no place I care about more," Don Henley said when I talked with him, soon before our visit.


We spent a full day at the lake, and another exploring Marshall—famous in the 1950s as the home of the New York Giants' quarterback Y. A. Tittle, and in the 1960s and 1970s as the home of the LBJ-aide-turned-journalist Bill Moyers, and viable now in part because quirks of the federal judiciary have made the courts of the Eastern District of Texas, headquartered there, a favored venue for those filing patent-claim lawsuits. We saw enough to get an idea of the difference that committed local patriots—Henley, Shellman, Michaels, their allies—could make in the fate of a region.

By quirk of timing, we apparently missed the next big challenge to Caddo's environmental and economic viability. The wind had been strong before our visit, and the winter had been cold. So the dark waters were mainly clear of the peril that threatened the lake: a plant called giant salvinia.

One by one, salvinia plants are tiny rather than giant. Their leaves look like miniature lily pads, and they are related to the familiar and harmless *Salvinia auriculata,* a common household-aquarium plant. But the similar-looking, ominously named *Salvinia molesta* is the horror-movie version. It originated in Brazil and has spread so rapidly worldwide that it is classified as a major invasive-plant species. The problem with the "bad" salvinia is how rapidly it grows. I suspect that every high-school math student has dealt with a "trick" question involving spreading lily pads. (Q: If lily pads double in size each day, and cover an entire pond in 30 days, when do they cover half the pond? A: On the 29th day.)

*Salvinia molesta* is that math question brought to life. It's capable of doubling its coverage not every day, but every five to seven days. This means that a tiny colony can cover an entire lake the size of Caddo within weeks. And when salvinia weeds cover the surface, they cut off the sunlight, meaning that aquatic life below them dies—other plants, fish, the ecosystem as a whole. The plants pile up; the lake dies, and reeks; what had been an environmental success story becomes a failure. In 2017, Laura Biel of *Texas Monthly* quoted a Caddo resident, Robert Speight, on what salvinia has meant for Caddo: "Ten minutes from leaving the dock, you can be in an area that just looks so totally primitive you wouldn't know what century you were in, let alone what day of the week it was. . . . All I can think about now when I go out is what salvinia is doing to the lake. The inner peace is gone."

That is the threat Caddo has faced with increasing frequency over the past decade. During our visit, wind and cold weather had kept the lake mainly clear of giant salvinia. But a year later it was back, and spreading too quickly for mechanical harvesters to hope to keep up with.

What is the main source of hope? It, too, is coming from the Caddo Lake Institute. Researchers at Texas A&M and elsewhere have found that a particular species of weevil eats *Salvinia molesta*—and, apparently, *nothing else*. If released into a salvinia-infested body of water, these appropriately named "salvinia weevils" will eat away at the invasive plant, but then not (it seems) mutate, develop new appetites, or start eating other forms of vegetation that humans value more. After our pontoon boat ride across the lake, Rick Michaels showed us the greenhouses where the Caddo Lake Institute is rearing weevils on industrial scale—and looking for new varieties that will survive local winters, which cruelly can be just cold enough to kill most of the insects without impeding the salvinia at all. "Doesn't this sound like the beginning of some sci-fi novel?" I asked him. "Breeding voracious weevils—what could go wrong?" "Yeah, I know," he said. "But it's the best answer we have for now."

Texas A&M, which had been leading the weevil research, had budgetary cutbacks—so Caddo Lake Institute offered more funding to fill the gap. Researchers there are working now with the Fish and Wildlife officials to build weevil greenhouses around the lake and to transport the weevils carefully to the lake once they're mature enough to survive. "They can't really cover any land distance on their own, so you have to walk them the few feet to the lake," Michaels said. "And maybe that would keep them from going some place we didn't intend."

"Caddo Lake needs everybody's love," Rick Michaels said as we drove back to Marshall. "It takes attention and affection, and that is what will save Caddo."

# *In the Air*

I knew as we headed north that the language we'd be hearing would change again. The slow southern drawl of Mississippi would tighten up and become more nasal as we turned toward Ohio and on up to Minnesota. And I was eager to listen for more versions of something that first struck me in Greenville and has become what I've come to think of as the Question.

The Question: Put yourself in a social situation, with people you don't really know but are trying to get to know a little more or maybe just have a conversation with. This is the question that comes after some version of "How do you do?" or "Nice to meet you," or "How are you?" We can call it the conversation opener or, more specifically, the second question.

I first realized we were onto something in Greenville, South Carolina. Two women, both transplants to Greenville, reported to us in surprised tones that the question people asked them after the first question was "Where do you go to church?"

They were flummoxed; we were flummoxed. Does that sound a little bit presumptuous, or personal, or prying, or audacious, or even offensive? Or is it exactly what those of you from Greenville would expect to hear? Well, besides a general consensus (in my unscientific polling) that this is the Question in Greenville, I also heard from people from smaller towns in Idaho, Virginia, Maine, Kentucky, and all over the South who confirmed that this is how they get their conversations rolling, too.

In Chicago, older people told me that the variant "What's your parish?" was so ubiquitous in their parlance growing up that even the folks who weren't Catholic knew exactly which parish they lived in. Some said the same for Boston.

Then there is St. Louis. I challenge each of you to ask someone from St. Louis about their question. Without fail—and I've tried it with hundreds of people—the answer is "Where did you go to high school?" If you draw towns into a Venn diagram of this question, the entirety of St. Louis fits inside that circle. I'm told the school question is also popular in Cincinnati and Charlotte, Louisville, New Orleans, Baltimore, and the island of Oahu.

What we are really intending with a question like "Where do you go to church?" or "Where did you go to high school?" is to find a rather gentle, regionally and socially acceptable way of sizing someone up. We are using the question to gather valuable information about their socioeconomic, cultural, and historical background. The question is a veiled probe of "Where do you fit in my world?" or "Let me understand who you are."

One person wrote me that the answer to "What's your parish?" is used "as a social marker for everything from your baseball team to your likely politics, to your geographical desirability as a candidate for a movie on Friday night." A woman from Texas said the answers carry a political overtone in her hometown of Waco, since everyone knows which churches are left- or right-leaning.

A second culturally loaded question asked in many sprawling metropolitan areas—like D.C., New York, Boston, Chicago, San Francisco, Los Angeles, and Houston—is "Where do you live?"

The more granular the answer, the better, say the folks from the big cities. Boston becomes Cambridge or Somerville, and then shrinks farther to the nearest square or subway station: Davis, Porter, Harvard, Central, Kendall, et cetera. Chicago becomes North Side or South Side, then a smaller slice, like Near North Side or South Loop. In our hometown of Washington, D.C., the generic answer of "D.C." is usually followed by some divvying up into the quadrant or sections of the district versus the suburbs of Virginia or Maryland.

One person from New York suggested that the question may just be an excuse to lead into everyone's favorite subject: real estate. Someone from the Low Country of South Carolina, in the southeast part of the state, said the calibration becomes "Which bend?," as in which bend of the river.

I've been asked the default question in Washington, D.C., countless, truly countless times: *"What do you do?"* or *"Where do you work?"* The question reflects the currency of the town. The answer, according to many who offered their interpretation, suggests a measure of a person's power and connections. I would add politics, passion, and money to that mix as well. It's a New York question, too, and probably common in other cities with a predominant industry, like tech in the Bay Area, or academia in Boston, or "the industry" in Los Angeles.

Some younger people told me that they shy away from that question because it reeks as too sensitive or judgmental among a generation of those who are having trouble landing jobs, or don't have a direction, or are just taking their sweet time figuring it out.

*"Where are you from?"* is a popular opener in Seattle, Austin, Madison, San Francisco, Los Angeles, Atlanta, and the entire state of Florida. It makes sense since so many people have moved there from elsewhere, maybe for a tech-rich environment or a guaranteed liberal culture, to stretch for the golden ring, or simply for the weather and absence of taxes.

Two places avoid this question: Alaska and Hawaii. Why? The Big Island of Hawaii is a relocation spot for the federal witness protection program. Alaska is well known as a place where people can start troubled lives over. "Where are you from?" can be an unwelcome foray into dangerous or uncomfortable territory.

*"What are you?"* This blunt question is after a description of ethnic or racial heritage. In Philadelphia or Boston, or more rural towns with big European populations, the question assumes that someone will say Irish, Polish, Italian, or German. Or maybe Hispanic or Native American. A lot of folks told me that they cringe when people ask this question.

At first, I thought it was a joke when I heard *"Who's your mama?"* Until someone explained that in New Orleans, where everyone seems to know everyone else, they know who your daddy is from your last name, but your mama, now, that's another matter. So the question really means *"Who are your people?"* or *"Who do you belong to?"* Folks from New Orleans also told me that a variant of *"Who's your mama?"* is *"How's your mama 'n' them?"* That's probably more for people you already know, and it strikes me as being soaked in southern personality.

Finally, there is a grab bag of geographically specific openers, many of which reflect a strong local culture or preoccupation. In fun-loving meccas of the country, like Burlington, the question *"What do you do?"* actually means "What do you do for fun?" Answers often circle around winter sports. In Denver, the question may be *"Where do you ski/bike/hike?"*

In Los Angeles, it's about cars and driving: *"How did you get here?"* The answer usually takes the form of "I took the 10 to the 405..." And there may be a follow-up: *"What do you drive?"* In San Francisco: *"What will we be eating?"* or *"What smells great?"* or *"What did you bring?"* In Chicago, in response to *"Who do you like?,"* there are only two possible answers: the Cubs or the Sox. In Birmingham, the question is *"Alabama or Auburn?"* In Laramie: *"Did you get your moose yet?"* I'm not kidding you.

In orange-growing Redlands: *"Do you have a citrus tree?"* There is an expectation, nearly an entitlement, that every backyard will have a citrus tree. Once, when I replied that our little rental house didn't have one, a kind of pained look fell across the face of my questioner, and he asked again, just to be sure: "Really, are you sure there's not even a small orange tree?" Later that week, I found a few bags of oranges, grapefruit, and kumquats on our front step.

A lot of people told me that they dislike every one of these possibilities. As a questioner, they feel intrusive. As a respondent, they feel boxed in and, often, judged. A few people suggested that they are more comfortable asking an open-ended question, one that invites a person to take any number of directions to answer. It's a question something like *"So, what's your story?"*

# Columbus, Ohio

Columbus, Ohio, was by far the biggest city we visited. It has well over a million people in the metro area, more than twice as many as the state's second-biggest conurbation, in Cleveland. The city itself is the fifteenth largest by population in the country, just behind San Francisco but ahead of Seattle, Boston, and Denver. Because of a dense concentration of Columbus-based retail and apparel brands, the Columbus area is a national leader in the size and value of its fashion-design industry. Ubiquitous national brands, like Wendy's, and semiubiquitous ones, like Bob Evans restaurants and White Castle burger shops, are based there as well.

But in terms of media presence and the pop-culture industry, Columbus looms nowhere near as large. It's still an "out there in the real America" city, as opposed to one of the focused-upon and minutely chronicled coastal centers. (Everyone can imagine a street scene from Boston or a vista of Denver from the movies or TV. Very few people outside Ohio have any mental picture of Ohio's state capital, or the city's now-thriving German Village and Short North or Arena districts, or the Franklinton area, which is in the middle of redevelopment.) "When you ask people where they're from, they can just say 'Pittsburgh' or 'Cleveland' or 'Nashville' without adding the state name, even though there may be a lot of Nashvilles in the United States," a Columbus resident named

Alex Fischer told us early in our visit. "But you always hear, 'Columbus, *Ohio*'—for a city this big!"

Fischer was making a point about the civic dream of allowing "I'm from Columbus!" to stand on its own as a statement. It seems an impossible dream, given the number of already-known other Columbuses on the map—including, for us, the Columbus that is the heart of the Golden Triangle in Mississippi.

We heard this theme a lot, and it is a clue to what we came to understand about the civic and cultural benefits that come from Columbus's mixed big-and-little status.

Like Sioux Falls or Greenville, Columbus seems to think of itself as a much smaller community than it actually is. You can imagine problems that might come from this mismatch of reality and perception—for instance, a city thinking it can address all its challenges in a person-to-person way, without realizing that it has outgrown that approach. Columbus is a major metropolis, with all the scale and resources that go with that status. In culture and operating patterns, it remains more intimately connected—and, thus, able to respond more quickly and with more practical-mindedness to challenges as they emerge, rather than being tied up in procedure or partisan standoffs.

What does this mean in practice? Following are two perspectives, starting with Alex Fischer's.


"When I first saw the downtown of Columbus, it looked like . . . nothing!" Alex Fischer told us in his office downtown. Fischer, a sandy-haired, athletic-looking man in his late forties, had first visited the city in the late 1990s and early 2000s, when he was putting together a research partnership with the Battelle Memorial Institute, which is headquartered in Columbus and—with an endowment from a local engineer and philanthropist named Gordon Battelle that has grown to some $6 billion—is one of the nation's largest, if least-publicized, research centers. "Of course I'd heard about Columbus, for fourth-grade memorization of the state capitals, but that was my first look at it. And I thought—*wow*." He didn't mean this in a positive way. At that time, the prospects for downtown Columbus seemed bleak. Department stores closing, small retail spaces vacant or occupied by pawnshops, life and business migrating to the suburbs, downtown streets deserted and often dangerous after dark. An old decaying state penitentiary sat in the middle of town.

Fischer and his family moved to Columbus nonetheless: the opportunities for him at Battelle and for his wife in the state government were too attractive to pass up. "But I often think about how different that first impression would be for someone seeing the city afresh right now," Fischer told me. The site of the former state penitentiary has become the city's showcase downtown redevelopment project, with an arena for the Columbus Blue Jackets hockey team and a billion dollars' worth of surrounding investment.

As it happened, seeing the city afresh was my own angle of vision on that visit, since Columbus was the most sizable U.S. city I had never previously set foot in. And what I saw, viewing it afresh, was a humming, stylish downtown very much like what we had seen in Greenville and Burlington. Retail stores with lots of daytime business, and restaurants and bars and theaters and brewpubs that were busy at night. Parks that were busy, with office workers on lunch breaks and some families. Old retail and warehouse buildings that had been converted into residential lofts and condominiums. All the elements of what we were beginning to think of as the "normal" healthy-downtown package.

Fischer proposed to explain the town's metamorphosis to us, from his perspective as CEO of the Columbus Partnership, an organization that connects business, civic, charitable, and educational institutions in the city.

"Up through about age forty, I feel as if I'd been able to *live* the experience of this new, cosmopolitan South that was coming into being," he said. Fischer had grown up in a small suburb of Nashville, done his undergraduate and master's degrees at the University of Tennessee in Knoxville, then worked on the Tennessee governor's staff in Nashville and at Oak Ridge National Laboratory. "Nashville, Charlotte, Atlanta— they really didn't exist then, in the form they do today. It was a lesson to me of how much can happen in a short time period—I mean, forty years, it's half a lifetime, it's a blink!" Fischer said that he was aware only in retrospect of how profound a transformation of the urban South he had been living through. From his childhood in the 1960s and 1970s until now, the South "went through a really major social and economic transition. There's still a long way to go on the social side, but it's profoundly different from the time when I was born."

When he got to Columbus, he thought it was time for a comparable transformation of cities in the Rust Belt. "The Midwest doesn't need to go through quite the same social transformation as the South," he said, referring not just to the legalized structures of segregation but also to other aspects of openness and tolerance. "But the cities and their infrastructure were built for an era and an economy that no longer exist"—the era of huge factories with thousands of workers streaming in and out at the end of each shift. Northern cities had to rearrange themselves for an economy of smaller, faster-changing, higher-value manufacturing sites; more offices and co-working spaces; less automobile-centric development and more walkable streets; and all the other traits of a twenty-first-century urban layout, rather than a nineteenth-century arrangement.

Fischer led us through the nuts and bolts of how Columbus was diversifying its economy. It had the steady base of state government and the university. Its away-from-the-coasts location gave it advantages as a transport and distribution hub. Battelle Research Institute, which had become an engineering and technology research center employing more than twenty thousand people and would be more famous if it were in Seattle or Palo Alto or Cambridge, produced a steady stream of spin-off tech companies, as did Ohio State itself. In addition to its retail and fashion chains, and the national restaurant companies that are based there, Columbus is a major financial center. The largest private employer in the area is JPMorgan Chase, with a staff of some sixteen thousand, followed by Nationwide Insurance, with some eleven thousand, and a very large hospital and medical-care sector.

Fischer pointed to dots on the map to illustrate the highlights: Over here, an enormous, historic downtown department-store building that had been shuttered in 2003 and reopened six years later as a modern office and retail space, after a public-private renovation effort. Over there, a new park, on the site of a former 1970s-era eyesore parking garage. Next to the park, downtown condos and apartments—practically unknown when Fischer got his first view of the town. "Even ten years ago, all of this was just wasteland," he said, gesturing through the window to what were now city blocks bustling with activity. "And I realize that now if the university or a high-tech firm is recruiting someone good from San Francisco, the feet-on-the-street impression of the downtown is going to be very different from when I first came here."

The recruiting point was more than rhetorical, because of Columbus's ambition to attract people who might otherwise assume they are headed for the biggest cities on the coasts. "Our branding is about being open and smart," he said. "We want to be a community that celebrates a diversity of lifestyles, in a community that is young and vibrant, with a lot of different perspectives and origins."

Fischer was well aware that every "smart" city wanted something similar. But he argued that Columbus's scale and culture gave it an edge. "I've spent a ton of time in Knoxville—which I love, but they just don't have our scale. I've never lived in New York or San Francisco or Los Angeles. Obviously they have the scale of economic activity, but that very scale overwhelms the right social connections we're able to maintain. That's the secret sauce for us. I'm not sure there are a lot of places big enough to do anything but small enough actually to get it done."

What was most interesting was Fischer's description of how and why Columbus had been able to rebuild its downtown and broaden its economy. He emphasized themes that, as he admitted even as he was talking about them, could sound like platitudes and clichés: "spirit of collaboration," "spirit of openness," "long-term commitment to the community." But by this point in our travels, I was recognizing the similarities to what we'd heard about successes in places from Michigan to Mississippi to South Dakota.

Fischer underlined that point: "If I had to give you one punch line for what's happened here, it would be the collaborative spirit of a group of business leaders who felt *something was expected of them*"—the kind of "local patriotism" and civic engagement we'd first heard about in Holland—"and got organized to say, How can we make this a better place? I know the term 'public-private partnership' is overused, but that's really what you saw here."

We traced the city's web of collaborations crisscrossing among business, government, philanthropy, start-ups, educational and civic institutions, the arts, and public-private partnerships. There is so much collaborating going on in Columbus that the edgiest among the collaborators have coined a new, shorter, more imperative word for it: "collab."

I first heard "collab" when I was walking along High Street in the Short North district of Columbus. The street is famously loaded with restaurants, shops, art galleries, and boutiques. I stopped in as many as I could. Near the top of the street was a place named Co+Op. I'm not sure how to describe it. An art gallery? A fashion-forward clothing boutique? A vintage clothier? A consignment shop? Yes, I think it was all of these. There was art on the walls, some old luggage and paraphernalia, a rack of newly designed clothes, some old (a.k.a. vintage) clothes. Food trucks sometimes park in the lot out front. Everything was for sale, at what struck me as high prices.

The manager back then, Kait Cutler, a millennial with bright red lips and dressed in fashion to match the shop, described the atmosphere of Columbus that draws many of her generation back. After six years of corporate life in Chicago, she said, she wanted to find a way to engage her creative side. Of Co+Op, she noted, "We *collab* a lot with Mouton," which is the wine bar and restaurant across the street. They held events together. Such edginess moves Columbus forward, but it doesn't always last, as I discovered when I heard the news, two years later, that Co+Op had shuttered. I recalled our years in Shanghai, where you'd have to be street-savvy when dropping off dry cleaning or shoes for repair, as there was a real chance the shop could disappear to new construction if you waited too long to retrieve your belongings. Mouton, at last report, is still going strong.

One of the food trucks that travels around town and sometimes parks in places like the High Street lot, was Ajumama, which means "ma'am" in Korean. I met owner Laura Lee when she was parked in a lot next to the indoor-outdoor Seventh Son Brewing facility, in the Italian Village section of Columbus. It was an early Friday afternoon, perfect for a late lunch with a little local beer. Lee cooked up one of the family recipes she'd adapted from her Korean mom's collection: *pajeon,* a green onion pancake, followed by *hodduk,* a sweet pancake with brown sugar, cinnamon, and walnuts. Lee says she's a stickler for ingredients, making her own kimchi and personal pancake mixes from scratch. They have earned her a bunch of awards and trophies, which sit on a shelf next to the order window.

Lee is a Columbus returnee from San Diego, where she worked as a sous-chef until deciding that Californians didn't appreciate her experimental creations. Several things have been working for Lee in Columbus, including a vibrant start-up food-truck culture and encouraging efforts from the city. The city recently eased up on licensing and parking rules and regulations for food trucks. Then they created a city-government position pluckily named "small business concierge" to cut through the red tape and provide advice for getting small ventures like Laura Lee's up and running quickly and successfully.

Another self-made Columbus transplant is Thomas McClure. We met for a glass of wine in the historic German Village neighborhood, walking distance south of the city center. He grew up in cattle country about two hours west of Dallas, with his Thai mom and American dad. To talk with Thomas McClure is to be swept up into his force field; he is all energy, speed, and can-do attitude. From an early age, McClure wanted to be in entertainment. A model and actor, he became a business partner in the talent agency that represented him. He started a runway show as a fund-raiser for local designers in Columbus in 2010; it quadrupled to twelve hundred attendees in four years. McClure says that cooperation and support happen naturally in the fashion industry in Columbus. Big brands, the likes of Abercrombie & Fitch, Designer Shoe Warehouse, Victoria's Secret, Lane Bryant, and others, get along with the little start-ups and boutiques, he explained, and operate as though there is room for all to work for the greater good of fashion in Columbus. Several times, we heard the mantra that Columbus is No. 3 in fashion design after New York and Los Angeles.

A more elaborate collaboration in Columbus takes place at the intersection of education, public institutions, and business. One afternoon,

I was leaving the elegant Columbus public library. The library's CEO, Patrick Losinski, had just told me about the Cristo Rey Columbus High School when, as if on cue, the school's development director, James Ragland, rounded the corner. The library can be a meeting place of sorts, intentionally or serendipitously; our near collision was the latter. Ragland was at the library to figure out some of the ways the school and the library might work with each other. He offered to take me on a tour of the school, which was right next door to the library, the next day.

The Cristo Rey Columbus High School is part of what is now a twenty-eight-school network that was founded in Chicago by Jesuit priest John P. Foley in 1995. The schools are strategically located in cities with a needy urban population, a supportive local Catholic diocese, and cooperative, deep-pocketed businesses. Columbus, as an energetic, creative, and generous city, fit the bill perfectly.

I went to visit Cristo Rey in its new home, formerly the Ohio School for the Deaf, which it purchased from the Columbus Metropolitan Library. The school's president, James Foley (no relation to the Jesuit founder of Cristo Rey, John P. Foley), told me that Patrick Losinski had told him that Cristo Rey didn't need its own library, since its students and teachers could use the public library right next door and thereby have "the best high school library in the country" at their fingertips. The building still had some of that new-car smell. The old wooden floors had been polished to a radiance; the paint was fresh; the big windows were sparkling; the rows of student lockers were unscratched. The massive $20 million renovation was still under way, focusing then on the upper-floor science labs and art studios. The majority of its funding had come from a creative combination of state and federal tax credits for historic building preservation and new job creation. Most of the rest came as a loan from the local Catholic diocese.

The mission of the schools, as Ragland describes it, is to break the cycle of poverty through education. The average annual family income of Cristo Rey students network-wide is about $35,000. Founder John P. Foley, S.J., says of the Cristo Rey schools, "If you can afford to come here, then you can't come."

The Cristo Rey students are needy. According to the school, some 83 percent of them were eligible for free or reduced lunch. Some 60 percent of the 188 students were African-American, 25 percent Latino, and the rest a variety. They were of all faiths. Ragland and the school's principal, Cathy Thomas, strip away the sterility that comes with reporting statistics like these by telling their students' stories: Of the ninth graders, three had parents who had died, two of them from violence. Lucky students come from two-parent households. Others have parents who are incarcerated. Some live with grandparents, others in foster homes. Still others drift in and out of homelessness. Some are in non-English-speaking households. "We reflect America," says James Ragland.

Cristo Rey found a creative way to fund most of the tuition, $18,000 per student to start, and projected to drop several thousand dollars per year as enrollment climbed. In Columbus, $5,000 per student per year is potentially available from Ohio's school-choice voucher program; if a student's home school is designated as a "failing school," that money can follow the student to a school of choice. When I visited, 59 percent of Cristo Rey Columbus students were eligible for vouchers.

The second piece of the business model is the hallmark Cristo Rey Corporate Work Study Program. Each student works five days per month—on a regular business day, not a Saturday—at a paid position in one of Columbus's many dozens of partner companies or institutions. The student's earnings, about $6,500 per year, are applied directly toward their tuition. Unmet differences come from donations, fund-raising, grants, and families, even if the latter is just a token amount.

The work-study program sets high expectations. Employers know that Cristo Rey will make site visits and will require daily time sheets, evaluations, and action where the kids need more help, training, or mentoring. Sometimes companies go well beyond this, bringing a student into staff meetings or arranging a meal with the executives.

Some kids translate their school-year work into summer jobs. Others become more realistic about the opportunities in their futures. When I asked one boy what his dream job would be, he immediately said, "Professional football player." (I've heard this answer from countless high school boys around the country, by the way.) And, I asked, if that might not work out? "I'd like to own my own business," he said. "Or maybe be a civil engineer."

Many of Cristo Rey's Columbus employer-partners do much more for the school's community. Nationwide Children's Hospital provides the students with preventative medical services at the school every Friday. The PNC bank offers a financial literacy course for the students and their families. Other programs were in process: the library is partnering with the school to create ESL and literacy programs for the families; nearby Franklin University and the school are talking about continuing-education programs for the students' parents.

Ragland describes the importance of the school's pervasive "culture of positivity": "The majority of their day is with us. The message is delivered in context from the janitor on down"—that word shows how seriously he takes the concept—"to the president." The role and place of the teachers is paramount; they are handpicked for both their teaching and their strong match of character to the beliefs and culture of the school. Principal Cathy Thomas says of the instructors that "their behavior is witness for the kids." The school offers generous packages to its teachers, including small classes, good pay, professional development, and retraining.

In year two, Cristo Rey Columbus High School was a work in progress. The entire school staff, the students, the families, the town's businesses and institutions are all invested and collab to make it work. To me, an early sign of success came while I was chatting with three of the second-year students. One began to get fidgety and started sliding down in his seat. The student next to him began subtly nudging him and giving him the Look, which clearly meant: "Sit up straight! Look her in the eye!"

A public-private partnership obviously entails a public element as well. Columbus is a strong-mayor town, both structurally and in the personality of the man who held the office in recent years. Michael Coleman, a prominent local lawyer and city council member, became Columbus's first Democratic mayor in thirty years, and its first African-American mayor, when he took office in 2000. He was forty-four when first elected and was easily returned for a total of four four-year terms, getting nearly 70 percent of the vote in his last two races. By the time we met him, he had become the longest-serving mayor in Columbus's history and the longest-serving black mayor of any U.S. city ever. Though still popular—he had four thousand guests at his sixtieth birthday party in 2014—he decided not to seek a fifth term, and he stayed in town to go back into law practice (and marry the woman who had been his unofficial companion through his final two terms as mayor).

When we met him in the mayor's office in Columbus, in the stately white-limestone, neoclassical-style city hall built in the 1870s, Coleman was halfway through what would be his final term. A smooth-mannered man, with modish big-frame glasses and a thin mustache, he leaned forward with a smile as he described the close calls he had had in office and the clever approaches he had figured out.

Part of the story Coleman had to tell was about the transformation of the city during his years there. "Our downtown used to make you *yawn* after five or six at night," he said. "Nobody was there. And, of course, now it's been turned around—a dynamic place, thousands of people living down here, all these new parks and business. During the weekdays, it's probably an eighteen-hour downtown. From Thursday to Sunday, it's twenty-four hours! And as I'm sure you've heard, it was the result of a public-private collaboration." We had indeed heard that, and could see the results for ourselves.

But the particular story Coleman wanted to describe was what happened soon after he began his third term in office, when the local, national, and international economies were all thrown into reverse by the financial crisis of 2008.

"When I think about what our city has achieved, I point to one seminal moment," he said. "It was a moment that made more difference than anything else, maybe in a hundred years. And it was a *tax increase*. A tax increase during the toughest economic times since the Depression. That's when we made the choice to become the Columbus of the future, when the citizens, together, voted to increase their taxes and invest in the long run."

At the national level, pushing taxes up when the economy is going down is, of course, a recipe for Herbert Hoover–style self-intensifying depression. Many cities and states are obliged by their constitutions to balance the budget each year, and so they have no alternative. At just the moment when their citizens have less money of their own—fewer customers at restaurants and stores, shorter hours at the office or factory, worse prospects of selling a house, more pressure from banks to repay loans—either the city must ask for more from them in taxes, or it must cut back the services it offers for schools, police and fire protection, road maintenance and other upkeep, and all the other ingredients of a healthy civic life.

"Historically, the city of Columbus has had a strong economy," Coleman said. "We had multiple legs to our economy—the center of government, the financial institutions, the schools, diversified business. We were a center of jobs for the entire state. So if you cut off one leg of the stool, the others were there, and it would still stand up. But in the fall of 2008, *all* the legs of the stool were cut. Every last one! We could have had fifteen legs to the stool, but *whoosh,* they were all cut, all at once."

As he was obliged to under the city's charter, by November 15 Coleman had come up with a balanced-budget proposal for the city council, paring expenses to make up for the expected shortfall of revenues. But barely had he submitted it when the collapse intensified. "Within thirty days, we had to reduce our revenue estimates by another *hundred million dollars,* beyond the shrinkage we already foresaw," Coleman said. The overnight change represented nearly a quarter of the city's total planned revenues.

"My initial inclination was to try to weather it," he said—that is, to keep making cuts in pace with the falling revenue. "I'd been mayor a long time; I knew we'd weathered the recession after the 9/11 attacks, and we had come back." But as the weeks went on, and the collapse continued, and the revenues continued to fall, and the proposed cutbacks intensified, Coleman said that he resolved to try a different approach.

"I had a lot of sleepless nights, because I thought the city really was at a crossroads," he said. "One path would be, we could just continue to cut the hell out of our services and expenses. We could lay off a few hundred policemen and a few hundred firemen, which is what I was preparing to do—on top of big layoffs already. And cutbacks everywhere else. But if we did that, I thought it would change the city for a generation. Everything we'd worked for would be at risk. We could go that route, but—we'd have a city that is more like Detroit."

Coleman hastened to add, "No offense to Detroit!" but he was using its declining years as a shorthand for a downward spiral of worse services and a more dangerous environment, which, in turn, drove businesses and more affluent residents away, which, in turn, drove revenues and services down further still. "You've seen these midwestern cities that just die," he said.

"So I thought we had a choice. And the other choice was—a tax increase." In specific, he proposed raising the city's income tax rate from 2 percent to 2.5 percent, a change projected to offset the latest $100 million shortfall in revenues. By state law, such a change required a majority-vote approval by the city's electorate. So as bankruptcies and layoffs were increasing, family budgets were tightening, and the city's unemployment rate was nearing its highest level in a generation, Coleman joined with members of the business community to argue in public that paying *more* for city government was the right next step.

The business community joined with the campaign. Why? I asked Alex Fischer, of the Columbus Partnership. "I think it was a question of trust," he said. "The mayor had a track record. The city finances were well run. We could all see that solving the problem by cutting was going to lead to a very different city."

When the vote came, in August 2009, turnout was relatively low, but 52 percent of those voting approved the tax increase, enough to put it into effect. The lead of the next day's story in *The Columbus Dispatch* spelled out the choice the city had made: "Police and fire recruits might begin training in December [after freezes on recruitment and training]. Recreation centers are likely to reopen in January. Your grass clippings will be hauled away free next spring. And if you earn your paycheck in Columbus, you'll begin paying higher taxes starting October 1."

———

"When you start these things, you know you're going to have seventy-five percent of the people against you," Michael Coleman noted about the political nightmare of selling a tax increase. "And all the more at a time when people are losing their jobs, scrambling to buy a loaf of bread. But we knew the city had two paths—one that has an upward incline but leads to the point of success, versus the path that sends us down into the valley. We chose to climb the mountain, and we got it done. It was the beginning of the new city you see around you now."

But how could this *possibly* have happened? What made the politics of Ohio's biggest city so different from those of the nation as a whole? Coleman said that the key was the ability of cities, his and many others, to insulate themselves from the paralysis of national-level politics.

"I've often been asked if I want to run for governor or senator," he told us. Before he became mayor, Coleman was the Democratic nominee for lieutenant governor of Ohio in 1998, losing (with his running mate Lee Fisher) to a ticket headed by Bob Taft. "There was a time when I was asked if I was interested in the presidency!" he recalled. "But *this* is where the action is." *This* meant city government, and being mayor in a strong-mayor system within a functioning civic culture. "There are a lot of broken pieces in government. But at this level, you can be more effective, because you have to be. I'm a Democrat, but I've worked very successfully with Republicans in the business community, and now with our Republican governor," he noted, referring to John Kasich. "I'd like to have the Congress see what they can learn from us."

Some of the assets of Columbus that Alex Fischer and Mayor Coleman talk about—deep public-private collaborations, size, the accessibility of its people—are vital to one of the town's stellar institutions: the public library. Patrick Losinski, who leads the Metropolitan Library System, described Columbus as being large enough to have international companies and small enough that he can call up a CEO and say, "I'd like to talk to you about some things around the library."

The community of Columbus has stepped up repeatedly for the public library. In 2010, facing a loss to the library budget from state revenues, voters passed by more than a two-to-one margin an increased tax levy for $50 million per year for better library services. This followed the previous year's city tax increase of half a percent. In 2013, the Metropolitan Library Foundation raised $500,000 at a gala fund-raiser. The library's board of trustees brings affiliations to powerful institutions like hospitals, investment companies, insurance companies, and the Ohio State University. Others, like the Friends of the Library, contribute in many different ways. The library's legacy and its story go way back.

In Columbus, word got around in the early twentieth century that Andrew Carnegie was funding the building of libraries. Columbus city librarian John Pugh hopped a train to New York City and knocked on Carnegie's door. Pugh and Carnegie bonded over their Celtic heritage, (Pugh's was Welsh; Carnegie's was Scottish), and Carnegie eventually gave Pugh a handsome $200,000 to construct the beautiful granite-and-marble Romanesque building. That is about the cost for a thorough cleaning of the library today, Patrick Losinski told me.

With the recent renovation of its original design, the main library is iconic all over again. It overlooks Topiary Park, a seven-acre park and garden that feature trees shaped to resemble figures from Seurat's famous Postimpressionist painting *Sunday Afternoon on the Isle of La Grande Jatte.*

I strolled the Tree Walk through the park looking for buckeyes, which I remembered as the state tree from my seventh-grade Ohio history class. I found them, but, disappointingly, they were the least healthy-looking among the whole collection. Someone offered—rather spookily, I thought—that perhaps it was because the trees were growing on the spot of a suspicious fire that burned down the abandoned buildings of the Ohio School for the Deaf in the 1980s.

Losinski left no doubt that the most important message to take away from the Columbus library was that on the stone engraving above the grand entry: "Open to All." Those words are there to remind every single person who enters of this nearly sacred message of public libraries in America.

By 9:10 in the morning, some of Columbus's homeless were already inside the library. I saw homeless people spending their days at most public libraries I visited around the country. They would be sitting, sleeping, reading, or sometimes eating at the library cafés. In Columbus, there are understood expectations for appropriate behavior: no sleeping, no bathing, and in case of strong odor, counseling on where to get to a shower. There are warnings and penalties for inappropriate behavior, which include a day's or a week's sabbatical from the library.

On the other end of the economic spectrum of customers— "customers" is the term of art favored by the Columbus library instead of the more common term "patrons"—as I traveled across the country, I became accustomed to spotting the young entrepreneurs who set up virtual offices at long reading room desks. They would take phone meetings outside in the gardens, often with lattes from the library coffee shop in hand. "Do you resent this?" I asked librarians around the country. "Not at all," the librarians invariably answered, adding that one day when their companies were flush, these titans might remember where it all started.

After visits to dozens of public libraries from Maine to Arizona, from Mississippi to Minnesota, I saw that America's public libraries, the place people used to go primarily to find books or do research, have become the heart and soul of American communities. I learned that in the library, I could discover the spirit of a town, get a feel for the people's needs and wants, and gauge their energy and mettle.

By my calculation, I would say there are three areas where libraries today reflect and serve the people: technology, education, and community. Here are the stories about the first two.

## Technology

Enter a library and the first thing you're likely to see are banks of computers. The computers are so popular that in many libraries, there are waiting lists and restrictions on time use. The Pew Research Center reports that today, about a quarter of American adults lack broadband Internet connection at home. Many library computer users are among them. (Disclosure: I worked at Pew for several years in the early 2000s.)

From Appalachia to the Bronx, I heard library directors' stories about discovering laptop users huddling near the library after hours to catch the strongest Internet signal.

"Behind the dumpster!" exclaimed Alan Engelbert, the library director from Charleston, West Virginia, when he learned that was where one man sought the best Wi-Fi signal in the wee hours of the morning. "Holy moly!" said Anthony Marx, the director of the entire New York Public Library system, relating, to an elite gathering in Aspen, what he'd blurted out when he'd seen a New York teenager sitting on the steps outside the library after hours capturing Wi-Fi to do his homework. Librarians all over the country know that this happens, and many leave their Wi-Fi on all night for just that reason.

Jim and I applied the same trick when we first visited Ajo, Arizona. We squatted at night in front of the library storefront in the town's historic plaza, the only reliable place in town to check e-mail or read the online news.

Some libraries lend out Wi-Fi hot-spot devices so people can carry connectivity home with them. In Erie, Pennsylvania, Erin Wincek, who has since become the library's director, told me that the library's ten newly purchased Wi-Fi hot-spot devices were spoken for immediately, creating an instant waiting list. The librarians ordered fifteen more.

In Columbus, I heard this true story about one of the most popular uses of libraries' computers: the job search.

A young man came into the library looking for help locating a job opening and filling out an application. He and the librarian spotted a good possibility, and the librarian helped him load the application onto the screen. They agreed that he would fill it out and then she'd come around again to look it over. A little while later, the librarian returned to discover that the man had completed the application, not by keying in the responses, but with a marking pen on the screen.

That is low-end technology use at the library. At the high end are the makerspaces. A makerspace is a communal twenty-first-century workshop where hobbyists, artists, entrepreneurs, artisans, designers, and dreamers share hardware and software like 3-D printers, laser cutters, wire benders, and hammers, to create and build. Around the country, we've been to makerspaces that are franchised like gyms, where you can take out a membership. We've seen others in forward-looking companies, where employees are encouraged to spend time with the most sophisticated tools, bringing ideas to reality. And there are makerspaces in libraries; they are free and open to all.

In my hometown library, the flagship Martin Luther King Jr. Memorial Library in downtown D.C., I joined a standing-room-only crowd to tour the makerspace, named the Fab Lab, with some thirty other people, from budding entrepreneurs to a mom with her homeschooled preteens.

Everything about the makerspace felt collaborative, accessible, and cool, including Adam Schaeffer, the young library associate in shirtsleeves and a wool cap, who introduced us to the eight 3-D printers, one of which was named Kevin Spacey. We saw the laser scanner and the laser cutter, which can etch metals; cut cardboard, wood, and paper; and even etch pumpkins, one of which Adam passed around. There was a wire bender, named Fender Bender Rodriguez. There was a milling machine that can make prototypes out of wood or plastics or even soft aluminum.

More humbly, there was a tool station resembling a basement workshop along one wall, with lots of superglue, duct tape, inspirational how-to books and magazines, and a collection of old-fashioned tools. If you're lucky, you can join Adam's Coffee Club, a coffee station using beans sourced from spots all around D.C.

Everything is free, except the coffee.

I returned to the makerspace a few times and watched one of D.C. library's makers-in-residence, Billy Friebele, working on some designs while he patiently waited for the 3-D printer to slowly exude the purple plastic that was transforming a photo of a vase he had photographed into an actual vase. It was one of the first experimental steps that Billy and his maker-in-residence partner, Mike Iacovone, who were sponsored by the Friends of the Tenley-Friendship D.C. branch library, were working on for the city of D.C., drawing residents into different, more intimate looks at some of the details of their street life. I had taken part in one of their exercises, a walk with about a dozen others around our neighbor-hood library, producing a digital group map-collage.

Lest you're still a skeptic about the propriety or relevance of maker-spaces being in libraries, note that nearly three hundred years ago, in the 1740s, Ben Franklin conducted some of his early electricity experiments in what we could today call a first makerspace of the Library Company of Philadelphia, which he'd founded. Miguel Figueroa, who directs the Center for the Future of Libraries at the American Library Association, told me that he sees makerspaces as a piece of libraries' expanded mission to be places where people can not only consume knowledge, but create new knowledge.

## Education

In Charleston, West Virginia, we watched another story, like Mayor Coleman's in Columbus, play out among citizens faced with voting on tax increases in hard times.

Charleston is a hard-hit town still recovering from the recession. In the fall of 2014, the town was facing a make-or-break levy for the library. The day before the vote, library director Alan Engelbert described some of the severity; staff numbers were already down from 160 to 42. "If somebody catches a cold," he said, "we have big problems." He said he couldn't even contemplate what would happen if the levy didn't pass.

The levy did pass, with a whopping two-thirds majority. On the morning of the vote, I was in the library when a burly man in overalls and a plaid shirt, with an ample beard, walked in and straight up to the front desk. "Just stopping by," he said, "to let you know I voted for the levy today!"

I asked Engelbert what would be his biggest dream for the library, beyond the essentials. He answered without missing a beat: the zero- to three-year-olds. "That," he said, "is the really big one."

Nearly every library director I met echoed Engelbert on their most important mission. One by one they said, with a sense of urgency: the children.

In keeping with this theme, Patrick Losinski showed me the brand-new branch library of the Columbus system in Driving Park, an economically strained urban part of the city named for an early horse-racing park turned into an automobile-racing park.

The library's glass front is stunning, it both catches your eye and draws you into the building. From the sidewalk or even from across the street, you can see the people inside sitting, or working at computers, or moving about. This design concept is a stark contrast to the magnificent Carnegie libraries, which impose rather than invite, and where I always need to square my shoulders before entering.

Front and center at Driving Park—you couldn't possibly miss it—is the children's section. The bright, airy Ready for Kindergarten zone is set with kid-sized moveable furniture, a comfortable carpet, and oversized letters and numbers to push around on a big magnetic wall. Children's sections today are about books and more: imaginary play, cognitive development, exploration, quiet corners, computers, and so on. (An important reality check if you visit the children's sections: Do the computers work? Is someone ready to help people navigate and to fix them when they break?)

All the children's sections have readiness for school in mind. When I asked Losinski to describe that in more detail for me, he left no room for imagination: "When a five-year-old walks into kindergarten, takes a book, and holds it upside down, you know there is no reading readiness there."

The sentiment about children and libraries was countrywide. In Kansas City, I heard: "Don't miss our new children's area. It's just been redone." In Eastport, Maine: "We just built a new children's wing." In Bend, Oregon: "Here's the children's area, right off the main entry." In Demopolis, Alabama: "You have to take the elevator, right over there, to the children's room. It's on the third floor. Don't miss it."

In financially stressed San Bernardino, the children's room is hands down the most attractive room in the library, with murals and an aquarium. The room is considered not only a draw for the children, but a gateway to the library for their parents. In Birmingham, Alabama, the librarian in the children's area was the first to spot me and offer help when he saw me wandering around.

Libraries use all kinds of (good) tricks to attract clientele. In Columbus, librarians at Driving Park look for moms with kids at the laundromats and quick-stop shops. In Winters, California, a small agricultural town in northern California where farmers grow grapes and tend orchards of stone fruits, nuts, and olives, a point person for the very active Friends of the Library looks for the babies to enroll in the Books for Babies program. She tracks the hospital birth announcements and goes stroller-spotting on the sidewalks of their small town. Each baby she finds gets a box with a T-shirt, a bib, a knit cap, information on the library, an application to join, and, best of all, books in a choice of Spanish or English.

The libraries' support for education grows with the children. Lots of libraries offer after-school homework help. Driving Park's comes with a snack. Many offer one-on-one reading tutorials for students. In Winters, the school librarians open the next-door public library early so the students can use the space. In Charleston, West Virginia, the close relationship between libraries and schools can be critical. Librarians, even with their skeletal staff after budget cuts, will stretch to assemble boxes of supplementary materials for teachers—books, DVDs, maps, and other extras—and deliver them to the rural schools.

In Birmingham, I sat in on the regular Wednesday after-school tech lab program for middle and high schoolers in the library. On this day, they were working on graphic design with their volunteer teachers, who were students from the University of Alabama at Birmingham. The endgame of this series of classes—after circuit-board soldering, computer-aided-design instruction, Arduino programming, 3-D printing, and more—was robots, always a favorite.

Summers are not vacation time in libraries. I've seen everything from special science programs to free and subsidized meals, in places from Dodge City to Columbus. And for older students, libraries offer GED classes and online college classes. In Redlands, California, the most popular volunteer program at the library is the adult literacy program—with trained community members conducting one-to-one teaching.

* * *

I came across a surprising treasure as I was thumbing through a book I picked up at the Columbus library bookshop. It was chockablock full of photographs about the history of aviation in Columbus, starting with the arrival in Columbus of the first airfreight flight ever in 1911, when one of the Wright brothers' planes carried a load of silk from Dayton; the fabric was bound for the Morehouse-Martens department store in Columbus. Columbus was also a waypoint for a record-breaking forty-eight-hour transit from the East Coast to the West in 1929: the Pennsylvania Railroad carried passengers from Penn Station to Columbus overnight; they flew on by day from Columbus to Oklahoma, then continued overnight on the Atchison, Topeka & Santa Fe to Clovis, New Mexico, and by day into Los Angeles. One of the inaugural passengers was Amelia Earhart. Then there were the airplane-versus-automobile races held at none other than Driving Park, home of the new library I had just toured, back when planes were so slow that cars were considered competition. And there was hometown boy Eddie Rickenbacker, the Tuskegee Airmen's base (for a while), and the opening of Executive Jet Aviation, which operated time-shares in 1964. Finally, I saw a throwaway line about all the aviators regrettably left out of the book because of space limitations, including Jerrie Mock. "Jerrie Mock?" I wondered, rushing to look her up.

Jerrie Mock, a housewife from Columbus, Ohio, became the first woman to fly solo around the world. The year was 1964. She piloted her single-engine four-seater Cessna 180 for twenty-nine days in the spring in a circumnavigation from Columbus to Columbus.

"How did I miss that one?" I thought to myself, especially since at the time, I'd been growing up in northern Ohio. I've since asked around a lot, and while everyone knows the story of Amelia Earhart, precious few have ever heard of Jerrie Mock.

Well, just look at the times and look at the women. Earhart was flying in 1937, the golden age of flight. Charles Lindbergh had crossed the Atlantic ten years earlier. There were air races, barnstorming, and round-the-world flights. Commercial airlines were new and exciting, offering luxurious long-distance flights. There were dirigibles and seaplanes. Amelia was a natural fit, dashing, adventurous, and modern. She flew a great silver plane, a Lockheed Electra 10E, and she was married to savvy book publisher and publicist extraordinaire George Putnam. Since then, of course, the tragedy and mystery of her ending have kept her story alive.

The times were less sympathetic toward Jerrie Mock. By the 1960s, when Mock was flying, the space age was arriving and the universe beyond the earth was taking over our imagination. Science was about rockets and computers. Astronauts like Alan Shepard and John Glenn were heroes and kings.

Betty Friedan's *Feminine Mystique* had been published in 1963, but despite Mock's audacious, first-woman-ever mission, she didn't look the part of one catching the wave of feminism. She was photographed by *The Columbus Dispatch* posing next to her plane, wearing kitten heels and with a corsage pinned to her dusky-blue Sunday-best coat. She referred to herself as a flying housewife and a lady pilot. She never developed an appetite for the limelight, and she shunned speaking engagements and public appearances.

Mock was a very new pilot for the daunting challenge of her undertaking. She earned her pilot's license at age thirty-three, only five years before her round-the-world flight, and her instrument rating just shortly before her departure. I worried all the way through Mock's journal of her flights, *Three-Eight Charlie* (a reference to the call numbers for her plane), even though I knew all would end well.

Drama began immediately. On March 19, 1964, Jerrie departed for Bermuda, her first over-water flight ever. Offshore from Virginia, she pressed on without establishing radio contact because she didn't want to disappoint her sponsors back in Columbus. Mock landed in Bermuda in fierce winds, which increased soon to 75 knots, hurricane strength, and was stranded there for a week.

From Bermuda to Africa, she twice found herself in the clouds over the Atlantic with ice forming on the wings. Stopping at tiny Santa Maria Island, in the Azores, she made one of her first instrument landings, necessary because a cloud cover settled only 100 feet above the water's-edge runway. By way of comparison, we always plan for a comfortable 1,000-foot ceiling, although we have landed in less.

Over Africa, the tumult continued. Sandstorms over the desert, failing brakes, unexpected weather changes, navigation equipment challenges. It seemed to me that Mock faced all of these with a cool practicality and survived them all with some derring-do and a whole lot of good luck.

Mock wasn't alone in her pursuit. She and another, more experienced pilot, Joan Merriam Smith, were in effect in a race with each other, flying toward their goals and a place in the record books. Smith had taken off from Oakland a few days before Mock, planning to trace Amelia Earhart's route. It's clear that the pressure of the competition led Mock to take some shortcuts. She landed in Casablanca with a faulty tail wheel that caused the entire tail section of her plane to vibrate roughly. She admitted that before departing from Columbus, she had known that the wheel was a problem, but she hadn't insisted on repairing it. She said in an interview with John Sivyer, which I watched online, on an anniversary of her flight:

"Rush, rush, rush. On an eleven-year-old airplane, certain things needed to get done. And there wasn't time to get them all done, chasin' this other female."

I was disconcerted to read Mock's accounts of how her husband, Russ, seemed to egg her on. This was how Mock portrayed Russ's comments about her delay in Bermuda:

"Look, weather can't be that bad for that long! Woman, you have to fly. That's why you got an instrument rating, so you could fly through fronts. Joan's leaky gas tanks are supposed to be fixed now, and the wire services say she's ready to go on. She'll get way ahead. Remember your sponsors, and take a few chances."

The racing also cost Mock some of the adventure she had sought. You can hear her poignancy in writing that she could take only five minutes to see the Pyramid of Cheops. And that she couldn't even stop to see the Taj Mahal. Other absurdities amused her. An immigration official in Cairo insisted that she produce an airplane ticket. Explaining that she didn't have a ticket since she was flying her own plane cost her precious time.

Jerrie did complete her adventure and finished first. Joan Merriam Smith had met with more weather delays and mechanical issues, which slowed her down. (And a sad footnote: about a year after she completed her own circumnavigation, Smith died in the crash of a small plane she was piloting in the San Gabriel Mountains.)

Jerrie Mock died in 2014, at age eighty-eight. She had lived long enough to enjoy the fiftieth anniversary celebrations of her aviation milestone at the Uvdar-Hazy Center of the National Air and Space Museum. She had been honored in the Rose Garden by Lyndon Johnson. And there is a statue of her at the John Glenn Columbus International Airport in Ohio. But I still think of Jerrie Mock as one who slipped away from us before we really knew her.

# *Louisville, Kentucky*

In Columbus, Alex Fischer mentioned a theme that recurred during our travels, especially in historic manufacturing strongholds of the Midwest. That was the potential of smaller-scale, higher-value, closer-to-the-customer "advanced manufacturing" as a source of business and employment possibility.

A trip we made to Louisville, Kentucky, early in 2016 provided a context for what this movement might mean. We jump ahead in the narrative to describe it.

\* \* \*

Through the years we lived in China, I felt as if I spent half my waking hours inside factories. And this was by choice. The factories that dotted the Chinese landscape and made modern China the workshop and the workhouse of the world were the settings for most of the country's historically dramatic trends. They were sources of catastrophic pollution; they were the vehicle for unprecedented economic ascent; they were the means of China's rise in relative wealth and influence around the world; they were the cause of both connection to and friction with the United States and other nations around the world. And they were unfailingly interesting, in ways good and bad. The small, old, dirty ones in the hinterlands, where workers might wear flip-flops while walking around ladles dripping molten iron, were a trip back to the harshest dawn of the industrial age. The vast, new, antiseptic ones, where workers with hairnets and face masks produced Apple computers on one line and Toshibas on the next, at a rate of thousands per day, were a trip into the future, and a clue to the economic imbalances of the present.

During our travels in America, I looked for factories, too. In older cities, their ruins are, if anything, too familiar as symbols of what once was but has now gone away. The crumbling structures that line Amtrak's Northeast Corridor routes and the lakefront in Duluth, the abandoned Bethlehem steelworks that are a spookily beautiful old-economy backdrop for concerts and art shows for new-economy visitors—these represent one very well-known, depressing face of American manufacturing. Plants like the steelworks and engine factories we saw in Mississippi or the tire and auto production sites in South Carolina are another—largely in the South rather than the urban North, mostly non-unionized, and heavily automated, so that as you walk through you see several industrial robots for each human industrial employee.

The question on my mind was: What would it take to foster a new wave of manufacturing? And this, too, we began to hear about, with something I had previously not paid much attention to: the "maker movement" and its role in fostering close-to-the-customer, fast-turnaround manufacturing within the United States. We saw it in action in Louisville.

I'm used to hearing excitement from people at American infotech companies—or from biotech innovators, or from people in other enterprises who believe the future is on their side. I'm used to hearing it in China. I've gravitated to tech topics and to fast-growing parts of the world because I like hearing from people with big plans and dreams. And as we traveled, we began hearing upbeat accounts from business officials and entrepreneurs engaged in American manufacturing.

The heart of their argument is this: Through most of post–World War II history, the forces of globalization have made it harder and harder to keep manufacturing jobs in the United States. But the latest wave of technological innovation, communications systems, and production tools may now make it easier—especially in terms of bringing new products to market faster than the competition by designing, refining, and making them in the United States. At just the same time, social and economic changes in China are making the outsourcing business ever costlier and trickier for all but the most experienced firms.

For Americans, the most important factor is the emergence of new tools that address an old problem. The old problem is the cost, delay, and inefficiency of converting an idea into a product. As with any new idea, before you can earn the first dollar from the first customer, you have to decide whether the product can be built, at what cost, and how fast, so that you can beat anyone else with the same idea. The need to reduce costs has driven much of this work outside the United States. The possibility of saving time may bring some of it back. By making manufacturing generally more attractive and feasible, new tools will—so I heard many times—lead to more good jobs in America than we would have thought possible only a few years ago.

"This would not have been possible ten years ago," Natarajan Venkatakrishnan, then the CEO of a unique and famous makerspace called First-Build, told me in 2016 in Louisville. FirstBuild is unique because it was created by GE, as a subsidiary of its appliance division and as a deliberate effort to bring the nimble maker spirit to its design process.

"What has changed is that the maker movement has figured out a group of technologies and tools which enable us to manufacture in low volume," he said. Venkatakrishnan, who goes by "Venkat," went on to explain the modern-day difference: Big manufacturers like GE built their business on high-volume, factory-scale, very high-stakes production, where each new product means a bet of tens of millions of dollars. FirstBuild is meant to explore smaller, faster, more customizable options.

"Now you can get a circuit board mill for $8,000," Venkat said. "If you are looking for a circuit board for an appliance, earlier the only chance of getting it was from China. Today I can make boards here and ship them out quickly. Similarly with laser cutters—not big ones but small ones, where I can cut metal right here. It's a huge advantage, and these things did not exist ten years ago. In those days, you couldn't hack the kind of creative solutions we are seeing now."

FirstBuild is an ongoing story of innovation and stimulation. It's unusual because it represents the collaborative efforts of a very old, very large, very successful worldwide corporation and a community of very new, very small, very local entrepreneurs.

The FirstBuild "microfactory" was established in Louisville, Kentucky, in 2014, as an offshoot of GE's appliances division, whose large "Appliance Park" manufacturing center is on the southeastern edge of Louisville. In 2016, FirstBuild was sold (along with the rest of GE Appliances) to the Chinese manufacturing giant Haier, but its management and operating practices remained in place. (Late in 2017, Venkat became vice president for global equipment at Starbucks.) To give an idea of its micro-ness: GE Appliances as a whole has something like twelve thousand employees, and Haier's worldwide head count is nearly eighty thousand. The full-time staff of FirstBuild when we visited was about twenty.

* * *

From GE's point of view, the micro idea started with an effort to reduce the "mind-to-market" cycle time, as Venkat told me. Refrigerators, freezers, dishwashers, clothes washers and dryers, air conditioners, and related heavy-duty, long-life-span products typically take about four years "mind to market"—from the first design concept or wish list to the first on-sale item in the store. But no matter the cycle's duration, weeks or decades, faster would always be better.

Faster means an edge on the competition. It means less tied-up capital. It means a better ability to offer new features or efficiencies. It means quicker response to shifting tastes and market trends.

The GE team began looking at start-ups. "We became interested in low-volume manufacturing," Venkat said. "What can we make that could be successful in units of ten?"

The low-volume idea was to make manufacturing faster and more varied by dramatically lowering the output level at which a product would pay off. You can think of the analogy in TV programming. When there were only three networks, the only shows that could make it were those that could draw a mass audience. But with cable, and then with online videos and podcasting, much smaller and more specialized audiences were "large enough," and we went from mass-culture *Gidget* and *Get Smart* to the much more varied, niche-sensitive, and more interesting modern range that encompasses everything from *Mad Men* and *Game of Thrones* to reality schlock. Another obvious comparison would be the shift from the standardized, fairly bland mega-brewery U.S. beer world of the mid-twentieth century to the rapidly diversifying craft-brew renaissance of today.

What does this mean, in practice, for other kinds of manufacturing besides beer? Essentially the approach is a combination of the well-known, intangible digital tools of the modern era with some very tangible, less-known-by-the-public maker-era tools that are transforming production.

That is: the products coming out of this microfactory use cloud-centric digital techniques we're all aware of, including crowdsourcing, online collaboration, crowdfunding, online sales, and open-source coding and design. But they also use the new production techniques, from the real world of real hardware, that have become available only in the past few years—and that keep improving thanks to Moore's law. These 3-D printers, laser cutters, and low-cost but high-sophistication multi-axis machine tools, as well as a range of other devices, allow people in smaller, less formal, much lower-cost workspaces to design, test, refine, and manufacture items that previously would have required factory production lines—and to find audiences that collaborate in the process of design and, so far, have provided eager markets.

The social and collaborative tools of the era—shared workspaces, partnerships with local schools—are also essential ingredients. The production tools are available for a modest cost to local people who want to use them. "It's like a manufacturing library," Venkat said, meaning that FirstBuild offers production equipment for shared use. "The 'books' are available. We're not going to read them to you, but you can find them here." I saw a number of University of Louisville students, including members of a rocket club, working on projects. Venkat pointed out that one advantage of being based in the Midwest is that "there's a long tradition of people being very hands-on here, of knowing how to make things." This is similar to what we had already heard in Holland and would hear again across the industrial Midwest. An explicit goal of First-Build, like many of the maker sites we've seen around the country, is to become a center for local individuals and groups with ideas for innovative hardware that might sell.

"We are trying to overcome the selection bias of needing to scale up for big-volume production," Venkat told me. "We don't have to design to a spec. We are making in small batches, low volumes. We can make one, then the next one, then the next one. We want to be open to as many ideas as we can."

If a new item sells in the tens or hundreds, that's fine in itself. If it seems destined for a volume of more than a thousand units, "we can scale it up to the mother ship, to Appliance Park," Venkat said. Meanwhile, the items come out in units of tens or hundreds. "We are like the pirates, and Appliance Park is the navy," Venkat said. "We're the agile, exploring part of the empire. If we find something valuable, we call in the navy. Meanwhile, we explore."

What do they make? "If it's smaller than a shoe box, you buy it from China," Venkat said, using an oversimplified but handy rule of thumb. "Bigger than a shoe box, you make it here." Most of the items I saw were culinary-themed: a new kind of "nugget" ice maker, a portable smoker, a sous vide cooker, new refrigerators, a compact pizza oven that gets hot enough to produce very good pizza, and, most startling to me, a high-speed home cold-brew coffeemaker, which can produce (very good) cold-brew coffee within ten minutes, rather than overnight, as in the traditional process. There's also an easy-load oven and a "smart refrigerator."

Many of the appliances have found market success. The induction cooktop hit its target on Indiegogo, a crowdfunding website, within twelve hours; the ice maker received $2.6 million in preorders, to become the ninth-most-funded project in Indiegogo history; and the pizza oven will become part of the GE Appliances "Monogram" series of premium products later this year.

So when people say, "Americans don't make things anymore," you should know. Actually, they do. And the idea of maker cities has legs beyond Louisville.

# Allentown, Pennsylvania

Allentown is the third-largest city in Pennsylvania, after Philadelphia and Pittsburgh. But to the extent that the city is known outside the state, it can thank an unfortunate bit of Rust Belt symbolism.

The symbol is Billy Joel's 1982 song "Allentown," which was a hit in the early music-video era and is more distinctly remembered than many others from that time. It used the name "Allentown" as a placeholder for that early wave of heavy-industrial shutdown and all the displacement that came from it:

> Well we're living here in Allentown . . .
> And they're closing all the factories down

This was unfortunate in the obvious ways—no one likes to be a nickname for failure—and with some additional twists. One is that the steel mills being closed in that era weren't even in Allentown. They were fifteen miles away, in Bethlehem; but for the purposes of the song, the word "Allentown" sounded and scanned better, and also worked better in rhyme schemes, so Allentown it was. "That was the hell of it," said Julio Guridy, who was born in the Dominican Republic but came to Allentown as a child in the 1970s. By the time we met him, he had become president of the city council, and as he walked us around town, he explained, "We have that song because nothing rhymes with 'Bethlehem.'"

For the Allentown of the current era, a generation-plus after Billy Joel's lament, shut-down factories aren't really the main problem, either economically or culturally. The labyrinthine former U.S. Steel workshops and furnaces in Bethlehem that were the real subject of Billy Joel's lament have been closed for so long that they're well into a second life. Now they are a popular concert venue known as SteelStacks, with the idled blast furnaces and rolling mills serving as an artsy-spooky, industrial-Stonehenge backdrop for rock, folk, and country music acts, with "historic" tours into the steel mill's ruins, plus an art gallery and a Sands casino nearby. Allentown has suffered its share of industrial layoffs, notably with what had once been the world manufacturing center for Mack Trucks. Now the truck factory is a center of advanced-tech and light-manufacturing start-ups—including a great brewery and a "meadery"—working on what had been the Mack shop floors.

The overall economy of the Lehigh Valley has expanded, diversified, and continued to grow. The presence of universities is one factor, the best known of them being Lehigh, in Bethlehem. Another is the importance of a range of specialty industries. Much of the Sam Adams beer that is sold and drunk anywhere in the country comes from a contract brewery in Breinigsville, just west of Allentown. The Rodale publishing and organic-products empire is based in Emmaus, just to the south. The most important economic advantage for the area has been that real estate stalwart: *location*. Allentown is far enough away from New York and Philadelphia to have much lower living costs than those cities do, and an identity as something other than just a bedroom commuter community. But it's near enough that some people actually do commute. And the big north-south and east-west interstates that cross paths outside town have made greater Allentown an attractive logistical site. Amazon, having calculated that one-third of the U.S. population was within a day's truck travel of Allentown, located its biggest East Coast warehouse nearby. Other grocery, furniture, and shipping companies are there as well.

Through the 1990s and early 2000s, the city's population both grew and changed, largely through a significant move of Latino families from New York and New Jersey. The new arrivals were mainly of Puerto Rican or Dominican background—"Nuyoricans," as Julio Guridy described them—and their flow accelerated after the 9/11 attacks. "It seemed safer here," Guridy said. "We had more land, more space, lower costs, and it was still easy to get to New York or Philly." By 2000, one-quarter of Allentown's population was Latino. A dozen years later it was more than 40 percent.

\* \* \*

The problem for Allentown was not so much the economy in general; it was the downtown specifically. Pennsylvania is more carved up into balkanized separate jurisdictions than any other state. With less than one-third as many people as California, it has five times as many local governing units: cities, townships, boroughs; water districts; school districts; counties—you name it. This theoretically keeps public officials closer to members of the public. It also makes it harder to set policies beyond a minutely local scale.

In the case of Allentown, the patchwork of jurisdictions meant that by moving development just outside the city borders—barely two miles from downtown, across a freeway in unincorporated county land— builders could escape city regulations, and merchants could have much lower taxes. So, starting in the 1970s, Allentown went through the destructive sprawl cycle familiar in so many American towns. New big-box malls and shopping centers sprang up in the suburbs; the customers followed them there; the downtown retailers struggled; the city's revenues shrank; and services from police forces to street maintenance followed; and, as a consequence, everything about downtown life got worse. The result was a bombed-out-looking, high-crime shell of what had been until the 1980s an architecturally attractive and commercially successful downtown area.

Every city has a symbol of either decline or recovery. In Allentown, nearly everyone we spoke with mentioned the closing, in the 1990s, of the celebrated Hess Brothers department store as the marker for the city's descent. In its post–World War II golden age, Hess was the anchor of the entire downtown. It had both high-end fashions and everyday family wear, a restaurant and a tea room, seasonal festivals, customers waiting when it opened its doors. We saw a picture in the Allentown *Morning Call* archives of throngs around Hess's on a New Year's Eve in that era, as if it were Times Square. "In 1970, Hess was the highest-grossing department store in the entire country!" exclaimed Ed Pawlowski, a balding man then in his late forties who had grown up in Chicago but had just won his third four-year term as Allentown's mayor. As we walked past the former Hess site, he noted, "It did $190 million in retail sales, right here in Allentown. It was the retail hub for the entire region, and people came from all over to shop there."

His mood grew more somber: "Then the malls got built, and slowly but surely they sucked everything out like a giant vacuum. We went from being a retail mecca to having dollar stores and tattoo parlors. We needed to do something to bring people back to the urban core."

\* \* \*

The "something" that the city did was similar to the "public-private partnerships" we had seen from South Dakota to South Carolina. The key was a new tax scheme called the Neighborhood Improvement Zone, or NIZ, which was approved by the Pennsylvania state legislature in 2009. This happened after years of effort by the Sixteenth District's state senator, Pat Browne, a Republican who was born and raised in Allentown and had come up with the NIZ idea as a way to restore Allentown's downtown to the splendor he remembered from his boomer-era boyhood. One of Browne's boyhood friends was J. B. Reilly, who had grown up on the same street. Reilly had become a major builder and developer; his company was behind many of the suburban projects that had sucked vitality away from the downtown. Soon after he reached the state senate in 2005, Browne began asking Reilly what it would take to attract developers like him back to the city. The NIZ plan grew out of those discussions, Browne told us when we met him in his district office in Allentown.

Under the NIZ, the city designated a multiblock downtown area that was once thriving, had become derelict, and could be the foundation for a healthy new city core. For any developers who put up their own money to erect new buildings within the NIZ area—hotels, offices, restaurants, theaters or arenas, apartments or condos—the plan provided that all state and city taxes generated in those buildings over the next thirty years could go to retire bonds to cover the costs of the construction. City and state sales taxes for items sold in new stores, ticket taxes on concert sales, even state income taxes for construction crews building new office centers and workers inside them once they were finished—all would go into a special fund, to pay down the costs of the original investment. The idea was to make developers more willing to consider projects downtown, since capital costs would be lower than elsewhere, and, in turn, to make future tenants more likely to lease space or open businesses in the new buildings, since the lower construction costs would allow developers to charge less in rent.

Is this, in effect, a public subsidy for private investment? Obviously, yes—very much like the "Megasite" deal that Mississippi made to attract big factories to the Golden Triangle or South Carolina's tax-concession and road-building deals when Michelin and then BMW were deciding where to locate their plants. The argument against all such policies is that they amount to "picking winners"—and, in Pennsylvania's case, effectively transferring potential tax funds from the rest of the state straight to Allentown. The contrary argument is that without the incentives and investment, there would be no new tax revenues to divvy up, since the investments would not have occurred. The downtown would continue to deteriorate, and the new business would go elsewhere: Mississippi would still be trying to hold on to jobs at the toilet-seat factory, South Carolina would be struggling to replace its lost textile-mill jobs, and the crime rate in downtown Allentown would continue to mount.

This is one of the long-standing arguments in U.S. economic history. I am on the side of those who point out that public investments and incentives for big, new promising areas of technology—like agriculture and transportation in the 1800s, aerospace and biotech and infotech in the twentieth, genomics and energy technology now—have been crucial elements in national economic growth and have greatly repaid their costs. Other people might argue that this has been wasteful corporate subsidy. But whatever the views on those larger discussions, the reality is that they were not the object of partisan debate in Allentown or elsewhere in the state. (The main blowback the plan created outside Allentown was an effort by other cities, including Reading, Erie, and Scranton, to get similar provisions for their downtowns.) "Partisanship has to be set aside if we're going to solve the problems of challenged cities," Browne said—a sufficiently bland-seeming sentiment, but one that the locals had put into action.

"I'm thinking of ten thousand people coming right here, downtown!" Browne added, looking forward to the debut of the city's new entertainment and sports complex. "What that will mean to everyone here . . ." Not far from Browne's office, at the heart-of-downtown corner of Seventh and Hamilton, a classic Main Street–style large public clock had been repaired and repainted, put back in working order (through a $20,000 private donation), and set to the proper time. "When people in the town looked and saw that the clock was running again, we felt like it represented that the town itself was getting a new start," Mayor Pawlowski said.

From Browne, the Republican creator of the NIZ plan, and the developer J. B. Reilly, also a Republican, to Mayor Pawlowski, a Democrat, and most others involved, people in the region seemed strongly inclined to give the plan the benefit of the doubt. By the time of our first visit in 2014, five years after the legislature approved the NIZ, more than $1 billion in projects had been committed to the downtown, which had seen essentially no investment in the previous twenty years. Tax revenue from new activities in the NIZ already totaled some $50 million. J. B. Reilly said that by the end of the year, three thousand more people would be working downtown than had the year before. "And for a city like Allentown," he noted, "that's just extraordinary."

The editors and reporters of *The Morning Call* had kept a close and skeptical eye on the project's finances, pointing out the lifelong friendship between Browne (the initiator of the NIZ plan) and Reilly (whose company made most of the investments and stood to receive most of the tax benefits), and probing repeatedly into whether Mayor Pawlowski had any personal stake in any of the developments. (Starting in 2013, the

FBI investigated some of Pawlowski's campaign and city hall associates on classic pay-for-play charges: taking payoffs in exchange for construction contracts. By 2017, at least half a dozen officials had pled guilty, and that summer Pawlowski himself was indicted, in a fifty-four-charge count that mainly involved allegations of influence peddling. But he ran for reelection to a fourth term as mayor, and that November he won. Two months later, his trial began.)

Since the time of our first visit, *The Morning Call* went through the strains and shrinkage common to many smaller publications, and one by one the reporters and editors who had followed the downtown and city-politics stories most closely—Sam Kennedy, Scott Kraus, Matt Assad—left for jobs outside journalism. The financial pressures on local and regional journalism are obviously another challenge for cities trying to revive a sense of public engagement and awareness, and a serious one. But in the editorials and reports *The Morning Call*'s staffers wrote while the downtown project was making its debut, and in updates they gave me as the years have gone by, they said that things were going about as well as anyone could have planned, and better than many people might have assumed.

\* \* \*

On one of our visits in the fall of 2014, Mayor Pawlowski took us on a walking tour around the under-construction and just-opened sites in the NIZ zone. The centerpiece of the whole project was the $200 million PPL Center, at the corner of Seventh and Hamilton Streets in the heart of the historic downtown. "We made sure that all the major component parts were made in Pennsylvania," Pawlowski told us. "Seven million tons of steel in there, all from Erie. Seven hundred and twenty football fields' worth of concrete, all local."

On a below-ground level of the center was a multipurpose arena; it would hold up to eighty-five hundred spectators for concerts and sporting events (including the home games of the Lehigh Valley Phantoms, the Flyers-affiliate minor league hockey team). On the other floors were restaurants, retail shops, office space, and an adjoining high-end Renaissance hotel. Around the corner was a new hospital and sports-medicine complex; in the other direction, condos in refurbished historic buildings. In that renovated high-rise, Pawlowski said, a law firm was bringing one hundred lawyers from a suburban location back to downtown. In another, a tech company would install a comparable number of engineers. Here was a cleaned-up park; there, a bike path; there, a brewery.

When we looked even a block or two in the wrong direction, we could still see the signs of a troubled downtown area. Pawnshops, blood banks, check-cashing operations. On other visits, we walked with Julio Guridy through some of the poorer, mainly Latino neighborhoods half a mile from downtown. The owner of a bodega said she was hopeful that the arena would bring new business to her area, as long as it was faster than the rise in property values that might push her out.

One warm August evening, we stepped away from the economic and political maze of Allentown's downtown plans. We went to watch the Lehigh Valley Iron Pigs, the Triple-A minor league affiliate of the Philadelphia Phillies, take on the Syracuse Chiefs, an affiliate of our Washington Nationals. It didn't really matter to us or to the hometown crowd that the Chiefs, like their parent Nats, were doing well in their league and the Iron Pigs, like the Phillies, weren't. We were going in the traditional American summer spirit of a friendly night at the ballpark—in this case, the fine new Coca-Cola Park, an eighty-two-hundred-seat stadium.

The stadium had opened in 2008 at the edge of Allentown, and its success had become an inspiration and a model for some of the really big plans for downtown Allentown. Coca-Cola Park is more than a lovely stadium. It is a stepping-stone in the economic and spiritual revival of Allentown and the Lehigh Valley after the loss of nearby Bethlehem Steel and other fundamental industries and businesses. Lots of people questioned the wisdom of building the $50 million stadium, doubting it could draw or sustain a crowd. But it did and it has. People come from all around the Lehigh Valley, and the stadium boasts the biggest attendance record of any minor league stadium in the United States.

The stadium's success was also used as an argument to undertake the construction of the downtown arena in the PPL Center, including the home rink for the Lehigh Valley Phantoms. If Coca-Cola Park worked for baseball, Allentown officials and the Phantoms reasoned, the downtown arena should work for hockey.

Fans poured into the stadium in droves the two evenings we went: groups of high school cheerleaders, Boy Scouts, employees from the nearby Amazon distribution center, buses of senior citizens from their assisted-living homes, pairs of twins celebrating their birthdays, couples celebrating anniversaries, service groups, Villanova alumni, an Episcopal church group from nearby Emmaus, the management staff from the Saucon Valley Country Club, groups with mysterious acronyms like HJSC and TCR, and the Pennsylvania credit union. They all popped up to cheers on the stadium's big screen, one after another.

The evening was hardly a splurge, at the family-friendly price of seven dollars a ticket or an upgrade to ten bucks, which included a five-dollar food coupon. We went all in. Some people came for the food alone. Lee Butz, whose family company built Coca-Cola Park and later the PPL Center, walked us around one evening and told me about one such friend of his. "He didn't really care that much for baseball," Butz said, "but he loved to have dinner at the park." Butz described the way his friend would sit at one of the little tables in the esplanade for as long as it took him to eat his dinner—that would be until about the end of the third inning—and then go home.

Making my own choice for dinner was difficult. Since we were in Pennsylvania Dutch country, there were all kinds of hot dogs and local sausages on offer. The longest lines were for the spicy corn on the cob— implausibly huge ears of corn dunked into vats of melted butter, then sprinkled heavily with Parmesan cheese and hot spices. Next up were funnel cakes.

Funnel cakes? I had noticed that the lines for make-your-own waffles at the free Marriott breakfast at our hotel were as long as the lines for funnel cakes at the stadium. Funnel cakes, waffles, one and the same? They looked the same to me. I thought it was perhaps time-of-day nomenclature: waffles for breakfast and funnel cakes after that. Locals whom I asked in Allentown launched into a heartfelt discourse, explaining that funnel cakes looked more like a pile of spaghetti than a well-defined waffle, proving again that regionalisms are alive and well across America. I went with corn on the cob for the shorter line.

Not a single stadium announcement went unsponsored. We heard the *Allied Bank* national anthem, the *Toyota* "Play ball!" call to action, the *Wawa* RBI batter of the game, the more creative *Dave's Vacuum* cleanup hitter and *ServiceMaster* clean sweep. The litany and the signage that covered every square inch of the stadium might be wearying in the big leagues, but the hometown crowd was enthusiastic; we felt we were walking through the yellow pages or Yelp of the Lehigh Valley.

Inning breaks offered a sideshow of acts: races between a slab of bacon and a hot dog (we're in pork country!); a blindfolded jump-rope contest; and a sumo match featuring wrestlers inside giant transparent plastic bubbles trying to roll each other out of bounds.

Only one such interstitial act struck me as heartless. A little boy who looked to be about eight years old was the lucky winner of two tickets to nearby Six Flags amusement park. Thrilled, he was invited onto the field by the local Vanna White stand-in, who offered him a choice: keep his two tickets or take a chance on one of three mystery boxes in front of him. He gamely chose the smallest of the boxes. "Vanna" held us in suspense, opening first the middle-sized box. It revealed a few tickets and some freebies. Then the big box: six tickets and lots of paraphernalia. Then, finally, the smallest box. The boy had exchanged his two tickets for nothing but a spool of black thread. A collective groan rose from the crowd as the little boy, visibly crushed, was rushed off the field with a "Tough luck, kid!" shrug.

Strolling the perimeter of the stadium, we saw playgrounds for the little kids, a grassy seating area for families to spread out, booths for fast-pitch and batting contests. There was something for everyone, or nearly everyone. Despite Allentown being over 40 percent Latino, we saw few Latino faces in the crowds. Julio Guridy, Allentown's city council president then, told me that I would be more likely to see Latino families at the town's parks, playing and enjoying soccer games, than at the Iron Pigs stadium.

We'd heard so much, from so many people, about the big blowout event that would announce the return of downtown Allentown, that when we took another tour of the premises of the PPL Center just a few days before the scheduled opening, we were protectively worried on the town's behalf. The locked-in deadline was the evening of September 12, 2014, when the celebrated and brand-new PPL arena would host its gala first event, a concert by the classic-rock group the Eagles. Tickets went for $200 and up, and the event was sold out a few hours after it was announced. But when we walked through the PPL hall, we mainly saw painters' tarps, audience-seating chairs still in their shipping boxes, scaffolding holding construction equipment, and other signs of a lot of work still to be done. "Don't worry!" Mayor Pawlowski told us. "It will be fine!" said Julio Guridy. "No problem," Lee Butz, the builder, agreed. "Okay!" I said, mock-cheerily. What I thought was "Oh sure."

But when September 12 dawned, bright and sunny, the arena was ready for the Eagles, and much more. (More than 125 future dates had already been booked, for events ranging from Cher and Tom Petty to rodeos and hockey games.) Two days earlier, Browne, Pawlowski, Guridy, Reilly, and other local officials had gathered for an official christening ceremony. They'd all stressed the corner they thought the city was about to turn.

"What this means to Allentown is hope," a city councilman named Ray O'Connell said. "Hope. Hope for a better Allentown. Hope for the families of Allentown. Hope for the children of the families of Allentown. Hope. And without hope, you have nothing."

\* \* \*

Big projects work best if they stimulate follow-on waves of smaller activity, in directions the original planners could not foresee. We saw signs of that kind of activity around Allentown, too.

The most visible industrial-age relic in Allentown is the remains of the Mack Trucks plant, on a bluff overlooking Little Lehigh Creek and the downtown. From the outside you'd take one glance and think: another Rust Belt abandoned factory. The Mack brothers founded their truck-making company in Brooklyn in 1900, but by 1905 they had moved to this site in Allentown, where they produced their famous trucks until the move to North Carolina in 2009.

The old shop buildings include an homage to the Mack Trucks era, with a historical museum full of antique models. But most of the shop floor is now occupied by small start-up operations of the sort we have seen in co-working and incubator spaces around the country. Most of them were for products that drew from the region's manufacturing and mill-working heritage—and one of Allentown's modern advantages, as the city saw it, of having an unusually large amount of manufacturing floor space available, unusually close to downtown.

"Our big idea here is 'walkable manufacturing,'" said Scott Unger, executive director of the Allentown Economic Development Corporation, which operates the old Mack factory. By that he meant something we were seeing signs of in one city after another: reversing the model of people having to commute to suburban or industrial-park workplaces, and instead building manufacturing or white-collar working spaces closer to downtown. "When Amazon expands in Seattle," he pointed out, "they moan about not having any public transit to their sites. But no subsidized system can offset the effect of sprawl. If you can place your plants where workers can easily get to them—and where trucks can get easily to I-78 with your products—you're ahead."

Different cities have different reasons for enacting land-use policies. Unger said that a big goal of Allentown's was to preserve old industrial buildings like the ones we were walking through. "We are ahead because of our manufacturing real estate," he told me. "Protecting manufacturing space is a crucial element of our land-use policy." Enough small, new companies, with enough young founders, would be interested enough in a bargain like this—ample factory space, low costs, walkable or bikeable distance to affordable housing—to give Allentown a chance at the next wave of enterprises. "A generation ago, people never wanted to go downtown," he said. "The new model is live/work/play" in a smaller area, for which he thought an old factory in an old town could be a good match.

We visited about a dozen different businesses: A cryogenics company, in which we saw vapors pouring from liquid-nitrogen tanks but whose specific product remained confidential. A polymers firm, bolstered by a National Science Foundation grant. A solar-tech company. Another making sporting products from composite materials. A brewery—and a distillery, and a meadery, which makes alcoholic drinks out of honey.

"We are looking for high-impact companies," Anthony Durante, program manager of this enterprise center, told us. "Not what you could think of as lifestyle companies, providing a living for one to three people. We are looking for companies that will employ twenty people, then fifty, then more. Will they ever go public? We don't know. Our job is to help them get started."

Again, as a model, this is familiar—familiar, that is, in stories from San Francisco or Brooklyn or Seattle or Austin. Here the model was being applied, with local adjustments, in an old-tech old manufacturing town.

In the late 1970s, the CEO of Mack Trucks was Alfred Pelletier, who was raised in Toronto, trained as a mechanic, started at Mack repairing trucks, and rose from the blue-collar ranks to run the entire company. His son, Doug, a tall, lean, athletic-looking man in his early sixties, unlike his father went off to college and then headed to the software industry rather than the Mack plant. He worked for IBM and then in the early 1990s founded a company called Trifecta, which became a very successful business-software firm that now has about a hundred employees. When he was starting the company, the natural site for its headquarters seemed to be a clean, safe, anodyne suburban office park.

Some twenty years later, when he heard about the new NIZ program for downtown Allentown, Pelletier considered moving his company there. "We were growing and needed to expand. I was thinking of buying a building somewhere else, but I heard a presentation on the new city center and thought, I'm in!" he told me. Rather than moving into one of the new corporate office buildings, he decided to acquire a classic but distressed downtown building, the former home of Schoen's Furniture Store barely a block away from the new PPL Center, and to develop it as a contemporary tech work space.

About two weeks before its formal opening, Pelletier walked us through his office, with the vintage industrial touches and fixtures now standard in the hippest work sites. All-glass walls overlooking the next-door park, and toward a historic church that once housed the Liberty Bell. Original beams on walls and ceiling, exposed brick, wood panels from old barns in the region, and restored, polished, century-old hardwood floors. Ping-Pong tables and a rooftop deck. Kitchens plus fridges, stocked with wine and local craft beer.

"I have always maintained that if we created a great work environment, it would help us to find and retain great local talent," he said. "We could always find smart people coming out of Harvard or MIT and they would move here. But the odds are that without roots in the Lehigh Valley, in a year or two they will return to Boston. But if we find great people *from* the Lehigh Valley, who in theory could go anywhere—we could show them a caring company culture and cool workplace that would convince them this is the place to stay and start a career." Pelletier said that as soon as his downtown plans were announced, he received six job applications from engineers at nearby firms.

"The next generation of workers and the young engineers that we want to hire want to live downtown," he said. "The Trifecta Building has created a new and great opportunity for all of us."

There was a long way to go, but it was a start.

If you've dipped into the world of gymnastics beyond watching the Olympics every four years, you may already know about the Parkettes. To the rest of you, the Parkettes probably sounds like a 1960s girl band. It's not. The Parkettes is a national training center for U.S. gymnasts in Allentown.

The Parkettes is indeed a product of the 1960s, and the story of its origin is a heartwarming classic American saga. Donna Strauss, petite like a gymnast, founded the club with her husband, Bill. She has clearly told her story many times before, but she launched into it as if it had happened yesterday.

As we walked around the cavernous thirty-five-thousand-square-foot warehouse-like building, the floor was bustling with girls flying from one of the uneven parallel bars to the other, muscling through sets of pull-ups, pounding at top speed to a leaping flip over the vault, and walking on their hands in military-neat rows across the floor, in ramrod-straight upside-down posture. Everything they were doing looked impossibly difficult to me.

In the 1960s, Donna and Bill were teaching in the Allentown public schools. This was the pre–Title IX era, of course, and as a PE teacher, Donna was keenly aware that while the boys in Allentown had their football, basketball, and wrestling teams, the girls' athletics options were spare. So she decided to start a girls' gymnastics program and asked the principal, a man named Carroll Parks, for help with practice space.

Principal Parks came through, daring to carve out floor time for the girls from the boys' basketball practices, and then opening the gym doors to the girls on Saturdays as well. He was such a motivator for Strauss and the girls, said Donna, that they named the now-legendary Parkettes in his honor.

The early gymnasts practiced at school, at a church, in a barn, and in a neighborhood backyard. The high school shop teacher built the girls a set of uneven bars. The program grew and flourished during Allentown's glory days, when neighboring powerhouse Bethlehem Steel, which had produced steel for such showcase structures of America as the Golden Gate Bridge, the Hoover Dam, and the Empire State Building, was still providing good jobs for the region.

In 1979, Donna approached Alfred Pelletier, then-CEO and chairman of the board of Allentown's Mack Trucks. The Strausses took Pelletier to see the gymnasts training in their borrowed space, which was then an upstairs floor of the Allentown Symphony Hall, and asked if he would help them raise money for a real gym.

Pelletier was impressed by the couple's dream of building a facility as safe, modern, and exciting as the one the Strausses had visited on a trip to Moscow shortly before the 1980 Olympics. There they'd seen their first foam filled "pit," into which gymnasts could safely fall from heights.

Pelletier pitched Allentown, and Allentown pitched in. Picture Thanksgiving weekend, 1981: A fleet of Allentown's Mack trucks, filled with leftover foam padding from the airplane seats that Mack also produced, pulls up to the almost-finished Parkettes building. Two hundred town volunteers are waiting, armed with their electric kitchen knives, to unload the foam and carve it into small chunks for bedding for the pits. Other townspeople show up to install subflooring beneath the vaulting tracks and under the mats, put in telephones, or do whatever the skills they possessed could allow them to do. Allentown built itself a gym that would become a world-class training facility.

I visited the gym on a hot late August Monday morning, the first day of the fall season for the elite girls' team. The youngest gymnast there was about nine, the oldest seventeen. The members of the elite team are Parkettes' best of the best. The girls mostly come from the surrounding Lehigh Valley, although some travel from as far away as Delaware or New Jersey. The parents drive the girls to practice every day, some telecommuting to their own jobs from laptops in the upstairs room the club provides for them. Then they drive back home at the end of the practice and start all over again the next day. The girls are homeschooled, an experimental idea the club rolled out in 2000, when it became clear that the highly motivated gymnasts were burning themselves out trying to keep up with five or six hours of practice piled onto conventional school life.

The Parkettes program boasts the flashiest list of achievements and all the hardware that goes with it: Olympians, national champions, world gymnasts, and full-ride scholarships to big-name universities. I watched the girls, even the little nine-year-old, carry themselves with laserlike focus on the floor, and this intensity also spilled over to a beyond-their-years maturity off the floor. If you planted this group of girls next to a randomly selected group of others their age at a mall and compared their composure, I bet lunch that you would agree with me. I watched the girls in every age group listen hard to their coaches, take direction, request clarifications, and stand straight when receiving criticism.

Much of the girls' attitude, you have to guess, is a reflection of the culture that Donna and Bill Strauss have created. I admit that before walking through the Parkettes' door that morning, I had steeled myself for the likes of Bela and Marta Karolyi, who make my stomach churn even when I'm just watching them on TV. So I was surprised when Strauss's demeanor seemed toned down and unwound. When I owned up to my preconceptions, she admitted that their manner has evolved over the years. At the beginning, the model was "mean and ugly," as Donna puts it, adding, "We thought that was what you do." But they grew to see that it doesn't have to work that way, and they have moved toward a different style. Realistically, of course, you can't expect that the atmosphere I saw on the first day of the season would always remain so peachy, and Donna agreed, noting understatedly, "It can get more serious."

So, how do the Parkettes play in Allentown today? I could hear the nostalgia in Donna Strauss's voice as she reflects on the boom times in Allentown. "It was a vibrant and strong city," she says, describing how coaches from visiting teams would come to town a day early just to shop at the flagship Hess Brothers department store. "We're still a heartbeat of the town," Strauss says. "But these days, Allentown is not the same."

Although Bethlehem Steel closed, the Hess store was shuttered, Mack Trucks company was sold, Strauss says, "We survived. We stayed alive." And as one of the newly retired superstars put it in her farewell speech before heading to Stanford: "Once a Parkette, always a Parkette."

# *In the Air*

We headed for Duluth. It was another homecoming of sorts, but this time for the plane more than for us. Duluth is the home of Cirrus Aircraft, where our plane, tail number 435SR, was made.

There is always quite a bit of conversation in the skies in this Upper Midwest area, where we were again finding ourselves. This was the area where I grew up: Chicago (home, of course, to the incredibly busy O'Hare airport), Ohio, Minnesota. I frequently listened to the controllers, for information or for amusement. Sometimes it was not so amusing.

"Say souls on board."

I first heard an air traffic controller say those chilling words, over upstate New York, long ago. We had been flying our younger son on a three-day journey from Seattle, where we were living at the time, to the East Coast for his last year of college. Lest you get the wrong impression, it wasn't a glamour trip. There were three of us bundled into our single-prop plane, duffel bags in the back, charts, maps, computers, and a small cooler for big appetites in the fourth seat. We wore headsets against the constant thrum of the engine and tried to stay cool as the late-summer sun glared in through the cabin windows.

We had flown away from the mountain ranges of the Northwest and through hours and hours of flat, deserted Wyoming. When the sun was overhead, I could look down and see the shadow of our plane tracking across the desert. Over Iowa, we stared down at the nearly comically iconic Norman Rockwell scenes as yellow school buses slowed down by picket-fenced yards, paused, and slowly pulled away again. Over Ohio, along the southern edge of Lake Erie, just before reaching my hometown of Vermilion, I looked for the cluster of islands I recognized from my sailor's perspective in my youth, spotting the village of Put-in-Bay and Canada's Pelee Island. We were nearing the home stretch over upstate New York when weather (shorthand for "bad weather") began organizing itself between us and Boston.

Big bands of cumulus clouds stretched from inside Canada to hundreds of miles south. Colossal, transmogrifying formations. Our cockpit screen flashed with tiny yellow crosses that signaled lightning. Jim reassured us that planes are made to withstand a lightning strike. We didn't speak much.

Jim began to plan a route with the military air traffic controller (ATC) from the Fort Drum airspace we were traversing. He was offering us a choice between a northern and a southern route, and we chose the northern one. Jim copied the ATC's directions: vectors, waypoints, altitudes, frequencies. And then the ATC asked for "souls on board."

I wasn't prepared for that. Six years of Catholic elementary school flashed before me. "Souls" to me whispers something heavenly. Why didn't he ask for a "passenger count," I wondered, the way they do on the airlines?

"Souls," I later learned, carries no existential overtones in aviation jargon, which is engineered for maximum efficiency, orderliness, clarity, and lack of ambiguity. If you were asked for "passengers," you might overlook the number of crew members, for example.

We headed on our northern detour, and the ATC wished us "good luck." I had never heard a controller say that before, either.


The vernacular of the air became second nature after hundreds of hours in the plane. I liked the precision of the special alphabet, from Alpha to Zulu to avoid the confusions that can come from mishearing the letters. The same goes with some numbers; nine and five, which can be difficult to distinguish, become "niner" and "fife," especially among old-time pilots and controllers.

I liked the regimen of order as you talk with ATCs: their name, your call letters, and your location, followed by your request, if you have one

> Pilot: Denver Center. Cirrus Four-three-five Sierra Romeo. Four
> thousand, five hundred feet.
> And the equally regimented response:
> ATC: November Four-three-five Sierra Romeo. Denver altimeter
> 30.14.

(The altimeter reading is necessary for determining altitude.)

It's reassuring to me that all pilots and ATCs, no matter their nationality or native language, are required to share the same, clear special language of the skies. They do make concessions sometimes. Once, flying commercially over Russia en route to China, back in the days when passengers could listen on the communications frequencies, I heard the ATCs revert to Russian from English. And many times in the United States, I've heard ATCs slow down and articulate a little more distinctly when they detect a heavy accent from a pilot.

We are always November 435 Sierra Romeo. (November, the phonetic version of the letter *N*, indicates a U.S.-registered aircraft, so their tail numbers begin with *N*. Canadian planes being with a *C*, or Charlie, and British ones with a *B*, or Bravo. And so on.) Pilots don't generally name their planes, the way boaters do their boats. No *Lucky Lady* or *Mist Chief*. Die-hard pilots often memorize their friends' tail numbers. Once when we were flying over the Hudson River, one of Jim's friends recognized ours and requested ATC permission to go to a "private" frequency so we could chat. It was kind of fun, a cool-kid moment between pilots.

Commercial airlines have their own monikers. Some are company names, like "United" or "American." Others are more creative:

> *Springbok,* South African Airways
> *Shamrock,* Aer Lingus

*Penguin,* British Antarctic Survey
*Bearskin,* Bearskin Lake Air Service Ltd., from Canada
*SpiceJet,* a low-cost Indian airline
*Songbird,* Sky King Inc., from Sacramento
*Gotham,* General Aviation Flying Services, from Teterboro, New Jersey

Once during our travels we heard Air Force One calling, so we knew that Obama was in the nearby skies. Most times, the presence of Air Force One was an inconvenience for us rather than a thrill. The plane exists within its own security bubble; if Air Force One is sitting on the tarmac at Palm Springs or Palm Beach, for example, there is a no-fly zone around it, called a TFR (temporary flight restriction) perimeter. We've had to fly around such a zone or sit on the ground waiting for it to lift a surprising number of times. It gets old, just as it does for residents of Washington, D.C., who are forced to idle at intersections while waiting for a motorcade to pass by. Another time, we heard the call sign of "Mexican Navy" talking to Minneapolis Center.

When the weather is perfect, we fly on visual flight rules (VFR), which means we can fly where and when we want, just as you hop into your car and head to the grocery store. We always file a flight plan, just so someone knows when and where we're going; it feels courteous and safer to me. And we often ask for "flight following," which means the ATC will keep an eye on us on the radar display and can warn us if another aircraft is in our vicinity. That, too, feels safer. The ATC might say, "Four-three-five Sierra Romeo, traffic at one o'clock, two miles, four thousand feet, a Cessna, westbound." We also have a traffic-alert system in our plane; it indicates the presence of another plane with a little dot once that aircraft approaches within a six-mile radius from us. On the display, we can see its altitude and direction of flight, and then we look out the windows to try to spot it. When a plane gets close, say within a few miles and converging, the robo voice warns, "TRAFFIC TRAFFIC!"

When the weather is not perfect, we file an instrument flight plan and fly IFR (instrument flight rules) and follow the ATC instructions on directions, altitude, change of course, and all that.

Night flying is another matter. It has its cons and pros. The cons are that it is, well, night. The dark is a little scary to me. The pros are many: spotting other planes by their lights against the dark sky is much easier than spotting them against all the distractions of daytime viewing.

The 747 pilot Mark Vanhoenacker wrote in his memoir *Skyfaring* that pilots would sometimes flash their landing lights as a greeting to each other as they flew over "the lonelier skies" of Africa north to south. I remember a Pan Am night flight across Africa, west to east, nearly forty years ago with our two very little sons. I think I remember right that we stopped in Monrovia, Accra, Lagos, and then on to Nairobi, to visit my sister who lived there at the time. I am sure I remember, when crossing over the Congo River and central Africa, that it felt indeed like the loneliest flight through the darkest skies I had ever made.

Once we flew at night on the Fourth of July along the Central Valley of California. We were flying over the tops of fireworks, which looked, from above, like mushroom clouds of so many small, spectacular colorful explosions.

There is a whimsical aspect to aerial navigation. Maybe because pilots have to be so serious about so many things, they go their version of crazy in naming waypoints. Waypoints? You can think of them as intersections in the skyways. If you're flying along an ATC's routing, you'll fly along a virtual highway, and then turn at an intersection called a waypoint.

There is always a secret or a message or a joke behind the five-letter waypoint names. Here are some of the categories I've identified:

Local pride: In Louisiana, you'll find CREOL, ZYDCO, VOODO, RYTHM. Near Santa Rosa, California, the hometown of Charles Schulz: SNUPY.

Geography: Over the Southern California coast you have NEWPO and BALBO (near Newport Beach and Balboa Island), JETTI (off San Diego), and KELPS and BAYVU just offshore.

Sports fanatics: Near Boston are CELTS and BOSOX. In Texas: GOALL, PPUNT, DRPPD, FTBAL, TEXNN, COACH, QTRBK, TAKKL, RECVR, FMBLE, and TCHDN. Near Soldier Field in Chicago: KUBBS and BEARS. In Washington, D.C.: GIBBZ, SKINS, and MONKK.

Foodies: Near Kansas City are SPICY, BARBQ, TERKY, SMOKE, and RIBBS. And in Vermont and New Hampshire: HAMMM, BURGR, and FRYYS.

Girls' names: SUSAN, SUSIE, SUSIQ, SUZAN, SUZEE, SUZEY, SUZIE, SUZIQ, SUZYQ, SUZYY, LIZIE, LIZZE, LIZZY, LIZZZ, ANNEE, ANNEY, ANNNE, ANNII, ANNYE.

Political junkies: By Andrews Air Force Base, you'll find DUBYA, BUUSH, FORRD, and RREGN.

Goofballs: Near Portsmouth, New Hampshire, there is a famous family of waypoints that includes ITAWT ITAWA PUDYE TTATT IDEED.

There are thirty-seven thousand waypoint names, and they can provide endless hours of diversion.

Sometimes, drama in the sky glues us to the radio. One August day, with storms scattered around the Midwest, we were flying south along the east coast of Lake Michigan, then turning west to skirt Chicago, now to our north, planning to head on to South Dakota. We heard this exchange between an ATC, speaking very distinctly and insistently, and a clearly lost pilot:

> ATC: "You need to head to MOTIF [the waypoint]. You need to deviate from Joliet."
> Pilot: "We *are* heading to MOTIF."
> ATC: "No, you're not. You're headed right for my holding stack at Joliet. You need to expedite course change to MOTIF!" [The exclamation point is mine, but I heard it in the ATC's voice. The pilot was heading straight for planes circling and waiting to land at O'Hare.]

Another time, we were flying over the airspace of Cincinnati Approach. The ATC was speaking deliberately:

ATC: November Four-nine-Alpha, say souls on board. [*Uh-oh,* I
   thought to myself.]
ATC: Say fuel remaining.
ATC: Tower does know you are expecting emergency landing.
ATC: Verify. Are you minimum fuel?

It seems like every time we fly through the chatty summer skies along
the East Coast corridor, there is some new and surprising announcement.

*"Crop dusters in the vicinity."* (So old-fashioned and charming.)

*"Birds reported in the area."* (This is dangerous; you don't want one to
hit your propeller, wing, or, worst of all, windshield.)

*"Jumpers!"* (Meaning parachute jumpers.)

*"Gliders."* (I always worry that they are not really in control; I also
wonder how quiet it must be up there, as if you're a bird.)

*"Motor glider."* (ATCs spend a lot of time monitoring them and seem
to give them extra space and margins.)

*"Drones."* (ATCs sometimes say, "Might be a drone" when they pick
up something unidentifiable flying at low altitude.)

*"Unmanned rocket launch."* (After hearing this, Jim muttered, "Jeez
Louise.")

# Duluth, Minnesota

Our trip in 2014 was not my first visit to Duluth, Minnesota, on the western tip of Lake Superior. Or the second, or the fifth, but more like the fifteenth. Until age seven, Deb had grown up in Minneapolis, and this had led to her spending some early-childhood time in Duluth. When she walks around Duluth these days, it is with a sense of familiarity that comes from an early imprinting. For me, without that midwestern background, Duluth has become an unexpected sort of second home.

In the late 1990s, when Duluth was one more Rust Belt symbol of the distress brought by industrial shifts, I'd gone there to work on a story for *The New York Times Magazine* about an ambitious mayor and his implausible-seeming plan to revive the city. Duluth's historic and economic rise, through the late 1800s and the first half of the 1900s, had been tied to the very heaviest of heavy industries. The taconite mines of Minnesota's Iron Range shipped their products to world markets through the port facilities at Duluth. Timber and grain moved out the same way. Early twentieth-century Duluth had the look of one of China's twenty-first-century manufacturing centers, with all the bones and innards of its economic foundation on clear display.

Then the long decline set in. The downtown decayed; real estate prices fell; young people moved away; the city looked bad. I went to visit the mayor, a sturdily built, dark-haired onetime local schoolteacher named Gary Doty, because I had heard about an intriguing aspect of his

economic modernization plan. In this locale far from the big coastal
university-innovation complexes, a place with a long tradition in the maritime trades but with nothing like the aerospace-industry heritage of Seattle or Wichita or Southern California, Doty hoped to foster a tiny start-up
company that intended to transform the entire industry of small-aircraft
aviation. At the time, the company mainly consisted of two young brothers from rural Wisconsin, Alan and Dale Klapmeier, and a small band of
co-workers and friends. Their idea was to produce an entirely new kind
of airplane that would outclass the familiar Cessna, Piper, and Beech-
craft brands of light aircraft and make small-plane travel safer, cheaper,
more comfortable, and more attractive to a wider audience.

In the aviation world, the Klapmeiers' story has now become as familiar as any "it all started in a garage in Palo Alto" tale from the infotech
world. The brothers' company, originally called Cirrus Design and now
Cirrus Aircraft, became a phenomenal success. The most obvious new
feature of their airplanes—that each one was equipped with a parachute
for the entire airplane, to bring it down safely in case of an emergency—
was only one of its many breakthrough redesigns. The first Cirrus model,
the SR20, went on the market in 2000, followed quickly by the higher-
speed, more powerful SR22. By 2004, the SR22 had become the best
selling small airplane of its type anywhere in the world, a distinction it
has retained ever since. By 2017, some seven thousand Cirrus airplanes
were operating worldwide, the company's models taking off and landing
in practically every country that has an airport. The factory has expanded
many times and still employs hundreds of advanced-manufacturing
workers in Duluth.

There have been bumps along the way: during the pressure of the
world financial crisis that began in 2008, the Klapmeier brothers had a
bitter falling-out, which left Dale in control of the company and Alan
with a new aviation start-up of his own. Although Cirrus's factory is
still in Duluth, the company is now owned by the Chinese state aerospace ministry, which was the most plausible source of capital when the
company almost failed during the financial crisis of 2008. But Cirrus
has been the center of a new aerospace industry in Duluth, and as an
example of willed acquisition of technological advantage, it has more
than fulfilled anything the city might have hoped for it.

Cirrus's arrival was part of Duluth's larger shift away from heavy industry and to an economy buoyed by education and medicine (the hospital complex is the largest single employer); by aerospace; by small advanced manufacturing; and by a robust tourism and recreation business. At the time of our latest visit, Duluth had won an *Outside* magazine poll and been named "Best Town" in the United States, outpolling competitors like Asheville, North Carolina; Provo, Utah; and even Burlington, Vermont. As with any online poll, this was hardly a scientific study, but the enthusiasm of people writing in on Duluth's behalf was a sign of its new fashionability. Its hotels are booked from early spring through late fall, with tourists coming from all over North America and much of Europe. Every spring its Grandma's Marathon attracts some nine thousand runners (the limit it has set for entries) to a course that follows the shore of Lake Superior from the start at the mining town of Two Harbors to the finish, in front of Grandma's Saloon and Grill in downtown Duluth's Canal Park. Locals proudly claim Bob Dylan as a favorite son, although that is a fact that morphed from his spending a few years there to the folk mythology of his being a hometown boy.

Even on a short visit you can see that Duluth has not come close to solving all its problems. A few blocks away from its most impressively restored structures, other parts of downtown remain derelict and decayed. The city has the opioid problems that any part of the middle of America does; on the streets downtown, you see people who are struggling. Duluth also has a much more difficult racial history, both with local tribes and with its African-American minority, than its far-northern location or the idea of "Minnesota Nice" might suggest. But compared with its situation a generation ago, and with what most people on the coasts would expect, Duluth is much more a story of resilience.

Downtown development in Duluth is improving fast, if unevenly. To the east, along Superior Street, there were specialty shops, restaurants, and outdoor-apparel stores. I was grateful to find puffy winter jackets on sale in early June; the last ice floes had melted on Lake Superior over Memorial Day weekend, and I wasn't prepared for the northern Minnesota summer.

When I headed west, toward the public library and the YMCA, it was a different story. There were sidewalk detours, deep excavation pits, and occasional scuffles at the bus stop. Sometimes I crossed the street to avoid these disturbances, and sometimes I just walked past. They never felt dangerous.

One afternoon, Jim and I went looking for a small corner park we had heard about, heading a few blocks uphill from Superior Street, on Second Avenue East. We found it and the memorial to a little-known lynching that took place in Duluth nearly a century ago.

Here's the story of that June night in 1920: A traveling circus was in town, a local young white woman was allegedly raped, and six young black men were rounded up and taken to jail. A mob of thousands of white people stormed the jail, seized the black men, "tried" them on the spot, and convicted three. Those three men—Elias Clayton, Elmer Jackson, and Isaac McGhie—were hanged that evening from a lamppost in the center of town. The police did virtually nothing to interfere.

Teachers, journalists, and local tour guides had talked some about the lynching over the decades. A 1979 book about the events, *They Was Just Niggers,* by Michael Fedo, was published and later republished under a more restrained title, *The Lynchings in Duluth.* There was a grave-marking ceremony for the three black men's previously unmarked graves. Approaching the eightieth anniversary, in 2000, Heidi Bakk-Hansen wrote about the incident in the *Ripsaw,* then an alt-weekly publication, naming the accusers for the first time. The piece, called "Duluth's Lingering Shame," inspired a big turnout at the anniversary vigil and sparked meetings about a memorial, as residents sought a way for Duluth to recognize and reconcile what they considered the worst incident in the community's collective past.

The consensus was a granite-and-bronze memorial, which was constructed in 2003. It occupies a small park kitty-corner from the site of the lamppost where the three men were hanged. In 2013, a scholarship was established in the names of the victims. Life-sized renderings of the three victims are set under words from Edmund Burke: "An event has happened upon which it is difficult to speak and impossible to remain silent."

From what we saw during our visit, the memorial achieved the goal that the people of Duluth sought, which was to create a respectful, artistic place where the public could think about, talk about, and come to terms with the events that had happened.

The Cirrus saga was my original reason for going to the city—and after my first visits as a reporter, I returned as a customer. I got in the early-purchasers' queue and bought one of the first SR20s off the assembly line; as Deb will attest, the two factors that swayed her to approval were the presence of the parachute and the plane's comfortable interior, which was designed to be like a nicer modern car (rather than an ancient pickup truck). I went to get that plane from the factory in Duluth as soon as it was ready, in November 2000, but I ended up on an unplanned stay for nearly ten days, caught by a persistent ice storm that made it too risky to fly back to our home of the time, in Berkeley, California.

For airplane reasons and otherwise, Deb and I kept finding reasons to return: in the summertime, for the boating; in the winter, to hear, in amazement (for me), about people sitting in igloos for ice fishing or roaring across the drifts in their snowmobiles. Deb knew all these stories and could readily add to them from her own experience, in a Minnesota accent she usually keeps under wraps.

We came back as part of our 2014 travels to see what else had happened in Duluth, and how its story fit into what we had been hearing elsewhere. So we asked Gary Doty, now gray-haired fifteen years after I first met him, what else he had been thinking when the Cirrus move was afoot, and what the turning points had been in the city's movement forward.

"There was this attitude around Duluth that nothing's any good," Gary Doty told us, about the days when he was growing up in the city and beginning his teaching career. "We're this little city stuck way to the north, far away from the Cities"—he was using the Minnesota term for the Twin Cities, Minneapolis and St. Paul—"and we're just going to have to plod along."

Doty, who was born in Duluth in 1948 and went to public school there and then the University of Minnesota Duluth, began teaching but got into politics quickly. He won a seat in the Minnesota legislature in his twenties, and in his thirties was on the county board of commissioners. He became mayor in 1992, in his midforties, and easily won three four-year terms.

Doty's predecessor, John Fedo, had through the 1980s begun the city's push toward being a tourist destination and an outdoor-recreation site, building an extensive biking and running trail along the lakeshore, and beginning the conversion of former commercial dock areas to what is now a very popular retail and entertainment district called Canal Park. We spent some nice days riding bikes along the lakeshore trail and prowling around the rocky water's edge and the bars and shops offering Etsy-like local products in Canal Park. Doty thought that his task was to concentrate on fundamentals—road repairs, sewers—and also to look for the new tech companies he might attract to the city. One of his big bets, and at least temporary embarrassments, was something called Tech Village. It embodied an idea that by the 2010s has become commonplace: setting aside downtown space as incubator or shared-work area for start-up firms. But Duluth's was slightly ahead of its time, or at least ill-timed. It opened just as the tech and financial crash of 2001 was setting in, and the place stood underused for several years.

"We had problems there," Doty told me a dozen years later. "But we couldn't remain stagnant." The arrival of Cirrus in the mid-1990s was a crucial turning point. "It really was the catalyst for more positive attitudes about the city," Doty said. "If that hadn't happened"—and its happening involved the same sort of courtship as Joe Max Higgins had done with steel and helicopter factories, and what South Carolina officials had done with BMW—"then we might really have been in a tailspin, and not even a parachute could have saved us."

But Cirrus did come, attracting engineers and designers (plus customers) from around the world and hiring mainly local tech workers to build its airplanes. Related aviation businesses began expanding at the airport. United HealthCare brought a service center into Duluth, which now employs more than one thousand people. Duluth Trading Company and the national fashion chain Maurices brought their headquarters to the city.

"People started saying, 'We're not that bad!' People would come up here to look around and say, 'Wow!' This was a gem they weren't aware of"—as long as they were prepared for what Doty tactfully called "four full seasons" of the year. "I complain myself if it gets colder than thirty below," he said. "But most people, once you get them here, they don't want to leave."

This might sound like any boosterish local talking about any city, as they did in Burlington or Greenville or even little Eastport. Indeed *Babbitt* itself, by Sinclair Lewis, the classic novel about urban boosterism, is set in the fictional city of Zenith, which is at least partly drawn on 1920s Duluth. But what struck me most about Doty's comments, and connected them with what we heard from the next generation of civic and commercial leaders in the city, was his emphasis on generational links and responsibility, and the way his contemporaries in the city's business and civic life were deliberately bringing along those of their children's generation.

Doty reeled off a list of the business, financial, and community leaders he had worked with. "As these people get older," he said, "they've backed off a little—but not until a younger generation was ready. There's a younger generation of people ready to take the reins. They're doing it differently, but they're taking over."

Who are these younger people? Doty mentioned the man who was then-mayor—Don Ness, who began the first of his two terms at age thirty-four, and whom we met a few days later—but also some young business leaders who were connected with one another and with their predecessors.

One example: the Benson brothers, Dave and Greg, grew up in the Cities and went to college in the early 1990s at UMD. If you saw them in Southern California, you might think they were surfers—shaggy-haired, rangy, weathered. Their sports were instead the northern plains variants: skiing, ice-skating, and skateboarding.

Soon after college, in 1997, they founded (with a friend, Tony Ciardelli) a company called TrueRide, which became a successful manufacturer of ramps, half-pipes, and other ingredients of outdoor skateboard parks. They started the company in Minneapolis but moved to Duluth because it was so much more affordable. They also liked Duluth's livable scale, and what locals consider its year-round recreational opportunities. The skateboard parks that TrueRide sold were made of expensive plastic and composites. The Bensons didn't like how much scrap was left over after they cut out the big sections for their skating ramps. They first formed a furniture works called Loll, then a kitchenware company called Epicurean, now an easily nationally recognized brand, which together made chairs, tables, cutting boards, kitchen utensils, and other products from the material they had been discarding.

On a wooded hillside outside Duluth, some of the company's design and manufacturing offices are housed in a building that had once been—no kidding—a factory producing cement burial vaults and then was closed as a hazardous brownfield site. The city government, under Gary Doty, and state officials agreed to help clean up the site if the Bensons based their businesses there.

As you approach from the back, you think, "This is what a Depression-era burial-vault factory, which was later condemned as a toxic waste site, would look like." Once you step inside the doorway, you're in an environment that the hippest firm in San Francisco or Brooklyn would envy: recycled timber, taken from the frigid depths of Lake Superior, for the walls, staircases, and beams (an approach we'd also seen with recovered lake timbers from Lake Michigan, in Holland); other structures made of the companies' own sleek plastic; one whole wall of glass, looking out on the woods, and bright, open workspaces. From this building, Loll and Epicurean ship their products to customers in sixty-one countries. As Dave Benson showed us around, employees went off to jog on lunch breaks; in the winter they ski or skate. Racks just inside the front door hold their sporting equipment.

"Ten years ago, there weren't many start-ups in Duluth," Dave Benson told us. "Now it's buzzing." If you saw this operation in San Francisco or Seattle, you would think: "Of course!" Where else could you combine the product-design talent that can appeal to a worldwide market, the emphasis on sustainability that has made the firm a leader in recycling techniques, and the production skills necessary to create a rapidly changing line of items? But you find it in Duluth—"Because we just like the quality of life here," Dave Benson said.

When we met them, the Benson brothers were in their forties. Another example, half a generation younger, comes from the two married couples who founded one of Duluth's most distinctive and successful craft breweries, called Bent Paddle. These four people—Bryon and Karen Tonnis and Colin and Laura Mullen—had either grown up in Duluth or gotten to know the city as students at UMD.

They'd had experience in the emerging craft-brew industry in Oregon and in the Cities, and starting around 2010, despite the surrounding financial crisis, they began laying plans for returning to Duluth and opening a production brewery and taphouse there. "We probably spent two years discussing all the angles of the right business and brewing plans," Karen Tonnis said. "Then six months of fund-raising, and six months of build-out before we opened our doors" in early 2013.

Why Duluth as a locale? "We all wanted to make our way back here," Laura Mullen said. "It would be an easier place to start our families and live the lives we wanted." Her husband, Colin, added: "From a beer perspective, it's all about the water. Duluth city water is basically very lightly filtered lake water. It's pure, it's very, very clean, it's unbelievably soft." As in Greenville and New York City, people in Duluth love their water. The water's quality, he said, "allows you to start from scratch and replicate whatever style of beer from around the world you would like," rather than being constrained by flavors or minerals in the local supply. (I am personally a fan of stronger-flavored ales; Colin Mullen said that the greater brewing challenge was to produce lighter lagers, like a pilsner modeled on one from the original Czech brewing capital of Plzen, one of Deb's family's ancestral homes.)

Within months of its opening, Bent Paddle was a business and critical success. Its on-site taproom was busy, but 95 percent of the beer it brewed was shipped to retailers across the state and elsewhere in the Midwest. By 2015, it was the sixth-biggest brewer in the state and had expanded to a second production site, a step that its original business plan had envisioned happening within seven (rather than two) years.

Obviously I am a sucker for microbrew start-up stories, but two aspects of the Bent Paddle saga struck me as being significant. One was in providing another illustration of the underappreciated role of "craft" eateries of all sorts—breweries, distilleries, coffee shops, farm markets, mustard or cheese or honey stores. The other was the practical importance of these enterprises in urban redevelopment. Operations of this sort have a bias toward less-fashionable, lower-cost, more run-down parts of a city, especially when they are starting up and short on cash. "Breweries are industrial operations, and they're expensive," a well-known beer-world writer named Jeff Alworth noted in *All About Beer* magazine. For making beer in particular, "you have to have quite a bit of space for the brewhouse, fermentation, and storage. . . . So breweries end up on the fringes, in bad parts of town where the rent is cheap."

The same might be true of any factory or big warehouse, he said. "But breweries aren't like the average industrial plant. They are people magnets, bringing folks in who are curious to try a pint of locally made IPA. In fairly short order, breweries can create little pockets of prosperity in cities that can (and often do) radiate out into the neighborhood. Pretty soon, other businesses see the bustle and consider moving in, too."

That process was very much the story of Bent Paddle's location, in a long-abandoned steelworks on the less-prosperous west side of town. "We liked this because of its great visibility from the highway," Bryon Tonnis of Bent Paddle said. "And, of course, we got the rent at a great rate. Now we see people coming to the neighborhood who say, 'You know, I haven't been here for years!'"

When the team announced their site choice, Duluthers of their parents' generation raised their eyebrows at the questionable-sounding address. "They thought, 'Wow, that's the shady part of town.' There's a shift that's happened that people who've lived here for a long time haven't quite caught up with," Bryon Tonnis said.

Soon after our visit to Bent Paddle and my mention of it on *The Atlantic*'s website, a Duluth native named Peter Hatinen wrote in to explain the part it had played in what he viewed as the spread of the city's revival to long-neglected parts of town.

"Bent Paddle," he observed, "cast its lot in the heart of downtrodden Duluth. . . . Since Bent Paddle has established itself, it has created a dynamo of entrepreneurial activity nearby. What is most important for the city is what is happening very nearby the brewery: a new restaurant, another brewery, and a new coffeehouse, all opening within blocks of Bent Paddle.

"The investment Bent Paddle has made and the traffic it has inspired are clearly driving this development."

The Bent Paddle founders were well aware of the importance of community connections, both in their own ability to succeed and in the effect they wanted their business to have. Local ties had helped them. One local bank took the lead in early financing, along with the SBA and the local Arrowhead Regional Development Commission, plus twenty-three private investors. The city government, then under Don Ness—himself barely older than the founders, and a craft-brew fan—gave streamlined approval to zoning changes. As they grew more successful, they expanded their local business contacts: chairs and tables in their taproom came from the local company Loll, tap handles and metal works were provided by local shops, and they made alliances with local farmers and coffee roasters for specialty brews.

Most striking to me was their awareness of the effect the brewery could have on the city's future. "A lot of people who grew up here, or got to know it from UMD, they would love to stay here, but they feel that they have to leave," Karen Tonnis said. "But now we're seeing young entrepreneurs"—like them—"who went to UMD and say, 'I love it, I'm going to stay, and I'm going to figure out the way how.' And I feel like there's suddenly more of a diversity of job opportunities here, as people embrace the history of Duluth and become proud of its possibilities."

Laura Mullen, another of the founders, said, "There are limits in a community this size. But you also see your place in connection with everyone else. We're excited about what we can do as part of a new entrepreneurial wave here."

The start-up boom is part of a general increasingly cosmopolitan air in Duluth. The sale of Cirrus Aircraft to the Chinese state aerospace ministry, during the company's financial straits soon after the world economic collapse, has brought several Chinese families to town. During our 2014 visit, Deb talked with a Chinese woman who had chosen the English name Heidi. Her husband was part of the Chinese management group at Cirrus, and they lived in a big English Tudor–style house, with a view downhill to Lake Superior. Her son, Tong, had just finished the fifth grade at the neighborhood school and was into football, which Heidi said she also appreciated for the teamwork, the mission of "war," the strategy and attack, the guarding, the getting the ball. Her almost-two-year-old daughter was in a playgroup with other neighborhood kids. Heidi said her adjustment to Duluth was easy, partly because she spoke English well and she drives. We had seen enough of Chinese corporate housing conditions to understand the miraculous transformation in the family's daily living circumstances. At Chinese aerospace headquarters in the southern China town of Shenzhen, most employees lived in cramped quarters in a densely populated and often-polluted city. Now for the AVIC employees in Duluth, it was as if they had their own country estate. Heidi confined herself to saying that she and her husband valued the family life and time together they enjoy in their American lifestyle.

\* \* \*

John Fedo, a relative of the author Michael Fedo, was the mayor in the 1980s who brought the lakewalk and Canal Park to the city. Gary Doty, in the 1990s, was the mayor who brought in Cirrus and other high-tech firms. Don Ness, whose two terms in office coincided with the Obama era in Washington, was the mayor of the entrepreneurial and outdoor-recreation boom.

Ness grew up in the city. In 2016, he produced a highly personal, heavily illustrated book called *Hillsider,* about growing up as an idealistic pastor's son in the city's Hillside neighborhood and his struggles as he entered into public life. He is a lanky figure, at six foot three, and while laconic, he has a natural talent for politics. He was student body president at UMD, won a seat on the city council at twenty-five, and was elected mayor at thirty-three. In his reelection run four years later, he was the first mayor in more than a century to face no opposition. He decided not to run for a third term, mainly to raise the three young children he had with his wife, Laura—and, I presume, to earn money before possibly reentering politics at some later stage.

Deb and I met the Nesses for dinner at one of the many popular restaurants in Canal Park, a gathering spot for tourists and natives alike, surrounded by water. Every three or four minutes as we spoke, a Duluther would come by to say hello to both of them. The first time I'd met Ness, two years earlier, on another aviation-related visit to the city, he had told me that being a mayor, "especially in a 'strong mayor' city system," was the best job current American politics had to offer. "It's a job that requires—and allows—you to create and implement a tangible agenda," he told me. "You can carry that out in a way that most positions in American politics just don't permit. One minute, you can be crafting a broader vision on economic-development strategy; in the next minute you are responding to a snowplow complaint. And it grounds you in what is happening in the community, and hopefully you can translate that into a broader concept."

This time, I asked him whether more years in office and more experience in politics had changed his view.

Not really, he said. "As mayor, I tried to convey a message that helped folks forge an emotional bond with the city. I wanted them to feel pride in the city, while still validating their concerns. Duluth is both gritty and beautiful—it was my goal to get folks to take pride in that paradox.

"In the 1980s," he explained, "it would be fair to say that Duluth was one of the ten most distressed cities in the nation. Our peer cities back then were Flint and Gary and Youngstown. There was a fear that we'd get into a spiral and not be able to pull out." If Cirrus hadn't come, everything might have looked very different. "Establishing the aviation sector was a critical turning point for our community," Ness said. "It's highly skilled manufacturing, it requires a high level of employees at both the shop-floor level and in engineers. And it demonstrated this region's ability to create a new industry that it can support." As Joe Max Higgins might have put it: We're making shit that flies!

Now, Ness said, the city didn't compare itself to any other city but, rather, had discovered "the authentic niche for what Duluth, on its own, can be." This he defined as being "a smaller midsized city, with exceptional outdoor-recreation opportunities and the natural beauty of the lake, with strong regional services like health care and higher ed, and a growing entrepreneurial economy. We're on the way."

# *Pittsburgh, Pennsylvania*

Well into our travels by now, we were getting a sense of a new measure for perspective on a town. That measure was through a town's art, a topic that doesn't come naturally to us. Jim and I are far from artists ourselves, much as I dream of how much fun that would be. But as the months of our travels became years, and we talked with more and more artists and planners and residents, we came to understand something about how the arts helped us (and residents and other visitors!) see a town.

Sometimes the art was celebratory and proud, like the bronze statues in Greenville or Rapid City or Holland that tell the story of the town. Sometimes, we saw art confront the dark side, like the memorial to the lynching victims in Duluth or the performances about the Civil War by students in the Columbus, Mississippi, cemetery. Later, we would see how art unleashes the human capital of a town, which lay ahead in Fresno; or attracts and allows creative energy to synergize and flourish, as in the artists' co-ops of the Franklinton area of Columbus, Ohio; or builds the civic strength of a town, which we would find among a new generation in San Bernardino; or is the basis for entire renewal of a town, like in Ajo, Arizona. We also came to recognize many cases where art is functional and just plain fun, as in Bend, Laramie, Erie, Sioux Falls, Dodge City, and many other towns where art was bicycle racks, benches, fountains, decorative wall murals, and more.

Two towns in the Midwest swing taught us two new perspectives on the scope and impressions art can make; one insight came from Pitts burgh, the other from Charleston, West Virginia.

Pittsburgh has long been a deeply philanthropic town, and much of its philanthropy has focused on enriching lives through the arts, with its big-ticket endeavors like museums, galleries, outdoor spaces, pleasant access to an attractive riverfront, stadiums, and theaters. Pittsburgh is known for its big-scale art. The city now has only half as many residents as it did during its heavy-industrial prime, but it has retained a concentration of locally minded philanthropies from its richest days—Carnegie, Mellon, Heinz, Frick—which have kept up its museums and concert halls. It has the cultural infrastructure of a city of a million residents, with only one-third that many people competing to enjoy them. Amid all that, we came upon something artistically unique, something that has, I would say, brought a new sense of compassion to its people.

The City of Asylum sits in a close in North Side section of Pittsburgh known as the Mexican War Streets; many of the streets there are named for battles or generals from the Mexican-American War. The gentrified bohemian row-house neighborhood is home to many writers, artists, and eclectic personalities.

In 2003, Henry Reese and Diane Samuels established the City of Asylum, an organization—for lack of a more precise word—that provides sanctuary for exiled at-risk writers.

Reese and Samuels pulled together donors and friends and bought a former crack house on a small lane called Sampsonia Way and fixed it up; City of Asylum now owns several houses in a row. The lane feels like a midwestern version of a *hutong* in old Beijing. Their first exiled writer was Huang Xiang, a poet from Hunan Province, also the native province of Mao Zedong. Huang Xiang became an advocate for democracy and human rights during the Cultural Revolution, was sent to a labor camp for three years in 1986 for "disturbing social order," fled China with his wife in 1997, and was granted asylum in the United States. He arrived at Sampsonia Way in 2004. The years of hardship and punishment had cost him broken bones, much of his hearing, and many of his teeth, but not his spirit or his poems, which his wife had squirreled away for safekeeping.

When Huang Xiang arrived in Pittsburgh and took a look at Mount

Washington, he said that in the tradition of the Chinese poets, he would like to carve a poem into the mountainside. Samuels didn't blanch, but she suggested instead that he might paint his poems on the outside of his house instead.

They set up scaffolding around the frame house and Huang went to work, painting his poems in his own "grass style" calligraphy. He was "writing his house," he said. The neighbors, of course, couldn't help but notice "House Poem." Before long, neighbors who didn't understand even a word of Huang's Chinese poetry began to slip notes through his mail slot, many with poems they had written themselves.

The City of Asylum began to grow and thrive. Five more writers arrived, from El Salvador, Burma, Venezuela, Iran, and Bangladesh, all with stories as dramatic as Huang Xiang's. There were concerts and readings open to the public by more than three hundred artists; the events spilled out into the street and vacant lots and under tents.

There were projects involving the neighborhood community, including one called River of Words. Exiled Venezuelan writer and poet Israel Centeno, a City of Asylum resident, created a community-generated public art installation within the Mexican War Streets. He chose one hundred words relevant in some way to Pittsburgh. Neighbors were invited to host a "word-in-residence," meaning that they would display a representation of their word on a wall, or door, or window of their house. Visual artists Carolina Arnal and Gisela Romero fabricated the words and traveled from Venezuela to install them. River of Words was wildly popular. "Vortex! I need to have vortex," claimed one neighbor. "Baseball!" claimed another. "Fear, talent, thought." The list went on. When we walked the streets around Sampsonia Way, we spotted the words, some bold, some inconspicuous, stenciled on garage doors or sitting above garden gates.

The City of Asylum has since developed a corner lot into a reading garden and renovated the long-abandoned Masonic Hall just down the street for musical and literary performances and films, a bookstore, a restaurant, and apartments and offices. Next up, they have an eye on former Salvation Army buildings.

We met Huang Xiang when he returned after his years on Sampsonia Way for the tenth anniversary program for the City of Asylum. He recited his poem "Wild Beasts." Or to put it more accurately, he didn't just recite the poem; he danced, shouted, waved, and lived that poem with his whole body and spirit. By the end, the entire audience was exhausted with him.

It seems natural that the City of Asylum should also thrive in Pittsburgh. The residents of the town were warmed up to appreciate and participate in such an edgy and ambitious artistic effort. The City of Asylum started out offering sanctuary to exiled artists, and it ended up bringing compassion to a city.

The story of Charleston is entirely different. It illustrates what happens when a town and its art make for synergy.

# Charleston, West Virginia

In the early 1970s, a young singer-songwriter named Larry Groce was launching his career in the music business. He had grown up in Oak Cliff, a working-class district of Dallas; moved to Los Angeles; started recording albums; and in 1976 had a Top Ten hit with the novelty song "Junk Food Junkie."

After that song came out, Dick Clark invited Groce onto his then very popular *American Bandstand* show. When Groce finished singing, Clark interviewed him about the "idea" behind the junk food song—but then asked him about his odd-sounding job title, which was "musician-in-residence" for the state of West Virginia. A few years earlier, when he was twenty-four and trying to get established in his career, Groce had heard from a friend about a federal program to send musicians to rural areas. "I first thought, 'Do they want me to go do a concert in West Virginia?'" he told us when we met him in his house in the capital city of Charleston. "They said, 'No, this is where you go live there for nine months.' I was in L.A., looking for something different. So I tried it." And he never left.

"I'd already made three albums, and I thought I could turn this into a career," he said. "When I was here, I started wondering if I could actually do that—from West Virginia, if I had representation elsewhere. That's why I came, and when I got here, I found that it *fit me*, personally."

After that half-accidental introduction to West Virginia in the early 1970s, Groce stayed, and he became one of major artistic and pop-cultural forces in the state. He continued his recording career: by the time we met him in late 2014, he had finished his twenty-third album, the latest in a list that includes several very successful children's albums for Disney. Since 2005 he had been the director of FestivALL, an annual ten-day arts festival in Charleston. In the 1980s, he owned and ran a ballet school in Morgantown. And for more than thirty years he has been the host of (and a performer on) the weekly National Public Radio music show *Mountain Stage*.

*Mountain Stage* is the main national-media production coming out of West Virginia, and it has been a significant force in country music. It was carried by 150 stations nationwide at the time of our visit, and in the next two years it expanded to 200. The list of artists who had their first live broadcast exposure to a national audience under Groce's auspices is so long and impressive that at first I didn't really believe it (but then I checked it out). The performers include Lyle Lovett, Mary Chapin Carpenter, Sheryl Crow, Barenaked Ladies, Alison Krauss, Ani DiFranco, Phish, Counting Crows, Lucinda Williams, and many more.

We got to see a live *Mountain Stage* performance at the Civic Center in downtown Charleston, before an enthusiastic and youngish full-house crowd, with Bob and Susanne Coffield of Charleston—he a lawyer, she an educator—who introduced us to many of the backstories of Charleston. It was two hours of music by a range of established and rising artists. James McMurtry—a singer-songwriter whom I first met when he was a teenager hanging around in his father Larry's bookstore in Washington—ended the show. Before him came the acoustic rock/folk/jazz band the Devil Makes Three, based in California; and the "progressive bluegrass" group Yonder Mountain String Band, from Colorado. And opening the evening, for a bewitching twenty-some minutes, were two teenage sisters from Indiana, Lily and Madeleine, who were just on their way up at that point and became much more popular in the following years. "They've got that sibling harmony!" Groce said when introducing them on the show. "There's no substitute."

A few days after the show, we went to see Groce and his family at their house, both to ask him about the program's history but also because his name frequently came up when we asked people in Charleston, "Who makes this town go?"

West Virginia in general and the Kanawha Valley region around Charleston are, of course, places where not enough has gone right for quite a long time. The coal industry has inevitably shrunk and is shrinking further; the big processing works that once gave the area the name "Chemical Valley" are mainly gone; other corporate headquarters have left; and the leading employers in the Charleston area are now the hospitals.

So what was it like to run a recording career from here? And to produce a national radio show from a state usually the object of condescension from coastal big-city tastemakers? Two themes ran through what Groce told us over the next hour or two.

One was about the possibilities and challenges of doing first-tier creative work in what the world considers second- or third-tier locations. This, obviously, was a major theme through all of our travels.

Whether they come out and say it or not, many of the country's most ambitious people assume that work of a certain level requires being in a certain place. This idea of a vast national sorting system for talent has huge ramifications. They range from politics to the distortion of real estate prices in a handful of coastal big cities. But as we continued to find, in countless other places across the country, people don't have to start out assuming that most of what they take home will immediately go out for the rent or mortgage. That is because they have calculated that—in Duluth and Greenville and Redlands and Holland and Sioux Falls and Burlington and Allentown and even larger places like Columbus, Ohio, and Charleston—they can build their company, pursue their ambition, and realize their dream without crowding into the biggest cities.

Some people have always preferred the small-town life; of course, America has always had diverse regional centers; and, of course, locational concentration matters in many industries. I had known that before we started these travels. What I hadn't known is how consistently, and across such a wide range, we would find people pursuing first-tier ambitions in what big-city people would consider the sticks.

As for Larry Groce, when he first got to West Virginia, he said he found it comfortable, because "the way people here looked, acted, and even sounded" reminded him of his grandparents' and great-aunts' generation in Texas. Which made sense, since many Texans of that era had migrated from Appalachia. As he stayed, he came to appreciate its practicality, its lack of pretension, and its person-to-person level of generosity.

Practicality: "It's one of those places that has never had a boom, so booms and busts are relative. If you're never up, you can't be down."

Lack of pretension: "Lots of people can make an album in the studio who can't do it live." (*Mountain Stage* is recorded before a live audience.) "That is very West Virginia, too: to deliver in person. We have hillbillies, but we'll tell you what a hillbilly is—you [outsiders] don't tell us." This was two years before J. D. Vance's book *Hillbilly Elegy* made the term a staple of political conversation. "A hillbilly isn't an ignorant fool. He's a straightforward, self-effacing, 'what you see is what you get' person. He relies on his friends because he doesn't trust a lot of other things. He is not necessarily formally educated. But he is smart."

Generosity: "If your car gets broken down, you want it to happen in West Virginia. This whole stuff about *Deliverance,* it's just the opposite. If something happens, you want it to happen here. People will stop and help." Groce told the story of a national network correspondent who came to interview people nearby and found them unwilling to answer questions. So he put up the hood of his car as if he were having engine trouble, and people came over to help him out and talk with him.

How does that affect his show? Groce seemed content with and proud of his show and its cultural reach, but he was fully aware that "since it is a national show, we have felt stereotypes people have about West Virginia."

He said, "One thing I've learned over the years, when you put 'Mountain' in the title of something, people think you're the fiddle-and-banjo show. Which we're not. Of course, if we were just an old-timey bluegrass country show, we'd probably get more national press, since we'd fit expectations.

"We see the expectations in the stories that are generated about this place. Have a mine disaster? The reporters are all here. Have a chemical spill? All here. Have something where it shows that some percentage of the children are poor or obese? Yes. But if you have Gabriel Kahane and Kate Miller-Heidke on one show, and then James McMurtry, it doesn't fit the categories, doesn't make sense."

If I am making Groce sound defensive in recounting this, I'm misrepresenting him. His tone was like that of a politician who understands, anthropologist-style, that the press simply can't help concentrating on elections rather than governing but nonetheless realizes that his or her job comes down to governing.

And the second theme Larry Groce reminded us of? His sense that West Virginia and Charleston, for all their travails, were moving in the right, rather than the wrong, direction.

How do the state's prospects compare with when he first arrived? we asked. "Lots of people who are older are looking backward," he said. "Fifty years ago, there were eighty thousand people in Charleston. Now there are fifty thousand. Back then Union Carbide employed a lot of people with advanced degrees who made good money. So people can get stuck in 'I remember when. . . .' Coal is dying, but it's like a dangerous animal that's dying. It's going to thrash."

However, he said, younger people, as well as those from elsewhere, didn't have that memory. They were starting new businesses and families and projects. "I think in the last ten years there has been a renaissance," he said. "It's easy to go to a place because the money is good. It's different because you like being there. I am optimistic about this place."

# 2015

*In the Air*

*Guymon, Oklahoma*

*Ajo, Arizona*

*San Bernardino, California*

*Riverside, California*

*Redlands, California*

*Fresno, California*

*Winters, California*

*Bend, Oregon*

*Redmond and Prineville, Oregon*

*Chester, Montana*

*The American Prairie Reserve, Montana*

## In the Air

Winter was coming. We wanted a way to keep traveling, despite the ice and wind and snow, and to extend our reporting beyond the eastern half of the country. It was time to head west, in the last weeks of 2014—for western travels the following year—which we're reporting here as the introduction to what we saw and learned in 2015.

⚜ ⚜ ⚜

*Potomac Clearance, Cirrus Four-three-five Sierra Romeo.*
*Ready to copy clearance, IFR from Gaithersburg to Hunting-*
*ton, West Virginia—Hotel Tango Sierra.*

We sat on the runway at Montgomery County Airpark in Gaithersburg, our normal base near Washington, preparing for a long trip to the West. We'd allowed plenty of time to reach our destination before nightfall—even though now, in late November 2014, night was coming early—and even though as we headed west across the Appalachians, we were likely to be buffeted by headwinds the whole way. We'd come out to the airport in plenty of time to weigh the baggage piece by piece, to make sure it was situated for the right weight-and-balance distribution between the rear seat and the luggage compartment in the tail, and to allow for careful checks of the oil level, the tire pressure, the updated navigation software.

It was only around noon, but with every hour, it was getting later, and darker, and colder. The preceding winter had been historically cold across the eastern half of the United States, as a "polar vortex" settled much farther south than normal and brought Arctic temperatures to much of the Midwest and the East Coast. On one of our visits to Greenville, South Carolina, the Reedy River had had a layer of ice, and the fountain in front of the downtown Poinsett Hotel had been frozen solid. Even southern Georgia had suffered a frost. From a climate scientist's point of view, this was one more sign of disruption in expected weather patterns: the Arctic was warmer than normal, pushing the vortex farther south. From our point of view, it was one more reason to try to get south and west before the upcoming winter, and the forecast of more polar vortices, set in.

That was the large-scale, strategic reason to get away from the Eastern Seaboard. The tactical one was an imminent snowstorm. If we could put a thousand miles between ourselves and the East Coast within the next day or two, we would escape the widely forecast crippling blizzard and whited-out cities between the Appalachians and the Atlantic Ocean.

Finally the controller from Potomac Clearance radioed back our authorized route, altitude, and takeoff time for the start of the trip to the west: "Four-three-five Sierra Romeo is cleared to the Hotel Tango Sierra airport"—he was using the phonetic term for HTS, the code for our destination airport in Huntington, West Virginia—"via, on entering controlled airspace, direct Westminster VOR, then expect radar vectors. . . ."

It was a formula I knew, and had anticipated, and had already entered into the plane's navigation equipment. I listened for the crucial words about the allowable takeoff window: "Cleared for takeoff. Clearance void if not off by time sixteen thirty-five, time now sixteen thirty. . . ." We had five minutes to get to the runway, and go.

We went.

\* \* \*

Over the Appalachians, the winds were stiff, the bumps were significant, the sky around us was gray and white with clouds. This is the kind of flying that amounts to "getting there," rather than "enjoying it." But the temperature outside remained several degrees above freezing—just as forecast, and as necessary so that the annoyance of a slow, bumpy ride did not become the serious danger of ice on the wings. The Appalachians are not stark and steep by the standards of such western ranges as the Sierras, the Cascades, the Tetons, or, of course, the Rocky Mountains. Nevertheless, their often-difficult weather and winds demand attention. An hour into our flight, we had finally crossed the mountains, and starting at Elkins, West Virginia, we could begin a slow descent to warmer temperatures and less ferocious winds as we traversed the state. We broke free of the clouds as we crossed over Charleston, West Virginia, again, where the airport is named for native son Chuck Yeager. We headed, as planned, for the Tri-State Airport in Huntington, on the banks of the Ohio River where the states of West Virginia, Kentucky, and Ohio all abut.

We'd gotten the last room in the motel, which was full of utility-repair and tree-service crews from across the Midwest who were being deployed in anticipation of the blizzard that would hit the following day. The next morning, trying our best to stay ahead of the storm, we headed west, across Kentucky.

Nearly two hours into that next day's trip, the weather was fine and the headwinds had weakened. But suddenly one of the six cylinders was showing a different temperature from the other five. Suddenly the engine seemed to be running a little rough. Suddenly it was time to land and find out what was going on.

Ten minutes' flight ahead of us was the airport in Murray, Kentucky, not far from the Missouri border, and the home of Murray State University. We landed and taxied over to a maintenance shop—one of whose staffers, we learned, was again fortunately an *Atlantic* reader who had been following our travels across the country. I said that I thought a spark plug might have failed. The head maintenance man said he could check—and if that was indeed the problem, he could probably fix it within an hour or two. He suggested that we drive into town for lunch.

We borrowed the "crew car," a veteran white Crown Vic that had previously been a police cruiser (complete with spotlights on both sides). Ninety percent of the time in small airports around the country, when there was a crew car it was a former police cruiser Crown Vic. We climbed into this one and drove into the old downtown for grilled-cheese sandwiches at Rudy's on the Square.

If it had been two years later, we might have felt obliged, as visiting journalists, to ask others here on the fringes of coal country about Hillary Clinton and Donald Trump. Instead we asked some residents about their town, and we mainly heard about new improvements at Murray State. As we'd noted so many times, when we asked people what was on their minds, we'd hear about schools or drugs or downtown-redevelopment projects or new companies that might come to town. Virtually never did anyone volunteer the staple themes from national politics—Do we trust the media? Which party do we dislike more?—that came to dominate so much of the national news and that are usually the first and last questions visiting reporters ask.

Back to the airport—and a failure of the spark plug on cylinder number three diagnosed and repaired. Off again toward the West—across Missouri, and on to Little Rock, for an overnight stay and a dinner with our dear friend and longtime *Atlantic* editor William Whitworth, who had grown up in Little Rock during the days of its school desegregation showdowns, then spent decades in New York and Boston as a jazz musician and a writer and editor with *The New Yorker* and then the *Atlantic,* and had returned to his home there.

On the way to Little Rock, we encountered a cloud bank just as we were crossing the Mississippi, from Tennessee to Arkansas. But we got a "pop-up clearance" to proceed on instrument flight rules; we kept going across rice fields and the catfish ponds of the flat Arkansas delta lands; and fifty miles outside Little Rock, we came into clear, calm air for an easy descent.

* * *

The weather stayed clear as we kept heading west the next day. It was bright, cold, and windy—a steady plains wind in our face, as we went across Arkansas and into Oklahoma. It was a Thursday morning as we took off from Little Rock—the fourth Thursday in November, Thanksgiving Day. Our two sons were with their in-laws, in California—one in Los Angeles, one in Santa Barbara. We missed them. We were headed westward but were only halfway across the continent from where they all were.

We were intent on a destination within Oklahoma, the very small town of Guymon. We'd planned an intermediate stop in the also small town of Okmulgee, which we'd chosen for its big runways and cheap gas. As we neared that airport and listened to the local air traffic control frequency, the only other plane we heard was a Cessna Caravan, a durable freight-hauling plane, doing practice takeoffs and landings there. Over the airwaves, we could identify by voice one grizzled-sounding American, who we assumed was the flight instructor, and two young students, who by their accents seemed to be from Africa. When we had landed and were refueling our plane, we saw them land a few hundred yards away— close enough to judge their appearance, not enough to meet or talk. Our guess was that the trainees were preparing for their commercial-pilot licenses (small airports all over America have foreign pilots-in-training, because the costs are lower and the facilities better here than anywhere else). This would probably afford the two young men some nice employment opportunities, perhaps as commercial pilots or perhaps as "freight dogs" if they went back home.

# Guymon, Oklahoma

Guymon had been on our map since we'd first come across Caroline Henderson. *The Atlantic* had published a series of letters Henderson had written from Guymon in the 1930s to a friend back in Maryland, describing her life and experience on her family's rural farm as the drought unfolded and persisted. *The Atlantic* called these "Letters from the Dust Bowl." Her farm was a most anticipated destination for us on this journey.

We landed in Guymon, with high winds tearing across flat, flat land in the early afternoon. The FBO manager had finished his turkey already and was back at the airport, with a (really nice!) crew car for us to borrow overnight. We don't mean to keep dwelling on crew cars at fixed-base operators, but they loom as a large factor in our travels. In many of the small towns where we land, like Eastport, there are no taxis and no car rentals. This was also the case in Guymon. And in the middle of nowhere, especially on a Sunday or holiday, you can find yourself with nowhere to go but back into your plane. So we were particularly thankful for the generosity of the FBO operator on this Thanksgiving Day.

I had tracked down Henderson's apparently only living relative. Caroline and her husband, Will, had one daughter, Eleanor, who had one son, David Grandstaff, now a geologist and geochemist. His profession struck me as fitting somehow, related, as he was, to a heritage of the earth.

Grandstaff recounted for me his visits to his grandparents' farm in the 1950s and 1960s; he'd spent summers and Christmases there when he was a boy. He also gave me the exact location of the farm—both the latitude and longitude and the road location, in the community known as Eva. The farm was at the intersection of Roads N and 9; the alpha and numeric at first sounded odd and later became comforting for being logical waypoints to keep us oriented along the straight, endless, and otherwise marker-free roads in rural Oklahoma.

Grandstaff warned me that the farm would look pretty desolate, not the way it used to. We could be sure to recognize it, he noted, by the barn with the fallen-down roof. Indeed, we discovered that there was more. The front porch of the house was gone; the doors and windows were gone or boarded up. We peered in where we could. Inside the dark rooms were some ghostly remains of a sofa and some chairs, an old fridge, a fine piece of cabinetry in the dining room, which Will Henderson had surely made, since he'd built the whole house. We could see the steps going up to the second floor, but even from afar they didn't look trustworthy any longer.

The barn, without its roof, was otherwise intact, and we found remains of outbuildings, one of which was probably a chicken coop that Henderson had written about, and the footprint of others. There was barren land as far as we could see. We unintentionally disturbed flocks of quail from the scrubby turf and saw an elegant hawk cruising aloft, as well as a bird that Jim swore was a great horned owl. There was no sign of the schoolhouse across the road, where Henderson had first taught when she moved to Oklahoma after college at Mount Holyoke.

Her dream of farming the land had coincided with the years of drought and dust, but Grandstaff reminded us of the decades of successful farming and pleasure Caroline and Will had enjoyed on their farm before the dark years of the Dust Bowl descended. Indeed, they had farmed since about 1908.

When I asked him why he thought they'd stuck out the drought for the duration—it lasted nearly the entire decade—he said he imagined they'd had no real alternative, since everything they had was in that land. And who would ever have guessed that the drought would persist for so long?

We drove back some twenty miles and what felt like most of a century from the Hendersons' farm at the crossroads in Eva to Guymon, where we searched with dwindling hope for some remnants of a turkey dinner. Nope, every restaurant was closed, we were told by the clerk at the Comfort Inn, the owner of a Mexican grocery, and the minder of the gas station, which had a few leftover chicken sandwiches in its cooler.

We raced to the Walmart, and were met at 5:30 p.m. by residents from miles around, who were lined up with their carts along every last aisle, with store employees standing guard to enforce traffic rules in the yellow-taped thoroughfare aisles. They were all ready for the 6:00 p.m. official start of Black Friday sales; we were warned to move out quickly. We grabbed a six-pack of Tecate. Then we found a lone quick food shop open and purchased two frozen burritos to microwave back at the Comfort Inn. Our Thanksgiving.

This part of the country is now connected to the nation and the world in a way hard to imagine when the Hendersons were fighting dust and drought and despair. Yet even now, the area has the distinct sense of being very, very far away from anything, and very much on its own. I found myself surprisingly moved by seeing the house in which Caroline wrote her chronicles of a terrible stage in the country's history, the very land that she and her husband and their daughter fought to preserve. (Let alone the improbability of the letters she wrote at her desk, in the same room we peered at through blown-out windows, making their way to editors in Boston, who made them known across the country.) Most of us fancy ourselves "brave" and "independent" in various ways. But to have even this rough idea of where and how these families lived, through all those years, gives a different meaning to the words "courage" and "independence."

# Ajo, Arizona

The word "remote" became vivid to us during our time in Ajo. The town in southwestern Arizona, population around 3,500, stands alone, surrounded by federal lands. To the east is the main reservation of the Tohono O'odham Nation—bigger than Delaware, smaller than Connecticut, and home to roughly 10,000 residents. To the south is the vast swath that FDR set aside as the Organ Pipe Cactus National Monument in 1937, and beyond that Mexico. And to the west is the Cabeza Prieta National Wildlife Refuge. The closest town, Gila Bend, considered just a hop up the road, is a forty-mile drive north through sparse desert, with hill and mountain views in the distance.

At night, we saw more stars than we knew were in the heavens. The quiet was broken by cries of what we imagined were small feral animals, and by the occasional A-10 training flights darting through the skies of the Barry M. Goldwater Range, the nation's third-largest bombing range. To add a city-folk measure, the town has one stop light, we had no cell coverage, and the nearest car rental we could find was in Phoenix, more than a hundred miles away.

Ajo has a small airport, which is unusual in that the town is almost entirely surrounded by various forms of "restricted" airspace. The most restricted of these, to the city's north, is known as R-2305, the Barry M. Goldwater Range, where A-10s, F-16s, and other aircraft conduct day-and-night bombing and strafing drills.

That's not so odd in itself. Much of the West is covered by military airspace, and you talk with the air traffic controllers to figure out when and how you can safely and legally cross. But this one on the way to Ajo was more stringent than usual. I called a couple of flight-service officials and asked how to make the transit; they all said they didn't know.

Then I prowled around online and found an account from someone who had flown all the way into Ajo a few years earlier. The punch line was that you can fly to the airport, as long as you follow a narrow state highway that edges along the air force range—all the while staying in contact with a military air traffic controller called "Snake Eye" and remaining over the road exactly 500 feet above the ground, which is very low.

Contact "Snake Eye"? Follow a road for forty miles, over terrain I've never seen before (and where jagged formations pop up all over), at 500 feet above the ground? Report passing between two peaks, at an altitude below their summits—and then craters? All the while with A-10s roaring around?

The pilot whose account I read was exhilarated by his trip: "It was a beautiful day for flying and I had an opportunity to experience the St Rte 85 corridor with an active restricted area and a strafing run down the highway. It does not get much better than this."

I decided it would be better to land at the last little airport outside the bombing zone, Gila Bend Municipal, and see how the road to Ajo looked from ground level.

Ajo is pronounced *AH-ho*. Many people assume that its name comes from the Spanish word for "garlic," but it's actually more likely an Indian-derived word for the red pigmented soil, *o'oho*. Ajo thrived as a copper-mining town for most of the twentieth century. Around 1911, the Calumet and Arizona Mining Company confirmed a large high-grade copper carbonate orebody, located a nearby water well, and developed a way to process the ore.

The company hired a mining executive named John Greenway, a former Rough Rider with Teddy Roosevelt at the Battle of San Juan Hill and Yale football star, to develop the New Cornelia mine. He was joined by his adventurous young wife, Isabella. By 1917, Ajo's open-pit oval-shaped mine, a mile and a half across and more than one thousand feet deep, nearly as deep as the structure of the Empire State Building is tall, was in full production.

Greenway was inspired by the City Beautiful movement of the era to build a well-planned town, managed in a socially responsible way. Ajo was noticed and referenced in journals of the early 1900s as a model company town.

Ajo's town plaza was and still is an oasis: a broad expanse of green lawns, surrounded on three sides by a Spanish Colonial Revival–style arcade of shop fronts, whitewashed and shaded by red-tile-roofed walkways. At the far end is the train station; the now-closed rail line connected Ajo to Gila Bend, where it then linked to the Southern Pacific Sunset Route. Across the street from the west end of the plaza are a pair of churches painted bright white, one Catholic and one Methodist. Palm trees are everywhere.

The residential part of the town was more modest. Housing for the mine workers was divvied up according to ethnicity, a system that, a century later, has brought the "model town" description under more critical scrutiny. The Anglos lived in the houses closest to town, and many of those houses still stand today. You can see some of the small slabs where the houses of Mexican Town and Indian Village once stood. St. Catherine's Indian Mission is now home to the town's history museum.

There were fully stocked company-run shops, schools, and all kinds of activities and cultural celebrations. Today's Ajo kids still lament the long-gone movie theater. People also recollect that the swimming pool was segregated by ethnicity back then, and the Indians' day was the last one before the pool's weekly draining and cleaning. The Greenways' own house—elegant but unpretentious—still presides on the top of the hill overlooking Ajo.

Fast-forward nearly seven decades: the New Cornelia mine had suffered from bitter labor disputes, as well as from the diving price of copper. The owners shut down the mine in 1985. What followed was a brutal and humbling collapse for the showpiece desert town. The population plummeted. Houses and shops were left to bake in the sun.

A trickle of old and new businesses have kept the town alive, including the community newspaper the *Ajo Copper News,* run by Gabrielle David, the editor, and her brother Hop, the publisher. (Before them, their mother, Ann, and father, Richard, were editor and publisher, respectively.) There are longtime locals, snowbirds and retirees from the North, tourists in campers or big SUVs on their way to the Mexican border or the Organ Pipe Cactus National Monument, and some survivalists. A number of border patrol families live in Ajo in new pastel-colored houses built by the U.S. government especially for them. There are warning signs not to trespass onto their streets. The prominent border patrol headquarters is about ten miles southeast of Ajo, and there's an all-vehicle compulsory road-stop station on the way to Gila Bend. We were waved through each time, after a few cursory questions and a quick look into our car. Outlaws traverse the desert; migrants and traffickers hide there; and while some people set out barrels of water, marked with flags, for those who need it, others report them. You see the occasional lone parked trailer that looks like something out of *Breaking Bad.* Border patrol vehicles are a constant presence on and off the roads through the desert around Ajo; there is no mistaking them.

Driving south into town, past the rural equivalent of strip malls, are a motel, a gas station, a few restaurants and RV parks, a supermarket, an Elks lodge, and lots of chances to buy Mexican car insurance. Then, rounding the corner into Ajo proper you come upon the stunning town plaza, with its palm trees and whitewashed buildings. Among the plaza shops today are a deli, a secondhand store, a gym, the library, a restaurant abandoned like a ghost ship, its tables still set with white tablecloths and stemmed wine glasses, and a grocery store that sells expired goods at incredibly cheap prices. We couldn't resist sneaking into the expired-goods store during our visits, for opportunistic shopping. Past-date gra-nola bars? Old soap? How bad could they be?

In 1993 came the beginning of a turning point for Ajo. A tri-national group of leaders from Ajo, the nearby Mexican town of Sonoyta, and the Tohono O'odham Nation convened out of concern for the Sonoran Desert, the environment they all shared. They called themselves the International Sonoran Desert Alliance (ISDA). For ten years, ISDA met with residents of all three nations—the United States, Mexico, Tohono. While remaining steeped in deep respect for the original mission of pre-serving the desert environment, it eventually shifted its focus to the eco-nomic development of their region through arts and culture.

ISDA and a multitude of local groups it has spawned have built a complex ecology of arts, environment, gardens, real estate, business development, health, and job training and employment that is leading the town toward a stable future.

One key to ISDA's and Ajo's forward motion has been the stewardship of Tracy Taft. An energetic yet understated former community organizer and educator from back east, she had already seen potential reach frui-tion in many other communities. Taft first came to Ajo to retire and to work as an artist with glass. She joined the ISDA board and became its executive director in 2003, tapping into her network of helpful friends and colleagues and wending deftly through bureaucracies to win count-less grants and support for ISDA from foundations, nonprofits, and gov-ernment agencies.

\* \* \*

Two major efforts have been the cornerstones of Ajo's sustainability: the renovations of the town plaza and, a few blocks uphill, the repurposing of the mining-era Curley School campus.

The project at the Curley School, named for Mike Curley, who was John Greenway's successor as mine supervisor, began with the renova-tion of a few buildings into modestly priced rental units for artists, sculp-tors, painters, photographers, dancers, and artisans of all sorts.

When you walk around the tiny front-yard spaces of the living quarters, you see stone sculptures, installations hanging from tree branches, and small decorative gardens, all evidence of indoor art spilled outdoors into the communal space. The resident artists do much of their work in the campus studios and workshops. Some sell their work in the gallery in the downtown plaza; one supplements her income with French bread she bakes for the town's Saturday market.

People with an artistic bent have always been attracted to Ajo. A lot of them said it was because of the light or the panoramas of the desert. We joined some of them for an impromptu happy hour out in the desert one evening, taking in the changing colors of the sunset over the dry hills and flatlands. Ajo is also attractive for being inexpensive. The asking price for a top-of-the-line house is under $175,000; a modest one goes for half that, and fixer-uppers for as little as $25,000.

You can't walk a block without running into sculptures of stone and metal, random fancy tiles, mosaics, hanging art, or extraordinary benches to rest on. People paint murals on walls and in entire alleys, from small to building-sized. Others craft creative railings or fences around their houses or gardens.

Visiting artists offer programs and classes: puppet makers, clowns and jugglers and mimes, basket weavers, bead workers, potters, quilters, and fiddlers. If we had stayed on, I know I would have begun to feel a little guilty, or at least left out, if I weren't contributing to the creative culture. I was thinking about jewelry or a delicate herb garden. And Jim could brew beer.

A new creation to reconcile part of Ajo's past is a tall concrete wall along the wedge of Triangle Park. Set into the wall are photographs, mosaics, and text to commemorate the mining-era residents whose lives came up short in sharing the prosperity and privilege of the times, the Mexicans and American Indians.

More renovations at the Curley School followed. At the top of the campus are the former elementary school classrooms, surrounding a courtyard. The business plan called for an income-producing conference center, with classrooms converted into guest rooms, meeting rooms, and cooking facilities. The outdoor play space would be desert-friendly gardens to supply produce and a henhouse for egg-laying chickens.

The construction was done by local workers, who are part of an ISDA apprenticeship program. The apprentices learn their skilled trades, do the work of the renovations, earn formal credentials, and emerge as ready-for-hire workers. The town has plenty of need for their services, such as addressing the stock of sorely aging housing, as well as the town's school, clinic, library, and other public buildings.

Some workers became bona fide artisans. One man designed and made intricate hanging lamps for the guest rooms out of the old industrial metal fluorescent ceiling lights popular in school buildings during the Curley era.

We stayed in one of the newly completed guest rooms. A group of a dozen young volunteers with the AmeriCorps National Civilian Community Corps (NCCC) were in residence, assembling beds, moving furniture, and painting many more rooms. They were smitten with Ajo, and vice versa.

* * *

Aaron Cooper has been at ISDA since 2010 and was a teacher at the Tohono O'odham reservation high school for five years before that. Recently, Cooper took over Taft's executive duties. We met Stuart Siegel and Emily Raine and their dog, Beau, who first stopped by Ajo on more or less a whim on their classic cross-country trip in their station wagon. They stuck around for a bit, despite Beau getting himself into considerable trouble while chasing a javelina into a cactus, and offered to help open the new conference center as volunteers. Two months later, they were weighing an offer from ISDA to direct the new conference center, which was still under construction. Ajo probably seemed farther away than two thousand miles from their former East Coast bustle, but Emily and Stuart decided to sign on. They were married about a year later in Ajo, now have a native-born Arizonan son, Jonah, and have moved from a rental to a house of their own.

Ajo needs more young people and families like those of ISDA to find their way there and settle down and help build the twenty-first-century Ajo. Jane Canon, a registered nurse at Desert Senita Community Health

Center, said she worried about who will replace her when she retires. Finding teachers for the school is a challenge. The excellent band teacher had to leave when her husband, who works for the border patrol, was transferred. We heard that the café had recently changed to new, young ownership. Maybe someone will open a microbrewery one day.


I was curious to get an idea of what the phrase "rural health care" looked like, so I visited the health center, which serves as the clinic for Ajo residents. The center is housed in a single-story sand-colored building that was originally the dormitory for single men at the New Cornelia copper mine. The miners' big rooms, which seemed about four times larger than any doctor's exam room I have ever visited, now hold examining tables, sinks, chairs, and counters placed liberally about as though to take up as much space as possible.

Ajo had a grand hospital back in the mine's heyday; it now stands vacant on the hill above the town plaza. Today, the nearest functioning hospital to Ajo is about a hundred miles away to the northeast, in the town of Casa Grande. There is another hospital on the Tohono O'odham reservation, about seventy miles away in the little town of Sells. It is designated for tribal members only, although I was told that it does receive non-tribal patients in emergencies.

Jane Canon had been at the clinic for sixteen years when I met her. She is also the clinic's manager for quality improvement and for outreach to the community and beyond.

She toured me around the clinic. It provides enviable one-stop shopping for many routine procedures that would have the rest of us traipsing all around our bigger hometowns for multiple appointments, including X-rays and lab work; there is also a well-stocked pharmacy, a dentist, and a behavioral health services team. The center also has a certified Spanish translator and a special phone line with third-party translators for multiple languages.

As Canon describes it, because of its remoteness, the clinic needs to be "self-ready" for a lot of circumstances, from an Ebola outbreak (unlikely) to backup for massive power failures (more likely). The local high school is set up with water, cots, and an emergency generator for electricity and cooling. And a strong community of support is nearby, including folks from the border patrol station and from Organ Pipe and Cabeza Prieta.

The Ajo clinic is registered as a Federally Qualified Health Center (FQHC). The FQHC designation earns the clinic extra reimbursements for the two-thirds of its patients who are on Medicare or Medicaid and allows it to participate in other benefits: being partners in an alliance of similar centers, receiving federal malpractice insurance coverage, and providing its patients with care from specialists, like a visiting cardiologist and ophthalmologist.

But it lacks the resources to serve everyone. For example, since there is no way to get prenatal care in Ajo, many pregnant women choose to put off those examinations and checkups for a while. And many will decamp to Tucson or Phoenix a few weeks before their due date.

I asked Canon about some of the worst problems for this rural community, and then without giving her a chance to answer, I guessed: drugs, alcohol, violence. She confirmed, and explained how these could spawn a vicious cycle of depression, lack of motivation, and even contribute to obesity and type 2 diabetes. The Tohono O'odham have the highest rate of adult-onset diabetes of anywhere in the world, a stunning 50 percent. If you're depressed and unmotivated, she told me, just getting up off the couch can seem like a major effort.

One target for improving the quality of life in Ajo is food. One of the last things I expected to find was a thriving local agriculture and food movement in the middle of the Sonoran Desert. Conditions are about as challenging as you can imagine: desert temperatures with freezes in the winter and 110 degrees in the summer; poor soil with low organic and microbial content, high alkalinity, and caliche (a natural cement); and four inches of rainfall annually, often arriving in downpours.

Undeterred, the Ajo community has built an intricate cooperative network around food. Working together are the school, the clinic, local gardeners, the farmers' market, local restaurants, the town's grocery store, student interns, adult volunteers, the food bank, the CSA, and the Sonoran Desert Conference Center, with its spaces for gardens, a chicken coop, celebratory events, teaching and demonstration space, and a newly finished commercial kitchen.

Ajo's CSA was founded and has been run by Nina Sajovec, an attractive and fearless anthropologist and community activist who made her way from Slovenia to Ajo. Slovenia! Her partner, Sterling Johnson, was born and raised on the nearby Tohono O'odham reservation. They are expanding and managing the main gardens, planting agricultural crops, and utilizing practices from the Indian reservation.

Sajovec described Ajo's food bank distribution experience to me, as well. Just that week at the First Assembly of God church, more than 120 cars lined up to receive bags of food. This week's offerings included potatoes, broccoli heads, three or four loaves of white bread, some hamburger or hot dog buns, lots of citrus, and some sodas. Food bank workers passed the bags in through the car door windows. "It works better that way," said Sajovec, because the experience is more anonymous for the recipients, who sometimes feel awkward.

I asked about the recipients. Largely the working poor, Sajovec told me, ranging from young women in their late twenties with three kids to older folks who come dressed in their Sunday best, including one woman who always shows up in a beautiful fancy hat and wearing lots of makeup.

And there's more: Ajo students work in the Edible Ajo Schoolyard garden, and some of their crops make their way to the school cafeteria. Canon told me that by 2016, obesity rates had dropped up to 11 percent among classes of the K–6 students, who are the ones participating in the program.

At the end of our final visit to Ajo, we saved time for a mad dash through the plaza's Saturday morning market. We bought several loaves of still-warm bread that we'd watched rising in the kitchen of one of the Ajo artists-in-residence the evening before. We bought jars of local citrus marmalade and regretted passing on the flowers, which we knew wouldn't travel well. Some of the market produce had come full circle from the gardens at the elementary school to the market stands, where the kids' parents shopped for it.

There are nearly 450 students in Ajo's schools, which span pre-K through twelfth grade, including the thirty-seven seniors who graduated in May

2017. The high school, which opened in 1956, and the elementary school, which opened thirty-five years later, are located in a series of low-slung single-story buildings. Each classroom has a doorway to the outside walkways, protected by overhangs should it ever rain here in the desert. The classrooms seemed dark to me, perhaps as protection against the desert heat and sun during most months of the school year. It's not a highly privileged school population. According to the Ajo school district, about 84 percent of the students in Ajo qualify for free or reduced lunch. Some 67 percent of students are Hispanic, about 17 percent are white, and another 10 percent are Native American, a population that fluctuates from year to year as some students move back and forth between Ajo and the Indian schools on the reservation.

Kids land in Ajo with a variety of stories. Some came with parents looking for jobs. One girl's single mom worked with the border patrol. One boy's dad had piled the family in the car and was driving south through Arizona looking for work. In Ajo, a tire went flat. With no place to purchase a new one, they scoured the yard sales until they finally found a used one. They went on their way again and, a few miles out, got another flat. At that point, the boy recounted, his father realized that a tire shop could be a going business. So he turned the family car around, drove back to Ajo, and opened a tire shop, which is still in business several years later.

Others have spent their whole lives so far in Ajo. One girl, a sweet and confident sophomore, described her household this way: Mom works in an office, Dad not sure, Grandma makes tortillas, Grandpa is disabled. Then, when I asked what she did when she wasn't in school, she dropped what to me was the bombshell: she takes care of her own one-year-old son. So far, it's working: she has a 4.0 grade average and is aiming for the University of Arizona. "How can it be working?" I asked. "I'm good at multitasking," she answered, as though it was just that simple. I shouldn't have doubted her abilities; in 2017, I heard that she had graduated and was heading to college.

Ajo's schools are fighting economic and cultural headwinds, but their recent progress has been impressive. Ajo High School's four-year graduation rate has grown from 50 percent in 2003, to 79 percent in 2010, to

92 percent in 2017. In 2011, not a single Ajo senior applied to a four-year college. Among the class of 2017, about half the students who graduated are heading to college.

The superintendent of the Ajo Unified School District, Bob Dooley, told me that Ajo High School grads are starting to return from college with positive reports to give their high school friends. "The kids who go to college are making it there now," Dooley said. And this is a big change from recent times, when the reaction to the challenges of college life used to be "What do you expect? You're from Ajo. You're wasting your time!"

Lauren Carriere, the principal, says it takes time to build the college-going culture. Families are excited when the kids are admitted, but they can turn reticent when the reality hits that their teens would actually be leaving home. We heard about that reticence in other heavily Hispanic communities around the Southwest, where family ties run strong and deep. Sometimes, Carriere says, the family will uproot and follow the student child all the way to Phoenix.

Like other small towns, Ajo needs to keep the professionally trained, skilled-up, and higher-educated grads. The employment options in Ajo make that hard now, although every new restaurant or studio or service that opens in town is a promise of change. The school wants to nurture more students who can make those changes for themselves and the town. "Can someone open a vet clinic? Can someone be a lawyer? Can they make an entrepreneurial spirit?" Carriere wondered out loud.

* * *

We couldn't leave Ajo without sharing the story of Isabella Selmes Ferguson Greenway King. You just know that with a string of last names that long, the woman must have had an interesting life. I first learned about Isabella in Ajo, where, nearly a century ago, she'd joined her second husband, copper-mining magnate John Greenway, to help develop the small company town. I ran across her again on a return visit to Eastport, Maine, about as far away from Ajo as you could be in the continental United States, and across the water from Campobello Island, where Isabella visited her lifelong fast friend Eleanor Roosevelt. Finally, I traced her steps a third time, near the end of our journey in Tucson, where she had embraced the West and its people by envisioning and building the renowned Arizona Inn.

The headlines of Isabella Greenway's life, with intentional adjectives: a rocky, disrupted childhood; unlikely opportunity as a newly privileged young woman traveling on the edges of early twentieth-century political and social power; drama and loss twice as a young widow of swashbuck ling, pedigreed men; fearless engagement as an entrepreneur and a businesswoman; the first woman elected to the House of Representatives from Arizona. This is all documented in a wonderful 2004 biography, *Isabella Greenway,* by Kristie Miller.

Isabella's parents suffered hard times ranching in the turn-of-the-century Dakotas. Her beloved mother, Patty, struggled with depression and alcoholism. Her dashing but impractical father, Tilden Selmes, died when Isabella was nine years old. Isabella bounced, often solo, among relatives in Kentucky and Minnesota. Improbably, Isabella's father was friendly with Teddy Roosevelt in the Dakota ranch country, a happenstance that marked Isabella's later life.

When Isabella was about fifteen, her mother moved them to New York, where they lived with generous relatives. Isabella attended fancy schools and met Eleanor Roosevelt. They were quick and sympathetic friends. The two spirited young women were favorites of Uncle Teddy Roosevelt and spent time in Roosevelt circles from Manhattan to the White House to Roosevelt's Sagamore Hill estate.

Eleanor chose Isabella as a bridesmaid, one of only two who weren't officially family, at her 1905 wedding to Franklin. Shortly after that, nineteen-year-old Isabella married another family insider, Robert Munro-Ferguson, who had been a brave and dashing Rough Rider with Teddy Roosevelt at San Juan Hill. At thirty-eight, Munro-Ferguson was twice her age.

San Juan Hill came back to haunt Ferguson in the form of tuberculosis. Just a few years after they married, he and Isabella moved with their two small children to New Mexico for the dry, healthy air.

They domesticated a remote mountaintop homestead, living in tents and homeschooling the children. Isabella became politically active in the World War I efforts, chairing the Women's Land Army and toiling with other women in the fields while the men went to war. When Munro-Ferguson's health further declined, they moved to Santa Barbara, where he died soon after.

Eleanor and Isabella always maintained a personal letter-writing relationship. It would ultimately last for nearly fifty years. They shared personal intimacies, including their sympathies for the frequent losses, anguishes, and betrayals that punctuated their lives. (Isabella had lost two husbands by the time she was forty; Franklin's polio and his affairs are well known; there were illnesses; the loss of parents, friends, children.) Kristie Miller and Robert H. McGinnis documented these letters in the book they edited, called *A Volume of Friendship: The Letters of Eleanor Roosevelt and Isabella Greenway, 1904–1953.*

In 1923, Isabella married John Greenway, a friend of and fellow Rough Rider with her first husband, and moved to Ajo. In 1926, John Greenway died suddenly in New York following a routine surgery, and Isabella returned to Ajo by train, suffering a miscarriage en route. Three thousand people attended his funeral.

After John Greenway died, Isabella lobbied hard to place a statue of him in National Statuary Hall, in the Capitol Building in Washington, D.C. It was a statue sculpted by Gutzon Borglum, who had carved Mount Rushmore.

In 1928, Isabella was elected to the Democratic National Committee. Four years later, she was rewarded for her effective lobbying on FDR's behalf with the chance to second his nomination at the Democratic National Convention. In 1933, Arizona's sole seat in the House of Representatives became vacant, and Isabella was elected to the seat with 73 percent of the vote. As a politician, she was loyal to her causes and her state, working for disabled veterans, the copper industry, and the underemployed. She won WPA projects for Arizona. And yet, in 1940 (having voluntarily left Congress while still popular), she publicly supported Wendell Willkie over FDR, who was making his third-term bid.

Isabella was equally fearless as a businesswoman. In the late 1920s, she started a furniture business called the Arizona Hut to employ disabled veterans. A few years later, she opened the Arizona Inn as a way to use much of that furniture. She bought and operated a cattle ranch. She bought a small freight and passenger airline called Gilpin Airlines.

Back in Washington, D.C., on a break from our travels in the winter of 2015, I hoped to see John Greenway's statue in the Capitol for myself. Poor timing; I missed it by weeks. It had just been replaced with a statue of Barry Goldwater. In 1953, Isabella had died at the Arizona Inn, where we were lucky enough to stay during our last night of our final cross-country flight.

# San Bernardino, California

We flew across central Arizona, into Southern California, and then through the Banning Pass toward San Bernardino. The aerial view over the desert and snaking through the mountains was beautiful. We could look down on Palm Desert, Palm Springs, and recognize the towns the way you would the streets in your neighborhood. It felt like home. The San Bernardino airport was another signal to me that we were home. It was right next to Redlands, where we stayed several times during these four years of flying. We had watched the airport change and ultimately grow, from its demise after the closing of Norton Air Force Base into a small, elegant FBO and a bustling repair center where old hulls of giant 747s are rehabilitated. The aircraft were painted with names that took your mind to far-off destinations: names like EVA, Uniworld, Arabiana, Meridiana.

San Bernardino is probably the hardest-pressed town in California, one of a handful of most-troubled cities in the United States. Its problems are economic, political, historical, and those of simple bad luck. How many other cities have suffered an economic setback because an existing interstate highway was moved someplace else? That happened to San Bernardino in the 1970s, before a lot else would go wrong.

Of all the U.S. cities and counties that went into bankruptcy after the real estate and financial crash of the late 2000s, San Bernardino took the longest to emerge. A federal bankruptcy judge began considering the city's plan for regularizing its finances only in 2015, long after fiscal-recovery plans for cities like Detroit and Stockton had been enacted and those cities had moved out of bankruptcy. San Bernardino's voters ratified the related necessary measures in the fall of 2016.

I've had some idea of San Bernardino's situation for almost as long as I can remember. My hometown of Redlands is San Bernardino's immediate neighbor—the place where many officers from San Bernardino's huge Norton Air Force Base, professors at its community college and Cal State campus, and doctors at its hospitals chose to live. Redlands had its small, locally owned shops, San Bernardino had the big malls and national stores.

San Bernardino had the McDonald brothers' original golden-arches hamburger store, which Ray Kroc took over and extended to a globe-girdling brand. That first McDonald's was only three blocks away on E Street from the campus of San Bernardino High School, home of the Cardinals. As visitors from Redlands High, we often went to McDonald's after tennis matches or speech tournaments, or just on outings to the big(ger) city. San Bernardino was one of the stops mentioned in the song "Route 66," composed just after World War II. Improbably, the very first performance the Rolling Stones ever made in the United States was at Swing Auditorium, right on the Orange Show grounds, in 1964—and one of the most daring things I did as a generally rules-abiding teenager was to sneak out and see their show. But San Bernardino was also a Hell's Angels haven, and the locale of frequent gambling and prostitution busts plus gang-violence outbreaks, and generally a tough town.

People outside the state often imagine the big divide in California as something like the old Mason-Dixon Line, separating its territory into north versus south. That is: the Bay Area of the north versus "the Southland," the tech industry versus "the Industry," redwoods versus palm trees, Stanford and UC Berkeley versus USC and UCLA. The more important dividing line more or less parallels the Coast Range of mountains and separates the state into west versus east, coast versus interior. On the western, coastal side are the biggest cities, the most famous companies and universities, the richest people, and most of the national mindshare of what "California" means, including its concentration of Democratic voters. On California's eastern, inland side are all of its deserts, most of its farmland, and a disproportionate share of its problems, from pollution to poverty to the worst consequences of the past decade's sustained drought. In political terms, this is also where most of its Republican districts can be found.

San Bernardino County is the center of the "Inland Empire" of Southern California, the non–Los Angeles part of the Southland, essentially the flyover country of the state—something I'm allowed to say because that's where I'm from. The county is the biggest one in the United States, although most of its expanse is Mojave Desert and most of its people are packed into its southwestern corner, closest to its border with Los Angeles County. San Bernardino County used to include what is now Riverside County, which peeled itself off as a separate entity in the 1890s.

San Bernardino was first settled in the early 1800s, became a major Mormon settlement in the 1850s (until Brigham Young called the group back to Utah before the Civil War), and through most of the 1900s developed as a big railroad and trucking center. Even when prospering it was a no-frills, no-nonsense, bungalows-with-small-yards blue-collar place. Just after it had been named an "All-America City" in 1977, San Bernardino lost, one after another, everything that had allowed it to maintain its blue-collar job base.

From World War II through all the Cold War years, Norton Air Force Base was where thousands of airmen and officers were assigned. When I was growing up a few miles away, enormous bombers and transport planes on the approach to Norton would pass over our schoolyards all day long; teachers would routinely pause during class to wait for sonic booms from the jets to subside. Through the 1980s, the base had supported well over ten thousand local jobs. As part of the post–Cold War base-closing movement, Norton was deemed unnecessary in 1988 and shuttered by 1994. Norton's closing, plus the demise of Kaiser Steel in nearby Fontana and the transfer of a major Santa Fe railroad maintenance yard back to Kansas, "ripped a part of the heart out of the San Bernardino area economy," the local economist John Husing told the San Bernardino *Sun*. "And really," he added, "in many respects the bankruptcy of San Bernardino today can be traced back to events in that period of time."

The city's population had long been more "majority minority" than the entire state's—San Bernardino is now about 60 percent Hispanic, versus about 40 percent for California—and significantly poorer. The median household income in the city is under $40,000, versus over $60,000 for the state and over $50,000 for the country. San Bernardino is the poorest city of more than village size in California.

When things went wrong for the country as a whole in 2008, they went worse for San Bernardino. Because its population was so poor to begin with and had lost so many previous sources of income, the debt levels on its real estate shot up during the subprime bubble of the mid-2000s and then home values fell extra hard, making the city one of the foreclosure centers of the country. Its unemployment rate neared 20 percent at the worst, and even as it improved it remained nearly twice the national level. In 2014, a WalletHub ranking put it dead last on a ranking of job prospects in 150 metro areas.

As if all of this were not enough, San Bernardino was also home to a uniquely dysfunctional city-governance system. The city is an unusual metropolitan parallel to the modern zero-sum gridlock of national politics that keeps the nation as a whole from matching attention and resources to serious challenges. In most of the country, you don't see this trickle down to the municipal level. Sadly for San Bernardino, national dysfunction has been matched on the local level.

Some cities we've seen run on the "strong mayor" principle; others have strong city managers. San Bernardino's unique and flawed charter gives it a "strong nobody" system of government. In theory, originally both an elected mayor and an appointed city manager had substantial authority to make decisions and address the city's problems. In reality, several interest groups within the city, most importantly the police and firefighters unions, had effective veto power over any decision they did not like. The odd structure had no real counterpart elsewhere in the country, and analysts had long pointed out its defects—and its consequences in depressing a sense of civic engagement and possibility. Back in 1981, a visiting panel from the American Institute of Architects said, "There is an almost tangible absence of consensus among the residents of San Bernardino about the sense of identity and unity of purpose—the spirit of the community-at-large."

The most important single result of its distorted system was clearest in the obscure-sounding but profoundly significant "Section 186" system of determining pay for the city's police and fire services. No elected or appointed official in San Bernardino had any direct control over pay for public safety workers—namely, police officers and firefighters. Instead salaries were set by a formula that, in effect, tied San Bernardino's pay levels to those of much richer cities across the state—for instance, Irvine and Santa Clarita, each which had a per capita income more than twice as high as San Bernardino's. (A team of researchers from George Mason University calculated that the per capita income of the cities San Bernardino was being indexed to was just over $62,000—whereas the income in San Bernardino itself was around $35,000.) Expenses in this category have made up more than 70 percent of the city's entire spending, but under the city's operating rules set down in the City of San Bernardino Charter, its officials were flatly forbidden to adjust, renegotiate, or trim the pay levels, even as they scrambled to cut costs elsewhere. The state's poorest taxpayers were locked into paying some of the highest salaries for their public servants. This city with a per capita income of $35,000 ended up paying its public safety workers total compensation of about $160,000 apiece, or about $40,000 more than the statewide average.

In 2014, there was a ballot measure to change this provision, and to set salaries by collective bargaining, as they are elsewhere in the state. The police and fire unions (whose members are not required to live in the city, and generally don't) fought back hard to block the measure, and won. Two years later, after court approval of the bankruptcy plan (which involved changes to the police officers' and firefighters' pay system) and large-scale efforts by the San Bernardino *Sun* and civic leaders to explain the situation—structural changes including a shift of fire-fighting responsibilities from the city's control to the county's—a charter reform passed. This "Measure L," which gives city leaders more control over salaries and finances, passed by a margin of 60 percent to 40 percent. The biggest hole through which the civic ship of state was taking on water had been patched. "This is the beginning of a new day for the city, one that a lot of people worked very hard for," Phil Savage, head of a civic committee that drafted the revised charter, said that evening, according to Ryan Hagen of the San Bernardino *Sun*. "This city can now become what it used to be and what it should be."

Could it actually become those things—what it was, what it should be? Here are the stories of a few teachers, civic activists, and neighborhood organizers already working to bring the city back. I start with Mike Gallo and Bill Clarke, two friends who have committed themselves to changing educational and job prospects for the city's young people.

By the time of our visit, when he was in his late fifties, Mike Gallo had become one of the wealthiest and most prominent citizens of San Bernardino. He is a stocky man with a mustache and brush haircut.

Gallo first came to town, in 1980, as a young second lieutenant at Norton Air Force Base. He left the military in the mid-1980s to work with Dan Goldin, later renowned as the longest-serving head of NASA, on a program to develop missile-launch vehicles at the TRW aerospace firm. This was during the Reagan administration's Strategic Defense Initiative buildup (known as the "Star Wars" program), when the Pentagon was funding a wide variety of missile-related programs. In 1992, Goldin left TRW to lead NASA; without him, TRW reduced its emphasis on the launch business. And in 1993, Gallo, who was in his midthirties, decided to do something different: he and some associates started their own firm. It was called Kelly Space & Technology, or KST, and its goal was to be a pioneer in the "reusable launch vehicle" business for military and civilian customers. KST became a bona fide technical and business success. It is still in the launch-vehicle business, along with a variety of other advanced-tech fields; it is still privately held and run by Gallo; and it operates in what are now the civilian facilities of the former Norton Air Force Base.

The company's story suggests the kind of person Mike Gallo is. Military- and defense-minded; trained as an engineer; and schooled in modern management practices, so that his conversation is peppered with references to the latest Harvard Business School report and motivational comments like "When you don't have a shared vision, you end up confusing activity with accomplishment. Because you haven't defined or, worse, prioritized your interests and investments, years later you end up just waking up tired, without any accomplishments."

Gallo talks passionately, and very quickly. In addition to calling to mind other civic leaders we'd met, like Chris Gardner of Eastport and Joe Max Higgins of the Golden Triangle, he also reminded me of some of the most forceful entrepreneurs I've come to know. These are people who built their business not on clever apps or software concepts but on tangible pieces of complex real-world equipment that have to be designed elegantly, manufactured precisely, and then sold (and maintained) one by one—with real-world life-and-death consequences if they fail. I didn't ask Gallo about either his national-level politics or his faith. But from the posters and photos in his office and the general vibe, I feel safe in assuming that he is an active church member who votes Republican.

That speculation interests me, because the mission that now engages Mike Gallo is creating better, fairer educational opportunities for the mainly poor, mainly Latino or African-American, mainly left-behind students in his adopted city's public school system, and helping build a local economy that can employ them.

Early in his time at KST, Gallo recognized that he was trying to build a high-tech company in an area with a low-skilled workforce. He became a founding member, and then the chairman, of the California Space Education and Workforce Institute, one of a list of regional-betterment efforts he became part of—including a role, at the request of Democratic governor Jerry Brown, to serve on the state's workforce investment board.

"I figure, why participate if you're not going to lead?" he responded, when I asked him why he did all this. "I don't just sit around. I don't sleep much. That's what I do. I do stuff."

Most of our modern economic-utility models have a hard time accounting for people who decide to commit so much of their attention, effort, and peace of mind to public-good causes of this sort. (Gallo's involvement is based on his belief in what is called "servant leadership," a doctrine about the duty to serve that has Christian scriptural roots.) This led Gallo to become more directly involved in local politics. He won a seat on the seven-member San Bernardino city school board in 2011. At his first meeting, he was elected the board's vice president; not long afterward, he became president. He came up for reelection to a four-year school board term in 2015 and had no concerted opposition.

Why did he bother to run in the first place, given the nightmare of school politics and the many other obligations he had? "I figure, you've got to get inside if you really hope to change the situation."

And what did he hope to change? "We have one of the poorest communities in the nation, fifty-four percent of the population on some kind of public assistance. And our public school system is requiring that our taxpayers further invest dollars that they don't have, for students just to barely get an entrance requirement for community college. That's tragic. I couldn't take that anymore. You've got to fix it."

Long before Gallo joined the school board, he'd set up a nonprofit—technically a 501(c)(3)—organization called Technical Employment Training, whose purpose is to train San Bernardino–area students for better opportunities there or elsewhere.

The San Bernardino drama is at surface level an economic story, but it is really a cultural and political one. It's a story of disengagement and suspicion: no one group feeling responsible for the others, or willing to extend any bond of trust.

That is what Mike Gallo said he most wanted to change. "We want to give our kids an incentive to stay here in our local region, rather than continuing the flight of our educated population somewhere else. We have to create that sense of hope, here, and opportunity and trust."

But why, again, here, with so much stacked so badly against him? When San Bernardino is a place he came to for work, not his original or generations-long home? And when almost any other city-government, school system, or student-parent population would start out far ahead in rankings? Why is this worthwhile—here?

"Why here? I *am here*. My kids are here. Now my grandchildren. You want to leave a place better off than when you found it. This is my place." There it was again, the comments about the hometown. From Sioux Falls to Eastport to Columbus to San Bernardino. Hometown was home.

Bill Clarke grew up in boomer-era Southern California in a non-college family. "My dad told me that I had to get a degree, and that I should get a job I really loved," Clarke related when I met him. "I was fortunate enough to do both." From the mid-1970s through the late 1980s, he worked for General Dynamics in Pomona, as a manager and trainer in their advanced-automation divisions. In the late 1980s, while beginning work on a doctorate in educational management, he switched to the staff of the local community college, San Bernardino Valley College, where he headed the training departments for advanced manufacturing and welding. And through all those years, 1974 through 2008, he spent the mornings teaching manufacturing-skills courses at Fontana High School.

These were the years when, with some ups and downs, Southern California was still generally booming, and the skills Clarke taught prepared students for higher-wage factory and construction jobs. But also during those years, "vocational education" and trade schools were falling out of public fashion, because of the conceit that white-collar positions automatically meant brighter prospects and better pay. (Why a "conceit"? The past decade has brought a reminder that skilled technical positions—in maintenance and repair of advanced machinery, in health-care fields and other laboratory work, in agricultural and food technology, in logistics and construction—are the era's fastest-growing "good" jobs.)

By 2010, San Bernardino Valley College had decided to phase out the machine shop Clarke had been running, and he was ready to retire from his teaching role there. By that time, he had become friends with Mike Gallo. "Mike said, 'Why don't you bring your equipment over to my place and teach here?'" Clarke told me. "I said, 'I don't want to teach anymore.' And then he said, 'Well, what if we started your own school?'"

The result was Technical Employment Training, Inc. (TET), a non-profit, 501(c)(3) trade school for adults that now operates in a building at the former Norton Air Force Base. Gallo became its CEO, and Clarke its president. Their ambition was to train the city's unemployed adults for middle-wage jobs available in the area's hospitals, warehouses, factories, and construction sites.

The nonprofit aspect of TET is important. When I spoke with Gallo, he inveighed against some for-profit trade schools as representing the worst in the student-debt syndrome. (They deserved more blame, he said, because they loaded debt onto mainly disadvantaged students, without carefully matching them to available jobs.) And Gallo and Clarke both emphasized the four-part strategy on which their TET approach was based:

- A "comprehensive, immersive training environment," in which students work in a machine shop six hours a day, five days a week, for six months.
- Nationally recognized credentials and certificates at the end of the program, so that the students' training is officially recognized and is transportable.
- A realistic, on-the-job training environment, in which students produce real products on real machinery and thus can go to employers with real-world experience.
- Placement connections with local employers, of whom the region's fastest-growing at the moment are in health care and logistics.

Multipoint plans naturally sound platitudinous. But TET's approach resembles strategies we had seen work elsewhere: for instance, the one at East Mississippi Community College. By early 2015, nearly four hundred local people had completed the full program at TET, Clarke said: "And we have put most of our graduates back to work in the high-tech manufacturing world. There are thousands of these high-tech jobs out there. We cannot train people fast enough for them."

TET was designed for adults who have already run into problems in the modern working world. Meanwhile, Gallo (as president of the school board), Clarke, and their allies were launching a parallel effort to prepare the city's schoolchildren to be ahead of the game.

Bill Clarke took me to see what this meant, in practice, at two public schools that would normally be classified as "troubled" or "have-not." As we drove up to Captain Leland Norton Elementary School ("Home of the Aviators"), we passed three police cars on patrol. There and at nearby Indian Springs High School ("Home of the Coyotes," where a large team of security officers were biking around the campus), virtually all students arrive with financial, educational, linguistic, or other family-background challenges. (It was at this same Indian Springs High School that Barack and Michelle Obama met families of the victims of the San Bernardino terrorist shootings in December 2015.)

These were the places where the San Bernardino school system made a commitment to training students for skilled technical jobs. Mike Gallo sent me a picture of a Norton third grader showing him the SolidWorks 3-D design program. He added in an e-mail, "This is the EXACT same program my rocket scientists use to develop the latest rocket test systems for NASA's space shuttle replacement vehicle. This is the student engagement environment and culture of high expectations that our students are now able to experience. This will transform San Bernardino and provide them with the passport to prosperity!"

At Indian Springs High School, Clarke showed me a fully outfitted machine-tool workshop in which students are trained and then certified for highly skilled trades. "We've built our elementary school lab, and middle school, and high school, so that soon students here will have a genuine pathway," Clarke told me. "By 2017, all seventeen thousand students in all San Bernardino schools will leave one of our nine high schools with real-world credentials in a growth-demand sector." These sectors, according to Clarke, include health care and medical technology (strong in the region), logistics and transportation (ditto), and manufacturing. This model—giving all students a "normal" education, but also equipping them with technical skills—is one we've seen in action elsewhere and have come to respect.

Can any of this happen? Are the odds too stiff? I don't know. By itself will it solve San Bernardino's problems? Certainly not.

But after spending time with people like these and in their classrooms and with their students, I do know two things. One is that the school system is now moving forward rather than back. The other is that in a famously "failed city" with a long-struggling school system, people are working hard to give others a better chance.

Another high school in town, San Bernardino's Cajon High School (Cajon is pronounced *ca-HONE*), lies near the foot of the San Gabriel and San Bernardino Mountains and is the "Home of the Cowboys." The school graduates about six hundred seniors each year. Some are bound for colleges from the Ivy League to the California state systems. Others will also head to the military or to jobs at places like the local Target or a Stater Bros. supermarket.

Cajon is a Title I school, which means it receives supplemental funds to help right the balance for its low-income and at-risk student population. After I spent a few days at Cajon in the spring, a mantra kept running through my mind: This school is changing lives, and sometimes even saving lives, *one student at a time.*

A variety of programs help keep the students in school and graduating. Cal-SAFE provides day care on-site for students with infants. Credit Recovery guides students to make up credits that have been lost somehow along the way. For some of the most troubled students, creative holistic solutions are there, like the Ladies Club, which offers "I am wonderful" classes to build self-esteem, an "angel closet" brimming with free clothing, and a Thanksgiving dinner served with turkey and the trimmings of social graces. The promise of a pink sash draping the commencement robe awaits those who succeed.

Some programs are run by the students themselves: Best Buddies, for students helping mentally disabled students; the Link Crew, for mentorships between upperclassmen and entering ninth graders; and University Prep Club, for older students to work with younger ones on college-prep skills and calendars.

The school also helps the students' entire families with a food bank, ESL classes for parents as well as students, and computer classes for adults. The California National Guard runs a Cadet Corps on campus.

And then there is AVID. The acronym stands for Advancement Via Individual Determination, a nationwide program with specially trained teachers to get students ready for college. "Get ready" means inculcating the students, most of whom will be the first in their families to go to college, with a mind-set that puts college on their radar and hones their skills both to get them to college and to be successful there.

The AVID program is a two-way street: students receive intense one-by-one attention from their AVID teacher (and as it turns out, from each other) and they commit to a complete package of reading, writing, talking, and thinking for their AVID classwork, as well as to taking some advanced-level high school courses, like AP courses.

This rote description doesn't begin to do justice to what I saw in the AVID class at Cajon High School and what I heard from the dozen or so students who talked with me. I learned about AVID from the program's teacher when I visited, Chris Peters—or "Peters," as the students all seem to call him.

The most dramatic statements came from the students. They talked about their home lives and the value of finding a "family" with their AVID class. They were aware of their pioneering first-to-college places in their families. And they were brimming with ambition.

Here, in their own words:

- "Before this advisory period, I didn't know the importance of a support system. I was gonna drop out, be on the street. In my home, there is selling drugs, alcoholism. All the drama. Something's wrong. I'm tired of being a peacemaker."
- "We're like a family. In class, we're more of a family. I never would have thought of it."
- "I'll be the first to go to college. I want to change the pattern of the family, to create a new era."

- "The program pushes us to explore yourself, make something of yourself. I want to find a cure for cancer. Or [go into] cardiology. Or neurology."
- "I want to do neonatal nursing."
- "My family wanted me to work at the local grocery store, without anything more."
- "I want to be a certified medical assistant. I want an MA in psychology. I want to be a counselor and a CPA."
- "I want to do criminal psychology. At home, I hear, 'I will kill you,' and they think that is pretty much okay. What makes people think that is okay? The cops come by our house all the time. I know I can do better. I will try so hard."
- "I want to do social work. My dad did drugs. I want to get others out of that."
- "I want to do police work. When the police come by, my family tries to cover for my uncles. I realize the police are there to protect people and the community. I was put there [in my family] for a reason. I'm not left off the hook."
- "I want to do computer engineering. My parents came illegally to the U.S. They heard about the DREAM Act on the news, and a social worker helped us with the process. I have a permit to stay and study."
- "I want to do criminal justice."

And how do their lives look several years out, once the students have gone on to chase those dreams? They pointed to the difficulty and importance of getting out of town (some families drove them out of the house; some held them too close) and the lessons they learned. Money is a prominent obstacle: lack of it first, then managing it if it comes their way. All the students, whether in real time or in hindsight, valued the personal attention from their teachers, like Peters, whose words replayed in their heads when they needed them.

*From a 2007 graduate:* "AVID was a true blessing for me. I really cannot imagine where my life would have gone without this stable program and caring teachers to help direct me. I was able to get into a four-year university after graduation. I decided to attend Cal State University, Northridge, and ended up graduating with a bachelor's in sociology last May, 2012. My parents were not very supportive with my decision to move over an hour away from home to attend college when Cal State, San Bernardino, was right next door; because of this, I had to figure out a way to pay for college and living expenses on my own. In all honesty, I can say that it was not always easy and I worked sometimes two or three jobs to support my choice of going away for school, but in the end I got much more out of the experience. It made me stronger, wiser, independent, and proud of myself. Not only that, but nowadays my parents respect my decision. College was a great experience, yet extremely busy and tiring."

*From a 2008 graduate:* "Upon graduating, I took the leap and decided to attend UC Santa Barbara. It was a tough decision. I was reluctant not only because it was 'far' away from home, but also because I knew I would be competing against people from privileged backgrounds. I figured these kids would be much better prepared than I, and that turned out to be true. However, this realization did not discourage me, and it should not discourage you. After holistically receiving the worst grades of my life during my first quarter at UCSB, I improved my GPA every single quarter subsequently and graduated with distinction honors as a history major in 2012. . . . My time at UCSB also broadened my horizons and showed me that a kid from San Bernardino can make it just as far as the kid from the suburbs in Orange County. This mentality is what pushed me to apply to law school and take another shot at success. I just finished my first year at the University of California, Hastings College of the Law. Law school is tough, so if you ever think about applying, then don't take the decision lightly. I am happy with my decision and am currently clerking for the Los Angeles County Public Defender's Office."

\* \* \*

Jim and I sat down to pizza and beer with a half-dozen millennials at a bar in San Bernardino. It was about eight months before the infamous shootings took place in December 2015.

About two years before that, the young people had assembled themselves into a loose organization, motivated by anger they felt about the awful state of affairs in their hometown, on the verge of declaring bankruptcy. "I was *pissed off*," Michael Segura told us. "By the time I was old enough to vote, everything was in such terrible shape in San Bernardino."

They clearly loved their town and were ready to pick up and do something about it. The Thinkers and Dreamers, as they describe themselves, were dreaming big. From early on, they said, "We are a movement, not an organization." They called themselves San Bernardino Generation Now (SBGN).

In their efforts to educate, engage, and eventually empower a new generation of leaders, some of those in SBGN turned to their strength: art. Several of the members were artists. They knew what they could do themselves as artists, and they knew the people to network with in the San Bernardino art world. They could imagine a way, through their art, to the "how" of building civic engagement.

Aiming ultimately to increase voter turnout, SBGN set out to educate by filming interviews with candidates about the issues that would be the most interesting to young voters. They went into high school government classes to talk about local government and voting. They invited candidates and government officials to community events that they built around music, food, and visual arts.

They made themselves obvious and accessible to other young people around town, painting murals in battered-looking areas, rehabilitating parks, planting gardens, picking up trash, and generally keeping on the move. They were not only actors in their own good deeds, but models for others to copy. People started showing up and joining their efforts.

These young people of San Bernardino Generation Now—men and women, Latino and black and white and Asian and multiracial in various combinations, some college-trained and some not—made a strong impression on us, probably because the challenge they took on was so immense. Their approach was initially artistic, but their goals were civic, cultural, and political.

We asked the same question of them, and about them, that we had of the likes of Mike Gallo and Bill Clarke: Why? Given all the obstacles in San Bernardino, why did young people like this bother—rather than simply moving someplace else? People with choices have often chosen just to leave environments like this one. Why did they soldier on?

In addition to modeling the change and behavior they hoped to see, two other themes came through the discussion.

*Anger.* Across the country, we saw "negative self-image"—stemming from being from someplace that most people mocked—as having powerful possibilities, both good and bad. The bad side is obvious. The good side is the "we'll show them!" motivation that rang through efforts in the Golden Triangle and so many other places, including San Bernardino.

*Faith.* Many of the people working to change this troubled town said that religion was part of their motivation. For better and worse, faith has always been one of the great non-"rational" motivators—along with family, nationalism, place-based loyalties, romantic love, and the like. But religious organizations are clearly a big factor in the effort to improve San Bernardino. For instance, a group called ICUC, Inland Congregations United for Change, and its director, Tom Dolan, have been inspirations for Generation Now. Among other lessons they conveyed was the non-obvious point that the group should not incorporate itself as a normal 501(c)(3) nonprofit group. As a normal nonprofit, it could not engage directly in local politics—and changing the political complexion of the city is an important part of SBGN's goal.

"San Bernardino is absolutely coming up," Jennica Billins said. "But I hope it doesn't come up just in the usual way, with some other people moving in. We'd like to make it work with our own people."

# Riverside, California

A generation ago, the nearby cities of Riverside and San Bernardino might have seemed to have almost comparable prospects. Each was the namesake, county seat, and main commercial center of its county. They're barely a dozen miles apart, both built along the usually dry bed of the Santa Ana River, with scenic mountains all around. Both had expanded during California's long post–World War II boom but also suffered the boom-related effects of sprawl development, congested traffic, water shortage, and, especially, smog. Each had a large, nearby air force base—March in the canyonlands outside Riverside; Norton in a gravelly, dry streambed within San Bernardino—that was an important boost for the economy of the town.

Riverside had started out on a different trajectory, with orange growing and tourism as the bases for its economy rather than the railroads, steelworks, and other blue-collar industries that were dominant in San Bernardino. Kevin Starr, the great chronicler of California history (and by chance a professor of mine in college, when he was a twenty-something graduate student), once called Riverside the classic citrus town of the West, and San Bernardino a classic transportation town. But through my childhood in the 1950s and 1960s in the town of Redlands, which was much smaller than either of these cities and located roughly a dozen miles from each of them, people spoke of San Bernardino and Riverside as parts of a natural pairing, rather than as stark contrasts.

A major element in Riverside's modern story was the state's decision, during the expansive governorship of Pat Brown in the late 1950s, to convert what had been an agricultural experiment station into a full campus of the well-respected University of California system. That has become the core of a major higher-education complex in Riverside, one that brings some forty thousand students and tens of thousands of faculty members and support staffers to town. San Bernardino has a community college and a branch of the Cal State system but not a comparable research university. When the two towns were on an even footing, the big federal legal center was in downtown San Bernardino. In the 1970s, Riverside attracted the U.S. attorneys' offices, several federal courthouses, and the associated legal business to its downtown instead. When San Bernardino officials were preparing their plans to escape bankruptcy in 2015 and 2016, this change of locale added an extra small humiliation: they had to get in their cars and take the short but traffic-choked drive down I-215 to present the plans to a federal judge sitting in Riverside.

San Bernardino's reliance on heavy industry made it more vulnerable to disruption during difficult times. But the surprise we found in talking with representatives of both towns was how much a cultural and governing difference mattered in Riverside's ascent, and in San Bernardino's long struggles.

At a small barbecue restaurant in Riverside, I met Ronald Loveridge. If he had done his work in a bigger East Coast town, more people around the country would probably recognize his name. Loveridge, who grew up in northern California and was student-body president and valedictorian at the University of the Pacific, in Stockton, went on to get his doctorate in political science at Stanford and then took a teaching position at the relatively new University of California, Riverside. In his early forties, he ran for and won a seat on the Riverside city council in 1979. "Why go from the academy to elected office?" he asked in an essay about his time as mayor—a question that was relevant since, to the best of his knowledge, no other full-time professor in the University of California system had held elective city office. He said there were a number of reasons to take the plunge, prime among them the nearly unlivable impact of smog in inland Southern California at the time.

I did know what he was talking about. As a high school student, I'd been to track meets where you fell over coughing, and tennis matches where you could hardly see the person serving from the other side of the court. Knowledge of those years tempered some of my horror at China's air pollution during our time there. But when Loveridge first came to Riverside, more than half of the days per year had Stage 1 smog emergencies, and almost a quarter had Stage 2, in which people were supposed to restrict their activity. (For comparison: now entire years go by with no Stage 1 alerts.)

Loveridge ran for mayor in 1993—and ran again, and again, and again, until he had been elected to five straight four-year terms. He finally stepped down as mayor in 2012, having spent thirty-two years in city office (while still teaching at UC Riverside).

What, I asked, turned the city around? Confronting the air-quality emergency was the immediate challenge, and dealing with it was, of course, not just a local issue but a statewide one. "Smog then, in the sixties and seventies, was unavoidable and terrible," he told me. "Republican, Democratic, conservative, liberal—you saw it, and breathed it. And it took years to cope with it. You'd work so hard, and people would say, Why is the air still so bad?"

As the state and the region began enacting increasingly ambitious air-quality programs, the next big challenge for Riverside was one common to many cities from the 1970s onward: its downtown, which had taken on the hollowed-out and derelict look of many cities where business was moving toward the suburbs. The situation was more acute in Riverside than in some other cities, because one property loomed so large.

This was the Mission Inn, a fantastical Spanish-Moorish-Hollywood structure built mainly in the early 1900s in the middle of Riverside's downtown, and very popular over the next half century as a stylish Southern California resort. Pat and Richard Nixon were married there, as was Bette Davis. Ronald and Nancy Reagan went there on their honeymoon. When U.S. presidents made swings through the West, it was a usual stop. In the main lobby, you can't miss the oversized chair made especially for President William Howard Taft. The Mission Inn hosted writers, Hollywood stars, Amelia Earhart, Andrew Carnegie, and Helen Keller. The hotel had the role later associated with Palm Springs—and as Palm Springs became more popular and developed, the Mission Inn slowly faded. In the mid-1970s, it was sold to the city's redevelopment agency. A decade later, it had changed hands several times, and it then closed altogether for some seven years—a huge, vacant, strange eyesore occupying a full block at the heart of downtown.

"I don't know a successful city that doesn't have a strong downtown," Loveridge said when I spoke with him. The city government helped find grants for, and a new owner of, the Mission Inn—which reopened in the 1990s and is now successful. We stayed overnight at the hotel, wending through mazes of hallways to reach our room, which overlooked the courtyard abloom in Southern California flora, where diners enjoyed old-time splendor. We toured the public rooms, including an art gallery, a music room, a chapel, an extensive collection of Asian artifacts, the Famous Fliers' Wall, festooned with copper wings commemorating famous fliers who had come to the hotel, and drooled over a set of rooms called "Authors' Row" where—you guessed it—famous authors have stayed to work. We lingered over beers in the Presidential Lounge.

Loveridge led an investment in public art through the downtown area, and walking and bike paths to bring students and families downtown, and other elements that were becoming familiar to us from cities across the country. In an effort known as the Riverside Renaissance, the city channeled more than $1.5 billion in public and private investment into downtown-recovery and other public works.

Near the end of Loveridge's term, he commissioned a survey from an independent polling organization, which found that some 85 percent of the people in the city felt it was heading in "the right direction." It concluded, "Riversiders, across racial, age, and income groups, are uniformly happy with their overall quality of life and proud to live and work here." I am wary of any report that says "uniformly," but there was little dissent about the city turning itself around.

———

A few days before I met Ronald Loveridge, Deb and I had spent several hours downtown with Loveridge's successor, Mayor Rusty Bailey, a fifth-generation Riversider from an orange-growing family who had gone to West Point and become an army helicopter pilot, then decided to come back home. An athletic man in his forties, he greeted us early in the morning as he dismounted from his bike, having ridden in from his home to city hall. We had breakfast at a coffee shop that was across a brick-paved walking street from the now-busy Mission Inn itself. As we sat and ate at an outdoor table, passersby stopped every minute or two to say hello to their mayor and ask him about local schools or redevelopment plans.

After we'd finished breakfast—big, gooey huevos rancheros for me, something neater for Deb, a fruit selection for the mayor—we walked toward his office in city hall, with its expansive outdoor deck and views of the whole city, across the local hills and out to Redlands. We strolled down the pedestrian-only Main Street mall, whose "Peace Walk" section was decorated at regular intervals with larger-than-life-sized statues of world figures from Martin Luther King to Mahatma Gandhi, and locally renowned leaders like Ysmael Villegas, who was born in the Mexican-American part of Riverside and died in combat in the Philippines during World War II. He was just a day short of twenty-one years old when he was killed; after the war, Harry Truman conveyed a posthumous Medal of Honor to his family.

A statue of Cesar Chavez is there as well, along with representations of farmworkers crouched over to pick crops like those that grew in fields around Riverside. Another depicts Dosan, born as Ahn Chang Ho, a hero of Korea's struggle for independence from Japan before World War II and a leader of California's sizable Asian-immigrant community. The city's population is slightly more Latino than the state's as a whole—just over half in Riverside, versus about 40 percent for the state, with about a third of Riverside's people being "non-Hispanic white" and about 8 percent each for African-Americans and Asian-Americans. (For the whole state in 2015, the figures were around 40 percent for both Latinos and non-Hispanic whites, 13 percent for those of Asian background, and 6 percent for blacks.) The Peace Walk and the statues that line it were products of Ronald Loveridge's campaign to revive the downtown.

"Aside from D.C., there's no other city with something like this," Loveridge, who had by then left office, said when the final statue on the walk, of Cesar Chavez, was unveiled in 2013. "It's a social justice walkway."

Why had Riverside been able to pull off its recovery act—the Mission Inn and surrounding retail areas, the once-decrepit and now viable Fox Theater, the tech start-ups, the medical and university complexes—when its onetime counterpart San Bernardino had struggled so badly? Rusty Bailey ran through the list of obvious reasons: the presence of the University of California, which attracted other institutions; the unique handicap of San Bernardino's governing structure; the series of economic blows San Bernardino had endured as all its major employers shut down. (March Air Force Base, in the canyonland outside Riverside, remained open, transitioning to an air reserve base, even as San Bernardino's mainstay Norton shut down.)

But then he emphasized two additional structural issues. One was Riverside's public ownership of the city utilities—water, electricity, and sewage—which was a legacy of early-1900s Progressive Era reform and which kept what would have been utility-company profits in the city's treasury. Riverside has this in common with a handful of other California cities, the best known of which is Pasadena. "There was that visionary community spirit from the start," he said. "It gave us a chance to control our fiscal destiny. There have been political raids on it over the past century," he noted, mainly from conservatives who thought this looked like city-scale socialism, "but we've been able to defend it."

The other factor was what Bailey called the "density of social capital," a phrase I'd also heard from Ronald Loveridge. It was the idea that Riverside had been, and remained, a place that people felt they were from, and *of.*

"It's a place for families," Bailey said—with parks, strong public schools, outdoor festivals, recreation centers. Starting around 2000, as housing prices soared in the coastal cities of Los Angeles and Orange County, Riverside became an attractive, affordable residential alternative for young families. "We've mainly been managing population growth through that time," Bailey said. Some forty thousand students attend the universities, professional schools, and community colleges in the area. "But," he pointed out, "it's retained its sense of place."

We'd gotten used to asking people around the country what cities were their models and targets. People in Sioux Falls said they were looking at Omaha. In Greenville, they were looking at Atlanta—but in a cautionary way, to avoid the effects of congestion and sprawl. Fresno was looking at Davis or Sacramento. Poor San Bernardino was too hard-pressed to think about more than itself. Rusty Bailey said that Riverside had now dared think of places like Pasadena and Santa Barbara as its next models—though he was quick to add, as anyone in California would, that such cities were now struggling with the effects of being so attractive to so many people, starting with astronomical real estate prices.

"We still want to be a place for families, where people can afford to live," he said—and then began telling us about how much a new light-rail system would enhance the livability and sustainability of the town.

I asked Bailey the same question I'd asked Don Ness in Duluth, and Knox White in Greenville, and other mayors whose city's success might seem to be the basis of their own future political ambitions. Did he want to run for higher office?

"Higher?" he said. "This is the highest office right here."

The entire California navel orange industry originated with two small trees that suffragist, abolitionist, and spiritualist Eliza Tibbets planted outside her Riverside kitchen door in 1873.

Tibbets was fifty years old at the time, having come from the East to Riverside by transcontinental train to San Francisco, then by boat to Los Angeles, then finally traveling overland to the Inland Empire to settle with her husband, Luther Tibbets. Luther had arrived a few years earlier to join a new utopian community that was based on ideals of political justice.

Tibbets's earlier life was, well, colorful. She was a member of the Swedenborgian church, whose adherents followed the teachings of the mystic and scientist Emanuel Swedenborg. She became a spiritualist, well known as an accomplished medium for her sought-after séances and fortune-telling. She and Luther had tried and failed to establish a new colony for freedmen and whites in Virginia in 1867. Then, as a suffragist, she'd marched with Frederick Douglass to Washington in 1871.

Riverside was remote in the 1870s; you forded the Santa Ana River to get to San Bernardino when you needed to find skilled labor, and to get a newspaper you drove a buckboard wagon to Los Angeles.

Just a few months into life in California, Eliza, searching for a stable cash crop for her family, contacted an acquaintance from her days in Washington, D.C., a horticulturalist with the Department of Agriculture named William Saunders, who experimented with imported plants in his greenhouse on the National Mall. Her timing was perfect. Saunders had just heard about a promising species of oranges from Bahia in Brazil. He received a dozen young trees and grafted buds from them onto rootstocks. Not all of them survived, but two that he sent to Eliza Tibbets, at her request, flourished in Riverside's soil and climate.

Thus began the story of Washington navel oranges in California. Part of the tale, apocryphal or not, is that Tibbets nurtured along the two little trees with dirty dishwater from her kitchen. Jim says that in his youth, he was taken on a ritual pilgrimage with his elementary school class from next-door Redlands to pay respects at the site of Eliza's original tree. I spoke with Eliza's great-great-granddaughter Patricia Ortlieb, an artist and psychotherapist who, with coauthor Peter Economy, memorialized Eliza in the heavily researched book, *Creating an Orange Utopia.*

The first fruit was picked in 1875, from the trees of Tibbets's neighbors, to whom Eliza had sold buds to graft. By 1882, half a million so-named Washington navels were growing in California, all as grafts from the two original Tibbets trees. The industry changed the state and the region. In Riverside, the allied industries of irrigation systems, grove expansion, orange sorting and packing, and refrigerated shipping catapulted the town's prosperity to the highest per capita income in the entire United States in 1893.

But the Tibbetses had missed out. Eliza and Luther—complex,

unusual, impetuous, litigious, and definitely not the best financial planners—had gone for quick money selling their buds for grafting instead of planting groves themselves. They also subdivided their land and sold off much of their property during the real estate boom that accompanied the explosion of the orange industry.

By 1887, the (first) area real estate bubble had burst. The Tibbetses continued their lifelong string of legal disputes and lost their remaining property in foreclosure. Eliza Tibbets died at a spiritualist colony near Santa Barbara in 1898.

Today, there is a stunning bronze statue of a ballerina-like Eliza Tibbets in the company of social justice heroes along Riverside's downtown Peace Walk. It portrays a beautiful young woman with a remarkably pinched waist and arms raised in hope and an uplifting posture. The loveliness of the statue is all the more striking when you compare it with any photo of Eliza Tibbets taken during her lifetime. She actually showed a stronger resemblance to Queen Victoria than to a ballerina.

Eliza Tibbets was buried in Evergreen Cemetery in Riverside, in a grave that remained unmarked until nearly a century later, in 1993.

# Redlands, California

Redlands, near both San Bernardino and Riverside, is my own hometown, a city I had in mind throughout this journey.

From the perspective of either of the bigger cities, Redlands has always had it easy. It is smaller and more contained than the other two; with a better-educated, richer, and whiter population than the other two cities; and with a greater proportion of its residential area filled with pre–World War II homes that range from California Craftsman–style bungalows to Georgian- or Victorian-style houses. In many details, from its streetside look, to its abundance of cultural and civic-uplift organizations, to its series of public concerts dating back more than a century, Redlands presents itself as a special, coherent community. This is all the more reason why Joan Didion's famous "Some Dreamers of the Golden Dream" article for *The Saturday Evening Post* in the 1960s came as such a shock to Redlands residents. "This is the California where it is easy to Dial-A-Devotion, but hard to buy a book," she wrote. "This is the country . . . of the teased hair and the Capris and the girls for whom all life's promise comes down to a waltz-length white wedding dress and the birth of a Kimberly or a Sherry or a Debbi and a Tijuana divorce and a return to hairdressers' school."

But nothing in Redlands' past or its self-conception seems immediately to answer a question that parallels Riverside's rise and San Bernardino's long struggle. That question is why Redlands, with its orange groves and its medical complexes and its beautiful small university, should have ended up as the home of one of the world's dominant middle-sized tech companies, whose growth and success have profoundly changed the town.

The company is Esri; its current name is derived from what started out in the 1960s as a two-person nonprofit called the Environmental Systems Research Institute. Esri is now very much for-profit (and still privately owned by its founders, Jack and Laura Dangermond), with tens of thousands of employees worldwide and some four thousand in Redlands itself. Most are well paid—if perhaps not by Silicon Valley standards, then certainly by the standards of the Inland Empire, where living expenses in general are much lower and attractive houses go for perhaps one-quarter what they would cost in Palo Alto or Menlo Park. Nearly all of these workers are well educated, as engineers, project managers, and sales officials for a high-tech company. Although people at Esri don't like this comparison, the company's mainstay ArcGIS software can be thought of as the heavy-duty professional version of Google Earth. The company was the commercial pioneer in the GIS field—the abbreviation stands for "geographic information systems"—and its customers include most national, regional, and city governments around the world, as well as most big companies, who use it for everything from planning new store-location sites to keeping track of pothole repairs and traffic flow in cities.

Most members of Esri's staff in Redlands come from someplace else—India, the United Kingdom, France, Germany, Canada, Australia, China, and computer science departments across the United States. They have brought to Redlands a high-end international and cosmopolitan note it would lack otherwise, except for the international medical talent attracted by Loma Linda's medical school and hospital and academic recruits at the University of Redlands. Through much of the twentieth century, Redlands' ethnic makeup had been an Anglo/Latino balance. Among the whites, there were large groups of Dutch immigrants and their descendants (as in Holland, Michigan); Mormons (whose forebears settled the area in the 1840s and 1850s before being recalled to

Utah by Brigham Young); and Dust Bowl–era émigrés from the Plains and the South. Among the Latinos, nearly all were Mexican, and many of those were from families that had been in the area for several generations, having first come north after the Mexican Revolution of the early 1900s. Now, a big tech company changes the faces of the people on the streets and in the parks and at the schools. The new arrivals have also meant a new demand for restaurants, entertainment, local retail stores, and other attributes of cities that seem economically alive—and museums, concerts, and other markers of a healthy civic culture.

Why and how? In the simplest terms, it is all because the founders, Jack and Laura Dangermond, had grown up in Redlands and met in high school there—and they decided that a relatively remote small-town setting was better for the overall life balance they wanted to have, and the corporate culture they wanted to create, than either Cambridge, Massachusetts, where Jack had done original GIS work as a graduate student at Harvard, or the San Francisco area, which was the default location for new tech companies even in the late 1960s.

Jack Dangermond's father was an immigrant from Holland, who worked as a gardener and ran a small nursery with his wife, who was American-born but whose parents were themselves also from Holland. (Jack's original degree was in landscape architecture.) Laura's mother worked in the local post office, and her father repaired televisions. Jack's parents knew mine, but I didn't come to more than a nodding acquaintance with him and Laura until we all were grown. I moved away from Redlands, they moved back, and I asked them: Why here? Why did you return, and stay?

Their answers have boiled down to a variant of the theme we first heard from Jeff Padnos and Bob Peacock and then encountered in different forms in different places along the way. "Why here?" we had asked Padnos about his little town of Holland and Peacock about Eastport? "Where else!" each had, in essence, replied, half jokingly and half in earnest. The Dangermonds have given a similar half-and-half response about staying in Redlands.

The half that's joking is Jack Dangermond's immediate riff-retort, "Who *wouldn't* want to be in Redlands?" When he's talking with me, it's followed by "And of course we know you'll move back here sooner or later." When he's talking with someone from Paris or Boston or Palo Alto, his tone seems nondefensive, as if signaling a willingness to laugh about the improbability of his company's setting.

The extended version of the argument, which I've heard on visits to Esri's headquarters and, for instance, when talking with him after he's completed hour-long keynote addresses to crowds of sixteen thousand international attendees at Esri's annual User Conference in San Diego (where Dangermond, lanky and loose-limbed in his early seventies, is as focused as Steve Jobs was during his Apple presentations), is that a remote location is a trade-off, but a valuable one. He and Laura get to live as "normal" a life as anyone in their positions might: he drives around in a beat-up car, he eats in the local restaurants, he's known as a benefactor and by far the richest man in town, but otherwise he has a surprisingly undistorted existence. He is something of a rock star at his annual conferences of many thousands, but in Redlands, he is quietly and quite anonymously Jack. And while the company loses some potential recruits who prefer the buzz of Palo Alto or West Los Angeles, and while Jack spends probably half of the year on the road with customers or at conferences, usually flying (on a commercial flight) from nearby Ontario airport, location reinforces the cultural model he has in mind for the company. Twenty-something singles are less interested in Redlands than in Santa Monica; thirty-something parents with young children like the idea of the town's lower-cost housing, five-minute commutes, strong public schools. This, in turn, has helped the company reinforce a lower-key, less-flashy, minimal-number-of-jerks cultural model—in contrast, say, to Apple's or Microsoft's reputation in their fastest-growing, elbows-out years. (In late December of 2017, Jack and Laura Dangermond attracted the attention of the environmental and philanthropic world, with the announcement that they had given $165 million to preserve, in perpetuity, thirty-eight-square miles of unspoiled California coastline, around Point Conception. "We're very intentionally setting out a model that we hope other people with money will follow," Jack Dangermond told me when I asked him about the donation. "We'd like other wealthy people to think, 'Let's do what the Dangermonds did.' We'd like them to copy us.")

Perhaps there is no larger Redlands model to draw from to illustrate the transformation of this one town, by this one company. Jack and Laura Dangermond liked Redlands because they grew up there—and when I think of small towns where we might live, this is naturally first on my list, for just the same reason. The broader significance is—once again—how often we came across stories like this, albeit about someplace else. Bob Peacock thought Eastport was the only place to be. Tracy Taft didn't start in Ajo, nor Larry Groce in Charleston, but once each of them found the right place, it was *theirs*. Even in an age of flux and seeming homogenization, regional imprinting is strong. And while we often hear of that in an immobilizing sense, as with people "trapped" in declining coal regions, such local patriotism turns up surprisingly frequently as an explanation for which towns or regions developed the way they did. You can't make a formula out of hoping that a locally raised couple goes off for schooling and then decides that the right place for a tech start-up is back home—and decades later, that company becomes a big international success. But these local attachments, plus local ownership, and the sense of "local patriotism" we felt in places otherwise as dissimilar as Sioux Falls and the Golden Triangle and Redlands, really matter in the fate of a town.

Ryan Berk, a millennial Redlander, grew up nurturing a passion for food and traveling, a route that took him around the world and eventually back to dream in his native Southern California.

Berk was one of the first to attend and graduate from the Grove School, the small Montessori-based charter school in Redlands. The school is centered on a working farm among the orange groves of the town. Students tend animals and grow crops, some of which they sell to local restaurants. Like all the other students there, Berk did internships and service work. And from his early teens, he was a dishwasher and busboy for a Thai family at their local restaurant.

After high school, Berk went on to culinary school. He saved up his money and set out to roam the world as a photojournalist, absorbing a core lesson he has since applied: food and local culture are essentially intertwined. Back home, Berk was again working at a restaurant, with some of its ingredients, frozen fish, packed in supercoolants. "Liquid nitrogen," Berk mused. "Why not use it to quickly freeze ice cream?"

Berk was not the first to think of this possibility, but he came to it on his own, he told me. He started playing around with the idea and discovered that, indeed, you could almost instantly freeze the liquid base into a smooth, creamy ice cream. And that was when it all came together: the lessons he described from the Grove School, to "just get out there and do it"; a passion for food; his self-described perfectionism for what he does.

I found Ryan Berk one sunny midday just before Christmas as I was stopping in at his À la Minute ice cream shop and he was heading out. With a small-town friendliness, seeming as if he had all the time in the world, he told me his own personal story, the new story of starting the business with his wife, Cassie, who runs the financial side of the company, and about how their business works.

The list of ice creams on the À la Minute board says a lot about the creativity of the owners and their commitment to being local. The flavors are inspired by local ingredients: honey from Soffel Farms, mint from Berk's own garden, local Redlands oranges, and nearby-sourced olive oil, apples, lavender, pumpkins, and more that come and go with the seasons. I chose the orange honey. I was in Redlands, after all. It was truly delicious, and I say that with confidence as an ice cream connoisseur.

Then Berk asked if I'd like to see his even newer shop, Parliament Chocolate, just a few blocks away. Parliament, as in "a parliament of owls," was named for an early tenant of the building, the White Owl Café. The chocolate shop had opened just a few days earlier.

Parliament Chocolate is the Berks' second dream. Once they had saved enough from ice cream, they turned to chocolate. Makes sense to me. He talked about the process of making his chocolate, from sourcing his beans on a recent trip to small farms in Belize and Guatemala, to outfitting the shop, to producing the exquisite finished candies. It was all in the details. "Look at that drain!" he said exuberantly, pointing to the floor and then to every carefully chosen fixture, tile, machine, and drawing in the tiny, gleaming shop.

I watched the Parliament chocolate makers tend big, rotating vats of chocolate, ladle small scoops onto trays, and decorate them like miniature works of art.

The five-minute amble from Citrus Avenue along Fifth Street to East Redlands Boulevard is irresistible. Between the À la Minute ice cream shop and Parliament Chocolate is Augie's Coffee House. Austin Amento, along with his father, an electrical contractor, bought Augie's, a small coffee shop, about five years ago. They didn't know much about the business but saw an opportunity in an uncertain economic climate. After a few years, they decided to go all in, to ramp up. Their mission and brand would set them apart: finding the best coffee beans; controlling every aspect of the bean roasting, the coffee brewing, and the costs; creating a new ambience for the customers.

The shop took on a fresh new look. The Amentos met with growers who came to California, and they eventually traveled to Colombia to see and buy for themselves. They went to San Francisco to learn about roasting. And they catered to their clientele, whom Austin describes as "everyone," meaning people from the University of Redlands, the high schoolers, and the tech crowd from Esri. Amento said that one of Augie's aims is to educate their customers as the Amentos educated themselves, switching brews as many as four times a day for comparisons and contrasts. Some customers, Amento told me, would come in that many times to learn about and to drink the different coffees. Augie's hooked me. Every time I went to the shop to buy beans, I was offered a coffee or tea on the house, which I found charming and personal, and a complement to the conversations struck up with other customers standing in line. "So, did you go to the beer fest at Sylvan Park last week?"

From ice cream to chocolate to coffee, microbreweries—including the granddaddy of them all, Hangar 24—and sandwich shops and small boutiques, Redlands is peppered with inventive start-ups and charming options. A lot of the loveliest classic buildings will never return, having given way to "modern" buildings of the 1960s and 1970s. But others show promise in preservation. Today's Starbucks is in a building preserved from the beloved former La Rosita drive-in. The old *Redlands*

*Daily Facts* building will be the site of the new Museum of Redlands. Soon to follow, everyone hopes, will be the redevelopment of the failed downtown Redlands Mall, now a deserted enclosed 1960s mall that serves the community only with its big outdoor parking lot. We heard that the plan calls for a mixed-use complex: street-level retail plus upper-story condos, a renovation model we met all across the country. Then there are new markets, talk of a train, biking routes already in place, and the protection of groves and green hills.

\* \* \*

I think my favorite institution in Redlands, where I've spent enough time during my life that I earned a pin from the town elders identifying me as an official "Redlander," is the YMCA (Jim would probably argue that his favorite is the Smiley Library.) The Y has a special feature: the annual circus production. For those of you who have always dreamed of running off to join the circus, here is your second-best chance: move to Redlands and join the YMCA. This is not just a tumbler's wannabe circus. It is the Great Y Circus, founded by a former performer with the Ringling Brothers and Barnum & Bailey Circus, Roy Coble, shortly after he moved to town in 1929. There are high-flying acts, trapeze stunts, maneuvers on the rings, unicycles, acrobatics, juggling, you name it, with performers as young as toddlers who train for several months each year and play to sell-out crowds inside the YMCA gym, which has extra-high ceilings designed to accommodate the show. Adults I know in town still have their childhood Y unicycles hanging in their garages.

I didn't sign up for the Y circus, but I did get a membership to swim in the pool regularly while we were in Redlands as a base for West Coast reporting and then writing. By now, I calculate that during our time on the road, I've swum multiple times in more than twenty pools, plus about eight lakes or rivers. To figure further, let's round up and say that thirty spots at ten times each at one thousand meters a pop, coming to three hundred thousand meters or nearly two hundred miles of swimming across the country.

I found YMCAs in more than half the towns we visited. Several others had pool complexes run by the city or the county or organizations like the Salvation Army.

You might be tempted to think a pool is a pool, but I have to tell you that you'd be wrong. A public pool, like a public library, often reveals something about the spirit and culture of a town, sometimes its bright side and sometimes its dark.

The ethos of the public pools that I experienced is to be democratic and generous. The staff there welcome strangers; they make day passes easy; they seem generally pleased to see you.

In Rapid City, South Dakota, when I scurried in for the last forty-five minutes of the open hours at the gleaming new Y, the woman at the desk said I surely wouldn't get my money's worth (five dollars) with so little time left in the day, so she'd catch me on the next visit. I swam as fast as I could for as long as I had, and when I left, she asked if I had enjoyed my swim. I returned the next day, careful to have allowed more time.

Swimming at public pools is a chance to rub shoulders with people I wouldn't ordinarily meet as a visitor in town. In Redlands, there was a woman I saw regularly who "lived" at the Y during a good chunk of every midday I swam there. She methodically lined up her overstuffed plastic bags along the locker room counter. She showered long and hot, and rested often on a comfortable chair. Her legs were red and swollen, and did not look good at all. She reminded me of the homeless people I frequently saw organizing themselves to spend the day inside public libraries. I asked about the woman once, wondering about her story. The staff told me quietly that oh, yes, they knew about her. "She doesn't seem to cause anyone problems" was the incomplete but discreet answer.

I saw cross sections of the towns at many of the public pools.

In Burlington, Vermont, the old pool in the old building's old basement was empty except for me and, improbably, a very big and strong African-American guy, a twenty-something swimmer, who left a big wake and seemed to be training seriously.

In Holland, Michigan, a town founded by Dutch Calvinists, I first saw many of the town's nearly 25 percent Hispanic population on a Saturday afternoon when many of the families poured into the Holland Community Aquatic Center, the children exuberant. The names of the swim team record holders on the bragging board included Dutch Vans and Hispanic Garcías.

In Columbus, Mississippi, a few stray octogenarians paddled around in the overheated pool. Only in Mississippi did I find a reminder that the Y was, in fact, the Young Men's *Christian* Association: a big bowl at the reception desk held what I first mistook for candy and later discovered were actually tiny paper scrolls, each with a typewritten proverb.

In the heart of Greenville, South Carolina, a short walk from gentrified Main Street, on one side, and the low-income urban neighborhood, on the other, is one of the more bustling public rec centers where I swam, the Salvation Army Ray and Joan Kroc Corps Community Center, where all slices of Greenville showed up. There are sports courts, a child-care room, a soccer field, tennis courts, gyms, a Boys & Girls Club, two pools, and, at the end of building, a chapel. There are moms in yoga clothes, older ladies in water exercise classes, and little kids from the next door A. J. Whittenberg Elementary School of Engineering, who regularly walk the few hundred yards to take lessons and swim in the pool.

In Austin, Texas, I swam in the brisk spring-fed WPA-era Deep Eddy Pool all through my graduate school years, and again later whenever we returned, summer or not. The deep end is full of serious lap swimmers, the shallow end packed with families with young kids, and the showers are set in an open-air tropical paradise where you can look up at live oaks while you rinse off.

At my neighborhood pool in Washington, D.C., a town that proudly boasts at least twenty-nine public pools, there is a woman who visits almost every summer morning at a picnic table in the park next to the pool, reading the paper or a book, her two corgi-looking dogs resting on the cool concrete beside her. She is there when I arrive and there when I leave. We say our hellos. (I was anticipating a British accent, but she actually spoke with a southern lilt.) One day I commented on the grapes she was eating, which she offered to share with me, and on the small pile of tangerines she had balanced into a pyramid. They reminded me of offerings at a Buddhist shrine. Every day since, even if she has come and gone early, she leaves a little something arranged on the picnic table for passersby like me to enjoy—a design from her orange peels, some fruit, and, once, a delicate bird's nest.

If you missed the 1950s, or if you hanker for them again, you can recapture them at a few of the pools I visited.

In Sioux Falls, I chose the Frank Olson Pool, run by the city's Department of Parks and Rec in a leafy residential part of town. It was filled with kids who had ridden their bikes to the pool, propped them against the chain-link fences, and were whiling away their afternoons until it was time to ride home for dinner. This was surely part of what people in Sioux Falls meant when they described their life there as "safe" and "easy."

In Bend, Oregon, the town's Juniper Swim and Fitness Center has one of the nicest aquatic areas I have ever seen, set within the natural beauty of this picture-perfect high desert town. There is a waterslide worthy of a theme park. The schedule of the fifty-meter pool cycled through open lap swims, team practices, masters swim sessions, and rec swims, with teenage lifeguards moving the center divider seamlessly and like clockwork around lap swimmers so no one's routines would be disturbed. I savored the rhythm of the summer days.

In tiny Winters, California, the Bobbie Greenwood pool sits right next to the public library and behind the high school. Bobbie Greenwood, a living legend of Winters, settled there as a young woman and built the pool out of her love of swimming, for all the Winters children to enjoy. I swam there for a rather embarrassing fee of one dollar (although I did have to change in the restroom and dry off with paper towels), as a group of ten-year-old boys darted back and forth between the library and the pool.

Dodge City, Kansas, recently built a brand-new pool, called—what else?—the Long Branch Lagoon, in keeping with the town's Wild West theme. When we visited, the center was quickly becoming hugely popular with the town's kids, with its waterslides, fifty-meter pool, kids' splash, everything! Best of all for me, the pool opened very early for lap swimmers and the small swim team; some of those swimmers were waiting eagerly outside the gates by 6:30 in the morning.

I had to be a little more resourceful to find my way to the lakes and rivers around America. Sometimes, I admit, I jumped in and swam just to say I did it. One of those occasions involved the very chilly Snake River in Clarkston, Washington, in the heart of Lewis and Clark country. The Snake River was a bit scary to swim in—which should not be surprising, given what one interpretation of its name conjured up for me.

As part of a Great Lakes personal swimming mission, I swam along the tame eastern shore of Lake Michigan in Holland. It recalled my hometown of Vermilion, Ohio, on the south shore of Lake Erie, with families, beach chairs and umbrellas, kids frolicking, and sailboats darting back and forth closely offshore. I also swam in Lake Erie, in Erie, Pennsylvania, with its eleven different Presque Isle beaches. I couldn't find a swimmable spot in Duluth's Lake Superior or on the edge of the Bay of Fundy in Eastport, Maine. But I did swim off the coast of Portland, where it was so cold that I braved my way in, warmed up a little, then rather soon jumped out before I froze to death. I understood why our host insisted on "spotting" me while I swam, lest I pass out and slip under from the cold, unnoticed. The edge of Lake Champlain was sparkling clear but rocky and cold, so I quickly gave it up and scampered over to Burlington's YMCA pool instead. And Chautauqua Lake was murky, foggy, and wavy in August, but I swam anyway.

# Fresno, California

When I was growing up, Fresno and the other main cities of California's Central Valley—Stockton, Merced, Modesto—were in my imagination just farther-north versions of Riverside or San Bernardino. Modesto, where the director George Lucas had grown up, was distinctive as the setting of the 1970s movie *American Graffiti*. But beyond that, I would have had trouble giving details on how the cities differed or how their prospects compared.

The Central Valley is an even starker illustration of California's coast-and-interior contrast than the Inland Empire of San Bernardino and Riverside, and of America's conjunction of wealth and poverty, as well. Starting around 2013, a tech-world venture capitalist was proposing that California be split into six states. (As a sign of California's human scale: if the population were equally divided into sixths, each one of the new entities would have more people than most of today's existing states.) That was not going to happen, but if it had, the proposed new state of Central California, with Fresno as its assumed capital and the Central Valley as its main territory, would have been one of the richest states in agricultural output, as by far the leading source of fruits and vegetables in the country, but the poorest in terms of per capita income. Within California, it has the highest unemployment rates and incidence of poverty, and the most serious pollution and public health challenges.

The first brief exploratory look we had at Fresno was not encouraging. We arrived near dusk and checked into a battered downtown hotel. Walking the streets after dark seemed dicey enough that we decided to stay in the hotel and eat sandwiches and granola bars rather than going on foot to look for restaurants. What we saw of Fresno's historic downtown the next day, especially the famed Fulton Street shopping mall that in the 1960s had been celebrated as an example of progressive urban design and in the 2010s was full of pawnshops and used-clothing bodegas, made us think that Fresno was mainly an example of the "before" stage of civic recovery.

But through the course of follow-up visits that year and afterward, there was no city about which we changed our minds more fully than Fresno. The first time we heard the cheesy civic-booster motto— "Fresno? It's Fres-*yes*!!"—all we noticed was the cheesiness. After a while we started saying it ourselves, with the understanding that the corny tone was self-aware and was part of the city's effort to turn its challenges and no-frills image into sources of "we'll show you!" motivation.

As we'd seen in Mississippi, in West Virginia, in San Bernardino, and in places in between, individuals and communities in smaller-town America can be acutely aware of being condescended to by big city fashionable America. That awareness—the realization of connoting the opposite of "the Bay Area" or "Cambridge" or "Westside L.A."— plays a part in their efforts at turnaround. When Governor Jerry Brown announced that construction for California's controversial (and in my view strategically valuable) north-south high-speed rail line would begin neither in the north, around San Francisco, nor in the south, around Los Angeles or San Diego, but instead in the middle, in Fresno, comedians and critical politicians began calling it "the train to nowhere." Nowhere, of course, is where the people of Fresno live. Sometimes condescension is spirit breaking. Sometimes it is motivating.

"Solving problems anyplace is valiant, but if you can solve them in Fresno, you can solve them anywhere," an entrepreneur named Jake Soberal, then in his early thirties, told us during our first visit to Fresno. By this time, we had learned to recognize an attitude we had observed in many other places, from Maine to Mississippi to southern Arizona:

namely, a determination to respond to difficult circumstances so as to shape, rather than just accept, a city's long-term fate.

Soberal grew up in nearby Clovis, went east to Hofstra and then the University of North Carolina for college, and worked as a big-city lawyer. He was the commencement speaker at Clovis High School, and he later told a business magazine, "I can distinctly remember sitting up there, this arrogant eighteen-year-old, thinking, you know, these folks really ought to enjoy this speech because they'll never see me here again." But he came back to Fresno to try to develop Fresno's own technology businesses and, crucially, also to train its community-college, non-college, and non-high-school-degree populations for better opportunities in the tech world. "If this project can work right here," he said, "in the middle of a lot of the biggest challenges facing American cities, what might it do elsewhere?"

Local boosterism is a familiar part of the American fabric. But the effort in Fres-*yes*! seemed worth notice as something more than self-delusion or salesmanship.

On our second trip to Fresno, we got an appointment with Ashley Swearengin and her staff. Swearengin, a striking blond woman with large, light blue eyes, then in her early forties, was in her second term as Fresno's mayor. Deb says her first reaction to Swearengin was "distractingly stunning" and her second was "embarrassed to have that reaction," given Swearengin's professionalism and laserlike focus. Swearengin was a liberal Republican in a strongly Democratic state, but she had proven very popular. She was elected with 55 percent of the vote in 2008 and reelected with 75 percent four years later. But because of California's term-limit laws, she could not do what Knox White had done in Greenville or Gary Doty in Duluth or even the controversial Ed Pawlowski in Allentown, and stay in the job as long as she retained support. She would be "termed out" in 2016, so she knew that the clock was running out on getting her long-term plans under way.

When we saw her in her office, she walked over to two large-scale maps on the wall, which she said summed up the city's challenge. The problem boiled down to: sprawl. One of the maps showed the city's structures by date of construction. The classic downtown, on a grid pattern with imposing banks and department stores, was built from the late 1800s through World War II. Then the standard postwar developments, with shopping centers and tract-home estates, sprawled their way north of town until they hit the natural limit of the San Joaquin River. (One of the northernmost, and newest, developments was, of course, named San Joaquin River Estates.)

The other map plotted out the city's residents by income. The poorest districts had the darkest blue coloring; the richest were in red. Not surprisingly for cities that were still in the sprawl-dispersion rather than downtown-recovery phases of development, there was a near-perfect correlation between the two maps. The older and closer to downtown the part of Fresno, the poorer and less white its residents were. (The city's population as a whole is roughly half Latino; the downtown districts, much more so.) The newer and farther away from downtown, the whiter and richer the residents.

I wanted to ask Swearengin about her plans. "Fresno," I began, "is famous as a victim of sprawl—"

"I'm not sure I'd use the word 'victim,'" she broke in. "We were the perpetrators! It wasn't anyone's malign intention. But these were the unintended consequences of not having a strategic view. No one was thinking that just because you're swinging hammers and punching out subdivisions, you're not creating employment levels—or an urban core." Among the most dramatic results was the devastation of what had once been the city's pride, its pedestrian-only Fulton Mall.

"This is why I ran in 2008," she said, as she pointed at the maps that presented a vision for the city's potential revival through changes in transport lines and downtown recovery. "Here you see the downtown as the city's heart, and Blackstone"—a main north-south drag—"as the spine, residential areas as the lungs. . . ." She continued on, through the parks and trails and bike lanes and gathering places that "would give life to the city."

———

There was a bittersweet aspect to Fresno's effort, because it involved—literally—bulldozing away a previous generation's attempts to save this same downtown.

In the early 1960s, Fresno commissioned the famed modernist landscape architect Garrett Eckbo to design a modern, art-adorned, car-free pedestrian strolling mall through the heart of the city's downtown. For a while it was celebrated as a work of both artistic and commercial genius. But then, as happened with so many other pedestrian-only, no-car malls across the country, the business and street life of Fresno relocated to the sprawl malls of the northern suburbs. The tracts of Fulton Street, once beautiful and busy, were still adorned with their original statuary but had precious few customers.

To save its downtown, Fresno decided during Swearengin's time on a step that had been applied in a number of other cities as well. Namely: bulldozing the expensive pedestrian model and reopening the streets to cars.

It was in Greenville that we'd first been introduced to the idea that allowing cars back into a downtown—on comparatively narrow streets, rather than huge speed-through boulevards—could actually be a formula for modern urban revival, by making stores and restaurants more easily available to more customers. "Fresno was the second city to have this kind of pedestrian-only mall," explained Craig Scharton, whose business card identified him as the publican of Peeve's Public House & Local Market, a holdout in the quasi-ruins of the old Fulton Mall. (The first was Grand Rapids, Michigan.) "We'll be the one hundredth–plus to dismantle it." All the evidence, he and many others said, had swung to the Greenville/Sioux Falls/Allentown/Riverside approach of controlled car access to a rebounding downtown.

"How will we know if this plan is working?" Ashley Swearengin said during one of our meetings. "Look down at our historic main street"—she indicated the blocks along the Fulton Street pedestrian mall—"and you'll see the greatest stock of historic buildings anywhere in central California. We've got good bones!" The problem, she said, was that most of the buildings now stood vacant, because the idea of being blocked off from car traffic no longer made sense.

"The city invested millions in public art, so no one wanted to take it out," she said. "But by the 1980s, the *Los Angeles Times* was already writing about the mall as a ghost town." By 2013, she had convinced the city council to support her idea of reopening the mall to car traffic—Fresno's version of Knox White's gamble in tearing down a highway overpass. Based on that vote, she said, investors had already begun to come in.

I told Ashley Swearengin, Craig Scharton, CEO of the Downtown Fresno Partnership Aaron Blair, and others I met in Fresno that I was still unconvinced by the comeback story. Then Jake Soberal took me on a drive and asked me to imagine what was not there yet.

Where is Fresno on the arc of recovery? I asked him.

"I drive down Van Ness," he said, referring to a main downtown street, "to work each day. And if you're a person from outside you probably think, 'Well, you've got some historic buildings here. But it's a pretty crummy downtown, compared to what's happening in other places in America.'"

I told him that was pretty much what I thought.

"But when I drive down that street," he said, "I realize that my friend Joe is doing a project *there,* and someone is doing a project *there,* and this building is under lease, and that building is about to be reopened. And I look at it and think, 'It's done!'

"I mean this earnestly," he added, "and I'm not being flippant. Downtown revitalization in Fresno is *done,* in terms of making the decisions. Now we just have to let it happen."

We first heard about the Kepler Neighborhood School during a conversation at Peeve's Pub, in downtown Fresno. That was not unusual, as Peeve's is the place to go when you want to know what's happening in Fresno. Or was. Much to our deep dismay, and certainly even more so to Fresnans', Peeve's suspended operations about a year and a half after we first visited. Peeve's was in the Fulton Mall, which was about to undergo a complete face-lift. Peeve's proprietor, the seemingly omnipresent Craig Scharton, became the manager of the Fulton Mall renovation project.

When Jim finished talking about beer, I asked Scharton about local schools, and he pointed us to the bar to chat with Steve Skibbie, who was pouring beers that night. Skibbie, his wife, Shiela, and their two young children live in the nearby downtown Lowell area of Fresno, a diverse, progressive-minded neighborhood that is one of those driving Fresno toward what local activists hope will be its best possible future.

That is how I found the Kepler Neighborhood School, a K–8 charter school named for the seventeenth-century German mathematician and astronomer Johannes Kepler. Shiela Skibbie founded the school with Valerie Blackburn in 2013. The two educators huddled for almost three years over research and charter writing; seeking teachers, a principal, students, a building, and a board; and persuading parents, the down-town neighborhood, and—unanimously—the Fresno school board to approve the Kepler charter.

Kepler's mission began with a deep commitment to service learning, which means, as the name suggests, combining community service with regular academic instruction. The Kepler community sees the school as an integral player in building civic and cultural strength in downtown Fresno, and they see its young students becoming self-aware citizens who can help make that happen.

How do you do this? A key ingredient is an understanding of the community where the school is located, plus concrete ideas of how the school will integrate itself and its curriculum into that community.

Within the school's walkable radius are the places in downtown Fresno that have become satellite classrooms of Kepler. For example, the Fulton Mall (home to Peeve's), for its makeover; the Lowell Community Garden for its urban agriculture; the Mural District for arts, burgeoning tech development, and makerspace; city hall; the trendy and bohemian Tower District for its new urban culture and performances; the school's home turf of the Lowell neighborhood for exposure to its urban chal-lenges (read: crime, gangs, drugs, slumlords).

Teachers in each grade build academics and real-world skills into special themes and projects within the neighborhood.

That year, the eighth graders' focus was called City Makeover. Stu-dents worked with historians to understand the plans for a full-circle evolution of the Fulton Mall from a downtown street to a pedestrian street and back again. They worked with engineers and architects to learn about construction and renovations for the street and its historic buildings. They learned about communicating with city administrators and politicians, and the politics of change. They learned how to write business plans for current and future commerce. And they confronted some real-world episodes, such as when the beloved Peeve's Pub shuttered.

The fifth graders' theme was called Cast Iron Chef. Principal Christine Montanez told me how the students made garden boxes and learned about seed selection and planting seasons, as part of a broader understanding of agriculture and food supply. She also described a series of disappointments and problems the students addressed: an unanticipated freeze killed their newly planted seeds, an irrigation pipe broke, and a roach infestation emerged.

Kepler takes its students out to serve the community and brings the community in. Students stage drama performances for a local community care center. They host local Art Hop nights to show off their own creations. They go out to the makerspace, Ideaworks, to learn woodworking. Kepler invites Revolution Foods to help teach the elective course Chefs and Seams (read: home ec). It sends kids for sports to a gym from the World Impact religious organization. Kepler fourth graders built owl boxes for Critter Creek, an animal rehabilitation center, which returned the favor by bringing owls and eagles to the school for demonstrations. The students marched the several blocks to city hall to meet with then-mayor Ashley Swearengin on National School Choice week, and then spoke about it on local radio.

Kepler draws students from all over the Fresno area, but it especially wants to draw in neighborhood kids, says Montanez. In many of the start-up schools I visited, I heard about the challenges of getting the school population going. It requires a lot of trust from parents to be the first on board with a new school. The student population of Kepler started with some two hundred kids. And then, as with many start-up schools I visited, Kepler's popularity exploded. Kepler more than doubled its enrollment, to 465, by the 2017–18 school year. In the spring of 2017, Kepler moved from a modest rented space in Cornerstone Conference Center to a renovated 1913 historic building, originally a car and truck dealership, just a few blocks away. The new structure has much more space, a beautiful façade of arched windows, wooden columns, and a terra-cotta tile roof.

It took me two visits to warm up to Fresno. On the first, which was really just a scouting trip, all I could see was the sketchy urban activity outside our downtown hotel. Jim started calling it a crack hotel. That was a little harsh, but you get the picture.

Nonetheless, we decided to return. We booked a different hotel for our next visit, which we arranged to coincide with Fresno's Rogue Festival, the popular fringe festival started in 2002 by local dramatist, director, and impresario Marcel Nunis.

Along our way, by then, we had been to art hops, local theater productions, plein air festivals, concerts, outdoor plays, parades, musical performances, and one-off exhibits. We had visited artist-in-residence programs like the one in Eastport. We learned about shared art studios and makerspaces, like the ones in the Franklinton neighborhood in Columbus, Ohio. We had taken self-guided tours of murals, sculptures, and galleries from Sioux Falls to Greenville, Rapid City, Ajo, and Holland, and we would later take others in Laramie, Dodge City, and Winters, California.

We had no idea what we were in for with the Rogue Festival. On opening night, the Rogue audience was lined up early along the sidewalk in front of the old Tower Theater. People were clearly primed for the pregame show of fire-breathers, men on stilts, and artists who walked the line handing out personal postcards featuring their work. Opening night was a teaser, where some thirty of the festival's performers (out of more than seventy) gave two-minute shotgun glimpses of what was to come later. The popular emcees, Jonathon Hogan and Amy Querin, appeared in a revolving collection of costumes, monitoring the show with stopwatch precision, walking out to slow-clap each act off the stage at exactly second number 121. Some of the performers were Fresnans, while others came from everywhere. This was indeed art on the fringe, with a savvy audience cheering on the artists who were pushing their own edges.

A few days earlier, we had met with Rogue veterans Jonathon Hogan and Heather Parish at a brewpub a few blocks down from the theater in the Tower District. They toured us around the festival venues, from gallery spaces to coffee shops, and talked to us about the importance of the Rogue Festival, the Tower District, and the art scene in general to Fresno.

Sure, the festival and the arts had revitalized the neighborhood and brought in a lot of business, but what the arts have done for the culture and self-image of Fresno may be the most important part. The arts had become a reason for creative people to come to Fresno and for those already there to reach for their own dreams. There was now license to *be creative* in Fresno.

How does this work? It starts with real estate. A nice house in Fresno costs a few hundred thousand dollars, rather than the few million, as in Los Angeles or San Francisco. In Fresno, you can do anything—start a family, start a business, start a school, start a studio—because *you can afford it.*

And being out of the shadow of the coast cities, Fresno was free to do things for itself and cultivate its own homegrown, edgy personality. "The Tower District is the bohemia of Fresno," said Parish. "And *Fresno is the bohemia of California.*"

On each visit, we checked in with a tech company called Bitwise Industries, located in the Mural District of Fresno's tattered-but-struggling-to-recover downtown. We were intrigued by its story because of the way it shed light on conditions distinctive to Fresno and the Central Valley of California, but also about the ways in which it reflected trends we've seen in every corner of the country.

The similarities involved Bitwise's basic setup, which resembled tech-promotion and start-up efforts we'd already seen from South Carolina to

South Dakota and including points in between. The familiar elements of this tech-fostering package include a physical space where start-up companies can get going at low cost and with shared facilities; the location of that space typically in a historic downtown area, as part of a larger downtown-renewal effort; courses on relevant skills, from coding to accounting to marketing; connections with more-established local businesses plus financiers and customers; and collaborative agreements with research universities, community colleges, and even K–12 schools in the region.

Bitwise is a "normal" tech-promoting effort in those ways. Jake Soberal, its co-founder and CEO, said he didn't like the term "incubator," since many of the businesses he worked with were already well established. Still, for descriptive convenience, the company's efforts resemble those of incubators elsewhere.

Bitwise was illustrative of its city and region, and about the challenges of trying to create a tech economy, with the high-wage jobs and spin-off business stimulation that presumably means, in a place far removed from the dominant tech centers of the East and West Coasts.

Soberal and his Bitwise co-founder, Irma Olguin Jr., described their organization as the "mother ship of technology" in the Fresno region. In practice, that means that their parent organization combines several of the start-up functions sometimes dispersed among different groups. The company's Hashtag Fresno component offers low-cost ($39 per month), tech-equipped workspaces for individuals or small teams. Its Geekwise Academy, a coding and tech-skills school, is developing an intriguing range of specialized programs. "This is the most significant thing we do," Soberal said of his courses for adult learners. "Most training programs take people from being out of the line, and put them in the back of the line," he said. "They get people all trained up for a poor job. We want to get them ready for the front of the line, for jobs in the highest-growth industry on the planet," by which he meant anything requiring coding skills. Its Shift3 Technologies does contract tech projects for firms in the region and elsewhere, employing local developers, designers, and marketers. And its headquarters building in the Mural District contains separate offices for more than two dozen tech firms.

In 2016, the company opened a new, much larger office-and-classroom space in a long-vacant building it had remodeled in Fresno's historic downtown. Soberal said that some forty tech companies will be housed there, along with more workspaces, classrooms, offices for lawyers or accountants or other allied professionals, et cetera.

For now, the focus is on the challenge of building a tech industry in a part of the country with an agricultural-centric economy, no major nearby research universities, and a reputation as a place that ambitious young people move away from rather than return to.

But what could be the business base for a tech economy that was more than a three-hour drive from either Los Angeles or San Francisco and, thus, would lack all the place-based advantages that came automatically to firms in San Francisco, Boston, or New York? I asked Soberal, How can you fight the trend toward the concentration of national and global talent in a handful of hyperexpensive but also hyperproductive big centers?

He had two replies, the first of which was that the global centers and the regional ones could prosper together—the latter using their advantage of such dramatically lower operating costs. "The per-person total cost of a very happy mid-career developer here is $80,000 to $100,000," Soberal said. "That's half, or less than half, of the cost in the Bay Area" or other big tech centers. "If we can get a critical mass of people here in Fresno who are competent and capable, national and global companies will choose to expand their operations here. The Silicon Valley and Boston and Portland will continue to grow. And so will Fresno—and Des Moines and Wichita. Software and tech have not been a zero-sum game."

You could think of this as the "outsourcing" part of the Bitwise/Greater Fresno tech vision. The other part was more intriguing, in that it matched the observation we've heard in the most successful-seeming cities across the country. That is the insistence on "knowing who we really are" in a given city or region—whether that was voiced in city hall, or public libraries, or schools, or about downtown design or infrastructure—and choosing strategies based on an honest assessment of an area's advantages and handicaps.

What Fresno really is, is the regional capital of one of the world's most important agricultural areas. "The economy is global, but significant strengths are local," Soberal said. "Industries tend to develop in a regional way." He went on to argue (1) that agriculture involves many of humanity's most important challenges, starting with sustainability in all its aspects; (2) that agriculture was still relatively behind in applying modern data tools to its operations; and (3) that, therefore, tech companies in the Central Valley had an opportunity to become the leaders in a field of ever-increasing importance.

"My guess is that five to ten percent of the tech need of the farming industry is now being met," he said. As compared to the flood of tech talent and investment capital that have vastly oversupplied the needs of the financial services industry or online commerce. "You could build a technology industry in Fresno based on that alone," he remarked, "not to mention the worldwide need in agriculture."

What kind of unmet need? I spoke with Derek Payton, a programmer who is CTO of a company called Edit LLC, which is based in the Bitwise building. He pointed out that modern farmers had an abundance of sensors—on soil moisture, sugar levels in fruit, you name it—but relatively poor tools for combining or analyzing data. You could contrast this with a hospital's intensive care unit, with displays of many important data all in one place. Payton's company was working on software to convert data from a wide variety of sources into a standard format so that it can be used for a kind of dashboard display.

"You think high tech, you don't think 'growing food,'" Payton told me. "You think 'Bay Area, self-driving cars, devices to make daily life easier.' But we've got a lot of farmers here with a lot of data they don't know what to do with. It can make a big difference to collect the data and put it in usable form."

And what would be a realistic ambition for Fresno? I asked Payton. "A realistic and positive scenario . . . ," he said. "It would be, when you think of tech in California, you'll think of the Bay Area, L.A., San Diego—and Fresno. There's definitely strong tech potential here."

At the north end of Fresno is a very different kind of school, ambitiously named the Center for Advanced Research and Technology (CART). This school began with the glimmer of an idea: that we could do better at educating students in the middle, who often "fall through the cracks," especially those who have trouble finding their way in a more traditional American high school environment.

The thirteen hundred CART students, eleventh and twelfth graders, come from fifteen schools around the city of Fresno and the smaller, more affluent adjacent town of Clovis. They spend half the day in their home high schools and the other half at CART. Rick Watson, who is CART's CEO (yes, CEO, not principal), said that in 1997 a group of educators and business and community leaders pulled together to imagine and assemble a career-track high school with a solid traditional academic footing, an infusion of technology, and, echoing Kepler, a spirit of real-worldism.

At CART, students choose from an array of courses that offer career-specific labs in fields from forensics to game design to law and order, robotics, biotech, engineering, business and finance, environmental science, psychology and human behavior, and many more. Each lab is taught by a team of three educators who have work experience in their fields, from TV to graphic design to pharmaceuticals.

Teams of students attack real-world projects from their fields; I heard about cloning carrots, making movies, designing online games, and building toys. CART takes advantage of its location among the high-tech business and agriculture efforts in the San Joaquin Valley; there are field trips to agriculture expos, aviation companies, and dairies. Students do internships or projects that take them to hospital operating rooms, senior centers, wildlife refuges, and the tech incubator Bitwise, which, in turn, offers them exposure to dozens of hot new tech companies.

CART's home is an airy former factory of the Danish water pump manufacturer Grundfos, whose U.S. birthplace was Fresno. The broad halls, big staircase, two-storied common area, and big-windowed classrooms create a space where kids can move freely and loosely. Banners depicting heroes like Eleanor Roosevelt, Bill Gates, George Lucas, Sandra Day O'Connor, and John Glenn decorate the halls.

I was talking for a while with Watson and the dean of curriculum and instruction, Bethany Garoupa, inside an all-purpose meeting room that looks out onto an open student gathering area, when a few students serenaded us with an impromptu (and respectable!) rendition of the Eagles' "Hotel California."

I toured the school with one of CART's enthusiastic student ambassadors. Harut Bareian is Armenian, part of Fresno's large immigrant farming population, which began arriving in the late nineteenth century. His home school is the Bullard High School in Fresno. He is on the biomedical track. Like many CART students, Harut has laid out his plan to attend community college for a few years before transferring to a four-year college. He dreams of becoming a pharmacist.

CART's hallmark career-track program couples with a mission that CEO Rick Watson considers equally important: developing the students' soft skills of confidence, self-esteem, and teamwork. This took me back to similar conversations at the Phinnize Fisher STEAM school in Greenville, which encourages the same kind of focus. There is nothing soft-sounding about CART's approach to soft skills. Teachers and administrators use terms like "take risks," "encouraged to fail," "get back on the horse," and "no one is expendable." In the team-based projects, a student who lets the team down badly can find himself demoted from responsibilities or even off the team.

While touring the school with Harut, I noticed a group of about ten people sitting around a table in the hall. I assumed they were visitors like me, who had also come to see the school. Wrong. This was a group of students from the multimedia track, dressed (better than me) for Professional Dress Day, meeting side by side with their equally young-looking teachers and mentors.

I sat with the group while the students talked through progress on their ten-week-long project, the production of a seven-minute video. This year's theme for the video teams was science fiction. The essential questions of their assignment: "How do imagination and technology contribute to our understanding of science, nature, and the human mind? How does the exploration of science and nature encourage us to dream of a better future?"

The soup-to-nuts tasks include writing an original story and script, casting actors, directing, filming, adding special effects, editing, promoting, and presenting the end product. The final package includes a documentary of the entire video production, with its many high and low points.

A few days later, Jim and I watched videos of about half of the previous year's twenty-two productions. The most remarkable part to us were the student-produced documentaries that accompanied each film. The students spoke about how doing this intense work taught them about perseverance, teamwork, satisfactions, and handling frustration, just the kinds of hard-to-measure soft skills that designers of education programs would wish for.

Just as the students from the AVID program in San Bernardino's Cajon High School reflected on the life-changing program and the attention from their teachers, the CART students sounded similar. The following words are from a CART graduate of 2014, a young woman who studied on the economics and finance track. Here is an excerpt from a blog post she entered on the CART website:

> Graduation is coming up in a few short weeks, and I can't believe that I'm about to be done with high school. In fact, it's hard to believe that I survived these past four years. I think I only survived these last two years because of CART.
>
> Attending CART is one of the best decisions that I have made in my life. While at CART, I have been challenged and pushed to become good in what I aim to do. I have struggled and stressed through projects, but reflecting back I can honestly say that I have enjoyed all of it, even if I didn't believe it at the time.
>
> This is my second year as a student in the Economics and Finance Lab. This lab and the teachers in it have helped me in more ways than I can count. I feel that I have gained so much knowledge in the business world that I am ready to be a part of it. During these two years, I have put together financial portfolios, gone on

two internships, created a non-profit, and am currently creating a for-profit business. None of these are things I would be able to do, especially not with such skill and precision like I have been able to, if not for CART. My teachers and this learning environment have provided me with plenty of real world experience that I feel I can jump into the business field now and survive.

In late March 2016, many of Fresno's leaders gathered for a "State of Downtown" gala to talk about plans for the Fulton Street mall. Mayor Swearengin was there, as well as the president of Fresno State, Joseph Castro; Aaron Blair of the Downtown Fresno Partnership; and others. The event was held in the downtown's historic, then run-down, now-being-renovated Pacific Southwest Building and drew a sold-out, standing-room-only crowd of many hundreds.

A centerpiece of the event was a video about the city's past and its future ambitions. "We are unapologetically Fresno," the announcer said near the beginning. "We are changing minds one visitor at a time."

"Unapologetically" was, of course, the key word. It's not one you'd hear in Cambridge or Brooklyn or Santa Monica—but it's one we had become hyperattuned to, from South Dakota to Mississippi to, now, the Central Valley. The rebuild-Fresno movement has unapologetically recognized the challenge of the city's self-image and determined to blast right through it.

I thought, as I watched the video, about what we had heard from people in Fresno on exactly this point.

From Ashley Swearengin, the mayor: "As mayor, I've run across this self-image question all the time. There are people who know every past failure of Fresno, and they can recite them routinely whenever we are discussing something new.

"But the generation now in their twenties and thirties does not reflect a defeatist attitude, like some of their parents. And the grandparents also don't have a defeatist outlook. They remember the city when it was on the cutting edge"—and the younger ones assume they can get there again, she added. To illustrate the generational split, the mayor mentioned that during a debate on Fresno redevelopment plans, a man in his twenties had tweeted a proposal for a new drinking game: Every time a middle-aged Fresnan responded to new proposals with a lamentation about crushed dreams in the past, the younger Fresnans would take a drink.

From Aaron Blair, who is from Ohio and had done urban-development work in Florida and Georgia before being recruited to come to Fresno: "When we came to look at Fresno, I also thought it had this little chip on its shoulder, which I actually like. Cleveland has some of that same feel to it, and so does some of the South. This is a situation I'm familiar with and like coming into. You want to see if we're good enough? Just watch! And I was excited by all the potential I saw."

Christopher Gabriel, a longtime stage actor turned local radio talk-show host, grew up and spent his early working life in big-city America—Chicago, Philadelphia, Los Angeles, New York, the Twin Cities—and came to Fresno after a stint in the also-revitalizing town of Fargo, North Dakota. "There was an energy and vibe in the room that was unmistakable," he said. "It wasn't just some feel-good moment. I've been to enough cities, I've seen enough of them rise from the dust, to sense that this was real. It was, Let's do this. Let's create everybody's collective legacy for the Central Valley.

"Sometimes people will hear me say that and react, 'Oh, you've just got this youthful energy about Fresno.' I'm in my fifties! I didn't move here just to go up to a larger market, or get more money. I moved here because I saw a city on the move, that has remarkable diversity, culinary and cultural and artistic. People here have been jaded, but if you can get outside yourself, you see an unpolished gem."

And once more from Jake Soberal: "What's the main thing making Fresno better? I believe that we have a generation of young people who do not want to adopt their parents' view of this place. Or the world's view. That is really, really significant. Increasingly we're able to count among those young people some of our most talented. Whereas before Fresno was famous for losing those people."

Soberal said that a number of local groups were interested in changing the prevailing views of the city, from the mayor to the downtown alliance. He supports those efforts, he said. "But the group of people involved in changing what others think about the city is smaller than the group of people who say, 'I don't care what you, Dad, might think about Fresno. There is real data that makes me excited about what I can do here.' That group is growing quite large, and the decisions they make are driven by data. They think, I can open a restaurant here, I can get a house here, I can build a company here. I don't care that you think Fresno sucks."

# Winters, California

A handful of times during our travels, we landed in a city on a hunch or a challenge. That was the case in Columbus, Mississippi, when high school English teacher Thomas Easterling enticed us there to compare his Mississippi School for Mathematics and Science with the acclaimed Governor's School for the Arts and Humanities, which we had seen and written about in Greenville, South Carolina. We took him up on the offer, and it worked out well. Both schools were amazing; both towns were surprising.

Our first visit to Winters, California, one of a pair we made before and then after our time in Fresno, began similarly. At a conference of California civic leaders, at the historic Ahwanee Hotel in Yosemite Park, we met Woody and Rebecca Fridae, both longtime teachers and civic activists in Winters. Woody was a former city council member and mayor; Rebecca, a leader at the public library. They talked about their town and enticed us to visit. "This is a town that is really trying to use every tool it can think of."

Before we arrived in Winters, we wondered whether the small northern California town would live up to the Fridaes' challenge and be "real" enough to illustrate the economic and cultural trends and tensions of the era. In photos, its downtown looked almost too perfect. The storefronts were restored brick structures from the classic era of American Main

Street design. Each springtime, the town held the month-long Plein Air Festival for artists. On one corner of the principal downtown intersection, where Railroad Street met Main, stood the Buckhorn Steakhouse, a frontier-themed fine dining establishment that drew customers from across California and beyond. Across from it was the Putah Creek Cafe, named for the oak-lined creek that twists around the town and looking as if it had been taken from the set of *Twin Peaks*, or even *Happy Days*. The signs on its windows advertised: LUNCH. DINNER. HOMEMADE PIES. On another corner was a public park, with benches and shade trees and a bandstand-gazebo. In the distance, past the creek, stretched vast stone-fruit and nut-tree orchards—walnuts, almonds, apricots, plums.

Up the block on Railroad were the offices of the *Winters Express*, a still-viable local weekly for a town of some eight thousand people. The *Express* was founded in 1884, and—as we discovered when we visited the town—had an office crammed with manual typewriters and other artifacts of a bygone era of publishing. A big pool table dominated the newsroom, and a game was in progress when we walked in. A few buildings down in the other direction, on Main, was the Palms Playhouse, occupying a Gay Nineties–era opera building and offering live-music performances several nights a week. Within a two-block range were two separate storefronts run by family-owned wineries, coupled with artisan cheesemakers.

With all its first-impression charms, would Winters be more than a copycat extension of the wine country an hour to the north, or a too-polished day-trip destination for the food and tech folks from San Francisco, barely ninety minutes west?

John Pickerel, a restaurateur and entrepreneur who moved to Winters to found the Buckhorn Steakhouse in the early 1980s, answered the question before we posed it. "The playhouse, the restaurants, the fancy bike shop, the wine outlets—they can attract people," he said. But the foundation of the local economy remains agriculture. "This town looks and feels like a midwestern town that just got dropped in California." He added, "And it's one of the highest-producing agricultural counties in the entire world—we're just off the charts."

Immediate evidence proving his point is the vast packinghouse of the

Mariani Nut Company, one of the world's leading walnut and almond producers and distributors, easy walking distance from the center of town.

At the time of our first visit, the viability of the area's agricultural base was newly called into question, because of the state's dire five-year drought. When Governor Jerry Brown was imposing mandatory water rationing on households across the state, and when city governments were jacking up utility rates and penalties for water waste, long-standing policies that favored farmers' claims to water became bitterly controversial. Even the calculations of how much water went to farms became embattled. If you measured all the moisture that fell on the state (or was drawn from the ground), farm use would amount to 30 or 40 percent. If you counted only purposeful human use—for drinking water, in industries, for irrigation, or other purposes, leaving out the flow that goes through rivers straight to the sea—the farming share becomes much larger. By any calculation, more water goes into agriculture in the state than into households and factories combined.

The nut orchards of Winters and its vicinity epitomized the tension: almonds and walnuts are extremely valuable cash crops because of rising demand around the world (notably China and the rest of Asia). They are more water-intensive, per pound of output, than most other crops. And the water to produce them was, especially in the drought years, drawn heavily from underground aquifers, whose levels were declining at an alarming pace.

Thus, at that moment in Winters, the farmers wrestled with the future of their industry, downtown businesses strove to keep it viable and attractive as a destination, and civic leaders, educators, and artists worked to preserve its heritage and strengthen its culture.

Almonds are indeed serious business in Winters, and we were told that you can tell a Winters native by the pronunciation of the word: "amun" rhymes with "famine." The joke goes that you have to shake the almond trees so hard to get the nuts to fall that you shake the "l" right out of the "amun."

Almonds and agriculture are serious business for even the children growing up in Winters. At Winters High School, nearly half the students are enrolled in agriculture classes. The options include an intro course in the history, economics, and production of California agriculture; ag business and management; farm practices and operations, including how to use and manage the machinery; animal and plant science. Lots of kids participate in the Future Farmers of America (FFA), with programs that incorporate public speaking, report writing, parliamentary procedure, and agriculture leadership training. Students in floriculture were already creating arrangements for a local business's Christmas party.

On a whiplash-rainy December day, I visited the school's off-campus "Ag site," just a few blocks from the main high school, which is next door to the public library and the town's swimming pool. The big warehouse space abuts the farm fields that were so soggy from the downpours of the so-called Pineapple Express roaring through the region (the beginning of what turned into at least a temporary respite from the years of drought) that we had to postpone our walking tour for a dryer day. The students grow tomatoes, pumpkins, ryegrass, grapes, peaches, and plums. Next year, with the help and guidance of local farmers, they planned to start an almond orchard. Inside the dry building, a group of freshmen was busy making black walnut and maple cutting boards, of which many would probably find their way under Winters' Christmas trees later that month.

Back at the high school, I talked with half a dozen upperclassmen in the school's small cafeteria about life in their small town, their school, and their families. They came from a variety of socioeconomic beginnings and upbringings: children of custodians and professors, of fruit packers, warehouse workers, librarians, mechanics, corrections officers, and managers. Some knew exactly what their parents did for a living, and others weren't quite sure of the companies where their parents worked. Some lived in blended families; others not. They were of means or of very little means. Some were first-generation Americans, and other families went very far back.

As in many California farming communities, the population of Winters is roughly half Latino. The median income here and in surrounding Yolo County is just at average level for the United States. That makes it higher than many other areas in California's Central Valley but much lower than much of the San Francisco Bay Area.

There were just five hundred kids in the high school. Most of them have been in school together since kindergarten. Not surprisingly, they talked about how they had bonded as a community of classmates after all these years.

They said their knowing one another so well—all the foibles and moments, good and bad—has made them close and accepting of one another. Their comments on one of the hot-button issues in American education culture struck me: if the occasional bullying comes up, they told me, the students take initiative themselves to stop it in its tracks with what they described as "we don't do this here" self-monitoring.

I asked about the occasional arrival of new students among their tight-knit classes, wondering how that might work out. They told me that it was a real event when a new student showed up. "We LOVE them. We fight to be their friend."

Being teenagers, the kids sharpened a wry sense of small-town life as they recited changes over the years. "It was a big deal when they took out the blinking light and replaced it with a stoplight!" one described, detailing the well-attended ceremony. And "Dollar General is coming! And a hotel!" "There used to be cool things here," another said, and they all added to the bygone list: a train, a movie theater, bowling.

The students admitted they knew their lives had been sheltered. And anticipating leaving for college soon, they spoke with a kind of push-pull tension. They were eager to go, but they knew it would be hard to leave; they wanted to get away, but they could imagine a day when they might want to return. The sequel to this thread came up repeatedly in our conversations with the next-older generation of Winters residents, some of whom had indeed returned to start new businesses. We also heard complements to the storyline from a number of young spouses who married into Winters families and are now raising their own families there: "If you fall in love with someone from Winters, be forewarned that you'll probably end up settling in Winters."

We came across two stories of entrepreneurs in Winters, which illustrated two paths forward for a community like this. Russ Lester is "just" a farmer, John Pickerel is "just" a restaurant owner, but each has adjusted his business practices and his efforts in the community toward the goal of making their community sustainable in economic, environmental, and social terms.

Russ Lester, a nut-tree farmer, was born in the 1950s in a part of the state then famous for its fruit and nut orchards, and now known as the Silicon Valley. "The Santa Clara Valley, where we had our farms, was known for its incredible prunes and apricots and cherries, and was called 'The Valley of Heart's Delight,'" he told us, when we visited him and his daughter on their walnut farm outside Winters. "Obviously that's all changed—it kind of looks like L.A. now." Lester is a stockily built, balding man with an inviting smile, who wore blue jeans, running shoes, and a California surf-shop T-shirt as he walked us through the orchards.

Even as the tech industry arose around him through the 1960s and 1970s, Lester's father resisted selling the family's land. But he could resist only so long. Property taxes kept going up, as adjoining properties became semiconductor factories, houses, and office complexes, and so did the family's burden of debt. "We were getting taxed at developed-land levels, and we were growing prunes, cherries, walnuts, and apricots," Russ Lester said. With several other farming families, the Lesters finally decided to pool their land in Cupertino and sell it and develop it, for what first became a mall named Vallco Park, which included a large mall named Vallco Fashion Mall (now defunct), and has become ground zero for the world's tech industries. "Right in the middle of where Apple's world headquarters is now, that's where I used to grow sweet corn that we sold at a roadside stand," Lester said. "I try not to go down there any more. I'm not anti-technology, but I think we have to eat before we play with our computers, and that we need to use our natural resources wisely."

With the money from the sale, the Lesters moved north, to the Winters area. In 1979, Russ Lester and his wife, Kathy, in their midtwenties, bought sixty-eight acres of neglected orchard that they began replanting with walnut trees. As a young person, working and living in the Cupertino and Santa Clara orchards, Lester and the rest of his family had been exposed to pesticides, herbicides, chemical fertilizers, and the other components of industrialized agriculture. After their move to Winters, he and his wife decided to switch to sustainable and organic practices. In the 1980s, his father was diagnosed with a form of lymphoma that had been linked to herbicide exposure. "Although research couldn't directly link my dad's cancer to the chemicals used in his prune orchards, watching his disease progress made me reconsider even the few pesticides that we still used," Lester wrote in a statement of principles on his company's website. "My wife and I decided, for our young family's health, to take the next step. My father's death in 1989 marked the end of our use of conventional chemicals."

The resulting operation, known as Dixon Ridge Farms and now covering more than 1,400 acres, attracts visitors from around the world and has been honored by the California state government for its commitment to sustainability in use of energy, water, chemicals, and other components. "Conventional farming uses a lot of chemicals," Russ Lester said. "With organic farming, you can use hardly any of those chemicals. And then you have *sustainable organic* farming. My definition of sustainable farming means that we should be able to keep on doing what we're doing today, producing good, healthy food, pretty much forever. We try to limit the inputs from off farm, and limit our impact on the environment."

For water use, the Lester approach involves not tilling the ground between the trees but instead planting legumes and clover. The resulting two-foot-high cover crop, plus walnut shell mulch (and twigs and pruned branches), reduces evaporation. Water is applied through an unusual irrigation system that utilizes low-pressure, rotary sprinklers suspended from hoses snaked through the trees, a process that minimizes waste and allows the cover crop to grow over the entire surface. Many walnut and almond growers pull out and replant their trees roughly every twenty-five years. "We have trees that are over a hundred and ten years old," Lester said. "With the shorter cycles, it's like walnuts on steroids—they produce a lot, and then they peter out, as you would if you were on steroids. You have to rip them out. If you manage them correctly, they can grow for a long, long time and still produce an excellent crop. And you're sequestering a lot of carbon in the trees themselves, creating a stable, healthy environment for various critters."

Probably the most celebrated aspect of Dixon Ridge Farms is its use of the by-products from one walnut crop to create energy for processing the next. Drying and processing nuts after harvest requires a lot of energy; Dixon Ridge has been a pioneer in using the shells and other by-products of the harvest to create both heat and electricity to operate the farm. Lester said that his farm has produced more than 1,750,000 kilowatt hours of electricity, worth more than $263,000, and will save more than 20,000 gallons of propane per year. Putting the charred shells back into the ground had additional benefits in carbon sequestration.

Where does this go next? Lester, a third-generation farmer, has five children. "Farmers are getting older, farms are getting bigger. If you wanted to get started in farming and had no farm roots, it would be very hard," says Lester. But we walked the land with his daughter Jenny, who said that she hoped to continue the tradition.

John Pickerel, of the Buckhorn Steakhouse, is an anchor of Winters' commerce and tourism. He grew up in a cowboy family, and looks the part. He was in his early sixties when we met him in Winters but appeared much younger: compact, lean, with a full head of sandy hair and a goatee. It's easy to believe that he was a wrestler in high school and college. He spent his childhood in the upper Mountain West—Idaho, Montana, eastern Washington, and Oregon—where his father was a rodeo bull rider, then a cattle buyer, then a feedlot operator, then a long-haul livestock trucker, among other pursuits. Pickerel was introduced early to the world of livestock, and to the practicalities of how to make farming-related businesses pay off.

"I'd ride with my dad on these long drives, like between Spokane and Montana, and he would tell me all his ideas about business," Pickerel told me, as he led a walking tour of the storefronts near his restaurant.

"He would say, 'John, it's not about how you sell the cows but how you *buy* the cows.' He'd explain how you needed to think about quality and cost."

Ever since then, Pickerel said, he has viewed the commercial landscape around him as an endless series of puzzles. He hears of a new store opening up in town and immediately thinks, *Show me where the customers will come from. Show me how you're going to make it?* He visits a bar or restaurant anywhere else and thinks, *What makes it worth customers coming here?*

Pickerel asked himself the same questions when he arrived in Winters in 1980, in his late twenties. By then, he had already started a restaurant in a larger nearby town. "I decided to open a restaurant in Winters because I'd heard this was a place that people would actually travel to, if you gave them a good reason," he told me.

"But when I came here," he said, "I could see the bones, and the charm—and I'd heard that people actually enjoyed driving to Winters." Driving west from Sacramento or Davis, or east from the vast Bay Area, much of the ride would be on relatively quiet roads through orchards or between hillsides and valleys. "So I thought, what if the drive itself added value to the experience they had? And making the experience of the restaurant something they would value and come back for?" Pickerel said that his rule of thumb was, you need to have two hours' worth of activity, for each hour it takes customers to get there. "That's been my mantra for every day since then, how can we add *value* that makes this trip to this place worthwhile." For Pickerel, that value came from the now-popular cut of meat known as the "Char Roasted Tri Tip" that he claims originated at the Buckhorn in the 1980s.

Pickerel's business success has spread far beyond Winters. By the late 1990s, he had opened Buckhorn Grills in ten other cities, while still basing himself in Winters. In 2009, two of his Tri Tip Grills opened in New York, in Rockefeller Center and Grand Central Station. ("I asked myself, *how* can you offer something that New Yorkers don't already have? I thought the answer would be tri-tip.")

Pickerel emphasized a theme we'd heard before in places as different as Holland and Eastport and Sioux Falls and Duluth and Redlands, and that would recur through our travels to come. That was the power of local loyalties, local attachments, a sense of belonging and rightness in being on a part of the earth you felt was *home*.

Pickerel's own life (and the lives of many others we met in Winters) turned out to be such an example. Pickerel had been ready to move back to his original home of Montana by the 1990s, "but I met the love of my life," who was from a larger town near Winters, and "this is where she wanted to be." In the next generation, their own children couldn't wait to get to bigger cities after finishing high school in rural Winters. "But they have come back to Winters, they're invested in the town, it's where they love," he said. "That's the best way to measure the sustainability of a town like ours—when young people come back, with education and experience, and add a twist to what we are doing. The kids come back, they bring their 'A Game,' they see that there are possibilities here."

# Bend, Oregon

It was inevitable, I suppose, that one of us would get sick sometime during our adventures. That fell to Jim, who came down with a frustrating, lingering flu when we hit Bend, in the high desert of central Oregon. In an unanticipated way, his illness, which turned into some kind of persistent cough and infection, became a chance for us to explore Bend differently from how we explored most other towns. We kept reporting, but we also built in more downtime to do the sorts of things that Bend offers.

Here is an odd combination of day-in-the-life activities that I won't even try to stitch together: hotels, baseball, marijuana, traffic roundabouts, and public libraries.

We were very lucky with our hotel, which mattered. I had learned a lot about hotels by the time we reached Bend, having stayed in dozens and dozens of them along our way. Most of our lodgings were utilitarian, but with exceptions, like in Bend, where the name Wall Street Suites (WSS) caught my eye.

The WSS began as the Plaza Motel, a classic 1950s motel, featuring pull-in parking for your big old family Buick right up to the door of your room. Across the street from the then-offices of the Bend *Bulletin*, still Bend's fine hometown daily, the motel was a favorite of visiting journalists. It was destiny, I thought, that we should end up there.

I had time to learn the history of the motel, from its dark past as "Felony Flats" to its bankruptcy in 2010. Two couples, Wendy and Pat Kelley, and Gretchen and Vernon Palmer, had scrambled to buy the derelict motel at an auction.

They poured their talents and experience into reassembling an amazing motel: interiors from old, repurposed wood, sliding barn doors between the rooms of the suite, handmade coffee tables from the wood leftovers, with locally welded table legs. We newly appreciated the artisanship after learning how welding was one of the emphasized, highly sought-after trades taught in the local community college. The owners beautified the parking spots with trees and planters, fire pits and communal seating, and personalized the room interiors with old family photos.

The WSS addressed head-on one of my travel pet peeves: a shortage of electrical outlets. We haul around a lot of electronic gear when we travel: laptops (three), iPads (three), cell phones (two), camera battery chargers (two), and a portable ADS-B/GPS receiver for the plane plus countless adapters and cords. In most hotel rooms, if the outlets are not already fully occupied by lamps and clocks, they are hidden inaccessibly behind chests of drawers. But at WSS, the outlets were abundant and convenient. No more iPads propped up by the hair dryer. No more Sophie's choice between our cell phones.

Further, at WSS, there were no chunky telephones taking up real estate on bedside tables. Who even uses hotel phones these days, anyway? There was plenty of low-voltage eco-friendly lighting, plus a bright skylight over the shower. And lots of extra soundproofing blown into the walls to make even passing trains sound romantic. And bikes to borrow. We stayed for about three weeks.

Our weeks in Bend included more classic Americana, the activities you would try to show off to international visitors. We biked gentle trails, hiked along the rushing river, established favorite brewpubs and food stores among several, wandered the town museum (in particular, admiring its collections of pet-cat photos), and walked in the parks where colorful hammocks hung in trees. Why, I don't know.

One fine day we were stopped on a downtown sidewalk by the mascot for the Bend Elks, the collegiate summer West Coast League baseball team. Vinnie the Elk and his sidekick were handing out free tickets for the opening game against the Corvallis Knights. Not to be missed.

We had already been to games for the Duluth Huskies, part of the Northwoods League, and the Allentown Iron Pigs, the Triple-A farm team for the Phillies. The college players for both the Huskies and the Elks are put up by local families for the summer, broadening the loyal hometown fan base.

Next to me in the bleachers along the third-base line was a young guy who worked at Enterprise car rental, and had himself played ball for his community-college team, probably less than a decade ago. He said the players with professional aspirations found the summer league especially valuable as a chance to hone their skills with wooden bats, like in the majors, instead of the aluminum bats that college teams traditionally use.

Exactly 1,073 people were on hand the night we were there. Families poured in, with toddlers new to the game and their older siblings, who lined up at the face-painting booth and then roamed free around the stadium. Guys in Hawaiian shirts struck up conversations with aging hippies, and the policemen who casually watched the gates slapped high fives with old-timers they called by name as they entered or exited the stadium.

During my walks along Wall Street from our hotel toward downtown, I would pass a small strip mall where one storefront had little signage but a leaf. After a while, it dawned on me that this was one of Bend's new, legal marijuana dispensaries.

One day, I stood outside debating with myself whether or not to enter. My inner dialogue went something like this: "I should go in." "What will I ask?" "It's reporting!" "Do I need some special language?" "I'm kind of afraid to go inside." "I'll go in." So I did.

Inside, the look was of a small clinic: pristine, organized, understated. A young woman asked politely if she could help me. I thought I should come clean with exactly why I was there: as a journalist, to understand the business—and, I added, I would like to talk with the owner.

Hunter Neubauer, a co-founder and co-owner of Oregrown, has an entrepreneur's spirit and a story like so many we found in Fresno, Pittsburgh, Greenville, Duluth, Redlands, and so on. He had sold medical devices for ten years, had felt hemmed in, and had gone after this opportunity. Knowledgeable, articulate, and politically astute, he started a PAC and went to D.C. to learn and lobby about cannabis issues. Responsibly risk-taking as a young family man, he'd raised local and family investment funds in order to start his venture with his business partner, Aviv Haddad.

Neubauer showed me around the shop, which brands itself as a grower and retailer of highly controlled farm-to-table cannabis for medical and recreational use. The retail space reminded me of a specialty coffee shop. He described the different varieties and products, from leaves to bars, which looked like candy. He told me about some typical customers: A mom from Alabama whose daughter has seizures. Guys with football injuries. Lots of patients with MS or PTSD. Cancer patients who want to distance themselves from traditional pharma drugs. Athletes. Recreational types. I was a little skeptical about so many medical users until I saw some of those customers come in as I was leaving.

Oregrown has since prospered in a broad sweep of ways. In the last few years, Neubauer and Haddad have established an eighty-four-acre farm, partnered with various companies (for apparel), tripled the space of their shop, added two dozen employees, won congratulations from their state representative as an anchor merchant in Bend, joined the board at the Bend Chamber of Commerce and underwritten the Young Professionals Network programming, supported athletes, offered public events, and helped beautify the city parks. When I replaced the word "cannabis" with "software" or "coffee," nothing about the story of the successful start-up and its entrepreneurial millennials seemed at all unusual.

When you start driving or, even better, biking around Bend, you quickly notice the roundabouts, more than two dozen of them, a progressive solution to the town's growing traffic volume: replace the traditional stop signs or lights at intersections with roundabouts.

There were lots of arguments for roundabouts. Safety: cars drive more slowly; accident opportunities are fewer and less severe; pedestrians only ever have to look to the left. Efficiency: no stopping at red lights, even when no one else is around. Environmentally friendly: less idling and stopping and starting means fewer pollutants; swapping big concrete intersections with green circles produces more oxygen.

Bend had to work out a few kinks, like how to move oversized emergency equipment through the circles smoothly and easing hesitant or confused drivers into different navigation habits.

The town also saw a chance to beautify the roundabouts with nature and art—specifically, with sculptures in the middle of the roundabouts. The first was installed in 2001. This effort matched many examples we saw of functional art, personalized for America's towns: park benches, bicycle racks, fountains, beautiful edible gardens, bridges, and retaining walls.

For the Bend roundabouts, artists submitted their ideas, the library displayed the prototypes, and the public voted. An early installation in 2002, officially known as *Rising Phoenix,* didn't go so well. People weren't sure what it was, and called it "the flaming chicken."

But more followed, and people got used to the sculptures just like they got used to navigating roundabouts. Some liked them; some didn't. But the art became affectionate points of reference, as in "I live near the flaming chicken roundabout."

\* \* \*

As part of their research into the community's library use and needs, the administrators of the Deschutes Public Library system, which includes Bend, filmed several Q&A sessions with residents about the library. For Todd Dunkelberg, the director of the six-branch Deschutes (sounds like *de-SHOOTS*) libraries, the results were a wake-up call about the library's visibility and people's familiarity with it. "People felt guilty about not knowing about their library," he admitted to me. That was a sentiment voiced by lots of librarians I met, who lamented that their libraries were "the best-kept secret in town." This connection to community—the third sturdy leg of the stool besides technology and education, where libraries engage to serve the people—was foundational in the Bend library.

In 2010, Dunkelberg and the Deschutes librarians set out to do something about it. The librarians assumed new titles—they were now "community librarians"—and headed out to embed themselves in local groups and organizations, carrying the message of the resourceful and activity-rich library. They also wanted to see how they might build partnerships for the good of the community.

At first, Dunkelberg said, the librarians met with a puzzled reaction: "Why are you here?" But after a few years of listening, learning, sharing stories, and collaborating, people would see the librarians coming and ask them, "How can we work with you?"

Bend was pulling a paragraph straight from Tocqueville's observations from his classic reporting trip around America. In *Democracy in America,* Tocqueville waxed on in astonishment at how many "associations" Americans made, for anything and everything: "Americans of all ages, all stations in life, and all types of dispositions are forever forming associations . . . of a thousand different types—religious, moral, serious, futile, very general and very limited, immensely large and very minute. . . . As soon as several Americans have conceived a sentiment or an idea that they want to produce before the world, they seek each other out, and when found, they unite."

That is still true, nearly two hundred years later. By now, the library staff in Bend is represented in more than sixty community groups, from the chamber of commerce to the City Club and the Homeless Leadership Coalition.

The library system made about twenty formal partnerships and countless informal ones. For example, working together with the library, AARP helps with tax assistance, and Goodwill teaches résumé-writing classes.

In its diverse offerings, the Bend library is one example of many. Across the country, libraries are figuring out ways to be relevant or interesting to their communities. There is a long list of the sorts of popular offerings you find nearly everywhere: art exhibits, book clubs, author readings, computer classes, story hours. I have practiced yoga and sipped lattes in libraries all around the country. In Washington, D.C., I saw a good seventy-five people dancing the tango in the big entry hall of the library.

Libraries offer citizenship classes, English-language classes, and programs on car-seat safety, self-defense, parenting, and even, as in Bend, fighting forest fires. Local lending is the most inventive program. In Denver, you can borrow hiking equipment and maps from public libraries before heading out into the mountains. In Vermilion, Ohio, on Lake Erie, you can borrow a fishing pole from the kids' section. In gardening-crazy Duluth, you can borrow seeds for your home plot, then replenish the supply when your crop yields. In Burlington, Vermont, I saw the summer-season tools available for borrowing: hoes, rakes, shovels, and a barrel of tennis rackets. In the winter, these are swapped for snow shovels, which the librarian told me are popular with ambitious teenagers who borrow them on snowy weekends to earn some money clearing sidewalks. You can watch movies in the newly plush basement theater, the former vault of the former bank building that is now the Kansas City Public Library. During the Minnesota summer, you can paddle your boat out to the floating library raft in one of Minneapolis and St. Paul's many lakes and take your books home in a watertight bag.

In many towns, local companies cooperate with the libraries, often in product-relevant ways. In Greenville, the French company Michelin sponsored an art competition, offering donated tire scraps to construct internationally themed creations. In Redlands, the library and the locally based software mapping company Esri partnered on a geography day.

Sometimes, libraries fix problems they notice. In Bend, when the older population felt disrupted by the usual flurry of activity from the younger library users, the librarians decided to open for an exclusive, older-patrons-only early-morning hour. Later, when the biggest volume of questions brought from users to librarians—because they are trusted—focused on meeting mortgages or paying rent, the library hired a social worker to train the staff in handling those sensitive, detailed conversations.

Similarly, people seek out librarians—because they are trusted—for medical issues. In Charleston, West Virginia, librarians described this typical scenario: a man comes into the library, rolls up his sleeve, and says, pointing, "Hey, I've got this spot on my arm. What do you think? Could you help me figure out what it might be?"

When Hurricane Sandy ravaged New Jersey, the libraries remained open for shelter. With Hurricane Harvey, the libraries in Houston were tweeting their openings within a few days, encouraging people to come by. When schools closed after riots in Ferguson, Missouri, and after the death of Freddie Gray in Baltimore, the libraries stayed open as a safe place for kids.

In Erie, Pennsylvania, the location of the new Blasco Library in 1996 became symbolic as a statement that Erie was on the road to recovery and rebuilding after the loss of thousands of jobs when the General Electric plant radically downsized.

Town planners and developers took a chance and located the library along the derelict waterfront, which the library's then-executive director, Mary Rennie, described as an area of "feral cats, rats, and sludge." Building on the water was an expression of local pride and confidence in the town's nautical heritage on Lake Erie. The library became a roaring success. Today, when the replica of Oliver Hazard Perry's tall ship, the U.S. brig *Niagara,* victorious in the War of 1812, sails into its home port of Erie, the librarians use the loudspeaker to alert the folks inside the library to rush to the windows to see it docking.

As a doctor's son, I'm always embarrassed to be sick. We were taught as children to shake it off or wait for nature's "tincture of time" to take care of nearly anything that was wrong. When I was in third or fourth grade, we were on a family trip to some park that had a Korean War fighter jet parked as a playground attraction. I was up in the cockpit when my dad called out, "Kids, it's time to go!" I told him I was afraid to jump all the way to the ground from where I was. He said it would be fine—and I jumped, and landed hard, and started complaining that my leg hurt. "It will be fine, just wait till tomorrow," he assured me. Three days later, I was in the emergency room, where X-rays showed the two places where I had snapped my ankle bones. (For everyone other than his own family, my father was actually a renowned diagnostician and a beloved local doctor.)

So I was embarrassed to be sick in Bend. But sick I was, and through the weeks we spent there, while Deb was out doing interviews, I spent a lot of time in the motel, coughing and running a fever and feeling bad. Finally, getting over my ingrained ethic about the "tincture of time," I went to a nearby "urgent care" outlet, to see if I could get some high-test cough syrup, ideally with codeine, so I wouldn't compound my problems (and Deb's) by keeping us both up with my coughing through the night. The nurses at the center looked at me with suspicion as soon as I said the word "codeine." At the time, the opioid epidemic was not nationwide news, but it was already a big problem in mainly white, long-working-class central Oregon, and I had unwittingly put myself in the suspect category. Eventually they heard me cough enough, and were convinced enough by whatever lung infection I had, to give me both the codeine-infused nighttime cough syrup and a giant dose of antibiotics, so that by the time we were ready to leave town, I felt fine again.

What I did manage to see in the town bore on what we had been learning about nearly every other place we'd visited. Which was: How had it come back? And where was it on the cycle?

The question may now seem irrelevant as applied to Bend, which by the time of our visit was already gaining a reputation like that of Portland or Santa Fe, as a desirable and hip post-industrial-woes city. But in the 1980s, Bend and its neighbors in central Oregon were mainly timber-industry towns, and when that business collapsed—because of overcutting, from one perspective; because of newly strict environmental regulations, from another; because of cyclical ups and downs in the housing industry, by all accounts—Bend had for a while the highest unemployment rate in the country, worse than midwestern and Appalachian areas that were enduring the more-celebrated declines of their coal or steel or auto industries.

The story of this region's travails was both plainer and more complicated than others we had seen and learned about. It's plainer in that it
was one more stage of the decline of a natural-resources economy. In
that way, it was similar to what happened when the sardine-canning
industry disappeared from Eastport, Maine; or when coal and chemical businesses declined around Charleston, West Virginia; or when the
enormous copper mine that was the main economic reason for being
of Ajo, Arizona, was shut down. Or what could conceivably happen to
California's Central Valley or other farming areas if historic droughts
and record heat continue.

In central Oregon, the crucial natural resource was, of course, trees—
timber from privately owned tracts as well as, significantly, the national
forests managed by the U.S. Forest Service and other federal lands run
by the Bureau of Land Management. Loggers were in the forests, lumber
workers were in the sawmills, truckers were behind the wheels of big rigs
taking logs and boards to their destinations, and construction workers
were on the job around the country putting wood products to use.

It could not last. The trees ran out; the Forest Service changed its
rules; the Endangered Species Act kicked in; and because of other factors, the timber-and-lumber industry that had built the communities,
created great fortunes, and employed most of the working people in
Bend, Prineville, and elsewhere would not regain its former scale. In
its modern history, even Bend—now the largest, most prosperous, and
most stylish of the cities in the area—had two episodes of severe downturn. One was in the 1980s, when it became clear that the timber industry really was gone and was not coming back.

For America as a whole, the job losses after the financial crisis of 2008
were more severe than anything since the 1930s. It was different in Oregon, where the prolonged downturn of the 1980s had been even worse.
For most of the country, the post-2008 recession differed from others
in that so many jobs vanished, and that they took so long to return. But
for Oregon, the job losses had been even greater, and the recovery even
slower, in the early 1980s. Then unemployment in Bend and its surrounding counties was over 16 percent, according to state and federal
employment statistics, when the national rate was nearing its recession-

era peak of just under 11 percent. The same pattern occurred in 2009 and 2010, when the national unemployment rate briefly exceeded 10 percent and that of central Oregon neared 20 percent.

This is not to minimize the impact of the post-2008 crash on Bend and its environs. This was one of several areas of the country (mainly in the Sun Belt) that had been riding a construction-borne boom. When that boom ended, unemployment was as bad in Bend as in any Rust Belt trouble spot you could name. "Bend suffered very badly during that crash, because it was so real estate dependent," Denise Costa, managing editor of the Bend *Bulletin,* told us. (Her husband, John, is the publisher.) "You would expect a city like this to have about seven percent of its economy in real estate—ours was about twenty percent, and it all went away."

A *New York Times* feature in 2009 presented Bend, in economic "freefall," as a "succinct symbol for the economic perils of 'lifestyle destinations' in the so-called New West, recreation-heavy communities where jobs have been heavily tilted toward construction and services and where many of the new residents were self-made exiles from California cashing in on their overpriced real estate."

Six years later, a variety of small businesses had started up locally or moved from higher-cost cities. A tourism, resort, and retirement industry gained strength, along with a medical treatment-and-research complex, and their success restarted the construction industry. The real estate vacancy rate was around 1 percent; the city had two thriving-looking downtowns: the traditional-style one, on Bond and Wall Streets, with strictly local outlets and an ever-growing array of craft-brew operations, anchored by Deschutes Brewery; and the restored Old Mill District, with a sixteen-screen movie theater and hotels and national-brand outlets and a river-walk recreation area where the millponds used to be.

The main local concern of the moment seemed to be managing the pace of growth—both in the short term, so as to avoid a repeat of the previous real estate bubble and bust, and in the longer run, to steer clear of a prospect that was always described to us as "becoming another Aspen." By this people meant a Mountain West shorthand for what could also be called "another Hamptons" or "another Nantucket," a place so successful in attracting moneyed residents that the people who work for them can't afford to live anywhere nearby.

Bill Smith, a developer who led the effort to convert the deserted lumber mill into the Old Mill dining and retail district, and his wife, Trish, who has led the local public-broadcasting board, the community foundation, the hospital and environmental boards, and similar civic causes, were the first people most Bend residents named when we asked our usual question, Who makes things go in this town? When I asked Trish Smith what she thought first-time visitors might miss or misunderstand about the town, she said, "It's easy to miss the *depth* of this community." Visitors would arrive, she said, and enjoy "the fishing or the snowboarding or the beer." It is a hotly contested title, but by many accounts, central Oregon has become the craft-brewing capital of North America. "And they don't realize that it's a place of substance, with libraries and parks and churches and the connections that give a community character."

What went in the right direction for central Oregon? Here are several answers.

\* \* \*

In one immediately obvious way, the central Oregon story differed from other regional-comeback sagas we had seen. The difference was in its educational establishment: there's no research university, or even a four-year degree-granting university, in Bend, Prineville, Redmond, or elsewhere in central Oregon.

This is an anomaly, because where you have tech-based hopes for economic growth, you almost always have a research university. The Golden Triangle of Mississippi has its challenges (and successes), but it also has Mississippi State. Sioux Falls, South Dakota, has a raft of private and public institutions. The Allentown-Bethlehem-Easton triangle of Pennsylvania has been buoyed by Lehigh University, Muhlenberg College, and others. Greenville, South Carolina, has nearby Clemson and in-town Furman and Bob Jones. And this is before we even get to Columbus, Ohio, with Ohio State, or Pittsburgh, with Carnegie Mellon and Pitt.

It is an anomaly that people in central Oregon are hyperaware of, and it is part of a years-long local push to expand a branch of Oregon State University–Cascades into a stand-alone four-year school in Bend. The proposed location for the new campus has been the subject of lawsuits and local controversy, but most people we spoke with expected that sooner or later the school will be built.

The region has gotten along without a university in significant part through an unusually active and ambitious community college, whose vice president told us that it was "university-esque."

Central Oregon Community College, or COCC, has its main campus in Bend and branches in Redmond, Prineville, and elsewhere in the region. Like other community colleges, it emphasizes an extra chance for people who can't afford a four-year college—or aren't ready for it, or are busy with children, or have other things going on in their lives. It is also like them in working closely with regional employers and entrepreneurs. In 2013, for instance, the FAA approved sites in Oregon for tests of new UAV (drone) systems. Matt McCoy, the COCC vice president for administration (and the man who said "university-esque"), told us that within a year, the college had a UAV-technology program planned, staffed, and running. The health-care industry is a major employer in Bend, and COCC has opened new health-technology programs. Its branch campus in Redmond specializes in advanced-technology manufacturing systems.

But COCC was also different from other community colleges we've seen, in ways that show the malleability of this educational model—and that indicate how an institution responds when it's bearing normal community college responsibilities and stretching to do more as well. For instance:

- COCC is the oldest community college in Oregon, founded in 1949, and one that has been exceptionally stable. It has had only five presidents in its sixty-five-plus years of existence. Faculty and staff members, once recruited, tend to stay.
- It has exceptional support from its community, including financial support. A local family donated the spectacular tract of land on Awbrey Butte where the main campus is now located.

Since 1955, local donors have supported the COCC Foundation, which gives out more than $1 million a year in scholarships. Usually four-year schools crowd out community colleges for "naming gifts," the large-scale contributions for buildings or scholarships named for the donor. COCC has done well with them. In 2009, during the worst of the recession, voters approved a big new bond for COCC. The resulting construction put hundreds of local people to work.

- COCC has created what looks like a campus, even though it is mainly a commuter school. Its setting is spectacular, nestled among evergreens, with hilly paths, big playing fields, and open, inviting dining spaces. A new 330-bed dormitory would be opening in the fall after our visit, part of a movement of community colleges to attract some out-of-region students by offering dorms. We toured the new dorm space, still under construction. It seemed to us to have a state-of-the-art design, with a number of different rooming configurations to choose from.

"When we say we are a 'community college,' we really mean that we are for and of this community," McCoy, who had been at the college for seventeen years, told us. We saw students doing a practice assembly the day before their graduation, and they indeed looked like a cross section of people seeking a second chance or better opportunities. Their ages appeared to range from the early twenties through the midsixties; there were more women than men, some young families with children, and some soon-to-be grads in construction-company or service-work uniforms from their day jobs; we noticed a less-white, more racially diverse mix than in the town as a whole. "We feel," McCoy said, "an obligation to help it toward a future of equitable, balanced growth." Yes, you can hear this sort of thing anywhere. But as in several other communities that had a productive and respectful relationship with their community colleges, we got the feeling in Bend that this was more than just talk.

Central Oregon's community college also played a role in Bend's evolution as a tech and start-up locale.

With its history as a resort town—skiing at nearby Mount Bachelor in the winter, rafting on the Rogue River, and hiking and bicycling in the summer—Bend may be a more obvious place than Redlands to come to the notice of high end investors. But start-up companies didn't get there automatically, especially in the absence of a university complex or any long heritage of "knowledge-intensive" (as opposed to natural-resources) businesses.

I talked in Bend with a Silicon Valley veteran named Dino Vendetti, who moved to Bend full-time in the early 2010s and—much in the fashion of the Bitwise team in Fresno or the Iron Yard's in South Carolina's Upstate region—has tried to foster a self-supporting high-tech community there.

Vendetti, who is in his fifties and has combed-back gray hair, would look at home as a veteran voice of experience at most venture capital conferences in Seattle or San Francisco. He grew up in Alaska, the son of immigrants; spent the early years of his career with Qualcomm, the globally dominant designer of chips for smartphones, which is based in San Diego; and then moved into the venture capital industry with Paul Allen's Vulcan Ventures in Seattle. He was successful enough that he bought a vacation home in Bend and began making regular visits there in the early 2000s.

"I always knew that I wasn't going to spend the next twenty years of my life in the Bay Area, with its hassle, or Seattle, with its rain," he told me in the office of his Seven Peaks tech incubator in Bend. "I wanted to be someplace with actually interesting people, and I'd assumed that meant near a university"—which Bend did not have.

Vendetti was still based in Silicon Valley when the financial crash of 2008 affected business there, as it did around the globe. As he observed the changes in business, technology, and culture—the growing caution of investors everywhere, the survival of the lowest-cost and most adaptable new enterprises, the ever-increasing power of cloud-based computing—he decided that the right next step for him was to move his home and business to central Oregon and see what he could accomplish there.

Vendetti gave me a long description of the challenges a second-tier tech center—or even a no-tier tech location, as Bend was in those days—faced in creating a sustainable modern-business environment. Without a nearby university, the most academically ambitious students would head elsewhere after high school, and not many would return. Without an established local investment or tech-talent community, local start-ups that did get going would eventually leave for San Francisco, Seattle, or another metropolis. "The more I got to know the Oregon market," he said, "the more I realized that just as start-ups were getting to scale, the big venture funds would pull them down to the Bay Area—especially if they wanted to go public." This had a perpetual lopping-off effect on the local economy, and it meant there wasn't a generation of successful businesspeople in their forties and fifties to encourage those in their twenties and thirties.

Vendetti began running a local-investment fund by himself, investing in software and medical-technology start-ups in Bend and Portland. He helped to develop a computer science major at the new Oregon State University campus. He evangelized for Bend enterprises on visits to established tech centers. He began arguing that the very absence of big technology companies gave Bend entrepreneurs an advantage—much as Greenville's history of many small textile firms, in contrast to the one big Milliken mills of neighboring Spartanburg, proved to make Greenville more agile and adaptable when the U.S. textile business plummeted a generation ago. "If we'd had one dominant tech employer, like a big printer division for HP, I think we would be less entrepreneurial now," he said. "HP would have hired up the talent as it arose. Instead, we've had a lot of smaller ones beginning to grow. We're kind of like a grape vineyard. You starve the plants for water, they have to send the roots deeper."

By the time we talked, in 2015, the general rise in the Bend economy included some forty-five software- and infotech-related businesses, plus twenty-five in medical technology and a similar number in aerospace-related businesses. More important, Vendetti said, was a change in individual and company choices. People who had left the area were returning or giving interested looks. Companies that were being priced out of bigger cities were considering moves to Bend, as well.

"There's always been some organic flow of talent into Bend, because it's one of those places where people want to live," he said. "But it's shifting and accelerating, as the Oregon market is maturing and things are getting ridiculously crazy in the Bay Area and Seattle. The costs, the complexity, the headaches of living there are at an all-time high. Silicon Valley can be an amazing place for your career during some phase of your life, but then as people begin to raise a family, places like Bend become ridiculously attractive."

Vendetti was not suggesting that the concentrated role of the big global centers would go away. It was not an "either/or" case he was making but an "and": that people would choose to do some work in Bend (or Fresno or Sioux Falls) as well as in New York or San Francisco or Los Angeles. "I don't think there will be any mass exodus out of Silicon Valley. But the disadvantages of *not* being there are diminishing." Partly that stemmed from the ability to hold on to talent: while big bonuses were luring engineers from Google to Facebook to Uber (as they did a generation before, from Intel to HP to Silicon Graphics), people who signed on with a regional company tended to stay there.

Vendetti is admittedly a booster, and at the end of our talk I asked him a "But, seriously now . . ." question. Were developments like those he saw in Bend part of any significant change in the regional distribution of opportunity? Or were they really just signs of a single town that had become lifestyle chic?

"No one can be sure," he said. "But my sense is, we're seeing a genuine shift. Historically, young people, in early or mid career just didn't *have* job opportunities in regional markets, like this one. So the motivated ones just had to stay in the major metros. But there's nothing like two major recessions in a decade"—the serious collapse of tech businesses in 2001 and the world crisis beginning in 2008—"to have people reassess what really matters. It's not a tidal wave, but a shift. I see people literally every week who want to find out about coming to Bend, for these life-change reasons. Usually it's because they're tired of being on the hamster wheel or want to build a family."

Vendetti argued that fostering the spread of tech companies to places like Bend served a larger national interest as well. Info tech and its related capacities are no longer a self-contained industry, he said. Anyone who tries to do anything, anywhere, is affected by their development. "So it's crucial that communities across the country be able to participate in the tech economy in a more meaningful way." The tech industry needed to do this as a whole, he said, and he felt he was doing his best to do his part in central Oregon.

Bend and the surrounding parts of Deschutes County still have economic challenges. But the problems of a fast-growth era, from gentrification to ever-more-visible economic extremes, are preferable to what they replaced, which were the challenges of a sinking economic ship. The contrast becomes clearer as soon you visit some of Bend's neighbors, like the small towns of Prineville and Redmond, which are still more heavily affected by the generations-long timber-industry collapse.

# Redmond and Prineville, Oregon

Central Oregon as a whole had struggled since the fall of Big Timber. We visited two more towns in the region: Redmond, which is emerging as an aerospace center, and Prineville, which has cast its lot with the distinctively modern industry of running data centers.

The Redmond story is again one about the incidental effects of personal decisions. When the Klapmeier brothers were working in a barn in Wisconsin to design what ultimately became the very successful Cirrus airplane, their West Coast counterpart, contemporary, and competitor was a man named Lance Neibauer. Neibauer, who when I met him in the 1990s had thick, dark hair and a wide mustache of the kind sometimes called a pornstache, was designing a plane that was meant to be a Ferrari or an Alfa Romeo, in relationship to the Audi or BMW the Klapmeiers were trying to provide. That is, the midwestern brothers were trying to create a product that would be safe, comfortable, and nicely finished. Lance Neibauer, on the West Coast, with a company named after himself called Lancair (pronounced *lance-air*), wanted to build a plane that was *fast*.

The first Lancair models came to market at about the same time the first Cirruses did. For a combination of reasons—luck; the appeal of the Cirrus parachute; the more-cramped test-pilot-style cockpit of the much faster Lancair; and, if not exactly luck again, good fortune, when the Chinese government decided to invest in Cirrus—the Klapmeiers' company made its way through the financial crises of 2001 and 2008 much better than Lancair did. Neibauer's company became a subsidiary of Cessna; its models were renamed the Columbia; and it stayed in business with a production rate roughly one-tenth that of Cirrus.

But much as the Klapmeiers' decision to move to Duluth became the basis for an aerospace complex there, and Jack and Laura Dangermond's decision to move from Cambridge back to Redlands transformed their hometown, so the partial success of Lancair helped make Redmond, the original base of the company, the site for further start-ups. Engineers and designers in Redmond already had experience with aircraft; the necessary machinery was on hand in local workshops; and people in the industry were familiar with Redmond, from their calls on Lancair during its most ambitious era.

As a result, by the time of our visit a cluster of small aviation companies had developed near Redmond's airport—including Stratos Aircraft, which employed several dozen designers and engineers working on the Stratos 714, a "very light personal jet" that would fill a then-tempting niche in the travel market. Corporate jets, from Gulfstream or Hawker or Cessna, were fast but cost tens of millions of dollars. Small personal planes, like the Cirrus, were much less expensive—but much slower and more exposed to the vagaries of weather (because jets can fly above most bad weather, while most propeller planes have to chug along at lower altitudes, right through it). A very small jet—essentially like our Cirrus, but pressurized (so it could fly high) and with a jet engine (so it could fly far and fast)—would be in the middle. Cirrus was also working hard on exactly such a project, with the Vision Jet, which Chinese financing allowed it to build, and which it introduced in 2015. "We think we'll be successful here," Carsten Sundin, who is originally from Norway and is now Stratos's chief technology officer, told me. "We think we can go 50 percent faster and 50 percent further than the competitive airplanes."

Private aviation is a notoriously risky market, not just for pilots and passengers but for entrepreneurs as well. Sundin told me that the company believed it could be sustainably profitable by selling twenty-five planes per year, which would mean capturing about 10 percent of the relevant world market. The interesting aspect to me was *why* this company, along with suppliers and other related firms, ended up where it was.

"Lancair and its descendants are connected in one way or another with all the aerospace activity around here," Sundin said. He himself, after starting out in Norway and spending his grade school years in Malaysia, had come to the United States in high school, as an exchange student to Roswell, New Mexico, and learned to fly there. His interest in aviation brought him up to Redmond, to meet with Lance Neibauer. He ended up liking the area and leapt at the chance to join Stratos when it started in 2008.

On my way out of Redmond, after touring the facility and sitting in a mock-up of the new plane, I saw a bumper sticker that concisely summed up the "locational theory" I had heard from the likes of Dino Vendetti and Carsten Sundin. VENI. VIDI. VELCRO, the sticker said. I came. I saw. I stuck.

Prineville is by far the hardest hit of these three cities. In its heyday, Prineville had been a very profitable timber center, but like many other cities in the region it had seen that business collapse. The other mainstay of the local economy had been the headquarters of the Les Schwab Tire chain, which had spread to hundreds of locations across the western United States from its founding location in Prineville. A laudatory article about the company in *Tire Business* magazine in 1995 pointed out that in a city whose population was only five thousand, some six hundred people worked directly for Les Schwab. But in 2008, just as the national economy was in post-crash freefall, the company moved its headquarters to Bend, eliminating hundreds of jobs.

In Prineville I spoke with John Shelk, a leader of the lumber industry in its heyday and now someone trying to imagine a future for the business and his town. When we met he was in his seventies, standing erect and with abundant white hair. We met at the modest offices of Ochoco Lumber, which was founded in the 1930s and of which his family had long been majority owner. In the decades after World War II, the Ochoco mills employed hundreds of foresters, sawyers, and other high-wage workers in its plants. The trees that they cut, barked, and fashioned into timber to ship around the country and the world came from the nearby Deschutes and Ochoco National Forests, which the U.S. Forest Service had opened to commercial lumbering operations in the late 1940s.

The industry collapse that affected the rest of the region affected Ochoco as well. By 2001, its sawmill closed for good. At the time, the mill still employed some 250 people, almost none of whom would ever find logging work again. Too many of the larger trees were gone; the environmental rules and standards had changed; such work as was left was more mechanized, with fewer employees.

"While we were developing our markets, especially in Japan, we assumed that the harvest from the national forests would inevitably decline," Shelk said. "But we never imagined that it would go immediately to zero," which was how he viewed the consequences of the new restrictions placed on loggers during the Clinton administration. The Clinton-era plans, he told me, "effectively eliminated commercial timber harvest on these forests, thereby dooming the remaining sawmills in central Oregon." After World War II, nearly a quarter of Oregon's entire economy was based on forestry. Now it's barely 2 percent; this is the Pacific Northwest's counterpart to the saga of Appalachian coal. In recent years, as a senior statesman of the timber industry, Shelk has worked with environmental and scientific groups, state and federal regulators, and both Republican and Democratic politicians (notably Oregon's Democratic U.S. senator Ron Wyden) to devise a sustainable-harvest plan to revive at least part of the region's forest-based economy.

Shelk drove me around the ruins of what had been his family's factory. Many of the buildings remained only as deserted hulks. Some had been bulldozed into clear lots. On the site of one, a new hospital now stood. "Of everything I see here, that's the one I feel good about," he told me.

A mile or two away were the vast warehouse-scale structures that were part of Prineville's next economic hope. These were data centers for Facebook and Apple, totaling well over $1 billion in investment cost and millions of square feet of space. They were drawn to the region by its low electric-power rates and its steady cooling wind—along with property-tax exemptions. Facebook cast itself as an active member of the community, opening its building for tours and for school-group events. Apple operated behind a wall of secrecy—no tours, no identifying sign or flag outside its buildings, no encouragement for local contractors or employees to say anything in public about their jobs or even where they worked.

We spent a day inside the Facebook site, which is mainly endless corridors of computers and cabling, and looked at Apple's only from the roadway—and from above, when we flew out of town. Together the firms represented this region's entry into the highly automated next economy: much greater capital investment than the old tire and timber facilities, comparatively fewer jobs. Building the new data centers creates hundreds of construction jobs in town; operating them requires many fewer people.

Still, it was progress. "We're celebrating here at the city," Steve Forrester, the city manager of Prineville, told *The Oregonian* after Facebook announced another expansion in 2017. The county's unemployment level had fallen from a catastrophic 20 percent in the late 2000s to around 6.5 percent—much worse than the national average, much better than it had been. "That's what this is about," he said.

# Chester, Montana

We headed north from Bend toward Walla Walla and on to the paired towns of Clarkston and Lewiston in Washington and Idaho. The towns were named for those intrepid travelers William Clark and Meriwether Lewis, whom we'd thought about often since landing near their route in South Dakota and again now along the Snake River.

Flying low over Chief Timothy Park, on an island near the confluence of the Snake and Clearwater Rivers, we peered down toward the nearly finished art installation by Maya Lin, the designer of the Vietnam Veterans Memorial in Washington, D.C. The installation is part of a project called Confluence, which memorializes six Lewis and Clark sites along the Columbia River system. This one was a Nez Perce–inspired modern hieroglyph, something she called a "listening circle"; large partial circles of stone rimmed a natural amphitheater and nestled into a grand landscape that has barely changed since Lewis and Clark paddled through there.

This destination fit into the most noble of three practices we had adopted during our travels. On the low-culture end, we typically landed from our long flights hot and thirsty, and headed straight for the nearest brewpub for local beer and burgers. Then, for middle culture, we found local sports events, maybe a wooden-bat baseball tournament. On the high-culture end, we sometimes searched for a cosmic experience of sorts at one of the sanctuaries or sacred spots that America offers in its natural parks, rivers, lakes, deserts, mountains, plains, and forests.

As visitors, we enjoyed the silence and the simple design, and the experience of walking around the Confluence circles and sitting on the stone ledges. And we wished we could camp in one of the little cabins in the park, which other people had figured out a way to do. To make my experience more personal, I took a dive into the Snake River once we were back in Clarkston. It was very cold, and I had to swim against the current. But just as I had once dashed quickly over the rocky shore into the Bering Sea on a dare from one of our sons, I jumped in here, figuring it could again be a now-or-never chance for the adventure.

We flew on through Idaho to Montana, with its places of rugged nature-inspired names, like Bitterroot, Sweet Grass, and, Beartooth.

When we're flying, our first impressions of an approaching town come at an altitude of about 2,500 feet above the ground. While Jim is busy landing the plane, and not noticing much except where the runway is and how he's lining up with it, I have a chance to look down at the layout of the town, at the grid of streets, or the line of the train tracks, or the course of a river, or the surrounding farmlands, hills, or forests.

As we descend slowly for landing, I might count the number of back-yard swimming pools, above ground or below, or see how many cars are in factory parking lots, or trace the angled geometry of mobile home parks or of new housing developments, or scope out schools and the amenities of their athletic facilities. Sometimes there are surprises, like the unmistakable smell of Kansas feedlots that wafts straight into the plane 1,000 feet up on a hot day, or the almost eerie silence on the radio when there is no one out there, anywhere, responding to our announce-ments of intentions to land. We've landed on runways that were little more than a skinny, patched stretch of tarmac with tufts of stubborn weeds and, at the other extreme, a onetime air force base with runways so long you could have a picnic on one end and not worry about planes landing on the other.

Second impressions for us come on the ground. The airports are usually, but not always, a little distance out of town. The least pleasant drives into town pass the indistinguishable strip malls of generic dollar and quick-mart stores. We could be anywhere. The best drives are along farms and woods that suddenly give way to a downtown. Then we know we're somewhere.

The approach toward Chester, Montana, was unique. We flew over jagged mountains, which then rolled away into the high plains, with fields of green, yellow, and gold. The rivers below us meandered. The rail tracks, arrow-straight for long stretches, looked efficient and important. The roads were few. In the skies, we flew for hours without sighting another plane.

We were going to visit a Chester native and college friend, Phil Aaberg, and his wife, Patty. Phil offered to collect us at the little Chester airport, and we gave him an ETA. He said he would listen for the plane as we flew over, then hop into his truck to fetch us. Indeed, he did exactly that, arriving quickly enough to watch us land.

As we flew over Chester, it was just as Phil had described: a no-stoplight town on the Great Northern Railway tracks, several square blocks of buildings, with the airport hugging the western edge of downtown. We were over it in a blink. I spotted Phil's old school, the pool, the grain silo, the tracks, and roughly where Phil and Patty lived with their son, Jake, in the same house where Phil grew up.

Phil is pretty much a Montana living treasure. With his full white beard and outdoorsman bearing, it would be tempting to call him gruff if he weren't actually closer to a teddy bear in real life. Already a serious music student as a young teenager, he would ride the train every few weeks to meet with his piano teacher in Spokane, a seven-hour trip, or ten if there were lots of stops.

Today, he is a pianist and composer with a collection of awards, performances, and collaborations that more than prove his bona fides to anyone who hasn't yet had the good fortune to hear his music. A Windham Hill Records contract, nominations for Grammys and an Emmy, and some twenty albums with names like *From the Ground Up* and *Live from Montana*. He built a studio in the back of his house from a metal grain silo.

We all went kayaking one afternoon on the Marias River, an expedition that began gently, with dreams of even a dip in the water, but turned surprisingly and quickly into a dramatic paddle-for-your-life ordeal as a fierce windy storm blew in. The hills right up to one side of the water's edge seemed steeper, and the marshy banks on the other seemed farther away and less hospitable. But you know we survived.


When Jim and I left Chester, we flew east, toward the American Prairie Reserve (APR). We landed in Malta, about a two-hour drive from the reserve. The trek in reminded us of an earlier time in Gansu Province in China, when we went in search of the town of Yellow Sheep River, where we were going to visit a small Buddhist boarding school for the children of the remote villages. We flew for two and a half hours from Beijing into Lanzhou, then drove two hours to Yellow Sheep River, then continued overland until the road ran out, and went on to the school by horse and, finally, by foot. At the end of that hot and dusty journey, the schoolchildren presented us with white silk scarves, the traditional Buddhist offering to guests.

This time in Montana, the paved road ran out before we reached our lodgings in the American Prairie Reserve, but we bumped along the dirt and potholes, grateful that rains had not made our route impassable, as we'd heard sometimes happens.

The APR is an ambitious, long-term attempt to return an enormous stretch of North American grassland to its original flora and fauna.

During our days at the APR, we hiked on the prairie, straining to see vistas all the way to the edge where the earth curved. We watched grazing bison up close, and peered into the holes dug by tiny prairie dogs, who would emerge to stand on their hind legs, as brazen as grizzlies, only in miniature. We stayed up late, hoping to see the northern lights. Alas, no luck. We trekked to a giant boulder left by an ancient glacier, named Indian Lake Medicine Rock, in the middle of the flat prairie. Millennia before us, someone (or several someones) had ventured repeatedly to painstakingly etch petroglyphs into the stone, and others more recently had left small offerings—an arrowhead, a striated stone, a tiny replica of a bison—balanced on the flat parts of the rock. All we could hear that day was the wind.

We went up the small mountain to the buffalo jump, trying to imagine the scene when the Plains Indians enticed some of the local herd to leap hundreds of feet over the cliff's edge to their deaths. Meriwether Lewis described in his journal how it worked: a man disguised in a buffalo skin waited between the herd and the edge of the cliff. Bands of his fellow Indians hid, completely surrounding the back and sides of the herd. When the Indians jumped up, startling the herd, the decoy would run ahead, leading the bison to the edge, then slipping out of the way, into a sheltered cranny, as the buffalo pounded forward, leaping over the edge.

# The American Prairie Reserve, Montana

The American Prairie Reserve is not a town. Indeed, it does its best to put urban influences far in the distance, so that at night the sky has the deep blackness, broken by pinpoint-clarity starlight, that you cannot experience within fifty miles of a big town. On the drive south from the nearest tiny airport, in Malta, we saw a few blocks' worth of western downtown, then a mile or two of residential neighborhood, then farmland, mainly with grazing cattle—then mile upon mile of prairie, as we drove south toward the Missouri River and rolling plains and prairie that in many vistas was, as we had seen at Chief Timothy Park, like what Lewis and Clark would have seen when they traversed this land more than two hundred years before.

That so much of this land still looks so much the way it once did—despite the paved roads, despite the fences for grazing, despite the dams that have been placed across the vast Missouri River, despite the dislocation of the tribes that once lived here to two large reservations (Fort Belknap and Fort Peck)—is the idea behind the civic innovation under way in this part of Montana.

Although it's not in a city, I use the term "civic" because in several unmistakable ways what was happening on the American Prairie Reserve resembled what we had seen in urban and small-town venues through our travels. People who had developed a connection to an out-of-the-way part of the country decided to invest their energy, resources, and even their working lives here. On problems that loom large nationally and internationally, they felt they were making progress. "We figure that we are maybe one-third of the way along the time line," Sean Gerrity, a Montanan who had returned from a career in Silicon Valley to run the reserve, told us about the work he and his colleagues had done for more than a dozen years. "I enjoy the long time line, and thinking how this will look in twenty or thirty years." This is not a wish you often heard expressed in national politics.

And the people behind the American Prairie Reserve were being creative—nonpartisan, public-private, working with businesses and ranchers and scientists and leaders of the neighboring tribes to realize their vision, which was nothing less than creating a natural reserve on the scale of the Serengeti National Park, in which the wildlife of the pre-settlement area would again prevail.

The ecological story behind the American Prairie Reserve was a scientific determination, around the year 2000, that there were only four extensive-grassland areas in the world that had *never been plowed* or reaped by mechanical harvester and thus, in principle, might have their original plant and animal ecosystems restored. One was in Kazakhstan, another in Patagonia, and a third in Mongolia—and all three of those were shrinking, as farming intruded on their borders. The fourth was in Montana, in the central region of the state, due north of Yellowstone Park in Wyoming, and was more intact than any of the others.

Part of this land along the Missouri River already enjoys protection as part of the Charles M. Russell National Wildlife Refuge, which was established under Franklin Roosevelt and is named for a famous western-landscape artist. Land to the west is protected as a component of the Upper Missouri Breaks National Monument, which was established under Bill Clinton and is named for the dramatic limestone escarpments in this "badlands" territory along North America's longest river. Some of the other nearby land is owned by ranchers, nearly all of whom graze cattle, in parcels separated by barbed-wire fences—and the rest by public agencies, from the Bureau of Land Management to the Fish and Wildlife

Service. Much of this is leased out to ranching families on long-term (and low-priced) leases.

Sean Gerrity, the native, who has the tousle-haired, ruddy look of a sailor, described the first twenty years of his career, through the 1980s and 1990s, in Silicon Valley, as the founder of a consulting firm that worked with companies like eBay, Cisco, and Netflix. As the year 2000 neared, he was interested in getting out of the tech rat race and wanting to go back home, and he heard about a scheme to restore these Montana grasslands, through the project now known as the American Prairie Reserve.

"We tried to get started in 2001 and early 2002," Gerrity told us, when we stayed with him at the lodge in the center of the reserve. "But, of course, that was the big tech recession. So we didn't really get any money until 2005—that was the start, when we bought our first piece of property."

Buying land from private owners and taking it out of ranching is part of the American Prairie Reserve's strategy. In the decade since that purchase, the organization has raised tens of millions of dollars, mainly from individual rich donors (like the Mars family, which still privately owns the Mars candy company), and used it to obtain control over more than three hundred thousand acres of land. About a quarter of that is land it has bought outright from private owners. The rest is public land on which it has taken over the lease and then taken the land out of grazing and converted it to wild use.

Bit by bit, the parcels have been put together—the fences pulled out and the strands of barbed wire removed, the migration paths reenabled. Ultimately the ambition is to assemble some five thousand square miles of contiguous land, or about three million acres. This expanse, roughly the size of Connecticut, would be big enough to support diverse populations of species large and small, from prairie dogs and ferrets to bison, antelope, eagles, and wolves. The sweeping scale means, as Gerrity put it, "that you could stand in one place and see only prairie for fifty miles in any direction, and it would stretch another fifty miles beyond that." It would also give the species living there more options as heat and rainfall patterns change.

"You have to *go big*," Gerrity said. "You can have an ice sheet covering half this territory in bad winters, so the antelopes have to travel eighty miles away. You can have long-term drought—and the animals are very adaptable, but they need the space." All in all, the cost of assembling this land might come to $500 million, by the American Prairie Reserve's estimate. Or—the comparison Gerrity uses in almost every fund-raising pitch he makes on visits to San Francisco, Seattle, or New York—about half as much as the cost of a new NFL-scale football stadium. (The Dallas Cowboys' stadium cost about $1.1 billion to build. The MetLife Stadium, for the New York Giants and Jets, cost about $1.6 billion, or three times as much as the aspirational budget for the American Prairie Reserve.)

Fund-raising is, of course, a familiar part of any vision for conservation, along with permanently removing land from commercial use. Groups like The Nature Conservancy have applied this strategy for decades. (The Nature Conservancy is the recipient of the Dangermonds' $165 million gift to preserve coastal land in California.) The more surprising part of the American Prairie Reserve approach is one that Gerrity says comes from his tech industry experience. This is a way to cooperate with local ranchers to encourage them to work with rather than against the reserve's long-term goals.

Many of the ranchers are from families who have run cattle on their fenced tracts for generations. Most of them are politically conservative. A noticeable fraction of them vocally resent the idea of outside money being used to make what they think of as their land a preserve or a showpiece. On the drive down from Malta, we passed at least a dozen anti-reserve signs in front yards and in pastures. They said things like "Don't Buffalo Me. No Federal Land Grab!" or the words "Monument. Reserve. Wildlands" with a slash across all of them.

Part of the friction is cultural. It involves resentment by people who feel that they have been the true stewards of the land, and that by raising cattle they are helping feed the world's billions. (We saw several large yard signs making this point, that without Montana beef the United States would have a larger trade deficit and more customers overseas would be hungry.) At least in one regard, time is very likely on the reserve's side: decade by decade, the farm population dwindles, and more of these ranches are likely eventually to go up for sale—and the reserve hopes to be able to buy them.

In the meantime, Gerrity and his colleagues are trying to address at least the economic conflicts between their plans and the ranchers' interests, through economic incentives to make cooperation with the reserve worthwhile. The best-known of these is a for-profit subsidiary of the reserve called the Wild Sky beef company. It guarantees ranchers a higher per-pound price for their cattle if they agree to a range of protective practices for wildlife. For instance, they can replace multistrand barbed-wire fences, which stop antelope as well as cattle, with fences designed to allow antelope to pass either over or under them. Also, they can stop poisoning and shooting prairie dogs, which ranchers view as a dangerous pest (since cattle can trip and break their legs by stepping into holes in prairie dog "towns") but naturalists consider an important part of the natural ecosystem and food chain of the prairie. "In Sweden, the government told people in the countryside, 'If you send us a picture of a live wolf on your property, we'll pay you three hundred dollars,'" Gerrity said as he described some of the incentive plans. "All of a sudden, the wolves are a valuable commodity." With similar plans in Montana, he said, "all of a sudden, as a rancher your portfolio is broader and more valuable, and there are new assets you want to protect."

"In my previous life in Silicon Valley, you were always *late* for something. For everything," Gerrity said as we were walking across the reserve on our last day there. "You had to ship that product before the competitor down the street was first-mover into that space. It could be anything. A pair of jeans. A new home-loan concept. A chip. Everything is *behind*. And what's worse is that as soon as you shipped that thing, almost immediately, its perishable date began, like yogurt. It was this endless hurry.

"This project is one hundred and eighty degrees different, and that is immensely satisfying. If we can make something happen, it will be permanent. When you add another piece of property, you can stop and think that, one hundred years from now, people will round that bend and see that view. It will be permanent. Nothing I ever did before can last in that way."

# 2016

*Dodge City, Kansas*

*Garden City and Spearville, Kansas*

*Erie, Pennsylvania*

# *Dodge City, Kansas*

Deb and I celebrated America's birthday in a city that evokes a certain kind of America—namely, Dodge City, Kansas.

Over the years, we'd crossed the southern plains often enough to understand the lessons they provided in history, climate, and geography. When you head westward, from the East Coast, you have a sense of going uphill, and into drier air. Mile by mile you leave behind the forested hollows of the Appalachian slopes, the farms and gently hilly pastures of southern Ohio and Indiana, the flatlands and sweeping corn and soybean fields of Illinois, which are broken at regular rectangular intervals by north-south and east-west roads laid out when the land was being distributed to nineteenth-century settlers.

Across the thick and slowly serpentine Mississippi River and toward the broad, brown Missouri, the land slowly rises, the vegetation becomes sparser and more burned-out-looking, until, as you near the 100th meridian, the historic dividing line between the wet and dry parts of the American heartland, the only green areas in sight are the ones sustained by mechanical irrigators. I've heard people in airliners wonder about the circular green spots they see in the Plains States; farmers know they show the watering radius of a circular irrigating system. In Ohio, we looked down on farm after farm with small manmade ponds popular for swimming, fishing, watering animals, and attracting wildlife. Water is too scarce for that farther west. At small airports, you see the effects of the westward progression as well. East of the Mississippi, airports usually have rope "tie-downs," where you can lash small planes like ours to the ground at three points: under each wing and at the tail. As you move into the plains and prairie, you stop seeing ropes and begin seeing chains, to hold the planes down in what are usually stronger constant winds.

Coming the other way, from the Front Range of the Rockies eastward toward the Atlantic coast, there is the opposite sensation—of sliding steadily downhill to wetter territory. The ground beneath you sinks in elevation, from more than five thousand feet above sea level in the Colorado and Nebraska plains to a few hundred along the banks of the Mississippi, and the vegetation gets denser and greener by the mile.

On this trip, we came up from the south, traveling across the plains of northern Texas and Oklahoma toward western Kansas. In the years I have flown this kind of airplane, I've landed it somewhere over fifteen hundred times. But every time, it commands my full attention, as I bring the airplane from several thousand feet above the ground and a two-hundred-mile-per-hour speed to the most benign return to ground level and low speed as I possibly can.

About thirty miles from Dodge City, ten minutes or so from arrival, we began the normal drill of preparation for landing. I tuned the plane's radio to get the "AWOS" or "ATIS," the weather reports that are broadcast nonstop from an airport's weather-monitoring station, and that confirm which way the wind is blowing and which runway I should be heading for. I turned on the auxiliary fuel pump and adjusted the fuel-flow setting from the fuel-minimizing "lean" rate for cruise flight to its full-rich level. That way, the engine would be ready for a quick, high-powered climb if we had to "go around" for another landing attempt because of an unforeseen problem on the runway—birds? a deer? another plane taxiing out by mistake? a tractor using the runway as a shortcut to its mowing site? We've seen them all, and more. I double-checked the elevation of the airport itself—2,600 feet above sea level for Dodge City, which is in the rising plains—so we could plan to be at "pattern altitude," which is usually about 1,000 feet above the airport, or about 3,600 feet in this case. Since Dodge City is a "controlled" airport, with air traffic controllers in a tower giving airplanes permission to take off or land, I listened on my second radio to ensure that communications with them would be clear.

Of the some five thousand airports within the United States, only around six hundred have control towers. At all the rest, pilots rely on communications through their CB-style "UNICOM" frequency to learn who is where and to keep out of one another's way.

At about the thirty-mile point, I made contact with the tower at Dodge City. The air traffic controllers there told me how they wanted me to line up for an approach—"make left traffic, runway thirty-two, report three mile left base"—which meant setting up at ninety degrees to the runway, then making a left turn toward a landing as our plane aligned with it.

And down we went, from our cruising altitude of 8,500 feet—higher than on the East Coast, because the ground itself was several thousand feet higher above sea level—toward the pattern-altitude target of 3,600 at a gentle 500-feet-per-minute pace of descent.

Part of my ritual for total immersion in the approach-and-landing process is to run through all the relevant numbers and specifications, often saying the results to myself aloud. "We're at fifty-five hundred feet, two thousand feet to go until thirty-five hundred." "We're at one hundred and twenty knots at pattern altitude of thirty-five hundred feet." "We're lining up with runway thirty-two, on final approach at eight knots, and I see the numbers three-two at the threshold."

The time this ritual seems most important is during an instrument approach in "actual" instrument conditions: that is, when you are pointing the plane downward, through a cloud, toward a runway you cannot see and amid terrain on either side that is also invisible. What keeps you safe is following the exact horizontal course and vertical descent path indicated by the dials in front of you, as you bring the plane down, down, down, until you reach the "decision altitude." At that point, you have either broken clear of the clouds and can see the runway or you must immediately climb out of danger in a "missed approach." "Twelve hundred feet going to six hundred," I will say aloud to myself when in a cloud following the glide slope down. If we descend to the decision altitude and the runway's not in sight, it's time to execute missed approach. I then shift the airplane into full-power climb and tell the tower, "Four-three-five Sierra Romeo going missed."

We landed in Dodge City just before the summer solstice. Temperatures hovered in the nineties, and hot wind blew across the prairies, keeping the immense wind turbines that populate this land churning. Flying in from the south, we looked down on the harvest of the wheat fields, which had reached about the halfway mark, and the occasional oil wells. Over north Texas, we had seen the roads cut through the fields by the ranchers, farmers, and oil drillers. In a Texas-patriotic gesture, one road through the fields had been cleared in the unmistakable shape of that great state. Surely the rancher couldn't have seen that from his perspective (and it was slightly lopsided), but we appreciated his tipping the hat to travelers like us, who, he knew, would fly over one day.

Finally, we saw the small city (population about 30,000) materializing in the distance. The real sign that we had arrived in southwestern Kansas came as we taxied to park the plane. I cracked open the door to draw a breeze into the broiling cockpit. The breeze blew in a much stronger version of the pungent and unmistakable odor of cattle from the feedlots, which had made its presence known during the descent. "The smell of money," as one Dodge City resident later remarked, a phrase I'm sure he had used a thousand times before.

We chatted with the folks at Crotts Aircraft, the FBO where we parked our plane, about the airplane paraphernalia decorating the lounge. With long distances across the flat lands, we found the flying familiar and commonplace in this part of the country. Crotts called us a few mornings later to say that it looked like some weather (which in Kansas means "bad weather") was coming, and offered to tow the plane from the tarmac into a hangar. That sounded like a good idea.

Sure enough, around midday something fierce blew toward Dodge. We watched it approach as we entered the new United Wireless convention center on the far west edge of the city, where the outskirts of the town's development stopped and seven bison, including three new spring calves, grazed on the land. We had come to lunch on chicken-fried steak and listen to the State of the City address by Mayor Joyce Warshaw, who itemized for an hour the many improvements and changes in Dodge City, from the arrival of new commercial air service to Denver to the city's 100 percent reuse of wastewater. The mayor had married into the Warshaw family of Dodge, early clothiers who left their telltale imprint in the brick front of one of the retail buildings still standing on Second Avenue in town.

To hang out in Dodge City is to be transported from one era to the next and back again. What put Dodge City on the map in the first place was cattle. Cowboys drove them up from Texas and in from the range to Dodge City, developed alongside the cavalry's existing Fort Dodge outpost. Then the railroads took live cattle or slaughtered cuts of meat on to markets in Chicago or farther east.

Gunfighters, buffalo hunters, drifters, railroad builders, traders, no-nonsense women, and soldiers from Fort Dodge just up the road—that was Dodge City, Kansas, in the 1870s. Wyatt Earp, Bat Masterson, and Doc Holliday—they are some of the characters who passed through or settled there. It was a famously lawless town with saloons, gambling, brothels, and shootouts. In a brief fifteen years, the stuff of legends flourished, and thrives even today as a tourist draw—especially among Germans, whose reruns of the 1950s TV series *Gunsmoke* have made a visit to Dodge City something of a pilgrimage.

Fast-forward two decades: electricity, water wells, sewer lines, a fire department, graded streets, and telephones arrived. Then, in 1905, another milestone of gentrification: a group of distinguished Dodge City residents, including a doctor and a judge (Edmond Madison, later a U.S. congressman from Kansas), was inspired by the women's club of Dodge City to write to Andrew Carnegie requesting support to build a library. Carnegie was already building five libraries in Kansas that year, and he granted Dodge City $7,500 for theirs. The city commissioned an unusual design in what was called the "free eclectic" style, with a rounded front, and the building was placed on a diagonal that still commands the corner view of commercial Second Avenue.

Today's Dodge makes the most of this heritage and the city's ongoing economic reality, in ways as kitschy as the refurbished Long Branch Saloon and as elegant as the city's logo, a silhouette of a group of trail riders on their mounts, which is featured on the way into and out of town and on many street signs. It also copes with being one of those American cities that is still immediately in touch with the dirty, dangerous, harsh work on which a meat-consuming society is based, thus shaping much of its economic and civic life. "This is a beef town," several people said with a tone of both pride and discomfort.

Modern-day Dodge City is a "red" part of one of the country's politically reddest states. In the 2016 election, just a few months after our visit, Donald Trump took 67 percent of the vote in Ford County, whose county seat and population center is Dodge City, versus just 27 percent for Hillary Clinton. But as with the political contrast and comparison of Burlington, Vermont, and Greenville, South Carolina—apparently opposite extremes in national politics that function very similarly at the local level—the red/blue categorization proves less valuable as a predictor of how people in this town deal with issues that are so poisonous at the national level, from immigration to environmental policy to the proper role of government.

One example is taxes. In national politics and at the state level, Dodge's residents often vote for tax-cutting conservatives. Locally they pin their city's long-term hopes on a daring tax-increase plan.

In 1997, the city's voters approved a permanent sales-tax increase totaling 1 percent, with the proceeds to be used for long-term civic improvements. This is known as the "Why Not Dodge?" initiative. Nearly everywhere you look in town, there's another project funded by the ongoing flow of Why Not Dodge? revenues. They include a large public soccer complex; the Cavalier Field and Legends Park baseball and softball complexes; an auto raceway; a new civic center; a large expo site; a brand-new aquatics park, the Long Branch Lagoon, which was in very heavy use during our visits; and repairs on a historic railroad depot.

In effect, a very conservative community voted itself an open-ended tax to pay for long-term infrastructure improvement. Why was this possible here, when its counterparts at the national level are gridlocked out of consideration?

"We may be 'conservative,' but we're progressive," Melissa McCoy, who grew up not far from Dodge City and is now the city's project development coordinator, told me. "There was a time when we had a really negative self-image as a town. But people thought, 'If we won't invest in ourselves, how can we expect anybody else to?' It was a matter of getting the community behind it and realizing that we needed to back ourselves up to get outside investment and support. Now we're starting to see it pay off."

I asked Mayor Warshaw whether there was any mystery or contradiction in a politically conservative community enacting a permanent infrastructure-improvement tax. Warshaw is herself a Republican; she ran (but lost) in the GOP primary for the Kansas state senate this year.

"Not at all," she said. "It's been *so* beneficial for the city. This community is incredible in embracing things that need to happen for the city. I think many people saw how important it was to raise taxes just a minute little bit to raise our quality of life here in Dodge."

Something similar was true of ethnic politics. Voters across Kansas, and in Dodge City, voted for candidates advocating a much tougher line on immigrants. In their own town, they operated very differently.

\* \* \*

The middle of the country is more of an immigrant magnet than you would guess from most stories about "flyover country." The cities and farms of the inland-America expanse from Buffalo, Pittsburgh, and Cleveland across to Denver and the mining towns of the Rockies attracted immigrant labor in the late 1800s. The cities, farms, and suburbs of interior America are doing so again now. Minnesota and South Dakota have been important refugee-resettlement areas. Almost every sizable city in the Plains States and the Midwest now also has a sizable Hispanic population.

The reasons for the migration differ region by region. In western Kansas, railroad construction drew a diverse workforce in the late 1800s, and now the meatpacking industry has done the same.

In southwestern Kansas, it's easy to see the demographic age pyramid typical of areas undergoing rapid and ongoing immigration. That is, the younger the age bracket, the larger its Latino proportion. The school-age population of Dodge City is 70 to 80 percent non-white, mainly Latino. The town's population as a whole is more than half Latino. But the business and political leadership, mainly older members of longer-established families, is mainly white. Nothing about this is surprising: through the long history of U.S. immigration, the first-generation arrivals concentrate on economic survival, leaving broader civic engagement to their children and grandchildren.

This imbalance brings the obvious potential for friction and resentment, of the sort given such clear voice during the 2016 presidential campaign. For instance, the school population looks very different from the people who are paying most of the school taxes and making decisions on the school board. But as we've noted throughout this journey, the more ferocious the anti-immigrant passion, the more distant actual immigrants tended to be, and the more theoretical—and, apparently, the more frightening—their menace was.

Put another way: in communities like those in western Kansas, whose economic vitality today and demographic prospects for tomorrow depend on attracting new residents, people have worked out a modus vivendi that resembles ethnic change through America's past. It has always involved strains, whether with the arrival of the Germans and the Irish in the 1800s, or the Italians and the Slavs at the start of the 1900s, or the Cubans and Filipinos in the middle of the twentieth century, or the Vietnamese and Salvadorans near the end, or the groups that have arrived since. Over time, American society has absorbed and flexed—and, in my view, benefited—from being able to accommodate and assimilate newcomers more easily than any other advanced society. That is how western Kansas seemed to us.

Dodge City had long had an ethnically mixed population, because of workers who arrived during its cattle-drive and railroad heydays in the late 1800s and afterward. But its modern makeup began changing when the big packinghouses started arriving in the early 1980s. The two major operations that dominate Dodge City's economy are those of Cargill Meat Solutions and National Beef.

"Packinghouse" is a nicer term for what once was called a slaughter-house, much as "meat solutions" is a nicer name for the company, and "harvesting cattle" is a nicer job-description term for the work of put-ting animals to death, one after another, through the workday. We didn't push for a look inside the packinghouses during our visits, because I have seen places like them before and understand their reality.

The economy that supports the packinghouses defines Dodge City: the associated feedlots that ring the city and in which the animals spend the final months or weeks of their lives, putting on weight; the trucks that roll in nonstop, bearing live animals into the huge buildings on the south side and carrying boxes of cut meat back out; and also the many thousands of people who earn their living inside. Something like a quar-ter of the beef eaten anywhere in the United States comes through the feedlots, packinghouses, and shipment centers of this corner of Kansas. Large quantities are also shipped overseas.

The employees in these factories are nearly all immigrants. In the 1980s, a substantial number were recent arrivals from Vietnam. Now they're mainly Mexicans or from Central and South America, plus an increasing number of Somalis and other Africans, plus some Southeast Asians and others. Pay rates vary but are much above minimum wage. For instance, a current listing for a starting position in "beef harvesting" at Cargill offers $15.50 an hour, with medical and 401(k) benefits, in an area where the living costs are very low. The work can, obviously, be unpleasant and extremely hard.

"I can tell you that no matter what wages you paid, you are not going to find any reasonable number of 'native-born' Americans who will do those jobs," stated a man who has been a manager for a large packing-house in the area; he preferred not to be identified. "Your Anglo com-munity is not going to work there, pretty much regardless of the wage. The entire meatpacking industry depends on immigrant labor, and always has."

The syllogism we heard from him and many others was: Without the meatpacking industries, these towns in western Kansas would have withered. Without immigrants, mainly from Mexico, the meatpacking and feedlot industry would not exist. The economic and cultural survival of places like Dodge City and Garden City depends on immigrants, some of whom arrive legally and many of whom don't. "There are some pockets of people here who are 'old school,'" the onetime packinghouse manager told us. "They'd like to 'take America back' and so on. But by and large, people here—Anglo and Hispanic and otherwise—recognize that we're in this together. The immigrants are the engine that keeps this community alive."

While we were in Kansas, we saw a study of the meat-based regional economy written by Brian Hanson, who works for a think tank called the Center for Rural Affairs. "Latinos and immigrants are not only bringing population growth to rural America, they are also bringing economic growth," Hanson noted in the study. "Economists have found that, nationwide, rural counties with larger proportions of Latino populations tend to be better off economically than those with smaller Latino populations. Rural counties with higher proportions of Latinos tend to have lower unemployment rates and higher average per capita incomes."

In Dodge City, the unemployment rate is among the lowest anywhere in the nation, somewhere below 3 percent. The city has a permanent website listing open positions, called DodgeCityHasJobs.com.

You might argue about the direction of the causal arrows: Are immigrants drawn to areas that already have strong economies? Or do they make economies stronger by their presence? Probably some of both is true. But the result is unmistakable. Across much of the plains and the rural midwestern region of the United States, what has kept communities alive is new arrivals, mainly from countries to the south.

I spoke with Greg Ruehle about the cultural side of the changed demographics in Dodge City. Ruehle, who grew up on a farm in Iowa, is CEO of Servi-Tech, a company that helps farmers across the Plains States increase their yields while optimizing their use of fertilizer, pesticides, and water, using technologies that allow precision foot-by-foot monitoring of growing conditions in the fields. Ruehle said that he and his family, who had come to Dodge City three years earlier, found it a great place to live. "It's an interesting culture, in part because there is such a big immigrant population here," he told me. "We're halfway through our son's third-grade year, and he was the only one in the family who knew the second verse to 'Feliz Navidad.' And you know what, that will serve him well!"

"If you ask about the population here, there are two answers," Ruehle told me. "There is the documented population, that's one number. The second number includes the undocumented population, which is bigger—we just don't know how much bigger.

"But Dodge City has found a way to make this work," he said. "No one fought it in the schools. I'm a pretty conservative guy, but I think we have to keep finding a better way to integrate this diverse population into our economy. If I say it in conservative circles, I might run the risk of somebody heating up the pot of tar, to tar and feather me. But it's the reality of our town."

An Anglo former meatpacking employee we met late in our stay summed up what we had heard from others, "The reality here in southwest Kansas is that we are heavily influenced by the Hispanic culture, and not just economically," he said. "They are part of the fabric of our community. If they decided to pack up and leave, Dodge City would be a ghost town. And we realize that the future success of the Hispanic community predicts the future success of our community as a whole."

One of those arrivals is Ernestor De La Rosa. When we met him, Ernestor was the assistant finance director and assistant to the city manager of Dodge City, and a sparkplug of civic life there. He is a handsome, slightly built man in his early thirties, most striking on first impression because of his large, dark eyes. If you listened carefully to De La Rosa for a minute or two, you could pick up clues that English was not his first language. But you would have to be listening closely. When Ernestor De La Rosa arrived in the United States, at age thirteen, he did not speak or read English at all. He was born and raised in Mexico and first came to the States on a visitor visa. Other members of his family were already in Kansas, working in the meatpacking plants. He eventually joined them in Dodge City; finished high school and then college; got a master's degree in public administration at Wichita State University, the innovative, leading school in this part of the Plains; and came back to Dodge City.

Starting in 2000, De La Rosa and other members of his family got in the queue for a green card. Sixteen years later, he was still waiting. But he was able to work in the United States now because of DACA, or Deferred Action for Childhood Arrivals, the Obama administration's 2012 executive order that allows people who arrived before age sixteen (as De La Rosa did) to get renewable work permits, and be exempt from deportation, while the U.S. government figures out some longer-term reform to its immigration policy. Of course, this policy was one of several that Donald Trump proposed changing as part of his crackdown on immigration.

"When I arrived, I was still a kid and didn't think about what was happening," De La Rosa told us. "I didn't think, 'I'm going to a different country, I need to learn a different language.' I didn't think about any of that. More than anything, I was enthusiastic about my family and the schools, and the help I got there. I couldn't be here now"—as a city official, a prominent young member of the city's new ethnic majority—"without the help and encouragement of my teachers after I arrived."

I asked De La Rosa whether he consciously thought of himself as part of a transition in the Latino community's local role.

"We already have many leaders working in many sectors," he said. "But I am hopeful that there will be more and more. If people see me working for the city, it might encourage others to step up. They might think, 'I could do that too.' We'd like to encourage young families to participate more in city and county affairs, and be more represented in all local events."

What did he think when he heard the "Build a wall!" chants?—which, by the way, were a more typical feature of rallies in New Hampshire or Michigan than of those in places where arrivals from Mexico had mainly congregated. "When we hear things like this," he answered, "it just sounds so irrelevant. It's not the story we are seeing here in Dodge City at all.

"Our people here work. They want to establish themselves here in Dodge City. They want to raise their families and have a future. It's unfamiliar to us, these comments being made on the national level. We are doing everything we can to integrate the newcomers and their families."

I asked De La Rosa about his long-term ambitions. He said that eventually he hoped to become a city manager, in Kansas or elsewhere. "I'd like to continue to help my community and encourage our Latino and other immigrants that you can do these things, even if you don't start with the proper documentation," he said. "I'd like to encourage them to pursue their dreams."

When I first arrived at Dodge City High School, I headed straight for the lake. That would be Demon Lake, the acre-sized pond at the side of the school grounds, where students practice their catch-and-release techniques on bluegill, catfish, and bass. Fishing in landlocked Dodge City, Kansas? No problem. With hefty funding from the Kansas Department of Wildlife, Parks, and Tourism, a lake was made with reclaimed wastewater and stocked with fish. I had never heard of high school fishing before—not even at my hometown high school, in a fishing town on the south shore of Lake Erie.

Jacque Feist, the DCHS principal, and her associate principal Mike Martinez met me on that hot late-June morning. Except for the brief diversion of some fire trucks responding to a false alarm, things were pretty quiet at the school. Some summer courses hosted a small number of students. Feist and Martinez described their school's operating principle: kids first, then teachers, then administration.

Martinez said he wants this school to be a place "where the kids can be themselves," adding, "If five or six kids are interested in snakes, we'll start a herpetology club, and they'll be crawling in caves." The school website lists more than thirty activity groups, from an animation club to a student-run business to the Demon Outdoor Club, which includes not only fishing but clay-target shooting and archery. Beyond those activities, the school curriculum, with its sixteen career clusters, whets kids' appetites in everything from welding to foreign service to communications.

The point of all this, Feist and Martinez explained to me, is to give every kid a place at the school and a sense that their interests—whether snakes or fish or art—matter and belong at the school. Translation: the students themselves belong at the school. The result: "Demon Pride."

Much of the reason that this inclusion works, according to Feist and Martinez, is the common ethic of the faculty and administrators and their solid grounding with Dodge City and its schools. Most of the adults at the high school have invested their lives and careers in the school and the community. Feist, who exudes energy, has been at Dodge City schools for three decades. Martinez, who looks impossibly young to claim it, has been there for two. There is little turnover among teachers, many of whom are homegrown or from nearby. Only one of twelve new teachers hired that year was from out of state. One measure of faculty and staff dedication: DCHS made history in 2016 by claiming the Kansas Teacher of the Year honor for the second year in a row. A larger-than-life-sized poster of the two winning teachers standing back to back, math teacher Justin Coffey and biology teacher Shannon Ralph, greets you in the school entry. In his own category, the twelve-year veteran school-bus driver Eduardo Escobedo won the "top transit-class school-bus driver" at the Kansas School Bus Rodeo Safety Competition.

The history of the student population is very different from that of the staff. Since the late 1980s, the demographic composition of Dodge City's students has dramatically changed. According to one estimate we heard from city officials, the Hispanic population in grades K–12 would have been about 20 percent in the 1980s, and is nearly 80 percent today. First Mexicans, then waves of others from Central American countries like El Salvador, Honduras, and Guatemala. Dodge City is, in effect, a "port of entry," says Robert Vinton, the director of the Dodge City Migrant Education program, even though it is nearly seven hundred miles north of the border. The high school is about 70 percent Hispanic, with another 7 percent designated as "other," which includes African and Asian immigrant populations; the rest are Anglo. In the high school,

36 percent of students are English-language learners. But now hear this: the heavily Anglo voting population of Dodge City passed an $85 million school bond to support the heavily Hispanic-population schools in June 2015 with 58 percent approval. For the high school, this means a new academic wing and expansions to some career technical centers, the performing arts space, and physical education facilities.

Keeping a school coherent throughout such dynamic changes is challenging. Each August, some twenty or thirty new immigrant students are likely to show up. They continue to dribble in through May. The latest wave came from Guatemala, many of whom—even at the high school level—were entering a classroom for the first time and were illiterate. At home, conditions are often poor, and many families arrive with a rough history.

Creating a safe and positive place for these students is important to the school system and to the city overall. That's because Dodge City is no longer a stop on the road for most migrant families. Think of Ernestor! The work opportunities, primarily at the meatpacking plants, are year-round and pay a wage that most workers consider solid. The families are in Dodge to stay.

Many of the children of Dodge City immigrants—unlike their parents—know only this way of life. The school administrators told me that their students today "don't see color," which speaks to the mature integration of races within Dodge City. One sign of this particularly struck me: while kids often tend to hang out with their own ethnicity or race, the norm I saw in Dodge City school halls, at the public library, and at the public swimming pool was groups of kids all jumbled up. However they were sorting themselves out, it didn't look to be on the basis of ethnicity or race.

I dutifully asked Feist about the usual problems in American schools: drugs, alcohol, bullying, and the like. "We have them all," she said. Any other answer would have been suspect, of course. A look through the school's website or newsletters confirms those problems, and many more, do exist and are aggressively addressed. Among the social services I saw: counseling for students who are pregnant, who are already moms, who have incarcerated parents; resources for everything from suicide prevention to intervention in self-cutting and alcohol abuse. There were also reminders that drug-sniffing dogs would occasionally be present.

\* \* \*

About four hundred students in Dodge City schools are designated as a special subset of minority: migrants. According to the federal definition, being a migrant child means you have been in the current school district for no more than three years and you are a child of a parent working in agriculture or fishing. Migrants are the newcomers. In Dodge City, employment mainly means working the line at National Beef or Cargill, in jobs that stop short of actual packaging of the product. No office workers, no administrative jobs. "Hands on with raw product," says Robert Vinton, in his no-frills language.

During a visit I paid him on a very hot July morning, Vinton described how the migrant population of Dodge City has changed over the years. He gathered several of his staff, all women, in the spacious but modest office in the old Dodge City Community College building. Here are some of the points they raised in building a profile of Dodge City migrants:

*Arrivals:* The children are arriving at older ages than they were thirty years ago; many are already in their teens. Some children come with families; others don't. There are many monikers that describe children's varying status. Some "border children" are smuggled in alone or with an older companion. Some are designated as "emancipated youth," having no parents responsible for them. Others are the "migrant out of school youth"—those up to age twenty-two who are working but who do not yet have a high school diploma. A sizable number of new migrants are designated as SLIFE kids. SLIFE is an unfortunate acronym that everyone struggles to deconstruct; it stands for "students with limited or interrupted formal education." They are the teenagers who have rarely or never been to school before.

Vinton occasionally referred to the migrant children as "kiddos." This was the second time I had heard this term used by a Dodge City education administrator; Mike Martinez had also used the word. "Kiddo" is a familiar term of endearment to my midwestern ears, and it struck me as a more humane way to refer to the children than "border children" or "emancipated youths" or "migrants."

*Language:* Most of the migrants speak Spanish. More than 50 percent of the students (not all of them migrants) in the DCPS are enrolled in well-established English-Language Learner (ELL) programs. The recently arrived Guatemalans have brought a new linguistic twist. While Guatemala is officially a Spanish-speaking country, roughly twenty-four indigenous languages are spoken there as well. For some who arrive in Dodge City, an indigenous language is their sole language. This forces the same kind of telephone-game translation system I saw applied in Sioux Falls, where a series of interpreters hot-potato a conversation from English to two or three other languages and back again.

The children learn English quickly, of course. I watched a conversation at the checkout desk of the Dodge City Public Library play out one day, as the English-speaking librarian talked to a young Spanish-speaking father about his overdue books. He needed to return the books or pay a fine before he could check out more, she tried to make him understand. He looked hopelessly puzzled until his very young daughter was finally summoned from the children's section to serve as translator.

*Academics:* The schools are balancing multiple pressures. They must meet their traditional goal for high graduation rates, provide a realistic "career path" for many students toward trades like welding or mechanics, teach some students to be basically functional in English, and address the extreme challenges from some entering migrant students. In Dodge City, there are some illiterate teenage children arriving who "don't know how to hold a pencil," Vinton told me.

*Culture:* Much of what we know in our bones arrives out of left field to new immigrants or refugees. How do you explain to those who have fled from desperate circumstances via a difficult journey and survived by keeping their heads down that it is all right to seek advocacy or to complain if someone—a landlord, for instance—seems to be taking advantage of you? How do you establish a foundation of trust to convince a migrant that legal rights allow you to speak up, and that it won't stir up trouble for you, especially in a newly politically charged era?

Support systems in Dodge City involve not only the schools, but also dozens of additional city and civic groups, ranging from the Salvation Army to the dental clinic to the emergency shelter, the health clinic, churches, and the credit union. Other centers help with testing, placement, community information, referrals to other agencies that can help with even more pieces of life.

Dodge City's public library, a foundational block in the support system, is called a "Family Place Library"; it offers all sorts of resources, workshops, and connections for parents and caregivers who are learning to raise young children, immigrant or not. There were scads of kids in the library each time I visited; they were searching for books, working on their summer reading programs, playing in the early childhood area, coloring and drawing. One day, I stopped by the big multiuse space in the lower level, where at least 250 kids, with adults in tow, had come for a demo and program with a traveling group from the Wichita Exploration Place. A few middle schoolers working at the library that summer were helping the kids run around obstacle courses, climb through tunnels, and try archery. I asked one of the young volunteers where she would be if not the library on that hot day. "Probably at the pool."

One staffer in Vinton's Migrant Education office described her home visits to families. She would, for example, arrive bearing shrink-wrapped packets of age-appropriate books for the half a dozen young children in a single family, calling each by name and handing them what she said are most likely the first books they have ever owned in their lives.

A staffer described the meal one family was eating when she arrived: cereal with water. I recalled this detail when I watched the 1960 Edward R. Murrow mind-set-shifting TV documentary *Harvest of Shame,* about poverty among migrant workers. A migrant woman identified as Mrs. Doby, the mother of nine children, described a typical family dinner: "Well, I cook a pot of beans and fry some potatoes, some corn or something like that. We don't have milk except when we draw a paycheck—we have milk maybe once a week." Teaching nutrition is also something the Migrant Education program tries to do today.

* * *

We were lucky enough to be in Dodge City on a so-called Final Friday evening for the monthly visual, culinary, and performing arts community walk around town; it kicked off at the Carnegie Center for the Arts, which is housed in the original Carnegie library building. That Friday's demonstrations featured Wanda Adamson, a quilter from the 850-strong nearby town of Jetmore. People milled about and then drifted down to the next venue, the Second Avenue Art Guild, to sample wine and cheese among the works of local artists. We talked with Jake Hendrix, a young millennial who was part of a large family of artists showing their creations that night. Jake still worked on the family farm and was also launching a start-up with his brother Rob, the Hendrix Keg Company, to make mini–beer kegs powered by carbon dioxide cartridges.

We also met John and Connie Chavez. He's a saxophone player with the Dodge City Cowboy Band, a community band since 1879 that still performs for the town each week during the summer. Later that week, on the Fourth of July, we joined much of Dodge and its tourists under a tent in front of the Long Branch Saloon, where actors in period regalia stage surprisingly alarming shoot-outs by day. That evening, Chavez and the Cowboy Band performed with a troupe of Hispanic and Anglo high-kicking cancan dancers. Like so many small towns in America, Dodge City goes all out with parades, barbecues, and spectacular celebrations. Afterward, we counted at least half a dozen fireworks displays along the flat horizons in Dodge, all visible from our third-story hotel room next to the casino on the edge of town.

Our final stop that evening was the old Dodge City railway depot, a Richardsonian Romanesque building erected in 1896, during the bustling rail days when the Atchison, Topeka and Santa Fe Railway stopped in Dodge City to move buffalo and, later, longhorn cattle from Texas. Today, Dodge City is an Amtrak stop for the Southwest Chief, which comes through town a few times a day. Mark Vierthaler, the new marketing director of the start-up Boot Hill Distillery, was, with a flourish, pouring his signature drink, "the Playa," a concoction he makes from light rum, lavender syrup, and elderflower liqueur.

That evening, we walked much of Second Avenue, to where the buildings turned over from earlier merchants, including the Warshaws, into bars, nail salons, or photographers' shops. Some shops sell clothing with a western flair and others offer *quinceañera* dresses for rent to fifteen-year-olds for their gala celebrations. Large murals of western scenes are painted on the broad sides of a multistory building. The old *Dodge City Daily Globe* building remains as today's office. Roger Bluhm, a heavyset man in his late forties with a shaved head, had worked at small newspapers around the country—Nebraska, Pennsylvania, Missouri, elsewhere—before coming to Dodge City as the *Globe*'s managing editor. He volunteered that he was a recovering alcoholic who had been sober for twenty-five years. He drank coffee continuously from a mug the size of a beer growler while we met with him. "This has been a city that has absorbed outsiders from the beginning," he said, about the response to immigrants and refugees. "It makes it go more smoothly now."

Downtown Dodge City has some way to go before it rivals everyone's favorite model downtown of Greenville, but it has potential and what lots of people would call good bones. Two new establishments are coming to town. A microbrewery called Dodge City Brewing Company will be built on the empty lot on Third Avenue, and it will be a welcome rival to the highway row of fast food stops for hungry tourists—KFC, McDonald's, Arby's, Burger King, Subway, Sonic, Taco Bell, and Applebee's, which has the most strategic location right outside the information center and the Boot Hill Museum and reconstructed Williamsburg-like shops.

The Boot Hill Distillery has undertaken an ambitious renovation of the former Municipal Building that is nearly finished; we took a tour of the gleaming distilling room and tasted a few of the spirits at the restored long bar.

# Garden City and Spearville, Kansas

We took a few field trips outside Dodge, the first heading east about seventeen miles to the town of Spearville, population eight hundred, deep in corn and wheat country. Prosperity has come to Spearville (sounds like spur-vul), recently, with the growth of wind-produced electricity, which has more than doubled in the last five years in the United States. "Out here," Mayor Kevin Heeke told us, "anything under a twenty-mile-an-hour wind . . . is a breeze."

Capitalizing on that natural asset, farmers have let energy companies plant rows of giant space-age-like turbine towers in their fields. With a two-hundred-plus-foot tower, topped by a one-hundred-plus-foot blade, and sweeping nearly an acre of airspace, the windmills have changed the landscape of the town.

Mayor Heeke described the farmers' and town's reaction. "People could see a way of generating income. The towers don't take up that much space. They farm right around them. It just goes with the city of Spearville." Farmers' incomes have as much as doubled. The city has benefited as well. We drove past new playgrounds, a new school, and other signs of economic health that the wind energy has brought to Spearville.

Another day, we drove west from Dodge City toward its neighbor Garden City. Dodge City, Garden City, and Liberal compose the so-called beef triangle of Kansas. Dodge envies Garden its big-box stores; Garden envies Dodge its impressive development and buildings, like the arena, the Boot Hill Casino, the Long Branch Lagoon water park, the raceway, and the classy athletic fields. Neither seems to envy Liberal.

As we headed to Garden City, about fifty miles west of Dodge, we passed farms, feedlots, and a wind-turbine blade distribution center. On U.S. 50, we routinely slowed behind trucks hauling cattle or harvested wheat. Also, small convoys trailed the transporter of a single 120-foot wind turbine blade like a presidential motorcade. When one of those trucks gets to an intersection, traffic stops in all directions as it navigates the turn.

We were meeting up with Sister Roserita Weber and Sister Janice Thome, nuns of the Dominican Order of Peace, who serve the poor in Garden City, to accompany them on their delivery rounds from the town's food pantry. The two sisters were sympathetic but no-nonsense. They dealt with tough cases daily, as they taught folks to drive, or helped them negotiate medical bills, or drove families the seven-hour round-trip to Wichita for services found only in the big city. They lived modestly in a midcentury split-level in the center of town, a place comfortable yet basic. A large statue of the Blessed Virgin Mary presided from a pedestal in a corner of the dining room.

The food pantry was set up in a small warehouse. We waited our turn to sign in and assemble our shares to distribute. A line of others waited behind us, showing the documentation entitling them to the free food.

I was expecting fresh foods similar to those in Ajo's food bank, which included at least some potatoes, broccoli, and citrus. But in the absence of a thriving local garden-to-table food movement like Ajo's, Garden City's donated goods came from some of their big-box stores or chains. A typical delivery that day included a few frozen entrées, bags of rolls, a pizza, a pair or two of brightly colored socks, a pack of cookies, and maybe a roll of frozen venison (although Sister Janice worried that none of her recipients—all Hispanic—would be familiar with venison or how to cook it). One lucky family would receive a frozen chicken.

Garden City, like Dodge and Liberal, is now a majority-minority city. Its population is already mostly Hispanic (estimates range from 50 to 60 percent), and trending upward as new employees find better-than-minimum-wage yet very difficult jobs at the meatpacking plants.

Sister Rosenta and Jim went in one direction, and Sister Janice and I started in the other. Sister Janice asked me if I needed the air conditioner on in the car. It was clear to me that the right answer would be no, since the AC would consume more fuel. If Sister Janice could take it, so could I. We each delivered to five or six families, those whose plans for a new life built around the meatpacking plants had slipped off the rails. Sister Janice and I started at the bungalow of a woman named Hilda. Her house was meticulously kept, with heavy wooden furniture, photos, and decor clearly from Mexico. In 1989, she had been badly injured in a car accident, which killed her only son and left her able to take care of herself and her housekeeping, but little more. Her husband had recently taken up with another woman, leaving debts on his way out. Hilda fell between the financial cracks, receiving a monthly settlement from her accident that was too little to allow her to do more than scrape by and too much to let her qualify for other benefits or move forward in her life. I asked if I could take a few photos, and she asked me back, immediately and rhetorically, if I would like to see her bedroom. She posed proudly next to the bed, her pièce de résistance, with its ornately carved heavy wooden headboard and an opulent red-and-gold damask medallion bedspread

Sister Janice and I drove on to another Hispanic family with a single mother. At the door of the small, dark house—the kind where you feel the floorboards give a little beneath you from the lack of a solid foundation, the dim interior not quite cool against the summer heat—we met the teenage daughter, who cared for her epileptic brother while her mom was at work, and she chatted with us about her summer. She said she wasn't doing much, except reading. Right now, she said, she was reading a book called *Bad Boy Next Door*. I later saw online that there are two books with that title, and a third more emphatically named *So Bad: Bad Boy Next Door*. She declined the venison we offered, as she didn't know how to cook it.

As we raced through the next stops, which were all trailers, everything began to blur. Here are two families' stories in short:

A woman from Guatemala fled with her husband from the guerrillas; they gained temporary political asylum in the United States; the husband lost his status and was repatriated; the woman moved quickly with the children when neighbors told her the INS was also looking for her. She has a number of kids (five or six; I wasn't sure), and for a while, she raised some chickens and earned $100 a week by babysitting. Then she became sick; she started bleeding, the source of which turned out to be a tumor. No one was home when we stopped by, so we left the box on the steps to the trailer door, piling the frozen items together and hoping some family member would arrive home soon before everything thawed.

Another Hispanic woman lived in a small, neat trailer, with flowers and a carefully groomed bit of outdoor landscaping. She said she had been serially beaten by her husband, who then started in on their eight-year-old daughter. One day, after the husband inadvertently left the family's only cell phone behind, the woman managed to call the police. They arrived, but so did the husband, who persuaded his wife not to press charges. He has since left her alone, but without a chance for winning a non-immigrant U visa (for those who have suffered substantial physical or mental abuse), since she disqualified herself by not pressing charges. Catch-22. With hopes of a path to moving on, she is working on a U visa for her daughter, also abused, but who, as a minor, can apply for the visa. If that works, the daughter might be able to piggyback her mother along as sole guardian of a minor. There were many complicated stories in Garden City.

Sister Janice's cell phone continued to ring during our rounds. People were asking her for all manner of help, like gas money to get to Dodge City or answers for questions on a job application. Sister Janice says she gets twenty or thirty calls a week, and considerably more at the point in the month when utilities get disconnected.

We went to another trailer park; this one was more dismal since it had been abandoned by many occupants who numbered among the twenty-three hundred workers who lost their jobs after a fire in the ConAgra Beef Company on Christmas night of 2000. Some vacant trailers were covered with graffiti, their windows shattered. Sister Janice told me that initiation rites from gangs included this kind of derring-do that ruined the property. The stories from the families who remained in this park were entwined and twisted, more and less hopeful.

As I tried to absorb the plights and probable destinies for families like these, the indefatigable Sister Janice dropped me off at her house while she pressed on to transport a family from a school's summer free-lunch program to their trailer. By then, I had only one recurring, clichéd thought: They are all one accident or illness away from total disaster.

# Erie, Pennsylvania

From Gaithersburg, our hometown airport just outside D.C., the flight to Erie is just over ninety minutes. If you're heading north from Washington, a shift in phase usually comes around the time you cross the Susquehanna River and the border with Pennsylvania. Maryland is already rural by this point—farms and forests if you're headed eastward, toward Philadelphia, or the hills and low mountains that become the Appalachians if you head west and north. We passed over the long, wavelike ridges that carried the veins that made this Pennsylvania's coal country, near Johnstown and Altoona. From above, the ridges have an almost man-made, planned quality to their look, evenly spaced and symmetrical compared with the surprises and chaos of other hills. Then as we left the mountains behind us and crossed over the flatter, forested land of the northwest corner of the state, we caught a glimpse of Lake Erie, from nearly fifty miles away.

To Deb this sight meant coming home, because of her childhood along the lake. For me it involved looking for our destination of Erie—and beginning to pick it out by the most distinctive part of its geography, the Presque Isle Peninsula, which sweeps out, like a six-mile-long comma, from the city into the lake. In the distance, with the sun reflecting off the lake, I caught sight of the peninsula and the city of Erie—and then began to wonder, as I often did at new destinations whose location was defined by coastline or mountain, why the place we were about to see was not more famous.

A protected harbor, in the lee of the Presque Isle Peninsula, was dotted with little white-sailed boats that moored at night at the small boat marinas along the water. Miles of flat, sandy beach along the far shore of Presque Isle were paralleled by a line of breakwaters out in the lake, constructed to moderate wave surges and erosion, and a matching line of lifeguard stations and snack shops along the shore. In the grid of the city itself, on the bluffs overlooking the lake, the houses visible through the thick, leafy tree cover had a classic pre–World War II small-town America look. To the far right of our view of the city—up the lakeshore, toward Buffalo—was a huge industrial expanse, GE's main locomotive plant. To the far left, down the lake toward Cleveland and running parallel to the shore, was the long runway of Erie's main airport, Tom Ridge Field, named for the local boy who had become a Republican governor of Pennsylvania and, after the 9/11 attacks, the first secretary of Homeland Security.

The winds were strong and from the west, so with guidance from the Erie control tower I guided the plane over the GE plant and then came along the shore—water to our right, close in city and distant farmland to our left, runway ahead in the sunlight, the whole giving us a first impression of another American gem.

The second impression came as we drove through the city, where the vista was less of beauty than of decay. Along West Twelfth Street, the main road from the airport through town, we passed one abandoned hundred-year-old red-brick factory after another. To the left, a former brass-casting factory. To the right, a machine shop. In the historic downtown, vacant shop fronts outnumbered the occupied ones. In front of a tattered 1970s-era hotel, a crowd of mainly white homeless people congregated. On the highway out of town toward Penn State's satellite Behrend campus, the largest industrial building in the area sat with a caved-in roof, sunlight streaming through the bare rafters—and presumably rain and snow during the long winters, too.

These were all signs of the Erie that, as we came to know, would dominate election-cycle coverage of this part of the country: the declining, mainly white Rust Belt settlements where the loss of jobs meant the rise of resentment and fuel for Donald Trump. In the eight months after our visit—four months leading up to the election, four afterward trying to explain its results—both TV and newspaper reports used Erie as a classic case of the modern dispossession that had led to Trump-era politics. A generation ago, the GE locomotive plant had had a unionized workforce of thousands, and Erie, its environs, and the entire state of Pennsylvania had been Democratic strongholds. Now GE was shedding hundreds of jobs every year, the surrounding supply chain that fed it was withering, and while the city of Erie eked out a Democratic result in 2016, the county, the surrounding area, the state as a whole, and, of course, the nation, through the Electoral College, had chosen Donald Trump.

Those were two faces of Erie, two faces of America: natural blessings, modern cruelty and challenge. But over several visits to Erie, we found other equally compelling threads of the story of Erie, matching much of what we had seen in our travels across America.

Erie's downtown is a shifting mosaic of old and new. The original stately and imposing former U.S. Bank of Pennsylvania building, constructed in 1839, sits around the corner from the beckoning modern glass entry and outdoor esplanade of the LEED-certified Erie Art Museum. These are two complementary wings of a single sprawling complex, which reaches all the way down to the depths of the old bank vault, whose abundant holdings range from a folk art collection of duck decoys, which the museum's founding director John Vanco (a collector himself) showed me lined up and organized in a back room awaiting their debut center stage, to an installation by local artist Lisa Lichtenfels, depicting and memorializing the counter of a beloved Erie diner, the Avalon, where she had been a waitress.

Across the street is Erie's still-bustling army-navy surplus store, and farther along, to the south, are trendy new restaurants and microbreweries, and the YMCA under renovation. And beyond that, the classic

Renaissance Center building, whose worn 1920s-vintage exterior belies the start-up, progressive energy within.

To the north, and in season, the farmers' market and downtown summer jazz festival spill over downhill past hospitals and medical facilities to the up-and-coming harbor's edge, with its new hotels, restaurants, a convention center, and kitschy pirate ships for tourists to ride. This is the heart of the nautical heritage of Erie. Greeting you at the Blasco Memorial Library, with its reading room overlooking the harbor, is an installation called "Aquatic Dancers," by local artist John Vahanian, which reminded me of sails floating over the broad staircase in the main atrium. Adjacent is the Erie Maritime Museum, recounting the region's lake-centric history from Oliver Hazard Perry onward, and the Bicentennial Tower. If you get to the top of the tower, you can see in all directions, from the old town and out beyond Presque Isle, and you can steep a little in the history of Commodore Perry and the lake battles of the War of 1812. Erie feels like a work in progress, but one that is clearly progressing.

During our time there, we met two of Erie's elder visionaries, who are putting their muscle and money behind plans for a vibrant, composed downtown for Erie.

A few weeks before our visit, we learned that Joel Deuterman, a successful entrepreneur who had built his company in a suburban office park outside Erie, had announced that he was moving his Velocity Network, a provider of high-speed Internet services, into the middle of downtown. We looked at the vacant building proposed as the headquarters, and across the street to others where Deuterman thought he might invest in restaurants, cafés, and other common areas. These projects may provide not only the workplace but also the shopping, dining, and, eventually, condo and apartment living that could keep workers nearby. "When I was younger, I thought that business was a kill-or-be-killed proposition," remarked Deuterman, who is now in his early fifties and has reached a reflective point in his life. "I came to realize that if I did things with an awareness of the common good, the benefits would also come back to me, and with a heck of a lot less effort."

Even more an Erie veteran and bulwark is the major financial building block of the region: Erie Insurance, the home-grown Fortune 500 company and largest Erie employer, which was founded by H. O. Hirt, an anti–World War I socialist, nearly a century ago and remains under that ongoing family management through his son-in-law Tom Hagen. Hagen's youthful vigor and informal, easy, generous manner is a model of what many people would hope to be in their eighties. He and his late wife, Susie, have been behind Erie in so many ways that recounting them would fill extra pages in this book. Once we learned of the Hagens, we saw their names seemingly everywhere in philanthropic leadership, from rooms in the art museum to the back wing of the Chautauqua Institution Amphitheater. One of Hagen's missions has been a commitment to redeveloping the city's downtown and business base, which he has done through investments of hundreds of millions of dollars in Erie Insurance buildings in formerly troubled areas of downtown.

Start-ups are moving into town as well. Radius CoWork, a high-tech shared work space of the sort you would expect to find in Brooklyn or San Francisco—and that we had come to expect to find almost everywhere—moved into the Renaissance Centre, just a few blocks from the solid Erie Insurance headquarters and Deuterman's newly planned site.

We took the creaky elevator to the ninth floor of the once grande-dame building; it's the kind of elevator with a metal expandable inner door that takes all your effort and a careful eye on your fingers to operate. Inside the offices, you feel the permanence of the original and the promise of what might be. The big old office spaces have been chopped up, rearranged, and then shored up with sheetrock into smaller offices. The decor is make-do. But the activity, that's a different matter.

There are designers, software engineers, creative types, business entrepreneurs, caterers, and video makers—many of them sporting remarkable tattoos, hair designs, and apparel.

Just a few doors away from Radius are the offices of the *Erie Reader,* a successful print publication in the model of *Seven Days* in Burlington. The *Reader* has been publishing since 2010. Its long-form reporting and opinions have made it a must-read among the progressive-minded population in Erie. The annual "40 Under 40" is an index of young business, cultural, and civic figures who have chosen to make something happen *here*. It is a competitive field, and the number of candidates for this recognition continues to grow.

These advances in Erie are fighting the currents of some serious traditional structural obstacles.

Pennsylvania's school-funding system is one of them. Compared with other states, it is uniquely unfair, in effect giving the cities with the least local resources (like downtown Erie) the smallest amount of state aid. The schools were nearly broke, and had pinched every penny they could to stretch the budgets. On the hot summer day we met with the then-school superintendent, Jay Badams, he apologized for the lack of air-conditioning, which they had turned off as a way of saving a little money.

School was not yet in session, but even driving past the imposing Gothic campus of Collegiate Academy, formerly known as Academy High School, we saw immediate evidence of the lack of dollars for upkeep and maintenance that the system requires. It had gotten so bad that not long before our visit, Erie's school system had threatened simply to close its public high schools unless the funding inequities were resolved. (A cruel twist of the knife: Pennsylvania requires districts to offer schooling only up to age fourteen. In practice, Erie would have paid to bus the students to the surrounding, much-better-funded suburban schools. After fighting for years to make the case for fairer school funding for Erie, while reorganizing and consolidating the school districts and also reducing spending, in early 2017 Badams took a job as superintendent of a district that covers schools in Hanover, New Hampshire, and Norwich, Vermont. "This is a town that is often hampered by its absolute refusal to move on from tradition," Badams said of Erie, in a departure interview with the *Erie Times-News*. "I'm proud of our school community . . . for leading the way. The district is going to go through this process of re-imagining itself and then seeing that to reality in a way that could be emulated by the rest of the city.")

In stark contrast to the challenges of the K–12 system in Erie is the explosion of its postsecondary opportunities. For starters, there are nearby major colleges: Penn State's Behrend campus, with over five thousand students and a separate R&D center and engineering and business schools; Gannon University and Mercyhurst University, both Catholic institutions of about four thousand students each; and the Lake Erie College of Osteopathic Medicine (LECOM), a private school of about two thousand students for osteopathic medicine, pharmacy, and dentistry.

This abundance of postsecondary opportunities has brought youthful drive and intellect to Erie and, with that, a natural spillover of optimistic attitude and culture. This new Rust Belt phenomenon of positivity and activity—similar to what you can find in Buffalo, up the road, or Youngstown and Cleveland, down the road—is well under way but is often drowned out as the more familiar older-school, older-generation refrains of despair and anger hang on.

"Dreary Erie," some folks say, the ones who still mourn the passing of GE. But as we have seen in places from West Virginia to Mississippi to the Central Valley of California, negative self-image can be a motivator as well as a handicap. "We're nothing but optimistic about this place," one of the young entrepreneurs said. "It's such a large canvas to paint on." And of their downcast parents' generation: "It's time to move on."

In Erie, we found another example of creating structural opportunity in answer to structural unfairness like the one represented by the public education funding system. It was the counterpart to the "Why Not Dodge?" campaign in Dodge City and the "NIZ" (Neighborhood Improvement Zone) funding scheme for downtown redevelopment in Allentown. Erie's version is known as "ECGRA." This stands for Erie County Gaming Revenue Authority, and it is usually pronounced as a word, *eggrah*.

We met Perry Wood, a young family man who grew up not far from Erie in the town of Franklin, at the ECGRA offices near the Penn State Behrend campus on the eastern edge of town. ECGRA, of which Wood is the director, was formed after Pennsylvania decided to authorize casinos and revive its horse-racing industry in 2004. Erie's is the Presque Isle Downs and Casino; named for the beautiful peninsular state park but located off the easily accessible interstate just south of town, it is a combined racetrack and casino.

Virtually all lottery and casino schemes devote at least some of their money to schools or some other public-benefit purpose. What is notable about Erie's, which has been open for about eight years, is the unique (at least to the experience of what we have seen) way the community has decided to use its share of the casino revenues.

The short version of a complex story is that 1 percent of the Presque Isle complex's total revenues come back to Erie County; half of that goes to retire bonds for airport expansion and other big-infrastructure projects; the other half, totaling roughly $5 million per year, goes through ECGRA for use toward the general goal of regional economic development. This share was about $1 million a year higher until neighboring Ohio opened casinos recently and drew off some of Presque Isle's traffic.

Erie has matched a familiar source of money (gambling) with a widespread civic goal (economic and technical renewal), in a novel and apparently successful way. "The structure of our gaming-revenue commission is unique, in having the flexibility to use the money for economic development," Perry Wood told us. "We're asking ourselves, What can we do to shape the future of this community? What can we do to make it more attractive to young people? What will make Erie a more vital community?"

ECGRA has done plenty:

- It supports a program called GO College, a college initiative project that helps Erie students through tutoring and college-search assistance.
- "Ignite Erie" is an across-the-board tech-start-up initiative designed to connect universities, technical colleges, entrepreneurs, and financiers to foster new businesses in the inner-city areas.
- "Tech After Hours" allows displaced workers, adults, and others to use school-system facilities after the regular school day, for

training as welders, machinists, builders, and other high-wage skilled trades.
- A youth summer-jobs program this year hired some 170 people from ages sixteen through nineteen in construction and land-scaping jobs "that give them both an income and some 'soft-skills' training," Wood said.

\* \* \*

After a while in Erie, we began to recognize the work that terms like "vital" and "future" and "attracting young people" play in the discourse by Wood and his thirty-something local contemporaries. At first glance, Erie seems to illustrate just the opposite. The population has long been shrinking; many of the factories look shuttered and closed; the historic downtown is in an obvious "pre-" rather than "post-" rebirth stage; and compared with the rest of the country and even the state, its people are, on average, old and poor.

That's why it was so impressive to find a group of next-generation Erieites—those who never expected to get a lifetime job at the giant GE locomotive plant and, therefore, aren't devastated as GE keeps shifting those jobs to Texas; those who look at the inexpensive real estate and still-present manufacturing infrastructure and see possibilities opening rather than closing. These are the people who think they can make this the next hot, successful city.

The point that comes back to us is the starkness of the contrast: on the one hand, the flattened terms—"angry," "resentful," "hopeless"—the language the media and politicians use to describe America in general; on the other hand, the engaged, changing realities people understand about the places where they actually live. The point may sound banal, but it has consequences. In the very same terrain that was just described as Rust Belt loserland in a big presidential-campaign rally, and whose urban landscape clearly shows the structural and human marks of trau-matic change, people are trying to anticipate and adapt to those changes, to improve their individual and collective futures, and generally to behave as if they are actors in their own dramas, rather than just being acted upon. Being active, rather than passive, is one working definition of today's American Idea.

Erie finds a hypercharged boost of optimism and energy from another sizable portion of its population: refugees and immigrants.

Erie has a long history of immigrants and refugees; it goes back to the early twentieth century, with an influx of Poles, Italians, Germans, Irish, and Russians. Now the faces have changed to include Africans, Asians, and Middle Easterners. Some 10 percent of today's Erie residents arrived as refugees. Those who make it to Erie are probably the most likely of the city's residents to want to be part of Erie's success and do whatever it takes to get there. After what they've been through, how could they not be part of the optimism?

I went to visit the starting point for Erie's continuing flow of new arrivals: the field office of the U.S. Committee for Refugees and Immigrants (USCRI). It was already beginning to bustle before 9:00 a.m. on a hot August morning. A woman wearing a bright African cloth wrapped at the waist, with two little children beside her, was sitting on the concrete step in front of the building, waiting for something or someone. Clusters of others, mostly talking quietly in Arabic, were waiting inside in the stuffy reception area. A few of the staffers behind the reception windows were greeting everyone who came in. Along the narrow halls, there were day-care rooms, and there was a play area outside. Beyond some parked strollers and water dispensers, a language lesson was in progress; the instructor was juggling a meld of English grammar and culture for a dozen or more men and women seated at long tables.

Behind closed doors in smaller offices, staff members were helping people with resettlement procedures. The to-do list is long: housing, employment, language help, schools, child care, transportation, health screenings, doctors, dentists, clothing, cash assistance, Social Security cards, and the steps to citizenship. Other topics are looser: neighborhoods, shopping, parks, the library, emergencies, calendars, deadlines, and cultural guidelines, like when it's appropriate to dial 911 and expectations for work or school attendance.

As the morning wore on, people continued to drift in; the building was filling up.

Upstairs in her office was Dylanna Jackson, who directs the program and has been working around the United States with refugees and immigrants for about two decades. She moves purposefully and quickly, every brown hair in place, addressing questions with the confidence of her experience. Jackson described the reasons for the current whirlwind. She called it the "summer bulge." Summer is traditionally a busy time for refugee resettlement, but in 2016 it was even more so, since the Obama administration had raised its annual goal of Syrian refugee admissions almost sixfold, to ten thousand people. "All the agencies are working as fast as they can," said Jackson, noting that more people had been moved more quickly into the pipeline. In Pennsylvania's Region 5, home to Erie, the arrivals numbered in the thirties and forties from November through March, fell to fifteen in April, and shot up to seventy-nine in June and ninety-one in July. That summer, the total since October 2015 for Region 5 was 520, and it was 2,645 for all of Pennsylvania.

Part of that summer bulge was the Zkrit family, who arrived in Erie early in June. In 2012, Mohammad Zkrit was living in Aleppo, Syria, with his young wife, Yasmine, and their two small daughters, and was working in a fabric factory. Then one day, his neighborhood was bombed by the forces of Bashar al-Assad. His house was destroyed, and he was injured. He showed us a video on his phone of the devastation, confusion, and injuries.

Zkrit and his family fled Syria for a camp in Lebanon. After a few months, the family moved on to Jordan. He had lost track of his brother in Aleppo, and to this day he doesn't know his fate. Seeing no future in Jordan, the family applied to the United Nations High Commissioner for Refugees to obtain refugee status. After three years in Jordan, they were offered the chance to resettle in the United States. Zkrit, thirty-six, and his wife, twenty-six, and their growing family of four young children boarded a plane in Amman bound for Chicago and, ultimately, Erie.

I went to visit the Zkrit family in their modest house on the east side of Erie, a few blocks east of State Street, which is the socioeconomic dividing line in Erie. The fancier folks live on the west side. Arriving at the doorstep of their new home is often the hardest moment for the refugees, Jackson had told me, especially for those who were lawyers, doctors, or other professionals in their previous lives. They were suddenly walking through the door into their new reality and a much more humble life, which would be at least temporarily permanent.

When Mohammad pulled up to the curb in his family's new used minivan, I was, I admit, a little surprised. Bought on time, the translator, Bassam Dabbah, explained. Of course. The family lived on the first floor of the house, which they rent for about $600 a month. For three bedrooms and one bath, it seemed like a bargain, until I did the math, figuring that at a starter job (once he gets one), Zkrit will probably earn somewhere between the minimum wage of $7.25 an hour and $10 an hour.

There was plenty of furniture around the house, all obviously secondhand. And a nice TV. The two older girls shared a room with each other and their favorite girlie toys, which they told me are Barbies. Anayat, who is eight years old, said she wants to be a doctor. Hanin, who is six, wants to be an airplane pilot. School would start very soon, and they would be able to walk the few blocks from their house. One-and-a-half-year-old Yahia, the Zkrits' only son, who toddled around the apartment sturdily, and tiny Rimas, just six months old, were both remarkably good and patient through my visit, I thought, especially for little ones without much diversion.

In Erie, as in Sioux Falls and Burlington, we repeatedly heard the range of work histories from refugees, from those who'd left behind menial jobs or no jobs at all to those who'd had to abandon professional jobs as lawyers, administrators, doctors, and teachers. They all arrive in the United States as equals and are all now scrambling to patch together whatever they can. Mohammad Zkrit says he will take any job he can get; he hopes to be happy in Erie and make his home there. "We are treated as human beings," he told me through his translator. "America is a dream country."

* * *

How would the Zkrit family, like others, make it a few years down the road? In Erie, the longer-term support system is a mosaic of organizations: churches, schools, YMCAs, cultural centers, public libraries, community centers, food banks, businesses, transport systems, medical services, and on and on.

I went on to visit one of these support groups, the Multicultural Community Resource Center (MCRC), which occupies the Old Penn Schoolhouse and has an annex next door at the former Tenth Street United Methodist Church. The MCRC began as the Hispanic American Council in 1975, broadening its scope nearly twenty years ago to include newer faces from Somalia, Congo, Bhutan, Iraq, Syria, and many other countries. The group's mission, which is funded by as many as two dozen organizations, from government and civic groups to corporations, nonprofits, and private benefactors, is to help refugees and immigrants settle into Erie long-term in just about every way.

On the day I visited, the buildings were humming. I knew by now to expect such high energy, buzz, and constant motion, which I had witnessed at refugee centers across the country. The MCRC runs at least fifteen different programs, including those addressing transportation, health-care navigation, notary public services, and language translation in Spanish, Bosnian, Russian, Ukrainian, Arabic, Vietnamese, Swahili, and Burmese. They touch a lot of cultural bases most of us wouldn't even think of, like truancy prevention and referrals for children at risk of being placed out of their homes.

The center's employment services arm, called Mosaico, is a for-profit subsidiary of the nonprofit MCRC. It matches employers and employees, and it supports both sides with language and cultural help. Many lines of work available are just what you'd expect: food services, construction, general labor, and the like. We visited the factory of one of the employers, Plastek, an internationally successful manufacturer of plastics packaging that makes many commonly used containers—for example, deodorant holders and detergent bottles. Workers I watched on the line could well have made some of the bottles or packages that Jim and I use every single day. Time and again we breached these few degrees of separation between us and America's refugees and immigrants around the country in such factories and plants. Today it was our plastic bottles in Erie; weeks ago it was our steaks in Dodge City.

Paul Jericho, the associate director for programs at MCRC, toured me around the center. Jericho told me that refugees fit in well with the growing entrepreneurial spirit of Erie. New arrivals have started more than one hundred new businesses in Erie, said Jericho. We saw a number of small shops and businesses along Parade Street, like general stores, car-repair shops, and construction or repair companies. As for training programs, Jericho said that one of their most successful has been preparing blackjack dealers for the Presque Isle Downs and Casino. About half the casino dealers now are refugees, whom Jericho trains in a small room off the nave of the former Methodist church.

The hard work pays off in Erie, which Jericho described as a good town for refugees. The modest cost of living launches them out of their entry-level jobs on a trajectory to renting apartments, buying cars on time, and purchasing their own houses after as few as two or three years. Many of the refugees I spoke with echoed these points, adding the much-appreciated Erie attribute that "it is safe," also as we had heard in Sioux Falls. Erie has its share of urban crime, but compared with the neighborhoods of Aleppo, Erie is very safe indeed.

Jericho carved out time he clearly didn't have to talk with me. All the while, his phone kept ringing and heads popped in and out of his doorway. Sometimes the calls were about legal troubles, like someone's DUI citation. Other times, he asked a visitor to return a little later. Jericho is a get-it-done person, like many others we've met who work in the chaotic and often unpredictable world of immigrants and refugees. He told me about driving refugees to Pittsburgh for help with serious eye issues and to Washington, D.C., so they could check out Gallaudet University.

Why Gallaudet, a college for the deaf? I wondered. Jericho said there are at least twenty-four deaf refugees from Nepal who live in Erie now. So far, no one has been able to figure out why there are so many.

By now, some refugees and immigrants in Erie have been around for a long time and have made new history in town, much the same way that Ernestor De La Rosa, the city official in Dodge City, did.

We met one of them in Erie, an outgoing young man with the air of a natural politician or public speaker. He was in his thirties, tall, with blue eyes and short blond hair. He introduced himself as Ferki Ferati. When I heard his name, I started to wonder whether he was from a Slavic or Hungarian family whose forebears had come to work in the mines or mills of industrial-age Pennsylvania. He short-circuited my speculation by explaining that he'd come to Erie relatively recently, as a teenage refugee from Albanian Kosovo, and that he guessed he might be the blondest, most American-sounding Muslim refugee we had encountered in our travels. He was born in 1983, the fifth of six children in a miner's family in Kosovo. As Serbian troops moved on Kosovo in the late 1990s, the family fled the fighting—first to Macedonia, and eventually a refugee camp in Fort Dix, New Jersey, when Ferati was fifteen.

As part of the resettlement process, screeners asked the arrivals where they would like to end up in the United States. "We want to be next to New York," Ferki Ferati told them. He meant the city; resettlement officials from Erie pointed out that their city was "next to New York," meaning the parts of New York State that were four hundred miles west of the Hudson River. "Technically, they were right!" he said. I could tell this was not the first time he had recounted his Erie-origin story, but its punch line was "And it was the best decision I ever made!"

Ferati went to Mercyhurst Preparatory School, which is affiliated with Mercyhurst University, also located in Erie. He went on to the university, excelled there, spent a junior year in Russia to learn that language— his fourth or fifth. Back in Erie he met a Russian woman named Katya, who became his wife, and on graduation from Mercyhurst considered a career in intelligence work. But, he related, "I couldn't find a job in my field because I was an Albanian with a Muslim upbringing who happened to be married to a Russian girl—and I have relatives in probably forty countries." As Ferati told the local alt-weekly newspaper, the *Erie Reader*, this was soon after the 9/11 attacks, and "the government thought I was diverse, but too diverse."

Ferki introduced us to Katya, who had a management job with General Electric. He explained that their story—stylish young professional couple, a refugee and an immigrant, choosing to start their careers not in Brooklyn or Boston or San Francisco but in one of the creakiest of Rust Belt cities—was not as anomalous as it might have seemed. The two of them might be better educated and more polished than many other newcomers to Erie, but a full 10 percent of the city's population of some one hundred thousand was made up of refugees. Erie was one of a number of midwestern and northern cities that had avoided population decline by making themselves welcoming and open to immigrants in general and refugees in particular.

In the summer of 2017, Ferati earned his doctorate and became the new—and only the second ever—president of Erie's Jefferson Educational Society. A civic nonprofit institution in Erie that offers seminars and lectures and an annual global summit of international thinkers and speakers, supports a research and publication arm, and hosts a local leadership program to polish young Erie's best and brightest, the society was founded by Erie legend and lifelong educator William Garvey in 2008. It felt to us symbolic of Erie's progressive, youthful culture that Ferki Ferati, a refugee from Kosovo, would be its second president.

*What We Saw and What We Learned*

*10½ Signs of Civic Success*

# What We Saw and What We Learned

And so we came home, and to the end of the journey, for now. America's contradictory evolution continues. Our own travels around the country and the world will go on. What we saw while crossing the continent during these years was reassuring and complex and evanescent, a picture of certain places at a particular time. Some will have gotten better, some worse, and all of them inevitably different since the weeks we spent in each of them.

But we learned something important, and surprising, and worth sharing, which was the reason, originally, for making this journey and now impels us to describe it in this book.

Through America's history, its people have been in motion, by choice and by necessity, for reasons good and bad. Its communities have grown and prospered, and have shrunk and suffered. The nation has been buffeted and surprised, it has been pushed backward and has found an uneven way forward. What is true of the country as a whole at any given time is misleading about many of its people. For instance, the decade after World War II was a golden age of "all-American" opportunity, but not for most Americans who were black. The years after the financial crash of 2008 slowly restored the wealth and productivity of the U.S. economy as a statistical whole, but, obviously, not the prospects or security of tens of millions of families.

Every bit of that historical contradiction persists. As we noted nearly every place we went and have already remarked about many of our cities, the problems of America's original Gilded Age have recurred in this century with a startling resonance and precision. Old ways of life and sources of income vanish practically overnight. New fortunes arise from enterprises and inventions barely imagined a generation before, and law and custom lag for years or decades in understanding how to blunt their unexpected bad effects. For the technologies of the previous Gilded Age, the bad effects included deadly pollution from smelters, mines, and factories; exploitation of child labor; a "life is cheap" approach to workplace safety, whether in the slaughterhouses depicted in *The Jungle* or urban sweatshops like the Triangle Shirtwaist Company, where 146 workers, mainly teenage girls, died in a daytime fire in 1911. For the technologies of this era: the prospect of all-hours tracking and the perfection of the surveillance state; the economic assault on traditional news media and the intellectual elevation of rumors and disinformation; the increased pressures toward economic polarization; the rise of new monopolies and the use of their money and power to prevent their own regulation; and countless other challenges. And the benefits, riches, possibilities, and cultural connection and expansion that come with this era's disruptions are also enormous, as they were a century ago.

Meanwhile, the national government of this era, like its predecessors in the era that Mark Twain and Charles Dudley Warner christened the Gilded Age in their 1873 book of that name, struggles to match the great resources of the country to its great challenges, or move forward at all.

Everywhere we went, Deb and I saw the imprint of the great national undertakings of the past. An astonishing amount of the public architecture of twenty-first-century America was laid down in a few Depression years in the 1930s, by the millions of people employed by the Works Progress Administration. The small airports we landed at were the result of midcentury defense-and-transportation building projects, as were the interstates we flew above. The libraries we found almost everywhere were the result of both public and private investment. The grid-pattern fields of the farmland Midwest had been laid out by the rules of settlement from the earliest days of the republic. The practices that made them the most productive farmland in the world were crucially spurred by land-grant universities and agricultural-research schools. The wildlands and ecosystems that have escaped development did so because of their protection as national parks or monuments.

To seize the opportunities, and cope with the failures, of this moment in American history, national efforts of the kind that more recently underlay the creation of the Internet, the GPS network, and DNA decoding might again be best. But for now, even if most parts of the complex American "system" work better than their counterparts in the rest of the world, America's national political system works worse. Thus the United States has a harder time taking the steps that would make adjusting to this era less painful and more productive. As the technological and economic imperatives pushing toward a "gig economy" erode the protections of the corporate-employment model—more side income via Uber and Etsy, fewer guaranteed pensions or health benefits national policy could respond, as it did more than a century ago when the industrial age eroded the protections of the family-farming era. Then, the response took the form of safety legislation, child-labor laws, union rights, and the minimum wage. Now it could take the form of extensions of health-care coverage and other safeguards harder to obtain without career-long jobs. As automation and world trade eliminate or immiserate some of today's jobs, schools can help prepare students for other kinds—as happened a century ago with the creation of high schools and then again after World War II with the GI Bill.

But that won't happen soon. Whichever party holds the presidency, the other will likely hold enough of the Congress to make comprehensive measures of any sort very hard to push through. That is why local resilience and adaptability of the kind we have witnessed deserve nationwide attention.

Sadly, history is not so mechanistic that we can say "Things eventually turned out all right in the transition from the first Gilded Age to the last time around, so let's wait for the reforms to happen again." This is not even to speak of the wars, the riots and revolutions, the economic booms and collapses, the deadly global epidemic of the Spanish flu, the reassertion of racial prejudice and violence, and the other calamities the United

States and the world endured in what appears in retrospect to have been an era of "reform." That those tumultuous decades would lead to reform at all was of course not fated, and it depended on the efforts of people who committed themselves as *reformers:* for labor rights, for women's rights, for movement toward racial justice, for environmental protection, for a less corrupt and more representative form of government.

Between the late nineteenth century and the early twenty-first, countless circumstances differ. But when we think about that earlier shift, three elements can show us what to anticipate and what to seize on right now.

The first, unpredictable element is the national shock that galvanizes effort. For me, the central document in American political psychology is William James's 1910 essay "The Moral Equivalent of War." America is capable of almost anything when threatened militarily, James argued; think what it could do if it could muster the same determination without the threat. The sin of commission for the United States after its greatest recent shock, the 9/11 attacks, was the invasion of Iraq, with the consequences this conflict will entail through the decades. The sin of omission may have been worse: missing the opportunity for real national improvement. Consider how Dwight Eisenhower used the then-terrifying "Sputnik shock" of the late 1950s: mainly as a spur to technological and educational investment. It is possible that the repercussions of the Donald Trump era may have a similar spurring effect—possible, but not ensured.

The second element is one that Paul Starr, of Princeton University, stressed in a 2015 *American Prospect* essay called "How Gilded Ages End." Democracy, he argues, finally depends on and is defined by the ability of political power to control strictly economic forces. Otherwise you're talking about a nationwide corporation, not a country.

American history of the era that began with J. P. Morgan and ran through the New Deal was about political power reasserting its preeminence. "Behind the myriad of specific reforms" that constituted the early twentieth-century Progressive movement, Starr writes, "was a common recognition—a collective revulsion against the privileges of great wealth allied with great power." He argued that the country is due for such an adjustment again. Through the past generation-plus, this struggle has been cast as a Republican-versus-Democratic issue. From Nixon onward, the modern GOP has channeled resentment about intellectual and cultural elites, as well as racial minorities, into support for the business elite. Thus white voters in West Virginia or Kansas support tax policies that disproportionately benefit financiers in New York and San Francisco. Much of the turmoil of American and world politics in this age turns on whether the genuine economic fears and grievances of the era help fuel a politics of solution, or instead one of resentment and backlash.

And the third element that marked the end of the first Gilded Age was fertile experimentation with new approaches and possibilities. Louis Brandeis's famous claim that the American states, rather than the central government, were the real "laboratories of democracy" came in a Supreme Court ruling in 1932. For several decades before that, states and cities across the country had experimented with new school systems, new tax and spending schemes, new ways of providing public services, new public health programs, new regulatory approaches, all toward the goal of responding to the crises of that age. "In Cleveland, Toledo, across the Midwest and Plains States, you saw these dedicated reformers," Michael Kazin of Georgetown University, a historian of the Progressive Era and a biographer of William Jennings Bryan, told me, when I asked about political parallels. "Some were Socialists, some Democrats, some Republicans—they were all trying something new." One of Bryan's goals, Kazin said, was to let the politically disparate but actively experimental reformers in one state know about parallel efforts elsewhere.

When the national mood after the first Gilded Age favored reform, possibilities that had been tested, refined, and made to work in various "laboratories of democracy" were at hand. After our current Gilded Age, the national mood will change again. When it does, a new set of ideas and plans will be at hand. We've seen them being tested in towns we never would have suspected, by people who would never join forces in the national capital but who work together "at home." Their projects, the progress they have made, and their goals are more congruent than even they might ever imagine. Until the country's mood does change, the people who have been reweaving the national fabric will be more effective if they realize how many other people are working toward the same end.

I thought frequently of what Philip Zelikow, a professor at the University of Virginia, said to me at the beginning of our travels: "In scores of ways, Americans are figuring out how to take advantage of the opportunities of this era, often through bypassing or ignoring the dismal national conversation. There are a lot of more positive narratives out there—but they're lonely, and disconnected. It would make a difference to join them together, as a chorus that has a melody."

That is the American song we have heard.

# 10½ Signs of Civic Success

After about a year on the road, Deb and I had evolved a pattern for our first few days in a town. We would make an appointment together at the local newspaper, to start on a note of respect and to meet the people most likely to have been thinking analytically about positive and negative trends. Also, the viability of a local paper (or, in some cases, a local-news website) was itself an early and reliable guide to how much "there" there was to a town.

After we found a place to stay—downtown if possible, in cities where downtown revival efforts had reached that point; otherwise in a "suites"-style lodging on the edge of town—we would fan out. Deb would go to the library and the YMCA or similar sports and civic clubs; all of these are surprisingly still-relevant bellwether institutions. I would go to the economic-development office and the tech start-up zone and the community college. We'd both visit schools; we'd find the local brewpub or distilleries and talk with their founders and owners. In good weather, we'd walk in the parks or ride on the bike trails or go to minor league baseball games. In bad weather or at night, we'd go to the arts zones and galleries or the brewpubs again.

By the time we had been to half a dozen cities, we'd developed an informal checklist of the traits that distinguished a place where things seemed to work. These items are obviously different in nature, most of them are subjective, and some of them overlap. But in our experiences, these things were true of the cities large or small that were working best:

*1. People work together on practical local possibilities, rather than allowing bitter disagreements about national politics to keep them apart.* We were traveling during the run-up to the bitter midterm elections of 2014, and then while the Supreme Court was ruling on same-sex marriage and Obamacare, and then as the 2016 presidential campaign, including the Trump insurgency, was gathering steam. People knew we were visiting from Washington, and some learned, by asking, that I had once worked for a Democratic president. Given the places we were traveling, I imagine that many of the people we interviewed were Trump supporters.

But it just didn't come up. Cable TV shows were often playing in the background, most frequently Fox News, and if people had stopped to talk about the TV fare, they might have disagreed with each other and with us. Yet overwhelmingly, the focus in successful towns was not on insoluble national divisions but on practical problems a community could address. The more often national politics came into local discussions, the worse shape the town was likely to be in.

*2. You can pick out the local patriots.* A standard question we'd ask soon after arrival was "Who makes this town go?" The range of answers varied widely. Sometimes it was a person in an official position of leadership, a mayor or city council figure. Sometimes it was a local business titan or a real estate developer. Sometimes a university president or professor, or a civic activist, or an artist or saloonkeeper or historian or radio personality. Sometimes a person with no official position but whose influence everyone felt.

What mattered was that the question *had* an answer. In one city in Appalachia, we asked a newspaper editor that question, and he said that no one came to mind but he would think about it overnight. In another southern city, the answer was the commanding officer at a nearby military base—but since the command rotated frequently, there was no permanent local patriot. The more quickly this question was answered, the better shape a town was in.

*3. The phrase "public-private partnership" refers to something real.* Through the years, I had heard about "public-private partnerships" but had thought of this as just another slogan. If it meant anything at all, it was probably a euphemism for sweetheart deals between big government and big business— the "public-private partnership" to build the latest fighter plane, for instance.

In successful towns, people can point to something specific and say, *This* is what a partnership means. In Greenville, South Carolina, the public school system includes an "Elementary School of Engineering," in a poor neighborhood. The city runs the school; local industries including GE, BMW, and Michelin send in engineers to teach and supervise science fairs, at the companies' expense. In little Holland, Michigan, a large family-owned scrap-recycling company works with the state correctional system to hire ex-convicts who would otherwise have trouble reentering the work force. In Fresno, California, a collaboration among the city, county, and state governments, the local colleges and universities, and several tech start-ups trains high school dropouts and other unemployed people in computer skills. The details vary, but the more specifically a community can explain what their public-private partnerships mean, the better.

*4. People know the civic story.* America has a "story," one that everyone understands, even if only to say that it's a myth or a lie. A few states have their guiding stories—California as either the ever-promising or the sadly spoiled frontier, Vermont as its own separate Eden.

Successful cities seem to have their stories, too. For Sioux Falls, that it's just the right size: big enough so that people who have come from the smaller-town prairie can find challenge, stimulation, and opportunity, but small enough to be livable and comfortable. For Columbus, Ohio, which is much larger than Sioux Falls, that it, too, is exactly right-sized: big enough to make anything possible, small enough actually to get things done. For Bend or Duluth or Winters, that they are in uniquely attractive locations; for Pittsburgh, that it has set an example of successful turnaround; for Eastport or Allentown or Fresno, that they are in the process of doing so. For many of the cities we visited, the civic story turned on the importance of strong local institutions: libraries, schools, philanthropies, public arts projects, annual events. For a surprisingly large number—in the Rust Belt, in the South, in the Plains States, in non-coastal areas of the West—it involved an awareness of being dismissed or disdained in the fashionable world's eyes, and thus being all the more determined to show what these people and this part of the country could really do.

As with guiding national myths, the question is not whether these assessments seem precisely accurate to outsiders. Their value is in giving citizens a sense of how today's efforts are connected to what happened yesterday and what they hope tomorrow will bring.

*5. They have downtowns.* This seems obvious, but it is probably the quickest single marker of the condition of a town. For a "young" country like the United States, surprisingly many cities still have "good bones," via the classic Main Street–style structures built from the late 1800s through World War II. In the mall-and-freeway decades after the war, some of these buildings were razed and many more were abandoned or disfigured with cheap aluminum fronts.

Most of the cities we visited were pouring attention, resources, and creativity into their downtowns. The Main Street America project, from the National Trust for Historic Preservation, has coordinated downtown revival projects in some two thousand communities across the nation. Of the ones we saw, Greenville's and Burlington's are the most advanced in this process, studied by planners from the rest of the world. San Bernardino's is still the furthest behind. Sioux Falls, Bend, Allentown, Fresno, Riverside, Holland, Rapid City, St. Marys, and many others mark points along the continuum. But downtown ambitions of any sort are a positive sign, and occupied second- and third-floor apartments and condos over restaurants and stores suggest that the downtown has crossed a decisive threshold and will survive.

*6. They are near a research university.* I feel bad even raising this point, because in contrast to all the others, there is very little a city can do to change its circumstances. It's not completely impossible, as central Oregon's long campaign to bring a branch of Oregon State University to Bend demonstrates. But it is both difficult and consequential because research universities have become the modern counterparts to a natural harbor or a location at a river confluence, in the economic benefits they confer.

In the short term, they sustain demand by bringing in a student population. Over the longer term, they transform a town through the researchers and professors they bring in. It's obvious once you think about it, but is still striking to observe how powerfully a university academic staff can broaden the international diversity of a community and raise its median education level. When you find a Chinese or German physicist in the Dakotas or a Yale literature PhD in California's Central Valley, that person probably works for a university. Rapid City is different from other towns of its size on the prairie not simply because of Mount Rushmore (and the city's downtown street-corner array of life-sized bronze statues of all the U.S. presidents) but also because of the presence of the South Dakota School of Mines and Technology.

And it's a cliché but true that research universities have become powerful start-up incubators. Stanford and its constellation of Internet ventures and Harvard and MIT with their biotech centers are merely the best-known examples of what you can see on the periphery of most other research universities. For instance: Clemson and the array of automotive-tech firms that have grown up around it in South Carolina, or UC Davis and associated agricultural tech ventures.

7. *They have, and care about, a community college.* Not every city can have a research university. Any ambitious one can have a community college. And while research universities are the most important parts of the U.S. educational system from a global perspective, I've come to think that community colleges matter most domestically right now.

Just about every other world-historical trend is pushing the United States (and other countries) toward a less equal, more polarized existence: labor-replacing technology, globalized trade, self-segregated residential housing patterns, and the American practice of unequal district-based funding for public schools. Community colleges are the main exception, potentially offering a connection to higher-wage technical jobs for people who might otherwise be left with no job or one at minimum wage. East Mississippi Community College has taken people from welfare and prepared them for jobs in nearby factories that pay twice as much as the local median household income. Fresno City College works with local tech firms and California State University, Fresno, to train the children of farmworker families (among others) for higher-tech agribusiness jobs. Obviously this does not end inequality, and badly run community colleges can make things worse by loading students with additional debt without improving their circumstances. Nationwide, only about 40 percent of those who start at a community college finish within six years. But we saw a number of such schools that were clearly forces in the right direction. The more often and more specifically we heard people talk about their community college, the better we ended up feeling about the direction of that town.

*8. They have distinctive, innovative schools.* Early in our stay, we would ask what was the most distinctive school to visit at the K–12 level. The question served a similar function to asking who in town made things run. If four or five answers came quickly to mind, that was a good sign. If not, the reverse.

The examples people suggested also ranged widely. Some were "normal" public schools. Some were charters. Some were special statewide public academies, like the Governor's School for the Arts and Humanities in South Carolina or the Mississippi School for Mathematics and Sciences, in Columbus (both of them publicly funded boarding schools for high school students, with counterparts in many other states). Some were religious schools or private academies. The common theme was the intensity of experimentation. In political speeches, phrases like "our failed public school system" come so naturally that people barely notice. Across our country, we saw cities experimenting with schools that could succeed—and we noticed in the few places where that was not so.

*9. They make themselves open.* The anti-immigrant passion that inflamed the 2016 election cycle was not something people volunteered as a threat or problem in most of the cities we saw. On the contrary, politicians, educators, businesspeople, students, and retirees frequently stressed the ways their communities were trying to attract and include new people. Cities as different as Sioux Falls, Burlington, and Fresno have gone to extraordinary lengths to assimilate refugees from recent wars. Greenville's mayor asked us to listen for how many different languages we heard spoken on the street, from residents or visitors.

Every small town in America has thought about how to offset the natural brain-drain tendencies that have historically sent its brightest young people elsewhere. The same emphasis on inclusion that would make a town attractive to talented outsiders increases its draw to its own émigrés.

*10. They have big plans.* For the United States as a whole, the very idea of ambitious "national greatness" projects seems preposterous. There's no money; the only big efforts the government can undertake are military; it now counts as victory simply to keep funding for the national parks, for NASA or NOAA, for health or science research from being cut. For better or worse, it was a different America that built the country's interstate highways and went to the moon.

Cities, because they *can* do things, still make plans. If I see a national politician with a blueprint for how things will be better twenty years from now, I think: Good luck! In fact, few national politicians even pretend about long-term visions anymore. When a mayor or community council shows me a map of how new downtown residences will look when they're completed, or where the new greenway will go, I think: I'd like to come back.

Of course, there's one other marker of a city that is working, perhaps the most reliable gauge. A city on the way back will have at least one craft brewery, maybe more, and probably some small distilleries, too. Until 2014, that would have been an unfair test for Mississippi, which effectively outlawed craft beers by setting maximum alcohol levels at the near-beer level. A generation earlier, it would have been an unfair test for the country as a whole. It was not until the late 1970s that Jimmy Carter, as part of his administration's deregulatory agenda, finally removed musty Prohibition-era restrictions on home brewing. This in turn allowed brewing enthusiasts to develop new products and expand their markets and businesses. By the early 1980s, local-brewing pioneers like Jim Koch of the Boston Beer Company on the East Coast, with his Sam Adams beer, and Ken Grossman of Sierra Nevada, in the West, were along with others laying the foundation for today's golden age of distinctive local breweries and beers.

In the late 1970s, the United States had only a few hundred breweries—mainly large, commoditized mass-producers. By 2017, it had more than five thousand—or in practical terms, one or more in any city with creative ambitions for its future. As with any start-up field, not all of these ventures were well thought out, and not all of them could survive. But enough have flourished to make craft breweries one of the most reliable signs of civic energy. A town that has them also has a certain kind of entrepreneur, and a critical mass of mainly young (except for me) customers. It sounds like a joke, but it explains a lot.

# Acknowledgments

Most authors say, as a courtesy, that they owe debts of gratitude to more people than they can properly thank. After more than four years of travel, in which we interviewed many hundreds of people in dozens of towns, we really do owe thanks to a larger number of people than we could feasibly list here. On our website for the book, we have a city-by-city roll of thanks for those who offered us time, hospitality, insights, and challenges.

Here are a few of those who supported the project as a whole.

John Tierney was our partner in travel, interviewing, thinking, and writing in the formative early stage of this journey, as part of the "American Futures" series for *The Atlantic*.

Rafe Sagalyn, our agent, has offered crucial intellectual and emotional guidance.

At Pantheon, our publisher, we have had the good fortune of working again with Dan Frank, our wise editor, and, among others on his team, Josie Kals and Betsy Sallee.

Our colleagues at *The Atlantic* offered material, intellectual, and emotional underwriting for these travels, which began under *The Atlantic*'s "American Futures" auspices. Among them we thank Yoni Appelbaum, Kasia Cieplak-Mayr von Baldegg, James Bennet, Katherine and David Bradley, Anna Bross, Bob Cohn, Jeff Goldberg, Kim Jaske, Corby Kummer, Margaret Low, Sue Parilla, Nic Pollock, Lyndsay Polloway, Sam Price-Waldman, Hayley Romer, Sydney Simon, Scott Stossel, and many others.

Early in this project we did several joint reporting trips with teams from *Marketplace* radio. We thank Tommy Andres, Bridget Bodnar, Deborah Clark, Sitara Nieves, Kai Ryssdal, Charlton Thorp, and their colleagues.

The mapping-software company Esri, whose story we describe in this book, offered technological and conceptual support. We are grateful to the leaders of Esri, Jack and Laura Dangermond, and also Allen Carroll, Hugh Keegan, Chris Thomas, and more.

Twice during the creation of this book—while doing West Coast reporting in 2015, and while writing the manuscript in 2017—we stayed on the campus of the University of Redlands, in California. Our friend Shelli Stockton, of the university, has our special thanks, plus Ralph and Nancy Kuncl, Char and Larry Burgess, and Bill Hatfield.

For their hospitality and generosity during the process of writing, including serving as our hosts for extended periods, we are very grateful to Sherry Smith and Marcus Corley, Carol and Ken Adelman, and Meena and Liaquat Ahamed.

For help in a wide variety of ways, from providing advice on local contacts to helping take care of the airplane in which we made these travels, we're grateful to: Jackie and Sidney Blumenthal, Lincoln Caplan, Melanie and Eliot Cutler, Jamie and Mary Cutting, Jack deGioia, Gloria Dittus, Patty Fabrikant, Julian Fisher, Barry Goldberg, Jorge Guajardo and Paola Sada, Peter Hirshberg, Steve Inkellis, Alan Klapmeier, Barbara and Robert Liotta, Steve Musgrove, Rita O'Connor and Ted Schell, Beth and Charlie Peters, Lucia Pierce, Shelly Porges and Rich Wilhelm, Hannah Stott-Bumsted and Guy Raz, Ric and Heather Redman, Dan Richard, Bob Schapiro, Kate and Tod Sedgwick, Derek Shearer and Sue Toigo,  John and Susan Sturc, Grant and Margot Thomas, Bonnie and Jim Wallman, Lynda and Bill Webster, Philip Zelikow, and Leah Zell.

Others we relied on city-by-city are mentioned in these pages and listed in detail on our website. Among those who initially opened doors for us and especially went out of their way to help are: Susan Backus,

Rusty Bailey, Bob Coffield, Joel Deuterman, Thomas Easterling, Dann and Que-Lan Engels, Ferki and Katya Ferati, Alex Fischer, Colin Fogarty, Rebecca and Woody Fridae, Chris Gardner, Sean Gerrity, Linda Godfrey, Donn and Kristin Grinager, Larry Groce, Tom Hagen, Joe Max Higgins, Jonathon Hogan, Dylanna Jackson, Paul Jericho, Sam Kennedy, Robert Litan, Patrick Losinski, Melissa McCoy, Rick Michaels, Don Ness, Jeff and Peggy Padnos, Heather Parish, Ed Pawlowski, Bob Peacock, Henry Reese and Diane Samuels, Craig Scharton, David and Rhonda Schwiet-ert, Raj Shaunak, Stuart and Emily Raine Siegel, Bill and Trish Smith, Jake Soberol, Ben Speggen, Ashley Swearengin, Tracy Taft, Natarajan Venkatakrishnan, Wyman Westberry, Knox White, Perry Wood, and Chuck Yarborough.

Many writers, thinkers, activists, and entrepreneurs affected the questions we asked and the lessons we learned, although they do not appear in these pages. Among them are Antoine van Agtmael, Jamie Bennett, David Borenstein, Stewart Brand, David Brooks, Steve Case, Liam Casey, Michael Crow, John Dearie, Richard Florida, Bruce Katz, Fred Kent, Jim Koch, Kate Levin, Amy Liu, Eric Liu, James Manyika, Stephanie Meeks, Lenny Mendonca, Mark Muro, Kevin Murphy, Tim O'Reilly, Wellington Reiter, Anne-Marie Slaughter, Stuart Stevens, Billy Townsend, and Jonathan Woetzel.

As always our deepest thanks are to our family: Deb's mother, Angie Zerad; the memory of our late parents Jean and James A. Fallows, and Frank Zerad; our sons Tom and Tad and their wives Lizzy and Annie; and members of the next generation—Jack, Tide, Eleanor, and Navy.

James Fallows has been a national correspondent for *The Atlantic Monthly* for more than thirty-five years and has reported for the magazine from China, Japan, Southeast Asia, and across the United States. He is the author of eleven previous books. His work has also appeared in many other magazines and in frequent public radio commentaries since the 1980s. Honors he has received include a National Book Award and a National Magazine Award. For two years he was President Jimmy Carter's chief speechwriter.

Deborah Fallows is a linguist and writer who holds a PhD in theoretical linguistics and is the author of two previous books. She has also written for many publications, including *The Atlantic, National Geographic, Slate, The New York Times*, and *The Washington Monthly*. She has worked at the Pew Research Center, Oxygen Media, and Georgetown University. She and her husband have two married sons and four grandchildren.

A NOTE ON THE TYPE

This book was set in Adobe Garamond. Designed for the Adobe Corporation by Robert Slimbach, the fonts are based on types first cut by Claude
Garamond (ca. 1480–1561). Garamond was a pupil of Geoffroy Tory and
is believed to have followed the Venetian models, although he introduced
a number of important differences, and it is to him that we owe the letter
we now know as "old style." He gave to his letters a certain elegance and
feeling of movement that won their creator an immediate reputation and
the patronage of Francis I of France.

*Composed by North Market Street Graphics,*
*Lancaster, Pennsylvania*

*Printed and bound by Berryville Graphics,*
*Berryville, Virginia*

*Designed by M. Kristen Bearse*